Ethics and Compliance in Financial Services

Wookjae Heo • John E. Grable

Ethics and Compliance in Financial Services

Case Studies and Practical Examples from North America

palgrave
macmillan

Wookjae Heo
Purdue University West Lafayette
West Lafayette, IN, USA

John E. Grable
Dept of Financial Planning
University of Georgia
Athens, GA, USA

ISBN 978-3-032-14448-5 ISBN 978-3-032-14449-2 (eBook)
https://doi.org/10.1007/978-3-032-14449-2

This Palgrave Macmillan imprint is published by the registered company Springer Nature Switzerland AG
The registered company address is: Gewerbestrasse 11, 6330 Cham, Switzerland

Dedication
This book is dedicated to our students and colleagues working in the financial services profession who have inspired this work. Your questions and insights challenged us to create a resource that bridges the gap between theory and practice. This book is dedicated to you as you strive to uphold the highest standards of ethics and compliance in serving clients and shaping the future of the financial services profession.

We also dedicate this book to our spouses, Choi and Emily, who offered encouragement and important nudges over the 18 months it took to write this book.

Preface: Bridging Ethics and Compliance in Financial Services

In our collective experience as educators and researchers, we have experienced a gap in the resources available to prepare aspiring financial advisors to deal with the ethical demands, regulatory frameworks, and compliance rules that govern the financial services profession. As faculty members in leading financial planning degree programs, we have heard firsthand a recurring concern from employers that new graduates often lack a practical understanding of the ethical guidelines, compliance requirements, and regulatory standards that define professional practice in the financial services profession. This issue is compounded by the fact that many academic programs accredited by certification boards like the CFP Board of Standards, Inc., require ethics and compliance training at the undergraduate and graduate levels. Yet, these programs often lack teaching materials to fulfill this mission. This book fills that critical gap, offering a resource tailored to upper-level undergraduates, graduate students, regulatory and compliance officers, career changers, and practicing financial advisors.

The knowledge gap is a challenge not only for students but also for instructors, who are left piecing together disparate materials (e.g., case studies from financial planning texts, online resources, and firm-provided content) to deliver a cohesive in-class learning experience. For career changers or those entering the financial services profession from unrelated fields, the situation is even more daunting, as accessible, comprehensive resources are virtually nonexistent.

Consider the reality faced by one of the authors, who teaches a course on ethics, rules, and regulations in the financial services sector. Before the publication of this book, the course relied on a patchwork of materials sourced from various websites and governmental resources. The result was a student experience that, while adequate, fell short of its potential. Today, students enrolled in the course have access to a resource that consolidates relevant material, transforming the learning experience. This book provides students with the tools and techniques needed to understand the ethical and regulatory landscape they will navigate as professionals.

We have also heard from the leadership of financial services firms of the need for a consolidated, authoritative resource to support their risk management and compliance functions. This need arises from the fragmented and often inadequate resources currently available to ensure adherence to the complex web of ethical guidelines, regulatory standards, and compliance requirements in the financial services profession. The absence of a single, comprehensive resource creates inefficiencies, leaving compliance officers to piece together guidance from a variety of sources such as regulatory publications, industry blogs, and internal firm policies. This fragmented approach not only increases the risk of oversight but also hampers the ability to train advisors consistently and effectively.

The growing complexity of the financial services regulatory environment also underscores the need for this book. Risk management and compliance departments must contend with an ever-changing landscape of rules, driven by shifts in governmental policies, certification board requirements, and emerging ethical challenges. Without a centralized, up-to-date resource, firms risk falling behind, potentially exposing themselves to legal and reputational risks. This book's emphasis on behavioral and psychological factors, such as cognitive, behavioral, and psychological biases that influence ethical decision-making, helps provide a more nuanced perspective regarding rulemaking and regulatory enforcement.

From the first day we started writing this book, our goal was to provide a comprehensive, practical, and accessible guide that demonstrates the ethical foundations and regulatory frameworks that shape the delivery of financial services. Unlike existing resources, which often focus narrowly on the legal ramifications of rules and the technical details associated with regulatory enforcement, this book takes a broader approach. We grounded each chapter's discussion in the theoretical foundations of ethics, compliance, and standards enforcement while emphasizing real-world applications. Through the use of real-life and hypothetical case studies, behavioral and psychological concepts that are associated with ethical decision-making are brought to life.

The structure of this book reflects our commitment to academic rigor and practical application. Each chapter explores critical aspects of ethical practice and regulatory compliance. Chapters focus on the behavioral and psychological dimensions of creating and maintaining client-focused ethical practices. Designed to be concise yet comprehensive, this book is ideal as a secondary text in introductory or capstone courses within financial planning, financial services, accounting, insurance, or investment management programs. The book can also serve as the core text for courses specifically focused on regulatory compliance issues.

By integrating real-world examples, behavioral perspectives, and a focus on making the material accessible, *Ethics and Compliance in Financial Services: Case Studies and Practical Examples from North America* offers a unique and timely contribution to the field. We hope that this book will empower the next generation of financial professionals to navigate the ethical and regulatory complexities of their profession with confidence, clarity, and integrity.

Book Learning Outcomes

This book includes 16 chapters. Each chapter focuses on a limited number of concepts related to ethical practice and regulatory compliance at the firm and financial advisor levels. The following list describes the set of learning outcomes associated with the book:

1. Define ethics in the context of the financial services profession as a set of conduct norms or standards that guide what is deemed acceptable and unacceptable behavior.
2. Explain the purpose of studying ethics within the financial services profession. This involves understanding the role of ethics in establishing frameworks for professional conduct and decision-making.
3. Identify historical precedents of ethical practice and regulation in the financial services sector across multiple regions, including the United States, Canada, Europe, Australia, New Zealand, Africa, and Asia.
4. Analyze the contextual factors that contribute to individuals and firms engaging in unethical behavior.
5. Evaluate the significance of ethical standards in maintaining trust and integrity in financial services by drawing connections between historical practices and modern regulatory frameworks.
6. Understand the importance of trust and client protection as a framework for ensuring the sustainability of financial markets and recognize the systemic consequences when these foundations are compromised.
7. Identify ethical theories that serve as a roadmap for delivering financial advice and services.
8. Apply philosophical perspectives to guide ethical behaviors and the decision-making processes of financial services professionals.
9. Demonstrate the practical application of ethics in the advisor-client relationship, including strategies for navigating ambiguity and managing conflicts of interest.
10. Evaluate ethical reasoning as a strategic and moral compass and use reasoning to reinforce trust and foster positive client engagements in financial services.
11. Apply ethical frameworks such as deontology, consequentialism, and virtue ethics, along with foundational values like beneficence, autonomy, and justice, to guide ethical decision-making in financial services.
12. Utilize a structured, step-by-step process for integrating ethical principles into day-to-day professional practice within the financial services profession.
13. Analyze real-world case examples to understand the practical application of ethical decision-making.
14. Identify and manage behavioral biases, including overconfidence, confirmation bias, and herd mentality, which can compromise ethical judgment in professional settings.
15. Employ ethics and decision-making bias checklists to enhance self-awareness and maintain ethical standards in high-stakes financial environments.
16. Integrate professional ethics and practice standard codes and regulatory frameworks with appropriate attitudinal and behavioral constraints to uphold ethical conduct in the financial services profession.
17. Analyze the intersection of cognitive, behavioral, and motivational factors to understand the decision-making processes of financial advisors and clients.
18. Navigate the complex landscape of personal values, ethical reasoning, professional responsibility, client expectations, and market pressures.

19. Identify financial, behavioral, and psychological determinants of fraud and recognize how rationalizations, pressures, and opportunities contribute to ethical lapses.
20. Evaluate common psychological tendencies, such as overconfidence, confirmation bias, and the pursuit of short-term rewards, that influence decision-making.
21. Understand the psychology and behaviors of clients, including their goals, anxieties, and biases.
22. Understand the role of financial services regulations in ensuring integrity, transparency, and fairness within financial markets.
23. Identify key regulatory standards relevant to financial services professionals, including requirements to act in a client's best interests, maintain transparent fee structures, and adhere to high standards of professional conduct.
24. Explain how regulations promote consumer well-being by fostering trust and accountability in financial advisory practices.
25. Describe the roles and functions of regulatory bodies such as the Securities and Exchange Commission (SEC), the Financial Industry Regulatory Authority (FINRA), and certification organizations like the Certified Financial Planner Board of Standards Inc. (CFP Board) in overseeing compliance and enforcing rules.
26. Evaluate the impact of regulatory frameworks on building professional integrity and fostering long-lasting, trust-based client relationships in the financial services profession.
27. Understand the historical development of financial regulations and the significance of regulations in driving ethical and compliant practices.
28. Analyze the evolution of regulatory frameworks behind current rules and anticipate potential future regulatory changes.
29. Identify landmark cases and regulatory milestones that have shaped the financial services profession.
30. Evaluate lessons from regulatory breakdowns and describe the catastrophic consequences of oversight failures and ethical misconduct.
31. Apply insights from historical cases to foster a culture of proactive compliance and continuous risk assessment.
32. Describe the roles of regulatory bodies, such as the Securities and Exchange Commission (SEC) and the Financial Industry Regulatory Authority (FINRA), in maintaining professional standards and accountability.
33. Develop a principled approach to financial advising, grounded in historical awareness, regulatory understanding, and ethical integrity.
34. Identify and assess potential compliance risks that could impact the operations, reputation, or legal standing of financial services firms and organizations.
35. Implement targeted mitigation strategies to reduce exposure to compliance risks and strengthen organizational safeguards.
36. Integrate risk management with compliance functions to create a cohesive framework that aligns regulatory requirements with strategic objectives.

37. Evaluate the importance of a holistic approach to risk management, understanding that it should not be treated as a stand-alone process but as an integral part of organizational compliance.
38. Define the concepts of integrity, fairness, accountability, and transparency as they apply to financial services engagements.
39. Demonstrate ways to incorporate integrity, fairness, accountability, and transparency into interactions with clients to foster trust and ethical decision-making.
40. Identify potential conflicts of interest, cultural sensitivities, and moral dilemmas that may arise in financial advisory relationships among clients, firms, and advisors.
41. Apply a structured model to anticipate, analyze, and address conflicts in financial services engagements.
42. Develop an understanding of ethical practice standards to enhance a financial advisor's ability to navigate complex client relationships.
43. Articulate the definitions, forms, and common characteristics of insider trading and market manipulation, and explain their detrimental effects on financial markets and public trust.
44. Describe the legal frameworks, key enforcement actions, and roles of oversight agencies responsible for preventing and addressing insider trading and market manipulation.
45. Analyze how insider trading and market manipulation undermine fairness, transparency, and integrity in financial markets and client relationships.
46. Interpret real-world case studies of insider trading and market manipulation to extract practical lessons as a way to enhance ethical awareness and professional judgment in financial decision-making.
47. Identify the psychological and behavioral factors that contribute to insider trading and market manipulation.
48. Explain the importance of a proactive compliance culture in preventing insider trading.
49. Explain the core requirements of major data protection regulations, such as the General Data Protection Regulation (GDPR) and the California Consumer Privacy Act (CCPA), and their impact on financial institutions.
50. Describe the elements of robust data governance frameworks, including secure data handling practices, explicit consent mechanisms, and consumer rights protection.
51. Analyze the ethical considerations financial services professionals must address to ensure confidentiality, integrity, and availability of sensitive client information.
52. Demonstrate knowledge of advanced cybersecurity measures, such as encryption, multi-factor authentication, and intrusion detection systems, to mitigate data privacy threats.
53. Articulate the role of compliance with data privacy standards in maintaining trust, operational integrity, and strategic risk management within the financial services profession.

54. Explain the three core dimensions of fairness in the financial services profession (procedural fairness, interactional fairness, and distributive fairness) and the significance of each when delivering services.
55. Describe the principles of procedural fairness, including neutrality, transparency, and adherence to due process, and how each ensures impartial decision-making processes.
56. Analyze the role of courtesy, respect, attentiveness, and two-way communication to make clients feel valued and understood.
57. Evaluate the equity of outcomes in financial transactions, focusing on the fair allocation of resources, benefits, and costs based on the contributions and needs of all parties.
58. Discuss how relationship marketing, consumer protection laws, and financial services regulatory frameworks contribute to promoting fairness in client interactions.
59. Identify methods to help clients overcome cognitive, behavioral, and psychological biases and decision paralysis that may expose them to potential mistreatment in financial transactions.
60. Evaluate real-world case studies involving unauthorized trading, hidden revenue-sharing, cultural collusion, corruption, data breaches, and sales misconduct.
61. Articulate how ethical and compliance failures erode client trust, damage firm reputation, and destabilize financial markets.
62. Explain the importance of regulatory oversight, transparency, and whistleblower safeguards in preventing and addressing ethical and compliance issues.
63. Describe the significance of fostering an ethical firm culture and protecting client data to maintain trust and integrity in the financial services profession.
64. Assess best practices for building and maintaining compliant and ethical organizations that integrate regulatory requirements, cultural interventions, and behavioral strategies.
65. Identify strategies to mitigate biases such as complacency, groupthink, and greed to promote ethical decision-making.
66. Demonstrate how ethical decision-making contributes to developing trust and market integrity through the broader themes of accountability and resilience.
67. Explain why fostering an ethical culture is a strategic firm imperative that goes beyond regulatory compliance.
68. Describe the impact of client culture in shaping client trust and public confidence.
69. Describe strategies that encourage ethical conduct among financial services firm employees.
70. Analyze the role of firm leadership in establishing, modeling, and sustaining ethical standards.
71. Discuss how an ethical firm culture affects individuals, families, businesses, and the macroeconomy in a competitive and litigious economic environment.
72. Identify the five core technologies that are reshaping financial services: artificial intelligence and machine learning (AI/ML), RegTech and SupTech, Distributed Ledger Technology (DLT) and tokenization, open banking and Application Programming Interfaces (APIs), and cloud/Software-as-a-Service (SaaS) platforms.

73. Evaluate the successes and limitations of technology adoption through various case examples, balancing the efficiency gains with regulatory, operational, and ethical constraints.
74. Analyze the behavioral dynamics that influence technology adoption, including trust, overconfidence, resistance to change, risk perception, and gaps in digital literacy.
75. Integrate insights from technology adoption and human behavior to understand how innovation can create new opportunities while also introducing new vulnerabilities within the financial services profession.
76. Explain how a structured and consistent evaluative lens aligns technology adoption at the firm level with global compliance rules and regulations.
77. Identify practice risks and describe how risks can be converted into defined controls to address audits and quality-of-advice assurance checks.
78. Outline a practical approach for financial services firms to enhance ethics compliance processes to ensure technology adoption aligns with organizational goals and regulatory expectations.
79. Assess how technology adoption, guided by ethical compliance processes, supports the broader objectives of financial services firms.

West Lafayette, IN, USA Wookjae Heo
Athens, GA, USA John E. Grable

Contents

About the Authors

Wookjae Heo is Assistant Professor of Financial Counseling and Planning in the Division of Consumer Science at Purdue University's College of Health and Human Sciences. At Purdue, he teaches undergraduate and graduate courses in financial planning—among them courses on ethics and compliance in financial planning—and contributes to curriculum and student mentorship. His research interests center on behavioral finance and consumer financial well-being, with a particular emphasis on financial stress and coping, life insurance demand, financial technology, and financial education. His work also involves the application of data mining and machine learning methods to solve problems in personal finance. He has published extensively on these topics (including studies on financial stress, risk tolerance, and financial therapy). He is also the author of the monograph *The Demand for Life Insurance: Dynamic Ecological Systemic Theory Using Machine Learning Techniques*, published by Palgrave. Heo holds a PhD in Financial Planning (University of Georgia) and held a prior faculty appointment in Consumer Affairs at South Dakota State University before joining Purdue in 2021. His peer-reviewed output includes more than 65 articles and book chapters across journals and edited volumes in financial services, consumer behavior, and applied finance; his Google Scholar profile shows broad citation impact. In addition to research and teaching, Heo is active in scholarly service. He serves on several journal editorial boards and reviews for multiple journals that publish consumer and financial services research. He also participates in professional associations and has held fellowships and invited roles internationally. His work blends quantitative methods (including machine learning and data mining) with applied techniques to improve financial decision-making and consumer outcomes.

John Grable CFP® teaches and conducts research in the Certified Financial Planner Board of Standards Inc. undergraduate and graduate programs at the University of Georgia where he holds an Athletic Association Endowed Professorship. Before entering the academic profession, he worked as a pension/benefits administrator and later as a Registered Investment Adviser in an asset management firm. Grable has served the financial planning profession as the founding editor of the *Journal of Personal Finance* and co-founding editor of the *Journal of Financial Therapy* and *Financial Planning Review*. He served as the interim editor for *Financial Services Review* in 2023/2024. Grable is best known for his work in the areas of financial literacy and education, financial risk-tolerance assessment, behavioral financial planning, and evidence-based financial advisory practice. He is active in promoting the link between research and financial planning practice where he has published over 150 refereed papers, co-authored several textbooks, co-authored a financial planning communication book, co-authored a financial counseling book, and co-edited a financial planning and counseling scales book. Since earning his doctorate, Grable has served on the Board of Directors of the International Association of Registered Financial Consultants (IARFC), as Treasurer and President for the American Council on Consumer Interests (ACCI), as cofounder, Treasurer, and board member for the Financial Therapy Association, and as an Academy of Financial Services board member. He has received numerous awards, including the prestigious Cato Award for Distinguished Journalism in the Field of Financial Services, the IARFC Founders Award, the Dawley-Scholer Award for Faculty Excellence in Student Development, and the ACCI Mid-Career Award. Grable was the first inductee into the Financial Therapy Association's Hall of Fame.

Introduction to Ethics in the Financial Services Profession

1

Chapter Outcomes
This chapter focuses on helping learners develop the ability to:

1. Define ethics in the context of the financial services profession as a set of conduct norms or standards that guide what is deemed acceptable and unacceptable behavior.
2. Explain the purpose of studying ethics within the financial services profession. This involves understanding the role of ethics in establishing frameworks for professional conduct and decision-making.
3. Identify historical precedents of ethical practice and regulation in the financial services sector across multiple regions, including the United States, Canada, Europe, Australia, New Zealand, Africa, and Asia.
4. Analyze the contextual factors that contribute to individuals and firms engaging in unethical behavior.
5. Evaluate the significance of ethical standards in maintaining trust and integrity in financial services by drawing connections between historical practices and modern regulatory frameworks.

Introduction

Before going deeper into this chapter, take a moment to reflect on what it means to act ethically by considering this scenario: You are deciding whether to sell (or buy more) shares in a fast-growing biotechnology company. Over lunch, a physician friend shares confidential information that the stock price is about to drop

Note: This chapter was copyedited using Grammarly™ and generative AI tools to enhance clarity, grammar, and overall readability. While these tools provided suggestions and assistance in refining the text, the ideas, content, and arguments presented remain the sole work and responsibility of the authors. Any errors or inaccuracies in the final version are also the authors' responsibility.

W. Heo, J. E. Grable, *Ethics and Compliance in Financial Services*,
https://doi.org/10.1007/978-3-032-14449-2_1

significantly due to the Food and Drug Administration (FDA) rejection of the company's new drug. Selling now could help you avoid a substantial financial loss. However, you also recognize that using this information may be unethical and illegal. How would you respond in this situation? Would you:

A. Sell your shares immediately to avoid significant financial loss, as the information is reliable and the decision is sound from a financial perspective.
B. Sell your shares but disclose to anyone who asks that you received confidential information before making the sale of the stock.
C. Do not sell your shares, even though the information could save you from financial loss, because trading on insider information is unethical and illegal.
D. Sell your shares by asking a family member to handle the transaction to ensure you are not directly involved and provide an arms-length transaction.

This is not an entirely fictional case. A comparable situation occurred in 2001. Martha Stewart, a prominent television personality, faced these choices. The case centered around her sale of 4000 shares of the biotechnology company ImClone Systems, just before the stock price plummeted due to negative news about the company's cancer drug, Erbitux. Martha Stewart was tipped off by her broker, Peter Bacanovic, about impending negative news regarding ImClone's drug. Bacanovic informed Stewart that ImClone founder Sam Waksal was trying to sell his own shares before the FDA rejected the company's application for approval of its cancer drug. On December 27, 2001, Stewart sold her shares in ImClone just before the stock price dropped by 16% following the news that the FDA had declined to approve the drug. Regulators immediately questioned this sale, as it seemed to have been timed with prior knowledge of the negative news. In 2003, Martha Stewart was charged with conspiracy, obstruction of justice, and making false statements related to the sale. The case primarily revolved around whether Stewart had acted on insider information. While not directly charged with insider trading, she was convicted of obstruction and lying to investigators. Stewart was sentenced to five months in prison, five months of home confinement, and two years of probation. Additionally, she was fined $30,000. She also resigned from her position as CEO of her company, Martha Stewart Omnimedia.

What would you have done? If you answered C, "Do not sell your shares, even though the information could save you from financial loss, because trading on insider information is unethical and illegal," you chose the correct (and ethical) course of action. Under current law, insider trading is not only unethical, but also illegal. Insider trading creates an uneven trading environment where individuals with access to privileged information can profit at the expense of ordinary investors.[1] Insider trading is prohibited under the Securities Exchange Act of 1934. If you chose one of the other options, here is what you need to know:

- Answer A (sell your shares immediately): Although financially tempting, this option involves using inside information to benefit from an unfair advantage, which is illegal and unethical.

- Answer B (sell and disclose the information): While transparency is important, simply disclosing that you received confidential information does not change the fact that you traded on that information, which is illegal. Full disclosure would not shield you from the legal consequences of insider trading.
- Answer D (sell and ask a family member to handle the transaction): This option would not release you from the responsibility for the trade. It is not enough to delegate the action to someone else. You would still be liable for trading on material, nonpublic information.

As this case illustrates, establishing and enforcing ethical standards in the financial services profession helps to maintain confidence and trust in the markets.[2] As will be discussed in this chapter, ethical considerations go beyond mere regulatory compliance. Ethical standards should be the cornerstone of all aspects of professional practice, from enterprise governance to customer relations.[3] The following discussion provides a brief overview of the historical roots of ethics as a professional obligation for financial services.

A Brief History of Ethics in the Financial Services Profession

The foundation of ethical practice in the financial services profession is deeply rooted in business history.[4] Many of today's regulations can be linked back to early banking practices dating back to ancient civilizations.[5] Throughout history, individuals have entrusted their wealth to custodians who have held an inherent asymmetric advantage in terms of knowledge and experience. Self-regulation was used early on to help balance conflicts of interest.[6] Over time, policymakers have increasingly introduced ethical obligations on those who provide financial advice to others for a fee to safeguard assets and market integrity.[7]

In medieval Europe, banking guilds introduced formalized codes of conduct, emphasizing principles such as transparency, fairness, and honor.[8] These codes laid the groundwork for modern regulatory frameworks (discussed in more detail in Chap. 5). The Renaissance period witnessed a surge in financial innovation. As an example, the Medici Bank of fifteenth-century Florence helped draft and enforce policies and procedures designed to ensure that bankers acted ethically.[9] Religious beliefs also shaped how bankers and financial advisors were expected to interact with clients.[10] The early Christian prohibition of usury illustrates the importance church leaders placed on conducting business with fairness and compassion.

Financial service business practices remained relatively unchanged for hundreds of years. This changed in the early twentieth century.[11] The Great Depression was a significant turning point in the way ethical practice is conceptualized.[12] The Great Depression was influenced by various factors, including overproduction, underconsumption, a decline in international trade caused by tariffs, income inequality, and weather anomalies. However, bank failures and the stock market crash of 1929 are generally recognized as its immediate causes. Speculation in the stock market, combined with a lax regulatory environment, led to an unsustainable asset price bubble.

When traders began to panic, the market corrected itself with a substantial sell-off that persisted for years. As a result, not only did wealth disappear, but consumer confidence in the financial system also plummeted. Simultaneously, thousands of banks across the country failed due to consumers withdrawing their deposits and borrowers defaulting on loans. This led to a contraction in the money supply, further eroding consumer confidence. As the economy spiraled out of control, the federal government felt compelled to intervene in order to support the economy. Policymakers took action to enhance investor protection and reduce the frequency of bank failures.

The result of the Great Depression was a realization that an unchecked market can create inequities in income, wealth, and living standards. This realization was a driving force in the creation of federal and state agencies that had (and continue to have) a role in enforcing regulations designed to create stability in the markets; reduce systemic financial risks; bolster investor trust through policies requiring firms to provide disclosures, transparency, and fair dealings; protect consumers against unfair, deceptive, or predatory practices; maintain market integrity by preventing market manipulation, insider trading, and other forms of fraud; encourage efficient capital allocation; facilitate credit availability; encourage investment; ensure institutions operate without taking excessive risk; and prevent financial crimes.

More recently, the 2008 financial mortgage crisis stands as one of the most impactful events in recent history. The crisis, which was triggered by the collapse of the U.S. housing market and risky lending practices, led to widespread bank failures, government bailouts, and a deep recession. The crisis also shook the foundations of the global economy.[13] Ethical lapses, such as excessive risk-taking and a lack of accountability, became increasingly evident during the crisis. The financial crisis revealed systemic weaknesses within the banking and brokerage sectors, which eroded public trust and confidence. In response, extensive regulatory reforms were implemented to address these issues and restore ethical standards. These reforms emphasized the importance of transparency, accountability, and risk mitigation, with the goal of rebuilding the fragile trust between financial institutions, the government, and the public.

Perspective

Unethical practices in the financial services profession can have a significant negative impact on consumers, the regulatory environment, and the economy as a whole. The following case offers a perspective on the consequences that an unethical corporate culture can create when aggressive financial goals are prioritized over ethical standards. The case also highlights the importance of regulatory frameworks and underscores the critical need to foster a culture that aligns business strategies with customer well-being and long-term sustainability.

In 2016, Wells Fargo was accused of engaging in widespread unethical practices that severely damaged customer trust. Over several years, Wells Fargo employees, under intense pressure to meet unrealistic sales targets, opened millions of unauthorized bank and credit card accounts without customers' knowledge or consent.[14] This fraudulent activity included creating fake email addresses, transferring funds without permission, and enrolling customers in services they neither requested nor needed. The scandal resulted in financial harm to customers, including unauthorized fees, damaged credit scores, and breaches of trust. Regulators uncovered a toxic corporate culture driven by aggressive sales quotas and a "cross-selling" strategy where employees were incentivized to push additional products to existing customers, regardless of ethical considerations or customer needs.

In response to the scandal, Wells Fargo faced significant legal, financial, and reputational consequences, including a $185 million fine, a settlement of billions of dollars in subsequent lawsuits, and the resignation of key executives, including CEO John Stumpf. The bank also faced intensified regulatory scrutiny that resulted in widespread reforms, such as eliminating sales quotas, enhancing oversight, and investing in employee ethics training.

This case highlights several critical lessons related to fostering a responsible and sustainable corporate environment. First, ethical leadership is essential in setting the tone for organizational behavior. At Wells Fargo, executives prioritized aggressive sales goals, creating an environment where unethical practices thrived. Second, bank employees failed to prioritize customer needs. Instead, they focused on short-term profits and self-justified bonuses. The bank's focus on aggressive cross-selling strategies directly harmed customers and demonstrated the dangers of incentives that are misaligned with client interests. Accountability at all levels is another critical takeaway from the case. The lack of internal firm oversight and responsibility allowed unethical behavior to persist unchecked. Only after regulators took action was any manager reprimanded or held accountable.

Additionally, the case underscores the significance of corporate culture. A toxic environment that prioritized high-pressure sales targets incentivized unethical practices. Rather than focus on fairness, integrity, and transparency, bank employees acted selfishly and unethically. The case demonstrates the need for strong regulatory oversight and compliance. The case also illustrates the long-term costs of ethical failures. Wells Fargo suffered extensive financial, legal, and reputational damage that outweighed any short-term gains from employee-driven unethical practices.

Important Ethical Principles: Integrity, Fairness, Accountability, and Transparency

Like other professional fields of practice, the financial services profession is guided by a set of core values intended to prompt integrity, fairness, accountability, and transparency when providing financial advice.[15] The rules governing the delivery of advice are based on a deontological ethical perspective.[16] Regulations, rules, policies, and procedures are almost always written using a deontology lens that focuses on whether an action is inherently appropriate. Rather than evaluate a behavior based on an outcome, a deontological evaluation measures an action by the integrity, fairness, accountability, and transparency of the action, not a person's intent or the behavioral outcome. When viewed this way, regulatory compliance becomes an obligation rather than a guideline, regardless of the consequences (good or bad) a particular action may produce.

Most people navigate daily decisions outside of a regulatory environment using an ethical framework based on consequentialism or what is known as a teleological perspective.[17] Using this ethical lens, the morality of an action is evaluated on the outcome. The central tenet of consequentialism is that the rightness of an action depends on the results it produces. The most common form of consequentialism—utilitarianism—asserts that an action is morally right if it produces the greatest good for the greatest number of people.[18] Utilitarianism prioritizes overall well-being over individual rights and duties. Whereas a deontology business model emphasizes adherence to absolute ethical principles, consequentialism focuses on achieving desirable outcomes, which allows someone to justify actions that would otherwise be deontologically wrong.

Integrity, fairness, accountability, and transparency are critical principles in developing and enforcing ethical frameworks used in the financial services profession.[19] In this regard, these principles represent a deontological perspective. That is, the law expects strict adherence to these principles regardless of the consequences. The following discussion reviews what these four pillars of ethics mean in practice.

Integrity

As a financial services professional, practicing integrity means planning, proposing, performing, reporting, and reviewing work with clients by being honest, transparent, and trustworthy. Integrity involves placing the interests of clients first, providing advice that is in the best interest of the client rather than pursuing personal (or firm) gain, avoiding conflicts of interest, and doing the right thing all the time.[20] Practicing with integrity means disclosing relevant information to stakeholders, including the way one is paid and the risk associated with products and strategies. Practicing with integrity also means that a professional adheres to all legal and regulatory practice guidelines, acts in good faith, and strives to build and maintain client relationships based on mutual trust and respect.

Fairness

A financial services professional is acting with fairness if the processes leading to client outcomes are equitable and balanced.[21] This means the financial professional treats all clients equitably, without favoritism or bias, and makes reasonable decisions. A fair financial services professional provides balanced and objective advice. The principle of fairness mandates that a financial advisor[22] give the same level of care to clients regardless of a client's wealth, income, or social status. A fair financial advisor does not discriminate based on personal preferences or prejudices. Practicing fairly also means that a client's best interest is of paramount importance.

Today, some firms define fairness to encompass the notion of providing equitable resource and opportunity outcomes as a way to redress historical injustices. Regardless of their scope, fairness principles and processes require a financial advisor to be consistent and inclusive.

Accountability

A core element of ethical practice is accountability. Accountability refers to taking responsibility for one's actions, decisions, and the associated outcomes.[23] An accountable financial services professional is willing to explain their thought process when making recommendations. They are also answerable for any mistakes or missteps that may arise during the advising process. A financially accountable advisor also acknowledges errors and works to resolve them, ensuring that the client's interests are prioritized. Practicing accountability also involves adhering to professional and ethical standards and being responsive to client needs. Accountability is the element that binds fairness, ethics, and transparency together. Accountability is what makes it possible for regulators to hold individuals, organizations, and governments answerable for their actions or inactions.

Transparency

Transparency in practice means ensuring that models, systems, and strategies are understandable to clients, regulators, and other stakeholders.[24] When someone says a financial advisor practices with transparency, they generally mean that the financial professional is open, clear, and honest about their practice procedures, including their services and strategies. Being transparent involves providing clients with complete and accurate information regarding fees, potential risks, performance, and the reasoning behind financial recommendations. A transparent financial advisor discloses conflicts of interest and proactively works to inform clients of any costs or charges associated with the delivery of advice.

Collectively, integrity, fairness, accountability, and transparency ensure that financial advice is delivered honestly and in the spirit of stewardship. Being an honest steward involves responsibly managing client relationships and resources. These concepts underpin the ethical delivery of financial advice. The following case narrative illustrates a situation in which one person acted unethically to undermine all aspects of integrity, fairness, accountability, and transparency.[25]

> The Bernie Madoff scandal is the story of one of history's most notorious financial frauds. The scandal involved a decades-long Ponzi scheme orchestrated by Bernard L. Madoff, who once served as chairperson of the NASDAQ stock exchange. Madoff attracted investors by promising consistently high returns through his investment advisory business, which he claimed utilized a proprietary "split-strike conversion" strategy. However, few legitimate investments were being made. Instead, Madoff funneled funds from new investors to pay returns to earlier investors, creating an illusion of profitability. As his operation

grew to oversee billions of dollars, Madoff drew in institutional investors, charities, and individual clients, many of whom entrusted their life savings to Madoff. The scheme unraveled in December 2008 during the global financial crisis when Madoff could no longer sustain the scheme due to mounting redemption requests and a lack of new capital inflows. Investigations uncovered that Madoff had defrauded thousands of investors out of approximately $65 billion. The scandal exposed significant lapses in regulatory oversight, as the Securities and Exchange Commission (SEC) had received multiple warnings about Madoff's activities but failed to act decisively. Madoff was arrested and later sentenced to 150 years in prison, marking a dramatic fall from grace for one of Wall Street's most respected figures. The fallout devastated countless lives, eroded trust in financial institutions, and underscored the critical need for stronger regulatory frameworks and vigilance in the financial services profession.

The Bernie Madoff case had profound personal, regulatory, and ethical consequences that reshaped the financial services landscape and public trust in investment practices. On an individual level, the fraud ruined the lives of thousands of victims, many of whom lost their life savings, retirement funds, and financial security. The emotional toll was severe, with some investors facing bankruptcy and irreparable harm to their well-being. Madoff faced significant personal consequences, including arrest, conviction, and a 150-year prison sentence. While this represented justice, it provided little solace to those he harmed. His family also suffered greatly, enduring public shame, financial ruin, and personal tragedies, including the suicide of Madoff's son, Mark Madoff.

On a regulatory level, the scandal exposed glaring deficiencies in oversight and enforcement within the SEC. Despite numerous warnings and red flags raised by whistleblowers, including financial analyst Harry Markopolos, the SEC failed to uncover Madoff's scheme until it collapsed.[26] This failure prompted a thorough review of regulatory practices, leading to reforms aimed at enhancing the SEC's ability to detect and prevent similar frauds. These reforms included increased resources for investigations, improved whistleblower protections, and the establishment of more rigorous standards for investment advisory firms. Ethically, the scandal highlighted the catastrophic consequences of greed, deception, and a lack of fiduciary responsibility. Madoff's actions violated trust and exploited vulnerabilities in a system reliant on transparency and integrity.

Ethical Considerations in the Twenty-First Century for Financial Services Professionals

The financial services sector is undergoing a profound transformation fueled by technological advancements in financial technology (fintech), blockchain models, and digital currencies (see Chap. 14 for more information on these trends). These innovations have redefined traditional advisory models, enabling personalized and accessible services while presenting significant ethical challenges.[27] Issues such as data privacy, algorithmic biases, equitable access to products and services, and the ethical deployment of technologies like blockchain technologies[28] and artificial intelligence (AI) require careful consideration.[29] For instance, while blockchain models promote transparency, their potential use in anonymizing transactions raises ethical questions. Similarly, AI enhances efficiency but risks perpetuating biases through inappropriate programming design and opaque monitoring.

Financial technology (fintech), which includes the innovative use of digital tools, technology, and software to improve the delivery of financial services and modeling financial processes, has democratized financial services and expanded access to underserved populations through tools like mobile banking, digital wallets, and microfinance platforms.[30] These technologies enable financial advisors to provide tailored advice using AI-driven analytics and user-friendly interfaces. However, this digital shift also exposes clients to risks, including cyberattacks and data misuse. While regulators continue to grapple with ways to oversee the use of fintech services, financial advisors must proactively balance seamless service delivery with robust protections for client confidentiality and transparent data use.

Regulatory oversight plays a critical role in addressing these challenges. The global nature of fintech innovations necessitates enhanced cross-border coordination[31] and regulations to ensure market stability, combat money laundering, and ethically deploy digital currencies.[32] Ensuring affordability and inclusivity is of paramount importance in preventing financial exclusion and inequality, particularly as automation and digitalization reshape the financial advisory landscape.

Ethical concerns in fintech extend beyond privacy and security. Workforce displacement due to automation is beginning to raise questions related to the fair treatment and reskilling of those who work in the financial services profession. In practice, algorithmic fairness must be prioritized to avoid biases and discrimination when AI is used to enhance decision-making. Financial advisors and firms also bear a moral responsibility to confirm their services remain accessible across all societal segments.

Addressing evolving ethical challenges requires focused leadership and a values-driven organizational culture. Leaders must model integrity, embed ethical principles into decision-making models, and promote accountability at every enterprise level. Continuous training on ethical standards, robust compliance frameworks, and a commitment to weighing profitability with client welfare are essential to sustaining trust and delivering responsible services. By embracing these principles, financial advisory firms and financial advisors can better navigate the complexities of technological innovation while maintaining the profession's integrity and advancing equitable financial access.

Ethical Decision-Making

Responsible financial decision-making requires financial advisors to carefully balance profit-seeking behavior with obligations to clients and society. As noted above, ensuring fair access to essential financial services fosters inclusion and economic equity. Doing so increases the likelihood that all individuals, regardless of background or socioeconomic status, have access to financial resources and advice.[33] Although still actively debated, sustainable investment practices, incorporating environmental, social, and governance (ESG) factors, may be a pathway to help align financial advice with broader societal values. Doing so may promote long-term macroeconomic stability while supporting ethical business practices.[34] Transparent communication is also vital, as providing clear, understandable information is a way to engage clients and encourage them to make better-informed decisions. As highlighted throughout this chapter, ethical decision-making is not just a regulatory requirement; it is a moral obligation. The financial services profession can foster a responsible, equitable, and sustainable financial ecosystem by embedding ethical principles into financial decision-making models and balancing profitability with actions designed to improve societal well-being.

Why Do Financial Professionals Engage in Unethical Behaviors?

The Martha Stewart and business management cases described earlier in the chapter indicate that unethical business practices, unfair dealings with clients, and fraud are ongoing professional problems. Unethical behavior arises due to a combination of systemic, behavioral, and personal factors.[35] This behavior is generally referred to as white-collar crime, which is a non-violent, business-related violation of state or federal statutes.[36] It has been estimated that white-collar crimes account for more than 5% of corporate losses each year.[37] In the financial services profession, 7% of financial advisers have misconduct records, with the proportion exceeding 15% at some large firms.[38] Approximately one-third of financial advisers involved in misconduct are repeat offenders, but only half lose their jobs after engaging in misconduct.[39] Firms that persistently engage in misconduct coexist with firms that have clean records. This can be explained by some firms "specializing" in misconduct and catering to unsophisticated consumers.[40]

A natural question arises concerning these statistics: Why do some financial advisors engage in unethical practices? The criminal justice literature provides some answers to this question.[41] At its core, unethical practice is driven by greed, opportunity, a sense of entitlement, arrogance, competitiveness, and rationalization.[42] High-pressure sales environments, where commissions or performance-based bonuses incentivize advisors, also create conflicts of interest, leading some advisors to prioritize their own financial gain over the best interests of their clients. A lack of comprehensive regulatory oversight or weak enforcement mechanisms may also provide opportunities for unethical behavior to go unchecked. Additionally, cognitive biases such as overconfidence or rationalization can cause financial advisors to justify questionable actions, believing they are acting in the best interest of their clients. Personal circumstances like financial stress or career pressures may further contribute to unethical decisions. Regardless, unethical behaviors harm individual clients and undermine trust in the financial services profession.

A financial advisor's personality has also been linked to engagement in unethical behavior.[43] Ethical violations tend to be engaged in by what are called "leaders" and "followers."[44] Leaders tend to be highly intelligent, aggressive, arrogant, cunning, successful, risk seekers, charismatic, and narcissistic (a personality trait characterized by an excessive focus on oneself, often to the exclusion of others[45]). Followers who engage in unethical behavior tend to be less confident, less aggressive, not as ambitious, easily dominated, prone to follow others, and less likely to accept responsibility for their actions. Whether classified as a leader or follower, criminal justice scholars have noted that those who engage in unethical behavior share the following characteristics. They (a) need to feel in control of the situation, (b) tend to exhibit bullying behavior, (c) are charismatic, (d) fear failure, (e) are ambitious, (f) lack integrity, (g) are narcissistic, and (h) lack a social conscience. Consider the following cases:

> Kenneth Lay, the founder and former CEO of Enron, exemplifies the dangers of an arrogant and controlling leadership style. Lay's management approach significantly affected his company's catastrophic collapse.[46] Lay fostered an environment in which his authority went unchallenged, often dismissing dissenting opinions and surrounding himself with executives who supported his vision. His arrogance was apparent in public appearances, even as the company's financial stability deteriorated. Lay frequently boasted about Enron's innovative business model and market dominance, downplaying or outright concealing the risks associated with the firm's aggressive accounting practices and complex financial structures. His controlling nature extended to micromanaging corporate communications and manipulating public perception, ensuring that stakeholders—investors, employees, and regulators—remained unaware of the company's precarious financial situation. This hubris blinded Lay to Enron's ethical and operational flaws and fostered a toxic corporate culture that prioritized short-term economic gains over transparency and sustainability. Ultimately, his refusal to acknowledge warning signs and his overconfidence in his ability to manage crises contributed to one of the largest corporate scandals in U.S. history.

> Dennis Kozlowski, the former CEO of Tyco International, provides another example of how an arrogant and controlling leadership style can undermine corporate governance, erode shareholder trust, and encourage unethical business practices.[47] Kozlowski's tenure at Tyco was marked by a blend of unchecked authority and extravagant personal excesses, reflecting his inflated sense of self-importance. He cultivated a highly centralized decision-making structure, which allowed him to exert significant control over the company's operations while bypassing traditional checks and balances. Kozlowski's arrogance manifested in a lavish lifestyle, funded in part by misappropriated corporate funds, including unauthorized bonuses and extravagant purchases, such as an infamous $6000 shower curtain rod and a multimillion-dollar birthday party in Sardinia. His sense of entitlement and disregard for ethical boundaries created a culture of excess and impunity at Tyco. By prioritizing personal gain over fiduciary responsibility, Kozlowski not only betrayed the trust of shareholders but also damaged Tyco's reputation and financial standing. His eventual conviction for grand larceny, conspiracy, and securities fraud highlights the dangers of allowing a controlling and self-serving leader to operate unchecked within an organization.

These two cases illustrate that unethical behavior often arises from individual traits, organizational culture, and systemic pressures. While personality traits like narcissism and low self-control predispose individuals to unethical decisions, the influence of a permissive corporate environment and high-performance expectations cannot be overlooked. This book will describe examples of dishonest behavior using a lens that encompasses all the factors described thus far. For the purposes of this book, these factors can be categorized into the following 11 elements that commonly describe engagement in unethical behavior (see the chapter appendix for a summary table).

1. Client Vulnerability: Some financial advisors may exploit a client's lack of financial knowledge, leading to unfair dealings and potential fraud. This exploitation can result in significant financial harm to clients.[48] Advisors may also exploit a client's lack of financial literacy, which can lead to fraudulent behavior.
2. Complex Financial Products: The complexity of certain financial products can be exploited by advisors to mislead clients, allowing a financial advisor to take advantage of a client's lack of understanding. This exploitation can lead to unethical practices and client harm.[49]
3. Conflicts of Interest: Financial advisors may prioritize their financial gain over a client's best interests, leading to biased recommendations. Conflicts can result in unethical behavior, as some advisors might be incentivized to promote products that offer higher commissions.[50]
4. Cultural and Environmental Influences: Operating in sectors and regions with prevalent unethical practices can normalize misconduct among advisors, as corrupted cultures will affect advisor behavior.[51] In some firms, unethical behavior may be normalized, leading advisors to engage in such practices because they perceive them to be standard professional behavior.
5. Inadequate Regulatory Oversight: Weak or inconsistent enforcement of regulations can create an environment where unethical behavior goes unchecked, allowing some financial advisors to engage in misconduct without fear of repercussions.[52]
6. Incentive Structures: Commission-based compensation can tempt advisors to recommend unnecessary transactions, prioritizing personal gain over a client's needs. A misalignment of incentives can lead to unethical behavior.[53] Additionally, compensation models that reward high-risk behaviors can prompt some advisors to act unethically, especially if they benefit financially by increasing the risk exposure in a client's account.
7. Information Asymmetry: Advisors may exploit their superior knowledge to deceive clients, knowing that clients may not have the expertise to detect unethical practices.[54]
8. Lack of Accountability: In environments where unethical behavior is not adequately punished, some financial advisors may feel emboldened to act unethically, believing there will be few or no consequences for their actions.[55]
9. Lack of or Inadequate Ethical Training: Without proper ethics and legal education, advisors may not recognize the implications of their actions, leading to unethical decisions.[56] A lack of a comprehensive ethical educational framework can leave advisors ill-prepared to handle complex moral dilemmas, increasing the likelihood of unethical choices.[57]
10. Pressure to Meet Sales Targets: High sales quotas can drive some financial advisors to engage in unethical practices to achieve sales targets, including misrepresenting products or services to clients.[58]
11. Repeat Offenders in the Profession: The presence of advisors with prior misconduct records who continue to practice can perpetuate unethical behavior within the profession. This recurrence suggests a tolerance for misconduct that can influence others.[59]

Chapter Summary

This chapter described the critical role ethics plays in maintaining trust and integrity within the financial services profession. The chapter provided a foundation for understanding how norms of conduct must be used to guide the delivery of financial advice. The chapter provided examples of ethical dilemmas and outcomes associated with acting unethically. A key takeaway from the chapter is that unethical financial advisory behavior has serious negative consequences for those working in the profession, consumers, and the overall economy. By establishing a framework for ethical thinking, this chapter sets the stage for deeper discussions related to fostering transparency, fairness, and trust in the financial services profession.

Chapter Resources

- Consumer Financial Protection Bureau: http://consumerfinance.org/
- European Securities and Market Authority: https://www.esma.europa.eu/
- Financial Industry Regulatory Authority (FINRA): https://www.finra.org/
- Securities and Exchange Commission (SEC): https://www.sec.gov/

Appendix

Table 1.1 summarizes a few of the determinants of unethical behavior described in this chapter. Future chapters will build upon the terms and definitions presented in the table when describing case narratives.

Notes

[1]Fairfax, L. (2022). ***Stakeholderism, Corporate Purpose, and Credible Commitment***. https://core.ac.uk/download/541429892.pdf

[2]Adaga, E. M., Egieya, Z. E., Ewuga, S. K., Abdul, A. A., & Abrahams, T. O. (2024). A comprehensive review of ethical practices in banking and finance. ***Finance & Accounting Research Journal***, ***6***(1), 1–20.

[3]Svetlova, E. (2022). AI ethics and systemic risks in finance. ***AI and Ethics, 2***(4), 713–725.

[4]Khaleel, F., Janjua, P. Z., & Ahmed, M. (2022). Ethical consideration of Islamic banks in Pakistan: an empirical analysis. ***Journal of Islamic Marketing, 13***(6), 1351–1372.

[5]Allioui, H., & Mourdi, Y. (2023). Exploring the full potentials of IoT for better financial growth and stability: A comprehensive survey. ***Sensors, 23***(19), 8015.

[6]Ferguson, N. (2008). ***The ascent of money: A financial history of the world***. Penguin.

[7]Davies, G. (2010). ***History of money***. University of Wales Press.

[8]Ferguson, N. (2008). ***The ascent of money: A financial history of the world***. Penguin.

[9]Hsu, Y. T. (2023). Medici influence in 15th century movements. ***Journal of Education, Humanities and Social Sciences, 8***, 982–987.

[10]De Roover, R. (1999). ***The rise and decline of the Medici Bank, 1397–1494*** (Vol. 21). Beard Books.

Table 1.1 The 11 factors used to describe why some financial advisors engage in unethical behavior

Term	Definition
Client vulnerability	Advisors may exploit a client's lack of financial knowledge or trust, leading to unfair dealings, potential fraud, and significant financial harm
Complex financial products	Advisors may exploit the complexity of financial products to mislead clients, taking advantage of their lack of understanding and causing harm
Conflicts of interest	Advisors may prioritize their financial gain over the best interests of clients, leading to biased recommendations and promoting products with higher commissions
Cultural and environmental influences	Unethical practices may become normalized in regions or firms where misconduct is prevalent, leading advisors to perceive unethical behavior as standard professional practice
Inadequate regulatory oversight	Weak or inconsistent enforcement of regulations creates an environment where unethical behavior goes unchecked, allowing misconduct without fear of repercussions
Incentive structures	Commission-based or high-risk investment compensation models can tempt some financial advisors to prioritize personal gain over the needs of clients, leading to unethical behavior
Information asymmetry	Advisors may deceive clients by exploiting their superior knowledge, knowing clients lack the expertise to detect unethical practices
Lack of accountability	Firms failing to punish unethical actions appropriately create a culture where advisors feel emboldened to act unethically without fear of consequences
Lack of or inadequate ethical training	Without comprehensive ethical education, advisors may fail to recognize the implications of their actions, making them more likely to make unethical decisions
Pressure to meet sales targets	High sales quotas may drive advisors to misrepresent products or services to clients in order to meet targets and secure bonuses
Repeat offenders in the profession	The continued presence of advisors with prior misconduct records perpetuates unethical behavior and suggests a tolerance for misconduct within the profession

[11] Goetzmann, W. N., & Rouwenhorst, K. G. eds., (2005). ***The origins of value: The financial innovations that created modern capital markets***. Oxford University Press

[12] Schularick, M., & Taylor, A. M. (2012). Credit booms gone bust: monetary policy, leverage cycles, and financial crises, 1870–2008. ***American Economic Review, 102***(2), 1029 1061.

[13] Chari, V. V., Christiano, L., & Kehoe, P. J. (2008). ***Facts and myths about the financial crisis of 2008***. Federal Reserve Bank of Minneapolis Working Paper, 666.

[14] Office of Public Affairs | Wells Fargo Agrees to Pay $3 Billion to Resolve Criminal and Civil Investigations into Sales Practices Involving the Opening of Millions of Accounts without Customer Authorization | United States Department of Justice. https://www.justice.gov/opa/pr/wells-fargo-agrees-pay-3-billion-resolve-criminal-and-civil-investigations-sales-practices

[15] National Academies of Sciences, Policy, Global Affairs, & Committee on Responsible Science. (2017). ***Fostering integrity in research***. National Academies Press.

[16] Mandal, J., Ponnambath, D. K., & Parija, S. C. (2016). Utilitarian and deontological ethics in medicine. ***Tropical Parasitology***, ***6***(1), 5–7.

[17] Savulescu, J., & Wilkinson, D. (2019). Consequentialism and the law in medicine. ***Philosophical Foundations of Medical Law***, 68. https://library.oapen.org/bitstream/id/d6e713af-d91d-47bf-848d-a7b4fac1f9a4/Bookshelf_NBK550266.pdf

[18]Classic Ethical Principles to Guide Responsible and Ethical Decisions. https://www.apps-explorer.com/classic-ethical-principles-to-guide-responsible-and-ethical-decisions/?amp=1

[19]https://par.nsf.gov/servlets/purl/10139705

[20]https://www.doctrine.af.mil/Portals/61/documents/Airman_Development/BlueBook.pdf

[21]https://d1wqtxts1xzle7.cloudfront.net/46191980/Fairness_and_financial_services_in_Austr20160603-13405-16fzpet-libre.pdf?1464943474=&response-content-disposition=inline%3B+filename%3DFairness_and_financial_services_in_Austr.pdf&Expires=1736081880&Signature=PGBq2x5eB0pZn-MQODq8eRsZqPOYYEUsTi0K4YlsXaUAh1M9~~HWbeZnU4K4HH1GK-lYTtfR70hFf61mmXmLkGMBWOcQ8Elg7~2Q5lEPGncv09qdsyjMe6ZbBIqCElLNvjmd6kcxUj2uPTxFJj-5Sw7opiqLYm2ClSWr0AH24LsKYJ2QpYd9uirNFS7SNFgOguIgOMAxlCr~2Onrv3CmSMEC41ra1-K05m3hXs-IoZ4N118iumuTgCZm3Zf0k6ke0pEhHV2jN-tGxIcKKtoj0B1TofS~H~ZRDEFTf4GQIf1FUpOoymdUilYx~W5prbNQyG3LmQ9UnkEwf2-DMFVjog__&Key-Pair-Id=APKAJLOHF5GGSLRBV4ZA

[22]Although the North American Securities Administrators Association (NASAA) adopted a model rule in 2025 that prohibits broker-dealer agents from using the titles "advisor" or "adviser" unless they are also registered as investment adviser representatives, in this book, a broad definition of financial advisor is retained. A financial advisor advises clients on managing their finances to help them achieve specific financial goals. This advice can cover many areas, including investment management, retirement planning, estate planning, tax planning, insurance needs, debt management, and wealth building.

[23]https://link.springer.com/referenceworkentry/10.1007/978-3-031-25984-5_58

[24]Schedl, M., Anelli, V. W., Lex, E. (2025). Transparency. In ***Technical and Regulatory Perspectives on Information Retrieval and Recommender Systems***. The Information Retrieval Series, vol. 50. Springer, Cham.

[25]https://www.fbi.gov/history/famous-cases/bernie-madoff

[26]https://www.sec.gov/news/studies/2009/oig-509/exhibit-0269.pdf

[27]Böhm, S., Carrington, M., Cornelius, N., de Bruin, B., Greenwood, M., Hassan, L., Jain, T., Karam, C., Kourula, A., Romani, L., & Riaz, S. (2022). Ethics at the centre of global and local challenges: Thoughts on the future of business ethics. ***Journal of Business Ethics, 180***(3), 835–861.

[28]Blockchain technology describes a decentralized digital ledger that records transactions securely across a network of computers. This technology makes data transparent, tamper-resistant, and verifiable without the need for a central accounting authority.

[29]Uzougbo, N. S., Ikegwu, C. G., & Adewusi, A. O. (2024). Legal accountability and ethical considerations of AI in financial services. ***GSC Advanced Research and Reviews, 19***(2), 130–142.

[30]Alexandri, M. B., Usman, I., Narimawati, U., & Taryana, A. (2023). Unraveling the fintech landscape: A systematic mapping study on the impact of financial technology innovation on investment decision-making in ASEAN banking. ***Khazanah Sosial, 5***(1), 113–124.

[31]Wójcik, D., Keenan, L., Pažitka, V., Urban, M., & Wu, W. (2022). The changing landscape of international financial centers in the twenty-first century: Cross-border mergers and acquisitions in the global financial network. ***Economic Geography, 98***(2), 97–118.

[32]Ramkrishna, V. M., & Loganathan, V. (2023). Is digital currency a payment disruption mechanism? ***Fintech and Cryptocurrency***, 173–191.

[33]Adaga, E. M., Egieya, Z. E., Ewuga, S. K., Abdul, A. A., & Abrahams, T. O. (2024). A comprehensive review of ethical practices in banking and finance. ***Finance & Accounting Research Journal, 6***(1), 1–20.

[34]Mehra, R., Patel, P., Shetty, A., Golla, A., Kanesathasan, A., Jacobs, K., & Young, M. (2012). ***Financial services for low-income women: Opportunities for economic empowerment***. International Center for Research on Women.

[35]Sutherland, E. H. (1983). ***White collar crime: The uncut version***. Yale University Press.

[36]Bucy, P. H., Formby, E. P., Raspanti, M. S., & Rooney, K. E. (2008). Why do they do it: the motives, mores, and character of white collar criminals. ***John's L. Rev.*, *82***, 401–437.

[37]Ibid.

[38]Hasnas, J. (2004). Ethics and the problem of white collar crime. ***Am. UL Rev.*, *54***, 579.

[39]Ibid.

[40]Egan, M., Matvos, G., & Seru, A. (2019). The market for financial adviser misconduct. ***Journal of Political Economy*, *127***(1), 233–295.

[41]McGrath, J. (2019). Why do good people do bad things: A multi-level analysis of individual, organizational, and structural causes of white-collar crime. ***Seattle UL Rev.*, *43***, 525.

[42]Bucy, P. H., Formby, E. P., Raspanti, M. S., & Rooney, K. E. (2008). Why do they do it: the motives, mores, and character of white collar criminals. ***John's L. Rev.*, *82***, 401–437.

[43]Blickle, G., Schlegel, A., Fassbender, P., & Klein, U. (2006). Some personality correlates of business white-collar crime. ***Applied Psychology*, *55***(2), 220–233.

[44]Ibid.

[45]Narcissist Couples Therapy for Healthier Connections. https://mantracare.org/therapy/relationship/narcissist-couples-therapy/

[46]https://www.sec.gov/litigation/complaints/complr17722.htm

[47]Ibid.

[48]Ibid.

[49]Samuel, G. K., & Richards, D. S. P. (2018). A probabilistic analysis of autocallable optimization securities. ***arXiv preprint arXiv:1804.00825***.

[50]Miller, S. (2014). Trust, conflicts of interest and fiduciary duties: Ethical issues in the financial planning industry in Australia. ***Capital Failure: Rebuilding Trust in Financial Services***, 305–331.

[51]Pham, M. H., Nguyen, H., Young, M., & Dao, A. (2024). Who Keeps Company with the wolf will learn to howl: Does local corruption culture affect financial adviser misconduct? ***Journal of Business Ethics***, 1–26.

[52]Egan, M., Matvos, G., & Seru, A. (2019). The market for financial adviser misconduct. ***Journal of Political Economy*, *127***(1), 233–295.

[53]West, A. (2023). Meaningful work and unethical work: The crisis in Australian financial advice. ***Business Ethics, the Environment & Responsibility*, *32***(3), 882–895.

[54]Lee, S. P., & O'Connor, M. (2007, January). How good is the advice you receive? The influence of social value orientation and knowledge asymmetry on the formulation of advice. In ***2007 40th Annual Hawaii International Conference on System Sciences (HICSS'07)*** (pp. 190a-190a). IEEE.

[55]Richards, D. W., Ahmed, A. D., & Bruce, K. (2022). Ethics in financial planning: Analysis of ombudsman decisions using codes of ethics and fiduciary duty standards. ***Australian Journal of Management*, *47***(3), 401–422.

[56]Ateeq, A., & Alqaidoom, M. (2024). The Impact of Integrity: Navigating Ethical Dilemmas, Conflicts, and Fraud in Contemporary Business. In ***Business Sustainability with Artificial Intelligence (AI): Challenges and Opportunities: Volume 2*** (pp. 295–302). Cham: Springer Nature Switzerland.

[57]Pham, M. H., Nguyen, H., Young, M., & Dao, A. (2024). Who Keeps Company with the wolf will learn to howl: Does local corruption culture affect financial adviser misconduct? ***Journal of Business Ethics***, 1–26.

[58]Wang, C., Xu, Y., & Zhang, T. (2023). Peer pressure and moral hazard: Evidence from retail banking investment advisors. ***Available at SSRN 4647853***. https://papers.ssrn.com/sol3/papers.cfm?abstract_id=4647853

[59]Egan, M., Matvos, G., & Seru, A. (2019). The market for financial adviser misconduct. ***Journal of Political Economy*, *127***(1), 233–295.

Ethical Theories and Frameworks in Financial Services

2

Chapter Outcomes

This chapter focuses on helping learners develop the ability to:

1. Understand the importance of trust and client protection as a framework for ensuring the sustainability of financial markets and recognize the systemic consequences when these foundations are compromised.
2. Identify ethical theories that serve as a roadmap for delivering financial advice and services.
3. Apply philosophical perspectives to guide ethical behaviors and the decision-making processes of financial services professionals.
4. Demonstrate the practical application of ethics in the advisor-client relationship, including strategies for navigating ambiguity and managing conflicts of interest.
5. Evaluate ethical reasoning as a strategic and moral compass and use reasoning to reinforce trust and foster positive client engagements in financial services.

Introduction

In the increasingly complex landscape of the financial services profession, ethical decision-making is not just an incidental concern of interest to regulators. Practicing ethically is the foundation for establishing a financial professional's credibility. Ethical standards serve as a benchmark by which the public and regulators assess a firm's stability, sustainability, and social responsibility. Consider a marketplace in which most participants (clients, advisors, and firms) act only in their own self-interest. In this market, cheating, withholding information, and pushing legal

Note: This chapter was copyedited using Grammarly™ and generative AI tools to enhance clarity, grammar, and overall readability. While these tools provided suggestions and assistance in refining the text, the ideas, content, and arguments presented remain the sole work and responsibility of the authors. Any errors or inaccuracies in the final version are also the authors' responsibility.

W. Heo, J. E. Grable, *Ethics and Compliance in Financial Services*,
https://doi.org/10.1007/978-3-032-14449-2_2

boundaries are the norm. If such a market existed, it would quickly fail. Failure would arise because engaging with another party becomes exceedingly difficult if trust is nonexistent. The risks are too high. Today, nearly all markets exist on the dual foundations of trust and protection. Even so, without clear ethical frameworks in place, the market can experience a crisis.

Consider what happened in 2008 with the subprime mortgage crisis.[1] This dark period in American history exposed significant failures in safeguarding the interests of market participants. Culminating in 2008, banks and other lenders aggressively issued high-risk mortgages to borrowers who lacked the financial capacity to repay. Some loans were extended using predatory terms. Lending practices were motivated by a desire for short-term profits. In this environment, lenders assumed borrowers were withholding critical information. Borrowers were assuming lenders were taking advantage of them by charging excessive fees. Regulators allowed the market to slowly disintegrate with the hope that by securitizing subprime loans into complex mortgage-backed securities (MBS), the bond market would be able to accurately apply a price to the risks taken by lenders.

An important watchdog failed in providing information transparency about the securitization process, which further eroded trust in the mortgage markets. Credit rating agencies operating under lender-paid models assigned inflated AAA ratings to securitized bonds. The rating agencies fraudulently misrepresented the actual risk of newly issued mortgages. At the same time, regulatory bodies, including the Securities and Exchange Commission (SEC) and the Federal Reserve, failed to provide adequate oversight or implement meaningful capital requirements on lenders. The lack of an honest watchdog and the absence of regulatory oversight allowed lenders to take on excessive leverage. This elevated market risks to such a point that market participants could no longer trust others in the market.

In the end, a mortgage bubble developed. It was at the height of the bubble that housing prices declined. This triggered widespread borrower defaults. These defaults began to shine a light on the unethical nature of the loans—loans that had been made to people who either lied about their financial situation or where lenders knew a borrower would be unable to make payments. The defaults rippled through the financial system. A liquidity crisis took hold in late 2008. Financial institutions, such as Lehman Brothers, collapsed. The ensuing contagion resulted in a global financial crisis. Millions of homeowners lost their properties to foreclosure, investors faced trillions in losses, and taxpayers ultimately bore the burden through unprecedented government bailouts. This case example underscores what can happen when market participants act unethically in a marketplace lacking adequate stakeholder protection. A lack of trust can quickly morph into a crisis.

Given its importance in creating a stabilized marketplace, it is important to understand what trust means. Trust is a shared expectation of honesty, fairness, and responsibility.[2] In practice, trust is the foundation upon which the functionality and integrity of financial markets are built. Trust is what enables transactions between parties who often operate with incomplete information and differing interests.

When viewed from a financial services perspective, trust is synonymous with a concept called mutual trust, which is the belief that each party in a transaction will act in good faith. At a deeper and more ethically grounded level, mutual trust evolves into reciprocal trust. Reciprocal trust means that each party not only believes in the integrity of the other but also actively upholds their own responsibilities to reinforce and sustain the trust relationship.[3] The following discussion looks at reciprocal trust in more detail.

Reciprocal trust implies a dynamic and ongoing commitment to ethical conduct, transparency, and the mutual fulfillment of obligations.[4] To exhibit reciprocal trust goes beyond passive reliance on assumptions and surface-level information sharing. Reciprocal trust is based on an active system of accountability and fairness. Given information asymmetries in the financial services marketplace (a situation that arises because advisors typically know more than their clients), clients depend on their financial advisors to operate using reciprocity.

Reciprocal trust is also a cornerstone of market integrity at institutional and regulatory levels. Consider situations where trust is absent. Even technically sound transactions can be hindered by suspicion and market dysfunction without reciprocal trust, which is what occurred in 2008 during the mortgage crisis.

The notion of reciprocal trust serves as the foundation for most regulatory frameworks. Stakeholder (for example, clients and trading partners) protection traditionally means ensuring that deceptive, negligent, or exploitative practices are avoided.[5] Operating at the level of stakeholder protection, firms and advisors are expected to emphasize shared responsibility, transparency, and fairness across all interactions.

Stakeholder reciprocity is another concept related to trust and protection. Stakeholder reciprocity is about avoiding harm and intentionally creating value and fairness in the marketplace.[6] To be reciprocal is to recognize the interconnected nature of financial systems in which clients, firms, regulators, and society are linked. In models of stakeholder reciprocity, market participants are responsible for protecting their interests and contributing to the entire system's ethical integrity.

Reciprocal trust and stakeholder reciprocity are deeply rooted in regulatory frameworks.[7] As the discussion thus far has highlighted, trust and reciprocity go beyond mere compliance with legal regulations. Figure 2.1 illustrates how reciprocal trust, stakeholder reciprocity, and ethics/professional conduct are related to each other.

Ethics defines the moral boundaries and expectations that govern professional conduct. Trust and reciprocity represent the shared norms that enable sustainable financial relationships. The application of these concepts also allows financial institutions to thrive in an overly complex and highly competitive marketplace. When internalized and consistently applied, ethical standards reinforce the credibility and stability of financial markets. The remainder of this chapter focuses on describing the critical role of ethics in establishing and sustaining trust, safeguarding stakeholder interests, and ensuring market stability.

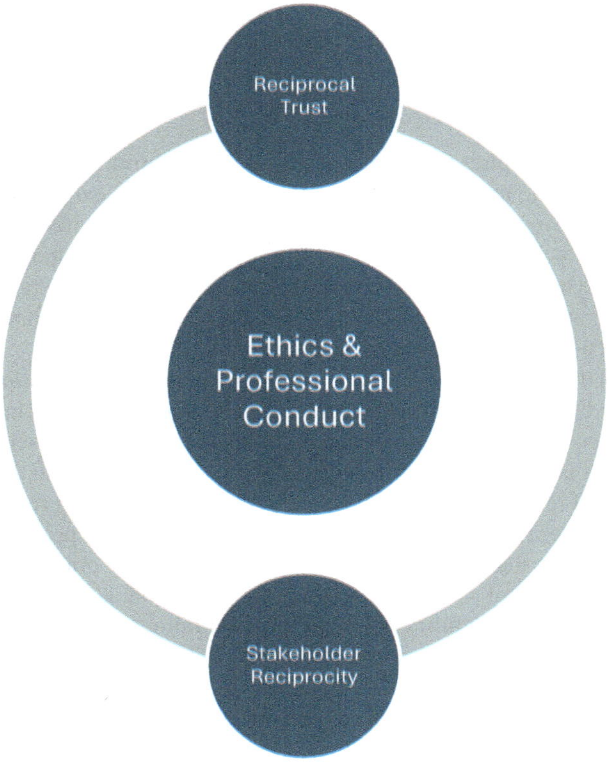

Fig. 2.1 The relationship between reciprocal trust, stakeholder reciprocity, and professional conduct

Perspective

The case of Enron Corporation is one of the most notable examples illustrating how a loss of trust among investors can lead to a market crisis. Enron, once a prominent American energy company based in Houston, Texas, was celebrated in the 1990s as an innovative leader in the energy trading and utilities sector. By 2000, Enron reported over $100 billion in revenues. The company was named one of America's most innovative firms. However, behind this facade of success, Enron's management was engaged in systemic financial fraud, utilizing complex accounting schemes to hide massive debts and inflate profits. The collapse of Enron in 2001, following the exposure of these practices, became one of the most infamous corporate scandals in history, severely undermining investor trust and damaging the credibility of U.S. financial markets.[8]

Enron's executives, including CEO Jeffrey Skilling and CFO Andrew Fastow, employed "mark-to-market" accounting to record projected future profits as current earnings, even when those profits were speculative.[9] They also created thousands of off-balance-sheet entities, known as Special Purpose Entities (SPEs), to conceal billions in debt and unprofitable ventures. Enron insiders often controlled these entities, allowing the company to present a misleadingly strong financial picture to investors and analysts. For example, Enron reported inflated earnings of $979 million in 2000, while its financial health was actually deteriorating due to unprofitable investments and growing liabilities.

The company's auditor, Arthur Andersen, one of the "Big Five" accounting firms at the time, failed to challenge these questionable practices, either due to negligence or due to complicity.[10] This failure further eroded the checks and balances designed to protect investors. Enron's stock price soared to a peak of $90.75 in August 2000, driven by false perceptions of profitability and growth, only to plummet as the truth became known.

In October 2001, Enron announced a $618 million loss for the third quarter and a $1.2 billion reduction in shareholder equity, prompting scrutiny from analysts and regulators. Whistleblower Sherron Watkins, an Enron vice president, alerted then-CEO Kenneth Lay to the accounting irregularities, but her warnings were largely ignored. By November 2001, Enron admitted to overstating earnings by nearly $600 million over several years, leading to a series of credit downgrades and investor panic. On December 2, 2001, Enron filed for Chap. 11 bankruptcy, marking the largest bankruptcy in U.S. history at the time.

The fallout was catastrophic for investors. Enron's stock, once a favorite on Wall Street, fell to under $1 by December 2001, erasing billions in shareholder value. Many employees had heavily invested their retirement savings in Enron stock through 401(k) plans. Employees lost an estimated $2 billion. Investors, including pension funds and individual shareholders, experienced devastating losses, with some institutional investors losing hundreds of millions.[11]

The scandal shattered trust in corporate governance and financial reporting. Investors who relied on Enron's audited financial statements and analyst recommendations felt betrayed by the failures of corporate executives, auditors, and regulators. The involvement of Arthur Andersen, which was later convicted of obstruction of justice for shredding Enron-related documents, further eroded confidence in the auditing profession. This loss of trust extended beyond Enron itself, as investors began questioning the reliability of financial statements across corporate America.

The Enron scandal had far-reaching effects on the credibility of U.S. financial markets, contributing to a broader "crisis of trust." The scandal amplified investor fears, leading to a massive sell-off of stocks, particularly in the energy and technology sectors. The NASDAQ, already weakened by the dotcom bust, experienced prolonged volatility as investor trust in U.S. corporate governance continued to diminish. The Enron collapse also revealed weaknesses in financial oversight, prompting Congress to pass the Sarbanes-Oxley Act of 2002.[12] This legislation introduced stricter corporate governance standards, including requirements for CEO and CFO certification of financial statements and enhanced auditor independence. While these reforms aimed to restore trust, they also increased compliance costs for companies, signaling to investors that the previous regulatory framework had been inadequate.

Furthermore, the complicity of Arthur Andersen and the failure of credit rating agencies to downgrade Enron's debt until days before its bankruptcy further undermined confidence in financial intermediaries. Investors began to doubt the objectivity of auditors, analysts, and rating agencies, many of whom faced conflicts of interest due to consulting fees or pressure from corporate clients. This loss of trust had tangible economic effects, deterring many retail investors from participating in the stock market due to fears of further fraud, contributing to reduced market liquidity and investment capital.

The Nature of Ethics in the Financial Services Profession: Historical Foundations and Contemporary Relevance

Ethics is a complex concept that defies a simple definition. Rather than being a fixed or universal standard, ethics encompasses a wide range of theories, interpretations, and applications that have evolved over centuries. At its core, *ethics refers to the principles, values, and standards that guide human behavior in distinguishing right from wrong, fairness from injustice, and virtue from vice.*[13] The application of ethics involves a normative inquiry into how individuals should act in personal conduct and within broader social, institutional, and economic contexts.

Ethics differs from laws in that ethics is not always codified or externally enforced.[14] Instead, ethics reflects moral reasoning and cultural norms that influence behavior in formal and informal settings.[15] Ethical reasoning requires individuals to evaluate the consequences of their actions, the fairness of decision-making processes, the intentions behind decisions, and the inherent dignity of those affected. In the financial domain, ethical thinking is essential for ensuring trust, protecting clients and other stakeholders, and upholding the legitimacy of institutions and markets.

Philosophers have thought and debated about the origins and implications of ethics for thousands of years. Table 2.1 shows some of the most notable ethical philosophers across time. The timeline starts with Aristotle, who argued in favor of virtue ethics that focuses on developing a moral character and cultivating habits that align with human flourishing (*eudaimonia*).[16] In this table, the timeline ends with Lawrence Kohlberg, who explored the developmental stages of moral reasoning. Kohlberg argued that ethical behavior and cognitive maturity are highly associated.

Upon reviewing the list of philosophers in Table 2.1, it is important to recognize similarities and differences. What unites these thinkers is a concern for human flourishing and moral development. Each, in their own way, believed that ethics can and should guide human behavior. Kant, for example, argued that people share universal moral obligations, whereas Rawls sought to change society to create fair social structures. Each philosopher also emphasized the importance of human relationships, justice, and fairness.

There are also differences in the way these thinkers conceptualized ethics. Ethics transformed from a focus on virtue and character under Aristotle to standardized rules under Kant, to consequences of behaviors under Mill,[17] to justice and psychological development under Buber and Kohlberg.[18] Internal versus external

Table 2.1 Ethical philosophers across time

Philosopher	Lifespan	Key contribution	Ethical focus	Approach type	Source of moral authority
Aristotle	384–322 BCE	Virtue ethics; moral character and human flourishing (*eudaimonia*)	Virtue and character	Virtue ethics	Human nature and rationality
Thomas Aquinas	1225–1274	Natural law; synthesis of Christian theology and Aristotelian ethics	Divine purpose and natural law	Theological ethics	God's law and reason
Adam Smith	1723–1790	Moral sentiments and economic fairness: early ideas of market ethics	Sympathy and fairness in markets	Moral sentimentalism	Human empathy and social norms
Immanuel Kant	1724–1804	Deontological ethics; universal moral duties and rational autonomy	Duty and universal principles	Deontological ethics	Rational autonomy and categorical imperative
John Stuart Mill	1806–1873	Utilitarianism; greatest happiness principle and liberal ethics	Consequences and happiness	Utilitarianism	Greatest good for the greatest number
Martin Buber	1878–1965	Dialogical ethics; "I-Thou" relationships and moral presence	Authentic relationships	Dialogical ethics	Mutual presence and respect
Viktor Frankl	1905–1997	Existential ethics; meaning-making and moral agency under adversity	Meaning and moral agency	Existential ethics	Individual responsibility and purpose

(continued)

motivations also mark differences across these philosophical traditions. Kant and Kohlberg, for instance, believed ethics arises from human reasons. Aquinas believed that law and social good come from a higher power.[19] Lastly, Frankl felt that one's

Table 2.1 (continued)

Philosopher	Lifespan	Key contribution	Ethical focus	Approach type	Source of moral authority
John Rawls	1921–2002	Justice as fairness; ethical foundations of social and economic equality	Justice and fairness	Political ethics	Hypothetical social contract
Lawrence Kohlberg	1927–1987	Moral development; stages of ethical reasoning linked to cognitive maturity	Moral reasoning development	Developmental ethics	Cognitive stages and justice reasoning

ethical perspective is individual, whereas Rawls and Mill viewed ethics from a collective perspective.[20]

One philosopher has come to dominate the way ethics is conceptualized in the modern financial services profession: Adam Smith. The following discussion reviews Smith's unique contributions to the way ethics is conceptualized and practiced today.

Adam Smith: Ethics at the Heart of Economics

Although some people think of Adam Smith as an economist or a market historian, the father of modern economics, Smith was primarily a moral philosopher.[21] Before he authored *The Wealth of Nations* in 1776,[22] Smith published *The Theory of Moral Sentiments* in 1759. This book focused on the ethical dimensions of human behavior, including sympathy, fairness, and the invisible mechanisms of social coordination.

Smith's economic theories were not intended to promote unrestrained self-interest or market chaos. Instead, Smith aimed to establish a moral framework for commerce. Under Smith's model, individuals should contribute to societal well-being by pursuing their own interests within a competitive and transparent marketplace. Smith described the benefits associated with the "invisible hand" of the market. The invisible hand has sometimes been mischaracterized as a justification for profit maximization and selfishness.[23] However, in its original ethical context, Smith described how self-directed behavior, constrained by norms of justice and fairness, can promote the public good.

Smith's critique of mercantilism (a system dominated by protectionism and producer-focused policies) was rooted in his commitment to the welfare of all market participants, not just property owners. Smith was particularly interested in the plight of consumers and workers. Smith envisioned markets as arenas for reciprocal benefit, not zero-sum power struggles. Thus, Smith imagined classical capitalism as a system deeply infused with ethical intent and civic responsibility.[24]

Understanding the historical and philosophical dimensions of ethics as conceptualized by Smith is not merely an academic exercise but a practical necessity for today's financial professionals.[25] Ethical reasoning, as noted by Smith, equips financial services professionals with the tools needed to navigate the complex interpersonal, institutional, and system-wide dilemmas faced on a day-to-day basis. This is true regardless of the philosophical perspective one adopts in relation to ethical standards. Ethical awareness requires sensitivity to the rights and interests of all market participants, along with a commitment to acting in compliance with the law and behaving with a moral purpose.

Developing an Ethics-Based Practice Perspective

In practice, acting ethically means working within the accepted boundaries established by society.[26] Being ethical means acting in accordance with the principles individuals are expected to uphold. As illustrated in Fig. 2.2, ethics encompasses a broader set of norms than laws. Unlike laws, ethical standards are not always legally binding. In many cases, failing to adhere to ethical standards does not lead to legal consequences. For example, murder is both ethically and legally wrong. However, there are situations when killing another person is deemed acceptable. This is an example of a situation when an action may be legally allowed but still be morally questionable. Here is another example. Telling the truth in all situations is an ethical ideal. However, withholding certain truths may sometimes be prudent and even legally permissible. Similarly, avoiding taxes through legal loopholes may comply with the law, but doing so is often viewed as unethical and dishonest.

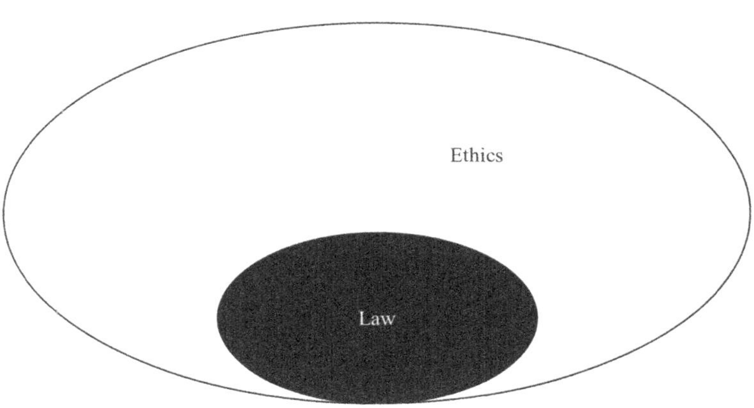

Fig. 2.2 Boundaries of ethics and law

Perspectives on Understanding Ethics

While the philosophers listed in Table 2.1 earlier in the chapter stand as the pillars of the way ethics is studied, it is possible to evaluate ethical approaches in more practical terms. Ethics can be understood through moral decision-making perspectives. One such perspective is egoism. Egoism is the belief that maximizing one's happiness and self-interest is morally right.[27] Egoism can manifest in two ways. The first is psychological egoism, which claims that all human actions are inherently self-serving. The second is ethical egoism, which argues that prioritizing one's interests is a moral duty. For example, making decisions that benefit oneself in the long run, even if actions seem selfish in the short term, can be seen as morally justifiable when viewed through an egoistic lens.

Another framework is utilitarianism. Utilitarianism focuses on the consequences of actions. According to utilitarian philosophers, an action is morally right if it produces the greatest happiness for the greatest number of people.[28] This perspective, championed by philosophers Jeremy Bentham and John Stuart Mill, emphasizes a results-oriented approach. A classic example would be diverting a runaway train to a track where a few people might die while saving hundreds of others. Utilitarianism prioritizes the greater good over individual loss.

In contrast, deontology is a framework based on the notion that the morality of an action is determined by its intrinsic nature, not by its outcomes.[29] Deontology emphasizes adherence to moral rules and principles. Consider this statement from Immanuel Kant: "Act only according to that maxim by which you can, at the same time, will that it should become a universal law." In plain language, this means that moral behavior should be directed by absolute right and wrong. Under a deontology framework, lying is inherently wrong and unacceptable regardless of the potential positive consequences of the lie.

Care ethics takes a relational approach to behavioral outcomes.[30] The care ethics approach emphasizes the importance of empathy, emotional connection, and individual interdependence. For example, respecting a friend's emotional needs by keeping their secret reflects a commitment to care and empathy, even if the situation could be resolved more easily by sharing the truth.

Virtue ethics is another perspective used to guide behavior. Rooted in Aristotle's philosophy, virtue ethics focuses on the character and virtues of the individual rather than specific actions or consequences of a behavior. Aristotle's concepts of *eudaimonia* (human flourishing) and the "Golden Mean" emphasize balance in virtues such as courage, honesty, and generosity.[31] Using this approach, moral actions stem from a person's virtuous character. For example, a kind person naturally acts generously because doing so aligns with their nature.

Yet another perspective is called rights-based ethics. This approach to decision-making emphasizes protecting and respecting the inherent rights of others. Those who follow a rights-based approach consider some rights universal and fundamental.[32] This perspective, which was influenced by John Locke's natural rights theory, asserts that everyone has the right to life, liberty, and property. These rights must be safeguarded by individuals and the government. In the United States, for example, the right to free speech is considered a fundamental right, which is protected even if one's speech conflicts with the majority's interests.

Core Ethical Principles

Regardless of one's ethical perspective, several principles are common across ethical theories and frameworks. At the core of all ethical frameworks is the notion of beneficence. Beneficence involves the moral obligation to promote the welfare and well-being of others.[33] Examples include providing optimal care for medical patients and implementing policies to support vulnerable populations regardless of cost or hassle. Nonmaleficence is another core concept embedded in ethical theories. Nonmaleficence focuses on avoiding harm. In the medical profession, this is emphasized in the Hippocratic Oath. In the financial services profession, the fiduciary standard aligns with the concept of nonmaleficence. For example, financial advisors who work under the fiduciary standard must act in the best interest of a client at all times and avoid enriching themselves at the expense of clients. Autonomy is another concept found in most ethical frameworks. Autonomy is the notion that an individual's right to make their own decisions is sacrosanct. This means that a decision-maker is given access to information and the freedom to make informed choices. Finally, justice emphasizes fairness and equality. From an ethical perspective, justice involves advocating for the equitable distribution of resources, information, and opportunities.[34]

Classification of Modern Ethics

Developing a basis for ethical decision-making and client interactions involves recognizing the complexity involved in conceptualizing decision points and potential outcomes. To make things easier, modern ethics philosophers describe ethical decision-making in one of three ways: metaethics, normative ethics, and applied ethics. These categories reflect the consensus of scholars. Each is described in more detail below.

Metaethics

Metaethics explores the fundamental nature of ethical concepts, focusing on the meaning of moral statements and the existence of moral truths.[35] Metaethics originated with G.E. Moore's *Principia Ethica* in 1903. In this book, Moore examined what moral terms signify and the essence of moral truth. Metaethics addresses profound questions, such as whether moral statements express objective truths or merely reflect subjective emotions or social norms. For instance, a metaethicist might ask whether a statement like "Murder is wrong" represents a universal truth or a belief shaped by individual or cultural contexts.

Metaethicists also examine the meaning of moral language, examining terms like "good," "evil," "right," and "wrong." In this context, cognitivism asserts that moral statements have truth values (true or false), while non-cognitivism argues that moral statements are expressions of emotion or commands without truth values.[36] Additionally, those who are interested in metaethics tend to examine large questions such as the origins of moral knowledge, including whether moral truths are intuitive, derived from observable facts, or based on transcendent principles. Other areas of inquiry include the motivation behind moral behavior and whether moral beliefs necessarily lead to moral actions. For example, a metaethicist might ponder whether "good" or "evil" exist independently or are human constructs.

Normative Ethics

While metaethics tends to look at big themes, normative ethics is focused on the standards of behavior that define what people should do to live a morally good life.[37] This ethical framework has roots that date back to Aristotle's exploration of virtues and how to achieve human flourishing. In modern times, philosophers like Kant (deontology) and Bentham and Mill (utilitarianism) had a role in developing what today serves as the basis of many regulatory frameworks. This branch of ethics addresses questions such as what makes an action "right" or "wrong" and what constitutes the "highest good" for individuals and society. For example, a normative ethics philosopher might ask if happiness, virtue, or love represents the ultimate purpose of life.

In more practical terms, normative ethics is focused on describing moral duties. In this regard, normative ethics is generally divided into three points: (1) deontology, which emphasizes duty and rules; (2) consequentialism, which focuses on outcomes; and (3) virtue ethics, which centers on the character and virtues of individuals. These approaches form the foundation for ethical norms in professional and societal contexts. Each will be introduced later in the chapter.

Applied Ethics

Applied ethics, as the name implies, focuses on relating ethical theory to real-world scenarios. Emerging relatively recently, applied ethics gained prominence with scholars like Tom Beauchamp and James Childress in the 1970s, particularly in the context of medical ethics.[38] Unlike metaethics and normative ethics, which explore theoretical principles, applied ethics is more pragmatic and directly addresses contemporary issues. For example, bioethics tackles ethical questions related to life and death, including whether euthanasia or stem cell research is morally acceptable. Environmental ethics examines the balance between protecting the environment and advancing human interests. Information ethics addresses challenges in the digital age, such as how personal data should be protected and whether social media platforms are responsible for managing misinformation.

Other areas of applied ethics include business ethics, which explores corporate social responsibility and ethical trade practices, and legal ethics, which examines fairness and justice within the legal system. Additional fields like military ethics, social justice, and education ethics tackle moral questions specific to their domains, such as the morality of war, addressing inequality, and ensuring fairness in education.

Normative Ethics and Professionalism

The diverse ethical frameworks discussed thus far provide a broad perspective on ways to navigate moral dilemmas. It is important to never lose sight of why ethics is important. Specifically, ethics is crucial in establishing trust, maintaining integrity, and ensuring that professionals act responsibly in professional settings. Among the three branches of ethics—metaethics, normative ethics, and applied ethics—normative ethics plays the most significant role in providing guidelines for professional ethics and regulatory compliance.

Normative ethics is generally used to guide regulatory policy. Normative ethics answers questions like "What is the right thing to do?" and "What are my moral obligations?" Answering these questions is essential when creating professional codes of conduct and compliance standards. For example, deontological ethics emphasizes adherence to rules and duties, which directly informs compliance policies related to fiduciary responsibilities, confidentiality, and fair treatment of clients.

Regulatory structures founded on normative ethics focus on whether an action is inherently right or wrong, not on whether the intention behind a behavior is good or bad. Normative ethics ensures that people behave in consistent ways by understanding their personal and professional obligations and acting accordingly.

Financial services professional ethics and standards require financial advisors (and firms) to act with integrity, fairness, and responsibility. Virtue ethics, a cornerstone of normative ethics, emphasizes the importance of cultivating moral character traits such as honesty, accountability, and diligence. These virtues are not just abstract ideals. These virtues directly influence how professionals approach their work, interact with clients, and make decisions in ethically challenging situations. Normative ethics helps the broader financial markets operate on a foundation of trust.

Through frameworks like consequentialism, normative ethics emphasizes the importance of considering the broader impact of actions. In a professional context, this perspective encourages balancing individual responsibilities with the collective good. Normative ethics promotes universal principles of behavior. The notions of fairness and justice, for example, ensure that transactions are not driven by self-interest without regard for consequences. Professional ethics and compliance programs often draw from these universal principles to ensure that employees in distinct roles and regions follow a standardized ethical framework. Creating a shared ethical framework reduces ambiguity and helps organizations establish a unified ethical culture.

Beyond rules and policies, normative ethics has a direct influence on the attitudes and mindsets of professionals. For instance, deontological ethics fosters a sense of duty and responsibility, while virtue ethics promotes empathy and respect in interactions. In the case of deontological ethics, responsibility is generally enforced through legal provisions, whereas standards of virtue are enforced through social pressure. When viewed positively, adhering to a strong ethical perspective encourages professionals to approach their work not just as a series of tasks but as an opportunity to contribute positively to clients, colleagues, and society. The following discussion highlights some of the most important concepts from normative ethics and their applications to professionalism:

Deontology (Duty-Based Ethics)

Almost all regulatory and compliance schemes in the financial services profession are based on the notion of deontology. Deontology emphasizes the importance of following moral duties and principles regardless of the outcomes.[39] Actions are judged by their adherence to rules or obligations, not consequences. The focus here is on doing what is inherently right at all times.

For financial advisors, deontology is reflected in the adherence to fiduciary and best-interest standards. Under these practice approaches, a financial advisor is obligated to act in the best interests of their client. For example, a financial advisor acting as a fiduciary must prioritize a client's financial well-being over personal gain. Other examples include compliance with professional codes of conduct and legal regulations regardless of intentions or outcomes. Consider the hypothetical case of Laken:

> Laken, a financial advisor, manages investments for her client, Tom, a retiree. Under her duty of care, Laken is obligated to act in Tom's best interests, prioritizing his financial goals over her own. A deontological approach, which emphasizes adherence to moral rules and duties regardless of outcomes, is reflected in Laken's actions. When a high-commission investment product becomes available, Laken could earn a significant personal profit by recommending it to Tom. However, the product carries higher risks and fees, making it less suitable for Tom's conservative retirement portfolio. Guided by her fiduciary duty, Laken adheres to the moral rule of acting solely in her client's best interest. She recommends a lower-cost, diversified fund that aligns with Tom's goals, even though the fund yields her a smaller commission. This decision reflects deontology, as Laken upholds her ethical obligation to Tom's interests, prioritizing duty over personal gain, regardless of the financial consequences to herself.

Consequentialism (Outcome-Based Ethics)

Consequentialism focuses on the outcomes or consequences of actions.[40] From a consequentialist perspective, the goal is to maximize overall good or happiness. This can be summarized as "the greatest good for the greatest number." From a financial services perspective, consequentialism underscores the importance of maximizing client wealth while ensuring broader societal benefits. For instance, an investment manager might decide to prioritize strategies that yield high returns for clients while at the same time contributing to the social good through sustainable investing. Similarly, corporate executives might adopt practices that balance profitability with positive social and environmental outcomes. This would align with corporate social responsibility (CSR) principles. The following hypothetical case narrative illustrates the concept of consequentialism:

> Mark, a wealth manager, oversees the portfolio of his client, Sarah, who seeks to grow her retirement savings. Guided by consequentialism, which emphasizes outcomes and maximizing overall good, Mark aims to maximize Sarah's wealth while ensuring broader societal benefits. Mark identifies a high-return investment opportunity in a sustainable energy fund that supports clean energy initiatives. The fund aligns with Sarah's financial goals, offering strong growth potential with moderate risk. Additionally, the fund contributes to environmental sustainability, creating positive societal impacts by reducing carbon emissions and fostering renewable energy development. By recommending this fund, Mark achieves the best outcome for Sarah (significant wealth growth). Mark's recommendation also generates broader societal benefits. His decision reflects consequentialism, as it prioritizes the overall positive consequences for Sarah and society.

It is important to note that a financial advisor may use consequentialist reasoning to guide decisions in a client's best interest, but in practice, the advisor will be judged primarily on adherence to deontological principles such as fiduciary duty, honesty, and fairness. Consider the case of Maria.

> Maria is a financial advisor who is working with a client nearing retirement. Maria believes strongly in keeping investment transaction costs low for her clients. For one client, Maria recommends a no-load index mutual fund, even though her firm's compliance rules require her to disclose and document at least three product options (one of which must be a firm-managed fund).
>
> While the consequences of Maria's recommendation turned out nicely for the client (the client saved thousands in fees), Maria ended up losing her job. During a routine audit, internal compliance officers discover that Maria failed to follow disclosure rules. In other words, she failed her deontological ethical obligation to the firm. Even though the client ended up financially better off, Maria was reprimanded for violating her professional duty to provide full disclosure. She was also terminated. Ultimately, Maria was judged by how well she fulfilled her professional duties and obligations (deontological standards) rather than strictly on the client's outcome.

Virtue Ethics (Character-Based Ethics)

Virtue ethics emphasizes the moral character of an individual rather than specific rules or outcomes.[41] This perspective focuses on cultivating virtues such as honesty, integrity, and fairness as a way to achieve a morally good life. When viewed with a virtue ethics lens, a financial advisor who embodies honesty and transparency will be in a better position to build long-term client relationships built on trust and transparency. Financial services professionals who consistently demonstrate virtues like accountability, fairness, and diligence uphold the ethical standards of the field, contributing to the profession's credibility and societal trust. Consider the hypothetical case of Emma:

> Emma, a financial advisor, works with her client, David, to build an investment portfolio. Committed to honesty and transparency, Emma embodies these values in her practice. When discussing investment options, she fully discloses all fees, risks, and potential returns associated with each product, even when it means revealing that a high-fee fund she could recommend would benefit her more than David. During a market downturn, Emma proactively contacts David to explain the impact on his portfolio, providing clear, jargon-free updates and a plan to mitigate losses. Rather than hiding underperformance, she openly discusses challenges and adjusts strategies in David's best interest. David appreciates Emma's candor and feels confident in her guidance. Over time, this trust fosters a strong, long-term relationship, with David referring new clients to Emma and remaining loyal through market fluctuations. Emma's honesty and transparency retain David's business and enhance her reputation, demonstrating how these qualities build enduring client relationships.

Application of Normative Ethics in the Financial Services Profession

Normative ethics provides a foundational framework for understanding how ethical principles can guide professional behavior. Deontology, consequentialism, and virtue ethics each offer a perspective directly applicable to providing financial advice. By emphasizing duty, outcomes, and character, these cornerstones of ethical practice ensure that firms and financial advisors act responsibly, foster trust, and contribute to the well-being of their clients and society. The following case examples illustrate how normative ethical standards are not mutually exclusive but rather complementary.

> To begin, consider a situation involving a senior compliance officer at a wealth management firm who uncovers evidence of trade allocation improprieties (commonly referred to as "cherry-picking") where favorable trades are funneled toward high-net-worth clients. Despite personal ties to implicated colleagues and awareness of the reputational harm disclosure could inflict, the compliance officer adheres strictly to the firm's code of conduct and regulatory obligations. The officer escalates the issue internally and facilitates full disclosure to the Securities and Exchange Commission. Although the firm is penalized, its proactive cooperation leads to mitigated consequences. This case underscores the essence of deontological ethics: a commitment to rules, duties, and the integrity of the financial system, even at significant personal or organizational cost.

> Now, consider a case from a consequentialist perspective. In this case, a fintech firm is preparing to launch a novel AI-driven investment platform. Firm leadership faces pressure to expedite the release in pursuit of early-market advantages and revenue capture. However, the Chief Technology Officer (CTO) raises red flags about the platform's untested response to volatile markets. A comprehensive risk-benefit analysis is conducted, balancing short-term profits against potential long-term client harm and reputational damage. The firm opts to delay the launch in favor of rigorous stress testing. When the platform eventually debuts, it coincides with a period of significant market downturn—and performs robustly, earning client trust and establishing the firm as a responsible innovator. In this case, ethical decision-making is framed not by rigid adherence to protocol but by the calculated evaluation

of consequences, reinforcing the critical role of consequentialist reasoning in risk management and strategic planning.

A third perspective, based on virtue ethics, shows how honesty, prudence, and empathy can enhance outcomes. This perspective is exemplified by a financial planner who is encouraged to sell a high-commission product to a near-retirement client. Recognizing the misalignment between the product's complexity and the client's conservative risk tolerance, the financial planner declines to recommend the product despite losing commission income. Instead, the planner proposes a lower-commission product that is more suitable for the client's portfolio. The financial planner's decision fosters trust, resulting in additional referrals and internal kudos, leading to a leadership role in the firm. Unlike deontology's focus on rules or consequentialism's emphasis on results, utilizing a virtue ethics perspective illustrates the importance of character, relational integrity, and fostering a culture where ethical conduct is internalized rather than imposed.

An Ethical Decision-Making Model: The Five-Step Framework

Craig E. Johnson, an expert in leadership ethics, developed a structured model to aid individuals and organizations in making principled decisions in complex, real-world environments. As shown in Fig. 2.3, the model brings together all the concepts discussed in this chapter into a workable practice platform. Johnson's Five-Step Ethical Decision-Making Model, outlined in *Meeting the Ethical Challenges of Leadership*,[42] integrates rational analysis with moral sensitivity. The process proposed by Johnson emphasizes the responsibility of leadership in fostering ethical practice.

The first step requires awareness and recognition of the existence of an ethical issue. Ethical decision-making begins by recognizing that a moral issue is at stake. If an action or decision could cause harm, violate ethical principles, or involve

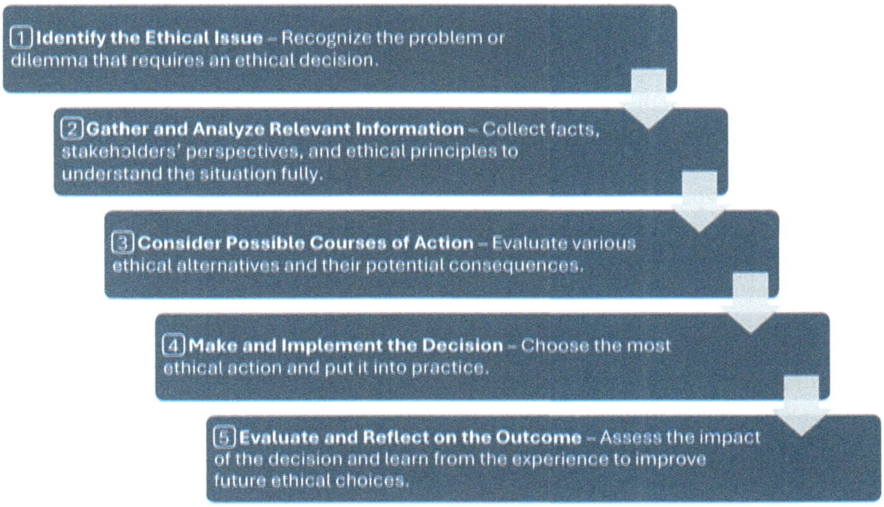

Fig. 2.3 Five-step ethical decision-making model

conflicting duties, a moral issue exists. Analysis at this step demands sensitivity to ethical signals such as stakeholder vulnerability, injustice, or breaches of trust. Failing to recognize an issue as ethical can result in morally negligent outcomes. Questions to ask include:

- Is someone being harmed or mistreated?
- Are core values or principles being challenged?
- Could this decision set a troubling precedent?

Once the ethical nature of the issue is recognized, the second step requires decision-makers to gather all pertinent information. This includes legal considerations, stakeholder perspectives, contextual factors, and factual data about potential outcomes. Johnson emphasizes the importance of comprehensive analysis over assumptions, encouraging decision-makers to consult experts, challenge biases, and scrutinize sources. Questions to ask at this step include:

- What are the relevant laws, policies, and norms?
- Who are the stakeholders, and what are their interests?
- What information might be missing or distorted?

At the third step, ethical reasoning frameworks, such as utilitarianism, deontology, or virtue ethics, are applied to assess the moral merits of possible actions. Johnson encourages the use of multiple ethical lenses to avoid moral myopia. Johnson stresses the need to balance personal values with professional and organizational ethics. To do this, a decision-maker should ask:

- What are the consequences of each option?
- What duties or principles must be upheld?
- Which choice best reflects integrity and character?

The fourth step in the model involves choosing a course of action and subjecting the action to ethical scrutiny. Johnson advocates "testing" the decision through various filters. One filter is known as the public disclosure test, which involves asking a question like "Would I be comfortable if this decision were publicly known?" The role model test can also be used at this point. The following question can be used to gauge the appropriate course of action: "Would I advise others to act the same way?" Answering these questions honestly reinforces personal accountability. Other questions to ask include:

- Can I defend this decision publicly and professionally?
- Does this choice align with the organization's values?
- How would I feel if I were on the receiving end?

The last step in the process involves implementation and reflection. Ethical leadership requires follow-through, ensuring that actions are executed transparently and with respect for affected parties. Afterward, the decision-maker should reflect on the results by considering what went well, what went poorly, and what can be learned for the future. Self-reflection fosters ethical maturity and continuous improvement in decision-making. Questions to ask at this step in the process include:

- Was the outcome fair and ethical in practice?
- Did I grow in ethical competence?
- What would I do differently next time?

The following case illustrates how Johnson's five-step ethical decision-making model can be applied in practice:

> Kristy Chen, a senior financial advisor at a mid-sized investment firm, is reviewing a new product. The product is an aggressive growth fund aimed at young professionals. While the fund promises high returns, it also carries significant risk due to heavy exposure to volatile emerging markets. During a routine compliance review, Kristy notices that the promotional materials downplay these risks and omit recent performance downturns. This raises concerns with Kristy about misleading clients. She immediately recognizes the ethical issue, which is that first-time investors may not fully grasp the fund's volatility. Furthermore, transparency and honesty appear to be compromised. Allowing such practices could set a dangerous precedent in the firm.
>
> To better understand the situation, Kristy gathers information by reviewing SEC disclosure regulations and the firm's compliance policies. She consults with the marketing team, the fund manager, and legal counsel. She also interviews junior advisors who have already pitched the fund. Her investigation reveals that the omissions were intentional and driven by pressure to meet quarterly sales targets. She identifies multiple stakeholders—clients, advisors, firm leadership, and regulators—who are all affected by how the situation is handled.
>
> Kristy then applies the five-step ethical framework to guide her decision-making. Kristy knows that from a utilitarian perspective, disclosing risks may reduce short-term sales. But doing so will protect clients from financial harm. Kristy leans on deontological principles to reinforce her belief that truthfulness and fiduciary duty require full transparency. Her reliance on virtue ethics highlights the importance of integrity and courage in challenging the status quo. Based on her analysis, Kristy concludes that the best course of action is to revise the materials and inform clients about the risks.
>
> Kristy drafts a memo recommending immediate changes to the promotional content and the issuance of a client advisory notice. Before submitting the memo, she tests the decision through several ethical lenses. She uses the "Public Disclosure Test" to confirm that she can stand by her actions if they became public. The "Role Model Test" assures her that her advice (as outlined in the memo) is the guidance she would give to a junior colleague. Finally, she uses an "Empathy Test" to reinforce that, as a client, she would feel respected receiving such a disclosure. Confident in her choice, she finalizes her recommendation.
>
> The firm accepts Kristy's proposal, revises the materials, and notifies clients. While sales dip in the short term, client trust is preserved, and the firm strengthens its reputation for ethical leadership. Reflecting on the process, Kristy feels the outcome was fair, as clients were informed and protected. She recognizes her growth in ethical competence and notes that in the future, she will involve compliance earlier in the product development process to prevent similar issues.

Challenges and Emerging Issues in Ethics and Compliance

The ethical landscape in the financial services profession is undergoing significant changes due to technological advancements, globalization, and an increasing reliance on algorithmic decision-making. The integration of artificial intelligence (AI) and robo-advisors into the delivery of financial advice is transforming the profession. For example, AI tools enable automated systems to manage investments and client portfolios more efficiently than human-managed funds. However, AI innovations also raise ethical concerns related to transparency, accountability, and potential unintended consequences.[43] It is reasonable to expect increased regulation to ensure that AI-driven financial tools are carefully managed to mitigate client risks and the possibility of ethical lapses. (See Chap. 14 for more information on technological challenges and opportunities.)

AI decision-making poses unique challenges in maintaining fairness in the markets. While machine learning algorithms are trained on extensive datasets to optimize financial strategies, these datasets may contain historical biases that perpetuate discrimination or disparities. For example, algorithms used for credit scoring, loan approvals, and investment strategies may inadvertently disadvantage certain demographic groups. To combat potential biases and reduce moral dilemmas, financial advisory firms must implement rigorous testing protocols. This can be accomplished through the establishment of company-wide ethical AI guidelines and continuous monitoring of systems to ensure that AI-driven models promote equity and fairness.[44] Regulatory bodies also play a crucial role in establishing oversight mechanisms to hold financial institutions accountable for their algorithmic decisions.

Additionally, globalization has introduced complexity to ethical decision-making (see Chap. 15 for additional details on globalization trends). As firms become more global in outlook and market strategy, they must navigate diverse regulatory environments, cultural differences, and evolving expectations about corporate responsibility. Regulatory disparities between regions can create challenges for multinational financial institutions. Financial advisors who work outside their country must balance compliance with multiple legal systems while maintaining ethical integrity. Differences in financial transparency, anti-corruption measures, and consumer protection laws further complicate ethical decision-making in cross-border situations. To address these challenges, global financial regulators are beginning to collaborate in developing ethical standards that ensure consistency, integrity, and trust across markets.

Chapter Summary

This chapter presented a principled framework for addressing the moral challenges that financial professionals encounter daily. Grounded in major ethical traditions, including deontology, consequentialism, and virtue ethics, the chapter connected historical philosophical ideas to the real-world dilemmas that emerge in client relationships.

At the heart of the discussion was the concept of trust. Trust makes financial transactions possible in an environment where information and power are often unevenly distributed. Trust must evolve from mutual trust (the expectation of good faith) to reciprocal trust, in which every party in the engagement takes responsibility for actively upholding integrity. In the same way, stakeholder protection must evolve into stakeholder reciprocity, where transparency, accountability, and ethical stewardship are shared among all stakeholders, including clients, firms, regulators, and society as a whole. These principles reflect the deeply interconnected nature of today's financial ecosystems.

To provide financial services professionals with a practical framework for applying these ideas, the chapter outlined the Five-Step Ethical Decision-Making Model. The model begins with recognizing whether an issue involves harm, fairness, or conflicting values. Next, the process requires gathering facts, including the perspectives of all stakeholders and relevant legal or regulatory considerations. Financial services professionals are called upon to then evaluate possible actions through the lens of ethical theories, select and test the most principled option, and finally implement the decision while reflecting on its consequences for both practice and relationships.

Ultimately, the long-term strength of financial institutions depends on weaving ethical reasoning into every layer of decision-making. By internalizing and applying these principled approaches, financial professionals not only fulfill their obligations to clients, firms, and regulators but also contribute to building a more resilient and equitable economic order.

Chapter Resources

- A review of ethical decision-making models: Suarez, V. D., Marya, V., Weiss, M. J., & Cox, D. (2023). Examination of ethical decision-making models across disciplines: Common elements and application to the field of behavior analysis. *Behavior Analysis in Practice, 16*(3), 657–671.
- CFA Institute: https://www.cfainstitute.org/standards/professionals/code-ethics-standards?utm_source=chatgpt.com
- CFP Board of Standards, Inc.: https://www.cfp.net/ethics/code-of-ethics-and-standards-of-conduct?utm_source=chatgpt.com
- European Financial Advisors & Analysts Association: https://www.efa-association.org/code-of-ethics/?utm_source=chatgpt.com
- Investment Adviser Codes of Ethics: https://www.sec.gov/rules-regulations/2004/07/investment-adviser-codes-ethics
- National Association of Insurance and Financial Advisors: https://belong.naifa.org/code-of-ethics?utm_source=chatgpt.com

Notes

[1]Jaffee, D. M. (2008). The U.S. subprime mortgage crisis: Issues raised and lessons learned. Commission on Growth and Development, Working Paper No. 28. https://documents1.worldbank.

org/curated/en/612021468130801823/pdf/577270NWP0Box353766B01PUBLIC10gcwp028web.pdf

[2]International Center for Academic Integrity. (2021). Fundamental Values of Academic Integrity (3rd ed.). https://academicintegrity.org/aws/ICAI/asset_manager/get_file/911282?ver=1

[3]Torche, F., & Valenzuela, E. (2011). Trust and reciprocity: A theoretical distinction of the sources of social capital. *European journal of social theory*, *14*(2), 181–198.

[4]Usunier, J. C. (2025). Reciprocity and Trust. In *About Commerce: Understanding the Interface of Deal-Making and Relationship Building* (pp. 191–214). Cham: Springer Nature Switzerland.

[5]Xiao, C. (2023). Why stakeholder theory is "non-exploitative." *Academic Journal of Management and Social Sciences*, *2*(3), 26–30.

[6]Bosse, D. A., Phillips, R. A., & Harrison, J. S. (2009). Stakeholders, reciprocity, and firm performance. *Strategic Management Journal*, *30*(4), 447–456.

[7]Fassin, Y. (2012). Stakeholder management, reciprocity, and stakeholder responsibility. *Journal of Business Ethics*, *109*(1), 83–96.

[8]https://www.fbi.gov/history/famous-cases/enron

[9]https://www.justice.gov/archive/opa/pr/2002/October/02_crm_627.htm

[10]https://www.sec.gov/news/press/2002-89.htm

[11]https://www.govinfo.gov/content/pkg/CHRG-107shrg94690/pdf/CHRG-107shrg94690.pdf

[12]https://www.cga.ct.gov/2006/rpt/2006-R-0122.htm

[13]Garnett, A. C. (1951). Distinctions and definitions in ethics. *Philosophy and Phenomenological Research, 12*(1), 69–82.

[14]Cook, M. L. (2019). Reflections on the relationship between law and ethics. *Adel. L. Rev.*, *40*, 485.

[15]Srivastava, S. (2024). *Ethics in Legal Profession: A Comprehensive Read!* https://www.toprankers.com/importance-of-ethics-in-legal-profession

[16]Belak, J., & Pevec Rozman, M. (2012). Business ethics from Aristotle, Kant and Mill's perspective. *Kybernetes*, *41*(10), 1607–1624.

[17]Hancock, R. (1957). Ethics and History in Kant and Mill. *Ethics*, *68*(1), 56–60.

[18]Grisez, G. G. (1958). Kant and Aquinas: Ethical Theory. *The Thomist: A Speculative Quarterly Review*, *21*(1), 44–78.

[19]Ibid.

[20]Cohen-Almagor, R. (2017). On the philosophical foundations of medical ethics: Aristotle, Kant, JS Mill and Rawls. *Ethics, Medicine and Public Health*, *3*(4), 436–444.

[21]Raphael, D. D. (2007). *The impartial spectator: Adam Smith's moral philosophy*. Clarendon Press.

[22]Smith, A. (1776). An inquiry into the nature and causes of the wealth of nations: Volume One. London: printed for W. Strahan and T. Cadell, 1776.

[23]Harrison, P. (2011). Adam Smith and the history of the invisible hand. *Journal of the History of Ideas*, *72*(1), 29–49.

[24]Bassiry, G. R., & Jones, M. (1993). Adam Smith and the ethics of contemporary capitalism. *Journal of Business Ethics*, *12*(8), 621–627.

[25]Wilcoxson, M., & Craft, J. (2024). "Honey, you've got to do what's right": common ethical decision-making challenges and strategies of licensed financial advisers. *Qualitative Research in Financial Markets, 16*(1), 183–211.

[26]Knapp, S. J., Gottlieb, M. C., Handelsman, M. M., & VandeCreek, L. D. (2012). *APA handbook of ethics in psychology, Vol 1: Moral foundations and common themes* (pp. xxiii-518). American Psychological Association.

[27]See: https://iep.utm.edu/egoism/

[28]Mill, J. S. (2016). Utilitarianism. In Seven masterpieces of philosophy (pp. 329–375). Routledge.

[29] Poff, D. C., & Michalos, A. C. (Eds.). (2023). *Encyclopedia of business and professional ethics*. Springer.

[30] Ibid.

[31] Putman, D. (1991). Relational ethics and virtue theory. *Metaphilosophy*, *22*(3), 231–238.

[32] Poff, D. C., & Michalos, A. C. (Eds.). (2023). *Encyclopedia of business and professional ethics*. Springer

[33] Ibid.

[34] Ibid.

[35] Fisher, A. (2014). *Metaethics: an introduction*. Routledge.

[36] Van Roojen, M. (2004). Moral cognitivism vs. non-cognitivism. https://plato.sydney.edu.au/entries/moral-cognitivism/

[37] Kagan, S. (2018). *Normative ethics*. Routledge.

[38] Beauchamp, T., & Childress, J. (2019). Principles of biomedical ethics: marking its fortieth anniversary. *The American Journal of Bioethics, 19*(11), 9–12.

[39] Dilbar, K. (2024). The Principles of Deontological Ethics. *Web of Teachers: Inderscience Research*, *2*(5), 56–59.

[40] Moore, E. (2007). Objective consequentialism, right actions, and good people. *Philosophical Studies: An International Journal for Philosophy in the Analytic Tradition*, *133*(1), 83–94.

[41] Duffy, J., Gallagher, J., Holmes, S., Gage, J. T., Agnew, L., Schilb, J., … & Barnett, S. (2018). Virtue ethics. *Rhetoric Review*, *37*(4), 321–392.

[42] Johnson, C. E. (2020). *Meeting the ethical challenges of leadership: Casting light or shadow*. Sage Publications.

[43] Yaramolu, L. S. K. G. (2025). AI-Powered Portfolio Management: Transforming Wealth Management Through Intelligent Automation. *Journal of Computer Science and Technology Studies*, *7*(3), 14–23.

[44] Eitel-Porter, R. (2021). Beyond the promise: implementing ethical AI. *AI and Ethics*, *1*(1), 73–80.

Ethical Decision-Making in the Financial Services Profession

3

Chapter Outcomes

This chapter focuses on helping learners develop the ability to:

1. Apply ethical frameworks such as deontology, consequentialism, and virtue ethics, along with foundational values like beneficence, autonomy, and justice, to guide ethical decision-making in financial services.
2. Utilize a structured, step-by-step process for integrating ethical principles into day-to-day professional practice within the financial services profession.
3. Analyze real-world case examples to understand the practical application of ethical decision-making.
4. Identify and manage behavioral biases, including overconfidence, confirmation bias, and herd mentality, which can compromise ethical judgment in professional settings.
5. Employ ethics and decision-making bias checklists to enhance self-awareness and maintain ethical standards in high-stakes financial environments.

Introduction

An important point from the previous chapter is that a financial advisor may use consequentialist reasoning to make decisions in the best interest of their clients, but in practice, advisors are primarily judged on their adherence to deontological principles such as fiduciary duty, honesty, and fairness. On the surface, this insight seems straightforward and reasonable. A financial services professional is required

Note: This chapter was copyedited using Grammarly™ and generative AI tools to enhance clarity, grammar, and overall readability. While these tools provided suggestions and assistance in refining the text, the ideas, content, and arguments presented remain the sole work and responsibility of the authors. Any errors or inaccuracies in the final version are also the authors' responsibility.

W. Heo, J. E. Grable, *Ethics and Compliance in Financial Services*,
https://doi.org/10.1007/978-3-032-14449-2_3

to comply with regulatory mandates, company standards, and other reasonable conditions. Even if the outcome for a client is positive, if the process to achieve that outcome violates any established practice standards, the financial advisor's decision-making process may still be regarded as inadequate and, in some cases, unlawful.

In reality, applying ethical principles to day-to-day situations is more difficult. It would be a rare person who would publicly admit to acting unethically or failing to protect others from wrongdoing on a regular basis. However, people are caught, almost daily, acting unethically. This is true not only in the broader society but also in the financial services profession. So, why is it so challenging to apply ethical reasoning in daily life? One reason is that most people who have encountered ethical theories rarely have the opportunity to explore ethics beyond the speculative level. As such, they lack the tools needed to help navigate complex decisions that could hurt others.

Imagine, for example, you are working as a financial advisor. Within a week, you receive numerous calls from current clients asking about a new investment opportunity. According to your clients, this latest investment opportunity has almost unlimited upside potential with minimal downside. They tell you that the government is about to enact new laws to protect this investment. They also inform you that their friends and colleagues are making a lot of money with the investment. They want you to place a sizeable portfolio of their portfolios in this new investment. What would you do next?

Or imagine you've just been promoted to a senior-level manager position in a large bank. Over the course of the next few months, you learn that some branch managers under your direction are using very aggressive sales approaches to increase sales. You sense that some of the sales practices are borderline unethical and possibly illegal. However, you've been receiving accolades from higher-ups about the astounding sales that have occurred under your direction. What would you do?

Financial professionals often find themselves in these types of situations where the "right" choice is not clear-cut. They get caught between competing pressures, obligations, and risks. In the first case, the financial advisor is confronted with clients eager to invest in a supposedly low-risk, high-return product that is being hyped through social networks and by other advisors. The clients are insistent and even hint that they will leave if their wishes are not followed. The ethical dilemma lies in balancing professional duty, which involves protecting clients from potentially unsuitable or fraudulent investments, with the immediate business risk of losing clients and income. The advisor knows that giving in to client pressure could compromise their fiduciary responsibility, but refusing could damage relationships and result in lost business.

In the second case, the newly promoted bank manager is praised for record-breaking sales numbers but becomes aware that the success may be fueled by questionable or even illegal sales tactics at the branch level. The ethical challenge here is intensified by organizational culture. Leadership rewards performance without questioning how results are achieved. Speaking up or highlighting risks could annoy superiors and jeopardize a promising career. Taking action could also result in retaliation on the part of other managers. However, staying silent could mean tacitly endorsing misconduct.

What makes these dilemmas so tricky is that they involve a tension between personal integrity and external pressures. Each person is caught between doing what is ethically responsible and protecting their career, reputation, and livelihood. In both cases, the "wrong" path may appear easier and more rewarding in the short term, while the "right" path requires courage, sacrifice, and a willingness to challenge powerful incentives and expectations.

The purpose of this chapter is to provide tools that can be used to help make the identification of ethical dilemmas easier. The chapter also provides applicable strategies that can be utilized to manage ethical dilemmas. The discussion that follows offers a practical roadmap for implementing ethical standards in practice, focusing on the concepts of deontology, consequentialism, and virtue ethics. By integrating these concepts with values such as beneficence, autonomy, and justice, the chapter demonstrates how financial services professionals can prioritize the interests of clients and other stakeholders above their own.

Perspective

To provide context for the material presented in this chapter, the following case deals with the collapse of FTX, a high-profile incident that involved financial advisors,[1] investors, and institutional players. The case demonstrates how cognitive biases can alter the way people evaluate the ethical implications of their actions, distort judgment, and undermine ethical standards.

FTX, a cryptocurrency exchange founded by Sam Bankman-Fried (SBF), was in 2019 the leading cryptocurrency trading platform used by millions of investors and financial advisors. By November 2021, FTX was valued at $32 billion. SBF was hailed as a crypto prodigy.[2] Financial advisors and wealth management firms recommended FTX to clients for trading and investing in cryptocurrencies. An ongoing media blitz was used to enhance SBF's reputation as a "genius." Marketing was supported by venture capital firms like Sequoia Capital and SoftBank.[3]

During the peak of the 2021 crypto market, when Bitcoin reached $69,000 for the first time, financial advisors at firms like Rocky Mountain Advisors (a hypothetical firm representing typical advisory behavior) faced pressure from clients to allocate assets to cryptocurrencies. FTX was a popular choice to implement crypto purchases because, on its surface, the firm looked innovative and safe. Financial advisors like Jane Durvy (a hypothetical advisor) were tasked with evaluating FTX for client portfolios, which included retail investors, high-net-worth individuals, and pension funds. Jane, a CFA® professional, was an experienced financial advisor, but for Jane, cryptocurrencies were a new investment class. She had limited expertise in these markets.

It turns out that Jane, like many other financial advisors, overestimated her ability to assess FTX's financial strength. Jane mistakenly assumed that FTX's high trading volume and SBF's credentials assured platform legitimacy. Advisors like Jane did not grasp the complexities of crypto exchanges or FTX's unregulated structure.

It turns out that Jane was succumbing to feelings of overconfidence and herd thinking. She relied on metrics like FTX's valuation and media praise rather than conducting thorough due diligence. When she tried to obtain information about the firm, she could not find reliable independent audits. Nonetheless, she dismissed this red flag as being due to the fast-paced world of cryptocurrencies. Instead, Jane sought out information to validate FTX's appeal, focusing on positive news, such as SBF's philanthropy activities and FTX's partnerships with major venture capital firms. She and others ignored warnings from skeptics and negative news reports.

The 2021 crypto boom also fostered a herd mentality, as retail and institutional investors rushed into the market due to a fear of missing out (FOMO). Social media platforms like Twitter (now X) and Reddit amplified FTX's marketing blitz, with influencers and celebrities, including Tom Brady, Larry David, and Gisele Bündchen, endorsing the platform. Financial advisors felt pressured to follow the crowd in order to retain clients and compete with firms offering crypto exposure. Consequently, the leadership at Rocky Mountain Advisors expedited FTX's approval for client accounts, bypassing traditional vetting processes. Jane justified her crypto recommendations by stating that "everyone is on FTX." Jane's reasoning reflected the herd behavior occurring in the crypto markets.

In November 2022, FTX collapsed due to a liquidity crisis triggered by a CoinDesk report that revealed that Alameda Research held a significant portion of its assets in FTT, FTX's native token. The report suggested the FTX was insolvent. A run on closing accounts followed, leading FTX to file for bankruptcy. The bankruptcy resulted in the loss of $8 billion in customer funds.

Later investigations revealed that SBF misappropriated client deposits to finance Alameda's risky trades and personal ventures, including political donations and real estate purchases. Clients of Rocky Mountain Advisors and similar firms faced substantial losses, with some clients losing their life savings and institutions pursuing legal action.[4] Advisors like Jane faced professional repercussions, including client lawsuits and regulatory scrutiny from the Securities and Exchange Commission (SEC) for inadequate due diligence. Ultimately, the SEC charged FTX with fraud, and SBF was convicted on seven counts of fraud in 2023. SBF received a 25-year prison sentence.[5]

The Process of Ethical Decision-Making

Recognizing Ethical Dilemmas

Recognizing ethical dilemmas when engaging in financial transactions begins by identifying potential red flag situations. One of the most common red flags relates to conflicts of interest. Conflicts can occur when personal gain conflicts with a client's best interests. For example, a financial advisor may recommend expensive products to earn higher commissions, rather than suggesting more suitable and cost-effective alternatives. Conflicts of interest can also include situations involving insider trading, where an individual has access to nonpublic information that is not disclosed to all stakeholders. Additionally, advising family or friends can blur professional boundaries, creating ethical gray areas.

Another significant red flag is a compliance breach. Compliance breaches include failing to adhere to regulatory obligations such as Know Your Customer (KYC) and Anti-Money Laundering (AML) rules, as well as data privacy protections. Ignorance of internal firm policies also falls under this category. For instance, bypassing established risk thresholds in pursuit of short-term profits is a clear violation of the red flag principle. Furthermore, stakeholder harm can occur when financial practices neglect or exploit certain groups, such as offering high-interest loans to vulnerable clients or prioritizing short-term returns over broader societal and environmental well-being.

Red flags are sometimes revealed based on client or colleague behavior. Suspicious trading patterns, including abrupt changes in client behavior or transaction volume, often serve as early warning signs that unethical behavior is present. At a minimum, red flags like these warrant further investigation. A lack of transparency, whether due to incomplete documentation or reluctance from clients or counterparties to share vital information, can indicate deeper ethical issues. Additionally, disproportionate power dynamics, where one party pressures employees or junior staff to overlook minor policy breaches "just this once," may reflect system-wide cultural issues and pave the way for more significant improprieties.

From a broader perspective, connecting red flags to client and stakeholder protection is of primary importance. Client and stakeholder protection is rooted in the moral obligation to consider all parties that may be potentially affected by a financial decision, including customers, employees, investors, and local communities. An ethical dilemma often arises when transactions or policies undermine this mutual safeguard, such as when information is withheld from counterparties or when the interests of one group are prioritized over those of another. When stakeholder considerations are overlooked, deeper structural conflicts may emerge. These conflicts include the neglect of low-credit customers and failure to maintain transparent risk disclosures.

Why is early recognition of these types of issues so critical? First, early recognition helps prevent escalation of unethical behavior. Noticing a minor compliance lapse early can forestall significant future consequences. Second, recognizing behavior early maintains trust and one's reputation by enabling prompt remediation, which is vital for a firm's credibility and the stability of the broader financial market. Lastly, identifying potential problems early supports legal and regulatory compliance efforts, allowing an institution to address missteps proactively before facing penalties, investigations, or lawsuits.

Consider the following examples. Suppose a financial advisor realizes their bonus largely depends on selling a high-commission financial product. The advisor must first recognize that this situation could compromise client welfare. Acting on this awareness can lead to a more impartial assessment of product suitability. In another scenario, if a compliance officer observes repeated minor anomalies in mortgage applications, they may conclude that discriminatory practices are occurring or that someone in the organization is deliberately engaging in data manipulation. The compliance officer must investigate these issues further, even if nothing nefarious is happening, rather than overlook the red flags. In both instances, the fundamental question is whether mutual trust and stakeholder reciprocity are maintained or being violated.

Several important issues arise at the firm level in relation to red flag monitoring. To foster a culture of early recognition within organizations, several practical steps can be implemented. First, institutional training programs can be used to equip staff to identify contradictory data, unusual client demands, and high-pressure selling tactics. Second, policy manuals can be revised to provide explicit definitions and real-life examples of conflicts of interest and compliance breaches. Making policy manuals clear is a way to help employees understand how to respond appropriately.

Additionally, organizations can establish confidential reporting channels that create a safe space for employees to raise concerns without fear of retaliation. Regular check-ins, such as team meetings or one-on-one discussions, can promote an environment where identifying and discussing potential ethical pitfalls is encouraged and expected, rather than avoided. For example, a financial advisor who realizes that their bonus depends in large part on selling a high-commission financial product must recognize that this situation could compromise client welfare. Acting on this awareness can lead to a more impartial assessment of product suitability. Discussing the issue with a manager can then provide the advisor with information about the firm's ethical culture.

Gathering Relevant Facts from Stakeholders

An ethical decision in the financial services profession relies on a thorough understanding of all relevant information, including financial data, client objectives, and the broader legal or regulatory landscape. In practice, this means collecting quantitative indicators, such as balance sheet figures and historical transaction records, as well as qualitative insights, including client goals and contextual factors that may influence the moral implications of a transaction. Incomplete or insufficient data can lead to poor judgments, especially when dealing with complex financial products where partial disclosures may obscure critical risks.

It is also essential to recognize the perspectives of all parties affected by a decision. This involves considering the firm's internal interests and shareholder expectations, while also taking into account the potential impact a decision might have on clients, market regulators, and the broader community. For example, when a firm is contemplating an investment product rollout, firm management should consider how the product's pricing or risk structure might affect financially vulnerable clients or strain regulatory trust. By systematically gathering and evaluating diverse viewpoints, a financial firm can achieve a more balanced ethical assessment that aligns with organizational goals and the principles of client and stakeholder trust and protection.

Evaluating Alternatives Using an Ethical Framework

Deontology, consequentialism, and virtue ethics offer behavioral perspectives that enable financial services professionals to evaluate moral decisions. Deontology (duty-based ethics) emphasizes the importance of fulfilling professional or fiduciary obligations, regardless of the outcomes.[6] This approach reflects the principle that specific rules or duties should not be compromised. In contrast, consequentialism (outcome-based ethics) focuses on maximizing overall benefits and minimizing harm for all stakeholders, making the net impact of each action the primary measure of its moral worth.[7] Meanwhile, virtue ethics (character-based ethics) highlights personal integrity, honesty, and trustworthiness, which is especially pertinent in fields that require ongoing trust from clients and the broader marketplace.[8]

While the previous chapter examined these theories in detail, it is worth reviewing the foundational concepts proposed in these theories given their importance and practicality in identifying and weighing ethical considerations. For instance, a duty-based perspective might prompt the question, "Does this course of action fulfill my professional obligations?" A consequentialist analysis would consider potential outcomes for clients, the firm, and other stakeholders. Similarly, a virtue-ethics approach would ask whether a decision aligns with the traits of a morally responsible advisor. These concise reference points enable financial services professionals to stay grounded when making ethical decisions without unnecessarily rehashing philosophical debates.

Since ethical theories can sometimes lead to different conclusions, financial services professionals must sometimes reconcile conflicts across perspectives.[9] An example is when deontology favors full disclosure of sensitive client information. However, a strict outcome-based assessment might reveal that disclosing too much information could cause unnecessary panic or reputational harm. In such cases, a trade-off analysis can clarify which perspective should take precedence or whether a middle ground can satisfy ethical responsibilities while considering stakeholder well-being and applicable laws.

In many financial institutions, policy documents and compliance guidelines implicitly align with one or more ethical perspectives. For example, fiduciary obligations reflect deontological principles, whereas cultural integrity tends to connect strongly with virtue ethics. This can cause confusion for front-line financial advisors. In situations where ambiguity exists, a financial advisor is well served by taking a "client-first" approach (deontological), followed by the maximization of collective benefits attitude (consequentialist), and ending with a cultivation of trustworthy behavior approach (virtue ethics). The following questions can be used to help guide behavior: "Am I meeting my duties to the client?" "What are the broader consequences for all involved?" "Does this reflect my firm's values as principled advisors?"

Making a Decision and Taking Action

Building on the theoretical foundations of ethical practice introduced in the previous chapter—particularly deontology, consequentialism, and virtue ethics—it is possible to develop a decision-making process that translates ethical theory into practical responses to real-world business dilemmas. Consider the following question: *Which should take priority, a client's interests or meeting a sales goal?* A duty-based (deontological) approach would emphasize protecting client trust above all else. An outcomes-based (consequentialist) approach, by contrast, would weigh the broader benefits and harms for the client, the advisor, the firm, and the market as a whole. In practice, the best solution often comes from blending these perspectives, while also considering organizational realities such as internal approval procedures and cross-departmental collaboration. If the analysis leads to the conclusion that "the client should receive additional information, supported by a clear communication strategy to limit external fallout," then the next step is to determine precisely how this plan will be implemented, monitored, and reinforced in day-to-day practice.

As noted above, making ethical decisions relies heavily on communication-based transparency. The ethical decision-making process begins when the chosen course of action is communicated clearly and openly, both internally and externally. From a client's perspective, briefly outlining the fundamental principles and data behind a decision helps them understand their interests. Open dialogue also fosters greater trust in the advisory process. Sharing the decision-making process internally among colleagues strengthens an organization's commitment to ethics. This, in turn, reduces the risk of misunderstandings or conflicting interpretations. Above all, presenting a coherent justification to senior managers or corporate leadership (explaining how a decision aligns with legal or regulatory obligations, benefits the company's mid- to long-term interests, and maintains public trust) ensures that an ethically based choice receives institutional support. To achieve this, a combination of formal documentation, verbal presentations, and question-and-answer (Q&A)-style guidelines can be employed across multiple communication channels. The following examples illustrate how Q&A guidelines can be used:

Client-Facing Q&A

Q: Why didn't you immediately invest my funds in this opportunity that everyone else seems to be pursuing?

A: My responsibility is to protect your long-term financial interests. Before moving forward, I need to evaluate whether this investment meets your risk profile, regulatory suitability standards, and your long-term goals. Acting too quickly without that analysis could expose you to unnecessary risk.

Q: How do I know you're putting my interests above your firm's sales goals?

A: I follow a fiduciary duty that requires me to put client interests first. Every recommendation is documented and reviewed to ensure it aligns with your objectives, not just the firm's business targets.

Internal Firm Q&A

Q: Why should we slow down the rollout of this product if it's performing well in the market?

A: Because compliance and suitability reviews aren't complete. If we push ahead prematurely, the short-term gains could be outweighed by regulatory penalties, client losses, or reputational damage.

Q: How can we be sure everyone in the department interprets the policy consistently?

A: We'll provide written guidelines, hold training sessions, and create a shared decision log. That way, decisions are transparent and traceable across teams.

Senior Leadership Q&A

Q: How does this decision serve the company's long-term interests?

A: By aligning with regulatory obligations and creating client trust, we safeguard the company against legal risks and reputational harm, ensuring sustainable growth rather than short-lived gains.

Q: What's the risk if we approve this strategy?

A: The primary risk is that clients or regulators could perceive the action as prioritizing sales over a firm's duty to client/customers. We're mitigating that by enhancing disclosures, documenting decision rationale, and building in oversight.

Achieving transparency, as these examples illustrate, does not signify the conclusion of the ethical decision-making process. Transparency instead serves as a foundation for ongoing monitoring and improvement. Ethical determinations rarely conclude with a single declaration. This is the reason it is important to collect feedback from clients, employees, and external auditors as a way to track decision outcomes. When unforeseen challenges or client concerns emerge, proactive remedies, such as adjusting alternatives and making clarifications, may be necessary. By creating a dynamic system that relies on monitoring and adjustment feedback, an organization can turn one or more ethical decisions from one-time "documented choices" into lasting "behavioral standards."

Post-decision Review and Other Considerations

Once a decision has been made, it is important to conduct a post-decision review as a way to examine decision outcomes and the decision-making processes. Various indicators, such as financial performance, client and stakeholder satisfaction, and regulatory compliance, should be evaluated at the firm level. This review should attempt to determine whether the decision functioned as intended. Additionally, it is important to consolidate feedback from clients, employees, and external audit groups to identify any overlooked issues or unexpectedly positive effects that may have arisen. This review should assess outcomes, other results, and whether adequate information and a rational procedure were applied during the decision-making process. Doing so lays the groundwork for making more robust ethical judgments when facing similar dilemmas in the future.

Moreover, the post-decision review should incorporate moral evaluations. New ethical challenges can emerge in response to stakeholder reactions or shifts in the market. Organizations need a system that enables firm staff to learn and enhance their capacity to respond. Such a system might include regular workshops, online training modules, or case discussions to keep employees informed about the latest legal and regulatory developments and evolving ethical issues. It is equally important to provide internal mechanisms, such as anonymous reporting channels or periodic meetings, through which routine dilemmas or minor errors encountered in the field can be openly discussed and addressed.

Achieving absolute ethical perfection is likely impossible, but efforts can be refined and improved continuously through systematic post-decision reviews. For feedback loops to work effectively, it is essential to foster a culture that encourages the sharing of information and provides a platform for discussing successful ethical practices and past shortcomings. For example, employees might come together to discuss how a particular dilemma was resolved or to identify what might have been lacking in a particular case resolution. This open exchange serves as a way to improve future decision-making processes. Additionally, cataloging best practices into manuals or training resources allows team members to avoid repeating previous mistakes and to expand their competence when making ethical judgments. Through this approach, ethical decision-making becomes less of a one-off event and more of an ongoing habit, thereby enhancing the institution's credibility and stability in the long run.

Table 3.1 shows the structured decision-making process as described above. The table describes each step and provides a reminder of some of the important factors to consider at each step.

Incorporating Behavioral and Cognitive Factors

The ethical decision-making process does not stop with the outline presented in Table 3.1. It is equally important to recognize how behavioral biases play a role in ethical decision-making processes. As will be illustrated below, people often fall prey to cognitive, behavioral, and psychological biases, even when armed with a solid theoretical understanding of ethical decision-making. These biases can infiltrate decision-making and skew outcomes in unexpected ways. Some common examples of these biases include overconfidence, confirmation bias, the availability heuristic, groupthink, the halo effect, self-justification, and the influence of emotions or intuition.

For example, a financial professional who overestimates their expertise due to overconfidence might ignore warnings or contradictory evidence and stubbornly stick to a specific conclusion. Similarly, confirmation bias can lead someone to selectively seek out information supporting their preferred outcome, thereby overlooking potential unidentified risk factors. These factors were at play in the FTX case presented earlier in the chapter. Consider the availability heuristic. This decision-making bias can be observed when a loan officer fixates on a recent, high-profile bankruptcy reported in the media. This singular dramatic case might lead the

Table 3.1 Ethical decision-making process and review factors

Step	Description	Important review factors
1. Recognize the ethical dilemma	Identify whether the situation involves potential harm, fairness issues, or conflicts between values (e.g., client interest vs. sales targets)	Nature of conflict (duty vs. outcome); who is affected (clients, firm, market); urgency and scope of the dilemma
2. Gather facts and perspectives	Collect relevant data, including stakeholder interests, legal obligations, and organizational policies	Regulatory and legal requirements; client goals and risk tolerance; market conditions and internal firm policies
3. Evaluate alternatives	Use ethical theories (deontology, consequentialism, virtue ethics) to weigh possible courses of action	Duty-based considerations (trust, fiduciary duty); consequences for all parties (short- and long-term); alignment with professional virtues (honesty, fairness)
4. Decision and communication	Select the most ethical course of action, and communicate it transparently to clients, colleagues, and leadership	Clear rationale documented; client explanation (principles + data); internal team briefings; senior management justification (long-term trust, compliance, sustainability)
5. Implementation	Put the decision into practice through organizational processes and safeguards	Approval procedures followed; cross-departmental collaboration; communication strategy for stakeholders; oversight mechanisms established
6. Post-decision review	Assess how well the decision worked and whether the process was effective	Financial outcomes; client and stakeholder satisfaction; compliance with laws/regulations; adequacy of documentation
7. Feedback and continuous improvement	Gather feedback and refine practices to strengthen future ethical decision-making	Input from clients, employees, and auditors; training workshops or case reviews; sharing best practices and mechanisms for anonymous reporting; cataloging lessons learned

loan officer to adopt overly cautious lending practices, even when statistical data indicates that the overall default rate in their community is low.

Groupthink (i.e., the tendency to engage in herding behavior[10]) can occur in a team meeting about launching a new financial product if no one is willing to voice a dissenting opinion.[11] Assuming that "everyone seems to approve, so it must be fine," the group may rush to move forward without adequate scrutiny. The halo effect[12] can also come into play. This bias arises when the probability of success for a projected decision outcome is too high (or given too much weight). For example, a financial advisor might overestimate a client's creditworthiness because of the client's polished demeanor. Giving the client a halo of financial capacity may lead the financial advisor to mistakenly conclude that first impressions are also financially sound impressions.

In addition to these common biases, self-justification poses a further concern. Financial services professionals may hold on to a previous decision out of fear that changing course could damage their personal or team reputation. Emotional or intuitive factors, such as anger, empathy, or gut feelings, can also override rational judgment. A strong emotional reaction might prompt a financial advisor to make a hasty recommendation that deviates from objective data or a more thorough analysis.

Case Studies in Ethical Decision-Making

Ethical decision-making generally occurs in the complex space between abstract moral principles and the specific realities of real-world situations. This section presents three cases, highlighting the tensions, ambiguities, and pressures financial services professionals face when dealing with ethical dilemmas. Each case, although hypothetical, is based on a real-world situation. Each case is distinct in its domain but shares the common challenge of moral complexity. Together, these cases provide a lens through which to examine the relationship between individual judgment, institutional expectations, and broader societal norms. By analyzing these scenarios, readers are encouraged to evaluate the decisions made and reflect on the frameworks and values that inform their own ethical reasoning.

Case 3.1 Insider Information and Overconfidence

In 2018, John Carter, a wealth manager at a large investment firm, received insider information about a pending merger between two tech companies. This tip came from a close friend who was, at the time, an executive at one of these companies. Known for his investing expertise and confidence in navigating complex financial regulations, Carter believed he could use this information discreetly to benefit his clients without violating securities laws. He assumed that his familiarity with SEC and FINRA regulations would enable him to structure trades that appeared compliant. For example, Carter timed transactions to avoid suspicion and used vague justifications for his decisions.

Based on his friend's tip, Carter gathered details about the merger, including its timeline and potential market impact. Carter's overconfidence bias played a role in the case, leading him to focus selectively on news that reinforced his belief that he could act on the information legally. For example, he assumed the tip was not material because it was shared casually. He failed to verify whether the information was public or to consult legal counsel. Basically, he failed to perform thorough due diligence. Carter executed trades based on this nonpublic information, generating substantial profits for his clients. However, the SEC was still able to flag the trades through routine surveillance. An investigation revealed Carter's connection to privileged and nonpublic information. Carter was subsequently charged with insider trading, fined $1.2 million, and barred from the securities industry for five years. His firm also faced reputational damage and settled with regulators for $3 million.

Case Analysis

When the SEC and his firm uncovered Carter's insider trading, Carter claimed that he anticipated substantial profits for his clients. He believed that regulators would not detect his trades. He also argued that, aside from personal accolades, his goal was to maximize his clients' profits, making his behavior consequently valuable and ethically sound. However, regulators pointed out that his reasoning was flawed. While Carter's actions did benefit his clients, his behavior caused reputational damage to the firm and a negative market reaction. Regulators reminded Carter of his deontological duty-based obligations. He was reminded that rather than acting from a consequentialist perspective, financial services professionals must adhere to securities laws, firm policies, and professional standards. Carter's duty was to avoid trading on nonpublic information and to prioritize the interests of his clients transparently. Carter's overconfidence bias caused him to rationalize his actions and conclude that what he was doing was in the spirit of the law. This distortion affected the interpretation of his ethical obligations.

Case 3.2 Commission Conflicts and Confirmation Bias

In 2020, Sarah Thompson, a financial advisor working at a mid-sized brokerage firm, recommended a high-commission variable annuity product to her retiree client, Mrs. Davis. Mrs. Davis came to Thompson seeking a stable retirement income. The annuity provided Thompson with a 7% commission, which was significantly higher than the commissions offered on other lower-cost products. Thompson presented the variable annuity as the "safest" option for Mrs. Davis's retirement plan. Thompson provided a glossy brochure that highlighted income guarantees, but during the presentation, Thompson omitted essential details about fees and early-withdrawal penalties. Trusting Thompson's expertise, Mrs. Davis invested $150,000 in the annuity.

Why did Thompson act the way she did? One reason is that confirmation bias influenced her decision-making. Thompson interpreted Mrs. Davis's initial reaction to the sales presentation as validation of her recommendation. As a result, Thompson unconsciously presented data that justified her recommendation while dismissing evidence of the product's drawbacks. This bias led Thompson to prioritize information supporting the high-commission annuity's benefits, such as its guaranteed income feature, while overlooking significant factors, including high fees, surrender penalties, and the product's unsuitability for Mrs. Davis's portfolio holdings and risk tolerance.

One year later, Mrs. Davis attempted to withdraw funds to cover medical expenses. She was surprised to learn of a 10% surrender penalty. Frustrated, she filed a complaint with the firm, which prompted a FINRA investigation. The investigation revealed Thompson's failure to disclose the annuity's risks. As a consequence, Thompson was fined $25,000, suspended for six months, and required to complete ethics training. The firm refunded Mrs. Davis's penalties and transitioned her to a lower-cost product.

Case Analysis

This case illustrates how sometimes a financial advisor's recommendations can cross the line into unethical behavior. Thompson had a responsibility to recommend a product that was in Mrs. Davis's best interest. When regulators questioned her, Thompson focused on the annuity's marketing materials and success stories from colleagues who had also used the product as justifications for her recommendation. She claimed that she did not have a conflict of interest. However, Thompson acknowledged that while she reviewed the annuity's prospectus, noting its guaranteed income and tax-deferral benefits, she only skimmed over the product's 2.5% annual fee and 10-year surrender period. These details were disproportionate to Mrs. Davis's $200,000 portfolio and need for liquidity. Thompson admitted that she did not research lower-cost alternatives, such as a firm-approved fixed annuity with a 1% fee, because the product offered a lower commission and did not align with her preference for variable annuities.

Thompson's duty was to act in her client's best interest and disclose any conflicts of interest. Confirmation bias led her to believe she fulfilled this duty by focusing on the annuity's benefits. Thompson neglected her obligation to prioritize low-cost, suitable alternatives and to disclose the influence of her commission. She approached Mrs. Davis's situation using a consequentialist perspective. However, confirmation bias caused her to underestimate adverse outcomes. Based on what happened, Thompson's firm instituted regular training and independent reviews to help detect and address similar issues before harming clients.

Case 3.3 Marketing Tactics and Groupthink

In 2025, a mid-sized financial firm, Apex Wealth Management, sought to increase revenue by targeting high-net-worth clients with aggressive marketing for a new high-risk hedge fund offering 13% annual returns. The fund carried significant volatility and illiquidity risks, which made the product unsuitable for many retail investors. During brainstorming sessions, Laura Evans, the firm's marketing director, proposed the use of bold claims, such as "An Unmissable Wealth-Building Opportunity," as a way to attract investors. However, two junior analysts, Mark and Priya, raised concerns that the fund's risks (potential 30% drawdowns and a three-year lockup period) were unsuitable for retirees or conservative investors. The group dismissed their objections, with senior members citing the fund's "strong historical performance" and accusing the dissenters of lacking ambition. Groupthink dynamics, including deference to leadership and fear of isolation, silenced further debate.

The team finalized a marketing campaign targeting all high-net-worth clients, regardless of their risk tolerance. The marketing materials downplayed risks and highlighted returns. Groupthink emerged within the team as they eagerly aimed to meet ambitious revenue targets, rallying around the marketing campaign's potential to attract wealthy investors. The firm's leadership's enthusiasm for the fund created pressure to conform. This discouraged dissenting opinions and views. Team members who questioned the marketing campaign's aggressive tactics or the fund's risks were sidelined. Without dissenting voices, the firm came to the false conclusion that the marketing strategy was ethical and client-focused.

Apex launched the campaign in early 2026, attracting $50 million from investors, including retirees who misunderstood the fund's risks. However, market volatility later that year resulted in a 25% loss, leading to client complaints. A regulatory investigation by FINRA found Apex's marketing materials misleading, citing exaggerated return projections and inadequate risk disclosures. The firm was fined $2 million, ordered to compensate impacted clients, and required to overhaul its marketing processes. Laura Evans faced a three-month suspension, and the firm's reputation suffered as a result.

Case Analysis

The ethical issue faced by Apex was the firm's responsibility to market products transparently and ensure client suitability. Groupthink skewed decision-making by prioritizing revenue over client welfare. The team ignored red flags, such as the fund's high leverage and lack of diversification. The team also failed to tailor marketing based on investor profiles. As a result of groupthink, the team (a) overemphasized the fund's upside, cherry-picking data from a bullish market period; (b) ignored regulatory guidelines requiring clear risk disclosure (e.g., SEC Rule 206(4)-1); and (c) assumed investors could "handle" the risks, neglecting suitability assessments.

The collective bias exhibited by the team prevented a structured evaluation of ethical pitfalls. The outcome might have differed if Apex had implemented a structured process to encourage diverse opinions. For example, assigning a "devil's advocate" role or allowing anonymous feedback could have amplified Mark and Priya's concerns, prompting (a) a revised campaign with clear risk disclosures and targeted outreach to risk-tolerant clients, (b) an independent review by the compliance team to ensure regulatory alignment, and (c) a suitability checklist to match clients with appropriate investments. Such measures could have mitigated ethical and legal risks while still meeting revenue goals.

Practical Tools and Best Practices

The checklist shown in Table 3.2 serves as a practical tool for use when evaluating ethical decisions. The checklist aligns with the principles described in Chap. 2 and the theoretical extensions offered in this chapter. Designed for quick reference, this checklist can be used to help ensure that actions are consistent with the core values such as fairness, responsibility, and respect for others. Use of this checklist should help those who are unaccustomed to making ethics-based decisions be consistent in their reasoning across various situations.

Table 3.2 Ethical decision-making checklist

Question	Answer	
1. Legality		
• Does this decision violate any relevant laws, regulations, or internal company policies?	Yes	No
• Could this action pose a potential compliance risk, even if it seems minor?	Yes	No
2. Stakeholder benefit assessment		
• What are the likely impacts on major stakeholders (clients, shareholders, employees, local communities)?	Yes	No
• Could a focus on short-term profits harm long-term firm or advisor reputation or trust?	Yes	No
• Are benefits distributed fairly, or is excessive risk being shifted onto others?	Yes	No
3. Bias check *(see more details in the next section on cognitive biases)*		
• Am I only considering evidence that supports my preferred outcome (confirmation bias)?	Yes	No
• Am I being influenced by recent events that may exaggerate outcomes (availability heuristic)?	Yes	No
• Is there a lack of dissent in the discussion, possibly indicating a case of groupthink?	Yes	No
• Am I letting a positive impression of a person or company skew my judgment (halo effect)?	Yes	No
4. Consistency with ethical principles		
• Deontology		
– Am I upholding my professional duties and avoiding violations of practice standards?	Yes	No
• Consequentialism		
– Does this choice provide the greatest net benefit for everyone involved?	Yes	No
• Virtue ethics		
– Does this action reflect core virtues such as honesty, fairness, and accountability?	Yes	No
5. Alignment with organizational policies and values		
• Is this decision consistent with the company's mission, vision, and ethical code?	Yes	No
• Does the decision reflect a culture of transparency, trust, and mutual respect?	Yes	No
6. Worst-case scenario		
• Has someone considered the potential damage or the extent of harm that could occur if something goes wrong?	Yes	No
• Are risk management or mitigation strategies in place?	Yes	No
7. Decision process and follow-up		
• Have I obtained all necessary internal approvals and cross-departmental input?	Yes	No
• Is there a plan in place for monitoring outcomes and addressing feedback after implementation?		

The ethical decision-making checklist shown in Table 3.2 can be used as a reference before meetings or at a point when a financial advisor needs to make an important decision. Consistently using a checklist like this one can help prevent ethical oversights or biased judgments.[13]

By design, the checklist focuses on pre-decision considerations and may not address the post-decision phase of the decision-making process. Therefore, after making a decision, it is essential to reflect on whether certain factors were overlooked or whether personal assumptions influenced answers. Reviewing these points can enable continuous refinement of the checklist, making it a more precise and effective tool for future decisions.[14]

Behavioral Bias Indicators

In addition to using the ethical decision-making checklist, it is recommended that financial advisors conduct a "bias check" before finalizing decisions. A bias check is a quick way to determine if one of the cognitive and psychological biases described earlier in the chapter may be at play in the decision-making process. On an organizational level, incorporating a checklist like the one shown in Table 3.3 into team meetings or review processes is also advisable. This approach helps reduce the likelihood that unconscious biases will affect decisions.

Organizations can enhance decision-making processes and mitigate the impact of biases identified in the bias-check questionnaire in numerous ways. Implementing peer reviews is one way for those who work in teams to identify potential risks or logical gaps that an individual might miss. Asking someone to play a "devil's advocate role" is another way to systematically challenge consensus-driven or confirmation-biased decisions.

Firms can also utilize statistical tools to minimize the impact of cognitive distortions by adding an objective, data-driven layer to the human decision-making process. For example, predictive analytics and machine learning algorithms can be used to analyze vast amounts of data, including client transaction histories, market trends, and default probabilities. The incorporation of statistical tools into the process of making decisions reduces reliance on anecdotal evidence or personal intuition. Quantitative indicators from statistical tools can also be used to help decision-makers assess the relative risks and benefits associated with specific decisions, lessening the influence of recent news events (the availability heuristic) or personal feelings about a particular client (the halo effect). Furthermore, when analytical frameworks are continuously updated and validated against real-world outcomes, these tools create a feedback loop that discourages decision-makers from ignoring negative signals or inconsistent metrics. By balancing statistical insights with human expertise, organizations can more effectively detect early warning signs of potential problems and mitigate cognitive biases that sometimes can slip through purely subjective assessments.

Table 3.3 Bias-check questionnaire

Bias-check questions	Answer	
1. Overconfidence		
(a) Am I overestimating the depth of my own information or expertise?	Yes	No
(b) Have I established a solid basis for supporting this decision, including expert or data-backed evidence?	Yes	No
(c) Did I neutrally assess the potential costs and damages that could arise if this decision goes wrong?	Yes	No
2. Confirmation bias		
(a) Am I selectively amassing only information that validates my preexisting conclusion?	Yes	No
(b) Have I looked for data that might challenge my conclusion?	Yes	No
(c) When colleagues or external parties offered dissent, did I reject or discount them too quickly?	Yes	No
3. Availability heuristic		
(a) Are recent incidents or sensationalized media reports unduly influencing my judgment beyond actual statistical probabilities?	Yes	No
(b) Have I checked precise data on how often comparable cases and/or outcomes really occur?	Yes	No
4. Groupthink		
(a) During the decision-making process, was there anyone who posed critical questions or oppositional ideas?	Yes	No
(b) Was the team so eager to converge on agreement that it bypassed in-depth analysis or robust debate?	Yes	No
5. Halo effect		
(a) Might my evaluation of someone's merits be unduly influenced by personal impressions such as courtesy, appearance, or brand identity?	Yes	No
(b) Am I scrutinizing how a non-financial attribute (e.g., way of dressing, speaking style, etc.) may overshadow core financial indicators?	Yes	No
6. Self-justification and related biases		
(a) Am I clinging to a particular decision or hypothesis merely to protect personal pride or the team's status, even though reevaluation might be warranted?	Yes	No
(b) Am I aware of potential flaws but hesitant to disclose them for fear of criticism?	Yes	No
7. Emotional or intuitive components		
(a) Have strong emotions (anger, sympathy, personal fondness) or gut reactions steered my conclusions without proper evidence?	Yes	No
(b) Did I consult a colleague or supervisor to gain an objective viewpoint, free from emotional sway?	Yes	No
8. Final check		
(a) Have I clearly differentiated "objective facts" from "subjective inferences or feelings"?	Yes	No
(b) If this decision proves mistaken, is bias likely to be a significant cause?	Yes	No

Seeking outside expert counsel is another tool that can be used to address potential blind spots within an organization. External consultants may identify ethical issues that internal experts overlook. By consulting an external specialist or a neutral third-party reviewer, firm executives can obtain candid feedback, avoid insular thinking, and reinforce the credibility of their ethical decision-making processes. In the end, this approach can help strengthen client trust and contribute to overall market stability, which are important outcomes associated with ethical decision-making.

Firm Culture and Training

Fostering a sense of psychological safety at the firm level helps create a firm culture focused on ethical decision-making. Such a culture is essential for increasing ethical awareness and reducing behavioral biases within an organization.[15] It may be possible, for instance, to establish a dedicated "ethics and compliance" bulletin board on the company's internal messaging platform to encourage employees to share even minor dilemmas or questions without fear of retribution (the system should be anonymous). Taking steps like this helps staff feel confident that voicing dissenting opinions or admitting mistakes will not automatically lead to negative consequences. When thinking about organizational culture, it is particularly important not to impose penalties for shared content. Allowing for the correction of past unethical conduct and the prevention of potential future unethical actions is one way to move a firm closer to normative ethical standards.

Additionally, conducting regular ethics workshops that include simulations and case studies can be very effective in building organizational culture. Through group discussions or role-playing exercises, staff can engage with real-life scenarios highlighting ethical pitfalls. Firm leaders and executives should actively participate in these sessions and candidly share their own experiences or mistakes. Doing so can foster organizational values aligned with virtue ethics, including honesty, fairness, and accountability. Finally, incorporating ethical indicators like the number of client complaints or the results of internal audits into the performance appraisals and reward systems can help foster a culture in which staff are recognized for their contributions to sales, profits, collaboration, and ethical compliance.

Technology and Bias Mitigation

Another way for organizations to enhance ethical decision-making while creating a culture of ethical responsibility is to incorporate AI-based compliance monitoring and decision-support tools into models of decision-making. In the future, AI promises to reduce behavioral biases significantly.[16] For example, implementing a system that automatically analyzes large volumes of transactional data to identify patterns or anomalies early in the decision-making process enables staff to quickly recognize warning signs (red flags) or misconduct that might otherwise go unnoticed. Decision-support features, such as scenario analyses and data visualization dashboards, can then be used to enable staff to make informed judgments based on long-term statistical trends and various interacting factors.

It is important to remember, however, that human oversight is crucial since AI and statistical algorithms can have inherent biases.[17] For instance, if training data are skewed toward a particular region or demographic group, a model's predictions can be distorted. Organizations can combat this by collaborating with experts to review statistical modeling processes and mitigate signs of discrimination or logical errors. Additionally, clarifying internal guidelines on the use of client data and ensuring explainability in predictive models is one way organizations can communicate the reasons behind certain decisions. Transparency helps to minimize the ethical and legal controversies that can arise when technology is used in financial decision-making processes.

Globalization and Cultural Differences

Globalization complicates ethical decision-making due to the varying cultural norms and legal frameworks that exist worldwide. For example, data privacy laws differ significantly between regions, such as the European Union, where the stringent General Data Protection Regulation (GDPR) applies, and other jurisdictions with less stringent regulations. Similarly, the interpretation of conflict-of-interest laws can vary, creating challenges for multinational firms operating across borders. Balancing universal ethical principles such as justice, honesty, and transparency with local customs is essential for firms and financial advisors who work worldwide. Firms can achieve a workable balance by adopting a flexible ethical framework that respects cultural nuances while adhering to core ethical values rooted in normative models. Engaging local stakeholders and conducting cross-cultural training can help firm executives navigate complexities, ensuring that decisions are globally consistent and locally relevant.

Chapter Summary

This chapter was written to connect ethical theories and models with real-world scenarios by providing financial services professionals with a practical framework for ethical decision-making. The chapter material built upon foundational concepts presented in Chap. 2, including deontology, consequentialism, and virtue ethics. This chapter illustrated how these and other ethical principles can be integrated with a firm's core values to enhance beneficence, autonomy, and justice. The chapter also outlined a step-by-step ethical decision-making process, supported by illustrative case examples. Behavioral biases were introduced, as were strategies to reduce the impact of cognitive, behavioral, and psychological biases. To help those who are asked to make ethically challenged decisions, two practical tools were introduced: the ethical decision-making checklist and the bias-check questionnaire. The first was designed to ensure decision-making consistency with legal, organizational, and ethical standards. The second was aimed at increasing self-awareness to identify cognitive distortions in the decision-making process. Together, these tools can be used to empower financial professionals to make sound, ethically grounded decisions while maintaining integrity and accountability.

Chapter Resources

- Accounting Insights, Professional Ethics in Financial Decision-Making: accountinginsights.org/professional-ethics-in-financial-decision-making
- Certified Financial Planner Board of Standards, Inc.: https://www.cfp.net/ethics/code-of-ethics-and-standards-of-conduct
- CFA Institute, Revisions to the CFA Institute Code of Ethics and Standards of Professional Conduct: https://rpc.cfainstitute.org/blogpage?q=155dc3ac7e51bc40757fbfd684648231f9d3c63b7814ba4e7bb544cde5f5
- Corporate Finance Institute (CFI), Ethical Decision Making in Finance: corporatefinanceinstitute.com/resources/career/ethical-decision-making
- The American College of Financial Services: https://www.theamericancollege.edu/about-the-college/the-college-at-a-glance/our-code-of-ethics

Notes

[1] Although the Investment Advisers Act of 1940 refers to a regulated financial professional as an adviser, for clarity, this chapter uses the term advisor.

[2] A timeline of cryptocurrency exchange FTX's historic collapse—ABC News.

[3] SEC.gov: https://www.sec.gov/newsroom/press-releases/2022-219

[4] Ibid.

[5] Office of Public Affairs | Samuel Bankman-Fried Sentenced to 25 Years for His Orchestration of Multiple Fraudulent Schemes | United States Department of Justice.

[6] Refolo, P., Sacchini, D., Raimondi, C., Calabrò, G. E., & Spagnolo, A. G. (2023). What type of person should I be? About the appeal to virtues in public health interventions. *Vaccines*, *11*(4), 767.

[7] Everett, J. A., Faber, N. S., Savulescu, J., & Crockett, M. J. (2018). The costs of being consequentialist: Social inference from instrumental harm and impartial beneficence. *Journal of Experimental Social Psychology*, *79*, 200–216.

[8] Misselbrook, D. (2015). Virtue ethics–an old answer to a new dilemma? Part 2. The case for inclusive virtue ethics. *Journal of the Royal Society of Medicine*, *108*(3), 89–92.

[9] It is important to note that no single ethical approach consistently yields the best solution. Focusing solely on outcomes can overshadow critical duties or moral constraints, just as unreasoning adherence to rules might create genuine harm or misaligned incentives. A balanced approach helps mitigate blind spots, encouraging professionals to consider the interplay between duties, outcomes, and character. By cross-checking multiple perspectives, decisions rest on more robust ethical grounds, reflecting a well-rounded moral insight rather than a one-dimensional stance.

[10] Baddeley, M. (2015). Herding, social influences, and behavioural bias in scientific research: Simple awareness of the hidden pressures and beliefs that influence our thinking can help to preserve objectivity. *EMBO Reports*, *16*(8), 902–905.

[11] https://leb.fbi.gov/articles/featured-articles/dangers-of-groupthink-and-the-internet

[12] Westbury, C., & King, D. (2024). A Constant Error, Revisited: A New Explanation of the Halo Effect. *Cognitive Science*, *48*(12), e70022.

[13] For significant projects, new service rollouts, or important screening sessions, including written responses to the checklist as a separate item in meeting materials or decision documents can be particularly beneficial. This approach ensures that everyone involved gains insight into the criteria and rationale behind the conclusions, allowing for any concerns to be raised and addressed immediately during the meeting.

[14] Since legal frameworks and social norms evolve, the content of this checklist should be revised periodically. Collaborating with internal audit and compliance teams to incorporate recent cases of

violations or legal risks will enable the organization to continuously strengthen its ability to address emerging issues.

[15]Kim, S., Lee, H., & Connerton, T. P. (2020). How psychological safety affects team performance: mediating role of efficacy and learning behavior. *Frontiers in Psychology*, *11*, 1581.

[16]According to the National Aeronautics and Space Administration (https://www.nasa.gov/what-is-artificial-intelligence/), artificial intelligence (AI) refers broadly to artificial systems—developed through software, hardware, or a combination—that can perform tasks typically requiring human intelligence, such as reasoning, decision-making, learning, perception, and communication. While there is no single universal definition due to AI's wide-ranging capabilities, common elements include the ability to operate under varying and unpredictable conditions with minimal human oversight, to learn and improve from data, and to emulate or approximate human cognitive functions.

[17]According to the U.S. Securities and Exchange Commission (https://www.investor.gov/introduction-investing/investing-basics/glossary/environmental-social-and-governance-esg-investing), ESG investing is a way of investing in companies based on their commitment to one or more ESG factors. While the term ESG has fallen out of use, proponents of the concept sometimes refer to the investment processes as sustainable investing, socially responsible investing, and impact investing.

The Ethical Mind: Psychology, Fraud, and Decision-Making in Financial Services

4

Chapter Outcomes
This chapter focuses on helping learners develop the ability to:

1. Integrate professional ethics and practice standard codes and regulatory frameworks with appropriate attitudinal and behavioral constraints to uphold ethical conduct in the financial services profession.
2. Analyze the intersection of cognitive, behavioral, and motivational factors to understand the decision-making processes of financial advisors and clients.
3. Navigate the complex landscape of personal values, ethical reasoning, professional responsibility, client expectations, and market pressures.
4. Identify financial, behavioral, and psychological determinants of fraud and recognize how rationalizations, pressures, and opportunities contribute to ethical lapses.
5. Evaluate common psychological tendencies, such as overconfidence, confirmation bias, and the pursuit of short-term rewards, that influence decision-making.
6. Understand the psychology and behaviors of clients, including their goals, anxieties, and biases.

Introduction

Ethical conduct in the financial services profession has traditionally been framed through the lens of regulatory compliance, fiduciary duty, and professional codes of conduct. Yet, the psychology underlying ethical and unethical decision-making

Note: This chapter was copyedited using Grammarly™ and generative AI tools to enhance clarity, grammar, and overall readability. While these tools provided suggestions and assistance in refining the text, the ideas, content, and arguments presented remain the sole work and responsibility of the authors. Any errors or inaccuracies in the final version are also the authors' responsibility.

W. Heo, J. E. Grable, *Ethics and Compliance in Financial Services*,
https://doi.org/10.1007/978-3-032-14449-2_4

rarely receives explicit attention, despite its profound influence on firms, advisors, clients, and society. Financial decision environments are uniquely complex. Financial decisions tend to be high-stakes, information-rich, and frequently characterized by asymmetries of knowledge and power. These features create conditions in which ethical lapses and fraudulent behaviors can emerge, not merely as deliberate violations of rules but as outcomes of cognitive biases, social pressures, motivational conflicts, and rationalizations.

Equally important is the examination of how psychological factors influence financial decision-making of advisors. Financial advisors are subject to the same cognitive biases and motivational dynamics as their clients, including overconfidence, loss aversion, mental accounting, and the allure of immediate rewards, which can affect judgment, risk perceptions, and ethical boundaries. By bridging ethical theory, fraud research, and behavioral decision science, this chapter provides a comprehensive framework for understanding the ethical mind in financial services. The aim is not only to identify risks to ethical conduct but also to equip professionals with a deeper self-awareness and practical insights for fostering trust, integrity, and sound decision-making in an evolving financial services landscape.

Perspective

Contrary to the popular belief that fraudsters are inherently devious or predisposed to criminality, evidence shows that most financial criminals originate from otherwise conventional backgrounds. The Association of Certified Fraud Examiners[1] reports that more than four out of five fraud perpetrators are first-time offenders. Individuals rarely join organizations intending to commit fraud.[2] Typically, fraudsters hold higher social status, are educated, and are generally respected within their communities.

Demographically, fraud is most frequently committed by individuals between the ages of 31 and 45, who work in accounting, finance, executive management, operations, and sales. These are roles characterized by privileged access to financial systems and, in management positions, the capacity for override of internal controls.[3] Men account for the majority of fraud globally, though gender distributions vary regionally. The dominance of male fraudsters in certain regions may reflect structural underrepresentation of women in senior roles rather than intrinsic differences in propensity to engage in wrongdoing.

Tenure within organizations is also significant. Over half of those who commit fraud had, at the time they were caught, been employed for three to ten years, and a quarter for more than a decade, before offending. Fraud typically persists undetected for several years, meaning that long-serving employees are often better positioned to exploit system vulnerabilities due to their familiarity with organizational processes. Patterns of fraud underscore a critical insight: fraud is usually committed not by career criminals but by trusted employees whose ethical boundaries erode over time when opportunity, pressure, and rationalization converge.

Research suggests that regardless of who commits a fraud or the place where a fraud has been committed, the following ten personal characteristics are common across fraudsters[4]:

1. living beyond one's means;
2. having an overwhelming desire for personal gain;
3. carrying a high amount of personal debt;
4. being closely associated with customers;
5. feeling that compensation is not commensurate with job duties;
6. possessing a wheeler-dealer attitude;
7. having a strong urge to outsmart the system;
8. exhibiting excessive gambling habits;
9. experiencing pressure from family or peers; and
10. feeling a lack of recognition for job performance.

The case of Scott London, a former senior partner at KPMG, illustrates these characteristics.[5] As the partner in charge of KPMG's Pacific Southwest audit practice, London oversaw major audits for clients such as Herbalife, Skechers USA, and Deckers Outdoor. Between 2010 and 2013, he provided his friend, Bryan Shaw (a jewelry store owner) with material, nonpublic information regarding earnings announcements and merger activity. In return, London received cash payments, luxury gifts such as a Rolex watch and jewelry, and other benefits. Shaw used the information to execute trades that generated more than $1 million in illicit profits, sometimes coordinating with London on strategies to avoid detection.

The misconduct drew swift regulatory and criminal action. The SEC charged London and Shaw with violations of Section 10(b) and Rule 10b-5 of the Securities Exchange Act, while the Department of Justice pursued criminal charges. London ultimately pleaded guilty to securities fraud and was sentenced in 2014 to 14 months in federal prison, a $100,000 fine, and 3 years of supervised release. Shaw, who cooperated with investigators, received a five-month sentence and was ordered to forfeit approximately $1.27 million in illegal gains. The scandal also had immediate consequences for KPMG. The firm resigned as auditor for Herbalife and Skechers, withdrew prior audit reports, and faced reputational fallout for the apparent breakdown of its internal controls and the breach of auditor independence. Table 4.1 shows how the fraud matched almost perfectly with the ten factors common across those who commit fraud.

This case underscores how financial fraud can unfold, as well as the psychological justifications criminals use to further their wrongdoing. London's actions were not a momentary lapse but a structured, prolonged scheme that undermined public trust in financial reporting.

The remainder of this chapter is focused on providing more context and insight into the psychological factors associated with financial crimes and engagement in fraudulent activities.

Table 4.1 The case of Scott London and Bryan Shaw

Factor	Example from the case
1. Living beyond one's means	London admitted he was under financial pressure and enjoyed a lifestyle that exceeded his income
2. Overwhelming desire for personal gain	London accepted bribes in exchange for insider information
3. High personal debt	Though not publicly detailed, financial strain was cited as a motivator
4. Closely associated with customers	As an auditor, London had intimate access to client financials
5. Compensation dissatisfaction	London reportedly felt underappreciated despite his senior role
6. Wheeler-dealer attitude	London engaged in secretive deals and rationalized his actions as harmless
7. Urge to outsmart the system	London believed he could avoid detection and manipulate audit protocols
8. Gambling habits	Not explicitly mentioned in court documents, it was apparent that London's risk-taking behavior mimicked gambling psychology
9. Pressure from peers	London's friend pressured him for tips and London succumbed
10. Lack of recognition	London felt his work contributions were overlooked, which fueled resentment

The Financial, Behavioral, and Psychological Determinants of Financial Fraud

Financial fraud is any intentional or deliberate act to deprive another of property or money by guile, deception, or other unfair means.[6] For a behavior to be fraudulent, the person engaged in the behavior must be knowledgeable about the truth or falseness of the behavior. They must also have had the intent to deceive. Furthermore, the victim must suffer injury or financial loss as a result of relying on the information provided.[7]

Differential association theory is perhaps the most widely cited explanation as to why people engage in criminal behavior. According to Sutherland (the person who proposed the theory), criminal behavior is not a trait-like factor but instead something that is learned through interactions with others.[8] Within this framework, those who commit fraud learn techniques, tools, and strategies from colleagues. They also learn to rationalize their motivations in such a way that perceptions of rewards and punishments fall in favor of committing a crime.

Building on Sutherland's work, Cressey developed what is now known as the Fraud Triangle (see Fig. 4.1).[9] Cressey concluded that fraud typically occurs when three elements converge: pressure, opportunity, and rationalization. Each factor is described in more detail below:

- Pressure refers to non-shareable financial or personal problems that create a perceived need for illicit gain. These pressures may stem from debt, lifestyle

Fig. 4.1 Cressey's Fraud Triangle

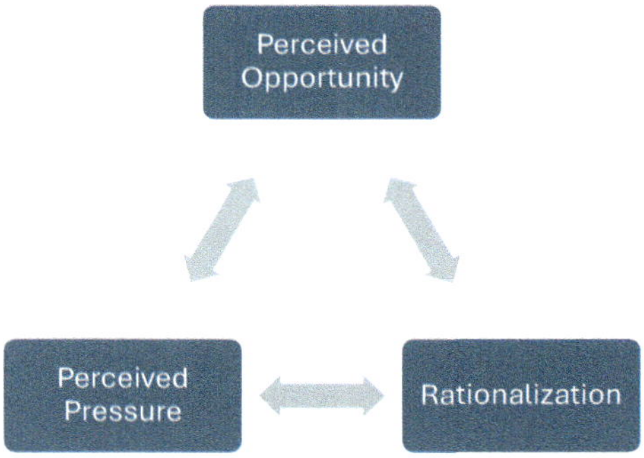

demands, business reversals, or social expectations. Pressures are often concealed due to fear of loss of status or reputation.

- Opportunity arises when organizational systems, internal controls, or positions of authority provide the means to commit fraud with a perceived low risk of detection. Individuals in roles with privileged access, oversight gaps, or the ability to override controls are particularly susceptible to committing fraud.
- Rationalization captures the cognitive justifications that allow otherwise law-abiding individuals to reconcile fraudulent acts with their self-concept. Common rationalizations include beliefs such as "I'm just borrowing," "I deserve this," or "the company won't miss it."

Cressey noted that fraudsters are rarely predestined criminals. Instead, they are ordinary individuals who, under specific conditions, convince themselves that their actions are acceptable or temporary. What made the Fraud Triangle revolutionary at the time is that it shifted the study of financial crime from a purely criminological model (i.e., people are born to be criminals) to one integrating psychological processes, organizational context, and ethical self-regulation. The framework provides a durable conceptual lens that is widely applied in auditing, compliance, and fraud risk management.

Perceived pressure and rationalization are worthy of further review. In the financial services profession, six types of non-shareable financial pressures commonly drive individuals toward fraudulent behavior. Violations of standards occur when financial difficulties stem from socially unacceptable behaviors (e.g., substance abuse). To conceal the actual cause of their problems, some turn to fraud as a cover. Personal failures, such as poor judgment or mismanagement of money, can create shame and embarrassment that discourage individuals from seeking help, making fraud appear to be a private solution. Business reversals, often triggered by external forces like recessions or declining client demand, can threaten a firm's (or person's) financial stability and prompt individuals to commit fraud in an effort to preserve their standard of living. Physical isolation is also important. Isolation deprives individuals of interactions with trusted colleagues or advisors, and without support, feelings of helplessness sometimes escalate into fraudulent actions. Status-gaining pressures arise when dissatisfaction with one's lifestyle fuels a desire for more wealth or material possessions, leading some to pursue illicit means of acquisition. Finally, strained employer–employee relations, such as perceptions of unfair treatment, inadequate compensation, or lack of recognition, may convince employees that their concerns cannot safely be voiced, leaving fraud as a rationalized outlet for resentment or perceived injustice.[10]

Rationalization is another factor of particular importance. Sykes and Matza developed what has since become known as neutralization theory as a way to explain how individuals justify or rationalize their unethical or illegal actions to neutralize guilt and maintain a positive self-image.[11] The theory suggests that those who commit fraud and other crimes use cognitive techniques to excuse their behavior. Through psychological self-manipulation, criminals can better engage in fraud without viewing themselves as criminals. In financial fraud terms, these techniques include:

- Denial of Responsibility: Claiming fraud was unintentional or due to external pressures, like financial distress or workplace demands (e.g., "I had no choice; I needed to meet targets").
- Denial of Injury: Arguing that no one was truly harmed, such as viewing fraud against large corporations or banks as victimless (e.g., "They can afford the loss").
- Denial of Victim: Blaming the victim, suggesting the victim deserved the loss due to greed or negligence (e.g., "They should've checked the fine print").
- Condemning the Condemners: Criticizing those who enforce rules, like regulators or auditors, as hypocritical or corrupt (e.g., "The system is rigged anyway").
- Appealing to Higher Loyalties: Justifying fraud as serving a greater good, like protecting family or employees (e.g., "I did it to save jobs").

By employing these rationalizations, fraudsters reconcile their actions with societal norms, enabling them to commit financial crimes while preserving their moral identity.

One additional factor not shown in the Fraud Triangle or discussed explicitly in neutralization theory that plays a role in describing the process of fraud is capability. Beyond situational opportunity, capability reflects an individual's unique position, skills, and personal attributes that enable them to exploit control weaknesses and successfully perpetrate fraud.[12] Capability includes organizational access not available to others, the intelligence to recognize and act upon vulnerabilities (notably, many fraudsters hold advanced education), and the confidence or ego to believe they can avoid detection. Additional traits such as persuasiveness, deceptive skill, and the ability to manage stress further enhance someone's capacity to commit or conceal fraud.

The Psychology of Fraud

While structural and situational factors, such as organizational controls and perceived financial pressures, have received significant attention in fraud research, comparatively few researchers have systematically examined the psychological characteristics that may predispose individuals to commit fraud. A very simple typology was introduced by the technical editor of *The Fraud Column* to address this issue.[13] The typology includes four recurring personality profiles: the egoist, the bully, the control freak, and the mouse. The thought is that these typologies encompass the majority of those who engage in purposeful fraud. The following summarizes the four typologies:

- The egoist is driven by self-interest and a belief in personal entitlement, often justifying fraudulent acts as deserved rewards.
- The bully uses intimidation and manipulation to override controls and exploit others, thriving in environments where fear suppresses scrutiny.
- The control freak seeks dominance over systems and processes, committing fraud to maintain or enhance their grip on power.
- The mouse is typically timid and risk-averse; they may be coerced or quietly drawn into fraud due to pressure or perceived necessity.

Moving beyond this simple typology framework, the following discussion highlights some of the other psychological patterns associated with fraudulent activity. To begin with, there are those who build "businesses" based on fraud. These people surround themselves with subordinates who can be easily manipulated.[14] Excessive competitiveness, the desire for control, aggressiveness, lack of discipline, insensitivity to others, disagreeableness, and neuroticism are other trait-like factors known to be associated with criminal activity. Much of the psychological literature suggests that certain personality dispositions may interact with situational factors to increase the likelihood that individuals rationalize or justify unethical behavior.

However, it is essential to remember that these traits are neither deterministic nor sufficient indicators of fraudulent tendencies. To date, there is no conclusive evidence that any personality characteristic reliably predicts who will commit fraud. Instead, personality acts as a potential facilitator rather than a direct cause, moderating behavior in contexts where opportunity and pressure exist.[15]

Corporate Psychopathology

Closely related to the typology of a financial services criminal is the notion of a corporate psychopath. A corporate psychopath is a person in the workplace—often in leadership—who exhibits traits like superficial charm, lack of empathy, manipulativeness, and a strong desire for power or control. They may appear charismatic and competent, but they often exploit others, undermine colleagues, and create toxic environments to serve their own interests.[16]

Consider the case of Bernie Madoff. The Madoff Ponzi scheme highlights how psychopathic traits and fraudulent behavior can come together with catastrophic consequences:

> In this case, Bernie Madoff exemplifies the archetype of a corporate psychopath in the financial services profession, blending charm, charisma, and apparent intelligence with extreme deception and manipulation. Initially perceived as a pioneering and trustworthy investment advisor, Madoff cultivated an image of financial genius, which enabled him to gain the confidence of high-net-worth individuals, institutional investors, and even members of European royalty. Behind this façade, Madoff orchestrated a massive Ponzi scheme, diverting funds from new investors to pay returns to earlier clients while fabricating financial statements to sustain the illusion of consistent gains. Madoff's psychopathic traits—grandiosity, callousness, deceit, manipulativeness, and emotional shallowness—manifested in his professional and personal interactions. He exploited trust, preyed on investor optimism, and maintained control through fear and intimidation, even among family members. His scheme persisted for decades mainly due to his impeccable reputation, which insulated him from regulatory scrutiny. Beyond financial deception, Madoff engaged in predatory and unethical behaviors, including betraying close associates and employees. The case underscores how individuals with high levels of corporate psychopathy can operate without restraint, achieve acclaim within financial circles, and simultaneously inflict catastrophic losses on investors and institutions, highlighting the critical need for behavioral and structural safeguards in financial oversight.

Table 4.2 shows how Madoff's psychopathic profile led to oversights in fraud detection, risk assessment, and compliance protocols.

Table 4.2 Madoff's psychopathic traits mapped to the Ponzi scheme

Psychopathic trait	Observed behavior in Madoff case
Charm and superficial intelligence	Built a reputation as a financial genius; gained the trust of high-net-worth investors, institutions, and royalty
Grandiosity and egocentricity	Presented himself as uniquely capable of consistently generating returns; he prioritized personal gain over others
Deceitfulness and manipulation	Ran a Ponzi scheme for decades; fabricated financial statements; misled investors and regulators
Callousness and lack of empathy	Exploited the trust of investors; stole from family and friends; showed indifference to victims' losses
Emotional shallowness	Displayed heartlessness in handling others' wealth; indifferent to crises affecting others
Impulsivity and irresponsibility	Created false narratives of investment strategies; ignored fiduciary responsibilities to clients
Superficial relationships	Used networking and social status to attract new investors while keeping personal and professional ties transactional
Predatory behavior	Targeted investors strategically; exploited optimism, trust, and lack of scrutiny to maximize personal gain
Intimidation and fear induction	Used temper and authority to suppress questions and maintain control over employees and investors
Lack of remorse	Remained unrepentant in prison; openly dismissed the harm caused to victims

Note: Adapted from Boddy, C. R. (2024). Insights into the Bernie Madoff financial market scandal which identify new opportunities for business market researchers. *International Journal of Market Research*, *66*(1), 149–167

Advisor Decision-Making: Psychological Factors

Cognitive biases, which are systematic patterns of deviation from rational judgment, play a critical role in shaping financial advisor decision-making.[17] While much of the literature on cognitive biases focuses on investor behavior, these same psychological tendencies can be used to describe how financial advisors make decisions, sometimes with ethically compromising consequences.

Biases such as overconfidence, loss aversion, and optimism can distort a financial advisor's perception of risk, control, and opportunity. When biases occur, so does the likelihood of misconduct or fraudulent behavior. Understanding common biases is essential not only for identifying circumstances in which advisors may act unethically but also for designing adequate controls, monitoring strategies, and prevention programs. By mapping specific cognitive, behavioral, and psychological biases to fraud-related behaviors, firms can strengthen compliance frameworks and cultivate a culture that proactively mitigates the human factors that contribute to financial misconduct.

Overconfidence Bias

Overconfidence bias occurs when financial advisors overestimate their knowledge, skills, or control over client outcomes.[18] An overconfident advisor might believe they can manipulate markets or client portfolios without detection or assume regulatory oversight will not uncover misconduct, increasing the likelihood of fraudulent activity.

Loss Aversion

Loss aversion can drive advisors to commit fraud to avoid perceived losses to their income, bonuses, or reputation.[19] For example, an advisor facing underperformance may falsify statements or misappropriate client funds to cover shortfalls and maintain their financial standing.

Recency Bias

Recency bias leads some financial advisors to overemphasize recent successes or failures, potentially rationalizing unethical behavior. For instance, an advisor may justify inflating returns or engaging in unauthorized trades because recent market gains make the behavior appear less risky or more likely to "work out."

Anchoring Bias

Anchoring bias can occur when a financial advisor fixates on past performance benchmarks, compensation targets, or previously successful schemes.[20] This may result in a financial advisor engaging in unethical behavior to maintain alignment with past conditions or compensation, even as market conditions or regulatory scrutiny change.

Confirmation Bias

Confirmation bias prompts advisors to selectively seek information that justifies unethical behavior, while ignoring red flags or regulatory warnings.[21] For example, a financial advisor may overvalue anecdotal evidence of a colleague's misconduct going undetected as justification for their actions or as evidence that they will personally not get caught.

Herding Behavior

Herding behavior can influence advisors to emulate peers who have engaged in questionable or fraudulent practices.[22] Observing others manipulate accounts or misrepresent returns without consequence may normalize unethical conduct and nudge some advisors to "join the herd" and engage in unethical behavior.

Availability Bias

Availability bias may cause some financial advisors to overestimate the likelihood of success in committing fraud based on recent cases of "successful" misconduct they have read or heard about.[23] Conversely, the absence of visible enforcement may lead some to underestimate the risk of detection, making fraud seem less risky than it is.

Status Quo Bias

Status quo bias can work in the opposite direction, where financial advisors continue ongoing fraudulent practices to avoid confronting the consequences of stopping. They may fear losing bonuses, client relationships, or reputation if they cease unethical actions already underway.[24]

Mental Accounting

Mental accounting can lead some financial advisors to rationalize misappropriated funds as "borrowed" client money or temporary transfers, mentally separating it from their overall fiduciary (or best-interest) obligations.[25] Mental accounting rationalization reduces perceived personal risk and increases the likelihood of continued misconduct.

Representativeness Bias

Representativeness bias occurs when advisors assume that prior success in minor ethical lapses predicts success in more significant fraud.[26] A financial advisor may overgeneralize from past experiences and underestimate the probability of being caught.

Endowment Effect

The endowment effect can cause a financial advisor to overvalue their control over client accounts or investment products.[27] Feeling "ownership" over these assets may lead to misuse, such as unauthorized trading, excessive fees, or misrepresentation of product performance.

Framing Effect

The framing effect can influence how some advisors perceive ethical dilemmas or the risk embedded in a fraudulent act.[28] For example, a financial advisor may frame inflating returns as a temporary corrective measure rather than fraud. Doing so reduces cognitive dissonance[29] and facilitates unethical behavior on the part of the advisor.

Regret Aversion

Regret aversion may drive some advisors to avoid reporting mistakes or cease unethical behavior for fear of losing clients, income, or status.[30] Instead, they may double down on fraud to prevent perceived regret, such as missing performance targets.

Optimism Bias

Optimism bias can make advisors occasionally underestimate the likelihood of criminal detection, assuming that audits, client complaints, or regulators will not uncover their misconduct.[31] This inflated sense of invulnerability increases the probability of engaging in fraudulent acts.

Building on the understanding of cognitive, behavioral, and psychological biases, it becomes possible to systematically assess how each bias may contribute to fraudulent behavior. By evaluating the likelihood and potential impact of biases, firms can prioritize monitoring efforts and allocate resources more effectively to reduce fraud and criminal activity. Table 4.3 shows the intensity of the cognitive biases discussed in this chapter as they relate to the likelihood of engaging in fraudulent behavior. Coupled with targeted detection strategies and preventative controls, ranging from enhanced supervision and transaction monitoring to training in ethical decision-making, the framework shown in Table 4.3 can be used by organizations to address the psychological drivers of misconduct and the situational vulnerabilities that fraudsters exploit. In this way, integrating behavioral insights with practical controls creates a proactive, evidence-based approach to mitigating advisor-driven fraud.

Understanding Client Attitudinal, Behavioral, and Psychological Triggers

Nearly all the discussion thus far has focused on the cognitive, behavioral, and psychological factors associated with fraudulent behavior on the part of financial advisors. The following discussion shifts to that of the victim. Specifically, what follows is a description of the factors that increase a client's susceptibility to fraud.

Much of the existing evidence suggests that fraudulent behavior in financial services exploits the cognitive vulnerabilities of victims.[32] For example, in cases of internet financial fraud, criminals use time-sensitive messages designed to activate peripheral mental processing rather than encouraging deeper, central cognitive processing. Phishing attempts rely largely on the victim's inability to process information effectively. Unlike the criminal behavior involved, personality traits (such as neuroticism) do not seem to relate to an individual's susceptibility to fraud. A person's mood and prior knowledge can influence how much attention they pay to and how thoroughly they analyze potentially fraudulent messages. The following discussion looks at the factors in more detail.

Fraud Victim Profiles

Financial services fraud victims exhibit distinct demographic, psychological, and behavioral characteristics, which vary depending on the type of fraud.[33] Investment fraud victims tend to differ from the general population in several ways. They are

Table 4.3 Financial advisor fraud risk based on cognitive biases

Cognitive bias	Likelihood to contribute to Fraud	Notes/examples in financial services	Suggested controls/detection strategies
Overconfidence bias	High	Overstating returns, taking unauthorized risks, and misrepresenting skill	Mandatory performance audits; cross-checks on advisor-reported returns; periodic training on regulatory limits and fiduciary obligations; peer review of client communications
Loss aversion	High	Misusing client funds to cover shortfalls, fabricating gains	Segregation of duties; daily reconciliation of client accounts; automated alerts for unusual transactions; incentive structures that reduce pressure to "protect" income at client expense
Recency bias	Medium	Rationalizing unethical trades based on recent market trends	Require documentation of decision rationale; independent portfolio review; and ethics case studies in continuing education programs
Anchoring bias	Medium	Reusing past schemes or holding on to prior fraudulent "templates"	Randomized compliance audits; rotating review personnel; tracking historical client interactions for unusual patterns
Confirmation bias	High	Selectively using data to justify fraud, ignoring warning signs	Encourage reporting of anomalies through anonymous channels; require multiple data sources for investment claims; and compliance review committees to challenge assumptions
Herding behavior	Medium	Copying peers' unethical behavior, succumbing to cultural pressure	Culture audits; mandatory ethics and compliance training; whistleblower hotlines; incentivize ethical behavior through recognition programs
Availability bias	Medium	Overestimating the chance of evading detection due to anecdotal success	Data-driven risk assessment of historical fraud cases; scenario-based compliance training emphasizing detection probabilities; regular regulatory updates
Status quo bias	Medium	Continuing ongoing fraud to avoid consequences or change	Regular rotation of client accounts; surprise audits; independent verification of long-term positions and historical transactions

(continued)

Table 4.3 (continued)

Cognitive bias	Likelihood to contribute to Fraud	Notes/examples in financial services	Suggested controls/detection strategies
Mental accounting	High	Treating misappropriated funds as "temporary" or separate from client accounts	Dual-control account access; automated segregation of client vs. firm funds; exception reporting for off-ledger transfers
Representativeness bias	Medium	Assuming prior minor lapses predict ongoing "success"	Pattern analysis of advisor behavior over time; statistical monitoring of deviations from standard practice; peer benchmarking
Endowment effect	Low-medium	Overvaluing client accounts, leading to financial abuse	Independent verification of portfolio changes; restricted access for high-risk transactions; mandatory disclosure of conflicts of interest
Framing effect	Medium	Rationalizing actions by framing outcomes as positive	Training in ethical decision-making; scenario analysis highlighting long-term consequences; and review boards for all client communications
Regret aversion	Medium	Doubling down on fraud to avoid admitting mistakes	Culture promoting early reporting of errors; supportive compliance reporting systems; tracking of repeated risk-taking patterns
Optimism bias	High	Underestimating the probability of detection, believing regulators won't catch misconduct	Enhanced surveillance and monitoring; independent compliance verification; surprise internal audits; automated anomaly detection in trade patterns

more likely to be male, married, and financially literate, yet paradoxically less persuasion literate.[34] Investment fraud victims rely heavily on personal experience and knowledge, are open to unsolicited sales pitches, and tend to be optimistic. There is also evidence to suggest that those with higher income and educational attainment tend to be victims of investment fraud, although the evidence is not conclusive. In contrast, lottery or sweepstakes fraud victims display almost opposite traits. They are more often female, widowed, living alone, and earn less than others. These victims typically have lower levels of financial literacy, are distrustful of professionals, have experienced multiple negative life events, and live in the present, often underreporting their victim status. Within this group, a smaller subset (so-called chronic lottery victims) repeatedly fall prey to fraud, potentially due to cognitive impairments, social isolation, or diminished capacity to process risk. Collectively, these profiles highlight that susceptibility to fraud is influenced not only by demographic factors but also by psychological traits, past experiences, and individual decision-making tendencies.

Firm Strategies to Reduce Fraud

Reducing financial services fraud requires knowledge about what prompts some financial advisors to cross into unethical behavior, as well as insights into what makes consumers susceptible to fraud. To begin with, it is important to recognize that fraudsters rely on highly refined persuasion tactics such as phantom fixation (appealing to greed), time scarcity (creating urgency), and social proof (leveraging perceived consensus).[35] Specifically, phantom fixation is used to lure victims with promises of large, often unrealistic rewards—such as lottery winnings, miracle investments, or exclusive deals. This tactic exploits greed and the desire for quick wealth, causing victims to overlook red flags.[36] Using time scarcity pressures victims to act quickly with phrases like "this is a limited time offer," "act now," or "your account will be locked." Creating urgency reduces someone's ability to think critically.[37] Finally, social proof involves showing that "others are doing it" to make a scam seem legitimate. Fraudsters may use fake testimonials, inflated follower counts, or pop-up messages showing recent purchases to create a false sense of trust and popularity.[38] To deal with these tactics, interventions must focus on equipping potential victims with the tools to recognize and resist manipulative techniques.

Persuasion training delivered through workshops, focus groups, or peer counseling programs can be used to teach individuals how to identify influence tactics and respond critically. Public campaigns, such as an "Ask Before You Answer," can be used to encourage proactive resistance by normalizing behaviors that disrupt a fraudster's script, using social influence principles to shift norms around engagement. Targeted outreach is also essential, as vulnerable groups (e.g., financially inexperienced individuals, socially isolated seniors, and repeat lottery fraud victims) may require customized guidance delivered through direct communication channels.

Additionally, message testing and behavioral interventions, including simulations of fraudulent solicitations in controlled environments, can be used to create prevention messages and strengthen resilience among consumers. For high-risk populations, particularly those with cognitive impairments, situational supports such as family oversight, peer networks, or automated alert systems can be used to provide an added layer of protection.

A financial services firm can implement these strategies through a structured, multi-layered fraud prevention program that addresses financial advisor misconduct and consumer vulnerability. The first step is to integrate behavioral science into compliance and training systems. For example, persuasion training modules can be incorporated into employee ethics programs and client education workshops, teaching advisors and customers to recognize tactics such as phantom fixation, urgency, and social proof communication approaches. Firm information can be delivered through in-person seminars and online learning platforms.

Second, firms can launch client-facing awareness campaigns modeled on an "Ask Before You Answer" principle, framing proactive questioning as a cultural norm.[39] This could take the form of email newsletters, mobile app prompts, or branch-level signage that encourages clients to pause and verify information before acting on investment opportunities.

Third, targeted outreach can be operationalized using client data analytics to identify at-risk groups, including novice investors with limited financial literacy and older clients with signs of social isolation. These groups could then receive personalized communications, invitations to protective workshops, or direct calls from trained advisors who provide education and reinforcement.

Fourth, message testing and behavioral simulations can be embedded into a firm's compliance and client service practices. For example, controlled phishing-style exercises or mock investment solicitations can be used to measure employee and client susceptibility, allowing the firm to refine messaging and strengthen safeguards.

Finally, for high-risk or vulnerable clients, firms can deploy situational supports such as trusted contact protocols, automated transaction alerts, or joint account monitoring with family members. Technology solutions, including AI-driven fraud detection systems, can complement human oversight by flagging unusual client behaviors or advisor actions for review.

Taken together, these initiatives can be used to enable a financial service firm to not only reduce the likelihood of advisor-driven misconduct but also build client resilience against external fraud attempts, creating a comprehensive defense grounded in behavioral insight, education, and proactive monitoring.

An Integrative Fraud-Reduction Framework and Implications

Understanding the motivations that prompt someone to commit fraud is essential for organizations aiming to prevent and detect misconduct. While conducting background checks on new hires can provide some deterrence (since most fraudsters are first-time offenders), organizations must acknowledge that anyone could potentially commit fraud.[40] This fact is enough to warrant financial services firms of all sizes to implement comprehensive risk mitigation strategies. Central to these efforts is the Fraud Triangle, which identifies pressure, rationalization, and opportunity as being particularly important in describing fraudulent activities. Since pressure and rationalization are internal to the fraudster and largely beyond an organization's control, anti-fraud measures typically focus on reducing opportunity and capacity. Effective risk-reduction strategies include implementing oversight, conducting frequent visits from headquarters, segregating duties, mandating leave, and enforcing strict authorization protocols. Additionally, fostering a robust perception among staff that internal controls are, in fact, robust and meaningful can act as a powerful deterrent.[41]

Financial fraud is frequently preceded by warning signs and behavioral indicators that, if recognized, can facilitate timely intervention and mitigation.[42] Financial advisors contemplating or engaged in fraudulent behavior often exhibit patterns of selective transparency and concealment, disclosing only information that supports their intended narrative while withholding critical details. Alongside information control, heightened defensiveness and evasiveness frequently emerge when fraudsters are questioned.

Gradual withdrawal from everyday social and professional interactions, coupled with increasing secrecy, further characterizes the possible onset of fraudulent conduct. Behavioral shifts extend beyond information management. Sudden, unexplained affluence and conspicuous consumption often signal illicit gains. External pressures, such as unresolved financial or personal stressors, may also spur fraudulent activity, while excessive professional dedication—manifested in avoidance of breaks or vacations (i.e., being a workaholic)—can indicate a financial advisor's attempt to control exposure. Additionally, within social and organizational contexts, fraudsters frequently manipulate colleagues and subordinates, fostering dependency and limiting oversight. Erosion of trust, elevated tensions, and strained interpersonal relationships often accompany ongoing deceptive practices.

However, focusing solely on opportunity and capacity factors is not sufficient to counter unethical behavior. Rationalization plays a critical role, as most fraudsters view themselves as moral and law-abiding individuals who must justify their misconduct before acting.[43] Organizations can make rationalization more difficult by cultivating a strong ethical culture, often referred to as "tone at the top." This involves communicating company-wide ethics policies, consistently reinforcing these standards, and ensuring employees understand the rules and the benefits of compliance.

Aggressively prosecuting fraud and providing safe channels for whistleblowing further reduces rationalization by demonstrating that wrongdoing has tangible consequences. Employee satisfaction and perceptions of fairness are also crucial. Undercompensation or perceived mistreatment increases the likelihood of fraud, while a positive work environment helps diminish the rationalization of unethical acts.[44]

Mitigating pressure is more challenging, particularly when it comes to personal financial stressors, which are largely beyond an organization's control. Nevertheless, companies can lower the risk of financial statement fraud, unauthorized trading, and similar behavior by setting realistic performance targets, avoiding undue pressure, and equipping employees with the resources necessary to achieve goals honestly.[45] In addition to these preventive measures, organizations must take recurring steps to educate employees at all levels to recognize warning signs and red flags of fraud, as early detection is vital to minimizing losses.

Ultimately, no single model fully captures the intricacies of fraud motivation, although the Fraud Triangle remains a fundamental framework. Since almost anyone can engage in unethical behavior under certain conditions, organizations must adopt a proactive and continuous fraud detection and management approach. This should combine strong internal controls, an ethical corporate culture, employee education, and vigilant monitoring to effectively reduce both the likelihood and impact of fraudulent activity.

Chapter Summary

This chapter examined the psychological, organizational, and social dynamics that underpin fraudulent behavior in the financial services profession. Building on Cressey's Fraud Triangle, the discussion highlighted how non-shareable financial pressures, ranging from personal failures and business reversals to status concerns and strained employer–employee relations, can create powerful motivations to engage in fraud. When combined with capability factors such as intelligence, positional authority, ego, and persuasion skills, these pressures increase the likelihood that a financial advisor may rationalize and commit unethical acts. Cognitive dissonance further explains how individuals reconcile their self-concept as ethical professionals with fraudulent behaviors, often through rationalization and moral disengagement.[46]

The chapter also emphasized the role of cognitive, behavioral, and psychological biases and persuasion tactics in describing victim vulnerability. Fraudsters frequently exploit psychological shortcuts, such as phantom fixation (greed), time scarcity (urgency), and social proof (perceived consensus), to manipulate clients and reduce resistance. Addressing these risks requires well-thought-out interventions. Prevention strategies include persuasion training, public awareness campaigns (e.g., "Ask Before You Answer"), targeted outreach to vulnerable groups, and behavioral interventions such as simulated fraud scenarios. For high-risk populations, cognitive and situational support, like peer networks, family oversight, and automated alerts, provide additional layers of protection.

Finally, the chapter outlined practical organizational strategies financial services firms can use to detect and deal with advisor fraud. These include embedding fraud awareness training in advisor development processes, normalizing ethical discourse within the workplace, designing detection systems sensitive to capability-based risks, and implementing client-facing education initiatives to reduce susceptibility to fraud. Together, these measures underscore the notion that reducing fraud requires a dual focus: addressing the internal pressures and capabilities that drive advisors toward misconduct and strengthening client resilience against manipulative persuasion tactics. By integrating behavioral interventions, organizational controls, and evidence-based prevention campaigns, firms can more effectively safeguard both their professionals and their clients.

Chapter Resources

- Association of Certified Fraud Examiners (ACFE): www.acfe.com
- Barclays LifeSkills: barclayslifeskills.com/help-others/lessons/introduction-to-fraud-and-scams
- Federal Trade Commission: www.ftc.gov
- *Journal of Accountancy*: https://www.journalofaccountancy.com/
- KPMG, Global Profiles of the Fraudster: https://assets.kpmg.com/content/dam/kpmg/ar/pdf/2025/profiles-of-a-fraudster.pdf

- Securities and Exchange Commission: https://www.sec.gov/about/reports-publications/investorpubsidentavoidfraud

Notes

[1]Association of Certified Fraud Examiners. (2014). *Report to the nations on occupational fraud and abuse.* Retrieved from http://www.acfe.com/rttn/docs/2014-report-to-nations.pdf

[2]Wells, J. (2013). *Corporate fraud handbook: Prevention and detection.* John Wiley & Sons, Inc.

[3]Association of Certified Fraud Examiners. (2024). *Occupational fraud 2024: A report to the nations.* https://legacy.acfe.com/report-to-the-nations/2024/

[4]Albrecht, W. S., Howe, K. R., & Romney, M. B. (1984). *Deterring fraud: the internal auditor's perspective.* Altamonte Springs, FL: Institute of Internal Auditors Research Foundation.

[5]Securities and Exchange Commission. (2013). https://www.sec.gov/newsroom/press-releases/2013-2013-58htm

[6]Association of Certified Fraud Examiners. (2024). *Occupational fraud 2024: A report to the nations.* https://legacy.acfe.com/report-to-the-nations/2024/; see also: Sprague, A. (2018). Considerations of Private Companies in Regard to External Auditing Including the Detection and Prevention of Fraud. https://core.ac.uk/download/217689116.pdf

[7]Fisher, K. (2015). The psychology of fraud: What motivates fraudsters to commit crime? *Available at SSRN 2596825.*

[8]Sutherland, E. (1947). *Principles of Criminology.* Philadelphia, PA: J.B. Lippincott Company.

[9]Cressey, D. (1953). *Other people's money: A study in the social psychology of embezzlement.* Glencoe, IL: The Free Press.

[10]The M.I.C.E. theory—introduced by Professor Jason Thomas—offers another way to think about fraud motivation beyond financial pressure. Standing for *money, ideology, coercion,* and *ego,* M.I.C.E. expands the traditional "pressure" leg of the Fraud Triangle by recognizing that not all fraud is driven by financial gain. Ideology reflects a belief in serving a greater good, coercion involves being forced into wrongdoing, and ego stems from entitlement or pride. (See: Kranacher, M., Riley, R., Wells, J. (2011). *Forensic accounting and fraud examination.* John Wiley & Sons, Inc.)

[11]Sykes, G. M., & Matza, D. (2017). Techniques of neutralization: A theory of delinquency. In *Delinquency and Drift Revisited, Volume 21* (pp. 33–41). Routledge.

[12]Wolfe, D. T., & Hermanson, D. R. (2004). The Fraud Diamond: Considering the Four Elements of Fraud. *CPA Journal, 74*(12).

[13]Allan, R. (2003). Fraud: The human face of fraud - Understanding the suspect is vital to any investigation. *CA Magazine-Chartered Accountant, 136*(4), 39–40.

[14]Duffield, G. M., & Grabosky, P. N. (2001). The psychology of fraud (Vol. 199). *Canberra: Australian Institute of Criminology.*

[15]Ibid.

[16]Boddy, C. R. (2024). Insights into the Bernie Madoff financial market scandal which identify new opportunities for business market researchers. *International Journal of Market Research, 66*(1), 149–167.

[17]Sale, V., Martini, A., & Chiarello, F. (2021). Cognitive Biases: A Text-Mining Driven Scientific Literature Approach. In *4th Economics, Business and Organization Research (EBOR) international conference "Changes in Uncertainty."* POL.

[18]Ul Abdin, S. Z., Qureshi, F., Iqbal, J., & Sultana, S. (2022). Overconfidence bias and investment performance: A mediating effect of risk propensity. *Borsa Istanbul Review, 22*(4), 780–793.

[19]Klontz, B., Chaffin, C. R., & Klontz, T. (2022). *Psychology of financial planning: The practitioner's guide to money and behavior.* John Wiley & Sons.

[20]Furnham, A., & Boo, H. C. (2011). A literature review of the anchoring effect. *The Journal of Socio-economics, 40*(1), 35–42.

[21]Nickerson, R. S. (1998). Confirmation bias: A ubiquitous phenomenon in many guises. *Review of general psychology, 2*(2), 175–220.

[22]Raafat, R. M., Chater, N., & Frith, C. (2009). Herding in humans. *Trends in Cognitive Sciences, 13*(10), 420–428.

[23]Tversky, A., & Kahneman, D. (1973). Availability: A heuristic for judging frequency and probability. *Cognitive Psychology, 5*(2), 207–232.

[24]Samuelson, W., & Zeckhauser, R. (1988). Status quo bias in decision-making. *Journal of Risk and Uncertainty, 1*, 7–59.

[25]Klontz, B., Chaffin, C. R., & Klontz, T. (2022). *Psychology of financial planning: The practitioner's guide to money and behavior*. John Wiley & Sons.

[26]Tversky, A., & Kahneman, D. (1973). Availability: A heuristic for judging frequency and probability. *Cognitive Psychology, 5*(2), 207–232.

[27]Thaler, R. (1980). Toward a positive theory of consumer choice. *Journal of Economic Behavior & Organization, 1*(1), 39–60.

[28]Plous, S. (1993). Psychological mechanisms in the human use of animals. *Journal of Social Issues, 49*(1), 11–52.

[29]Cognitive dissonance is the psychological discomfort people feel when they hold two or more conflicting beliefs, values, or behaviors at the same time. To reduce this tension, individuals often change their attitudes, rationalize their behavior, or ignore contradictory information.

[30]Loomes, G., & Sugden, R. (1982). Regret theory: An alternative theory of rational choice under uncertainty. *The Economic Journal, 92*(368), 805–824.

[31]Marks, A. B. (2009). *Corporal punishment and its association with anxiety in youth*. Unpublished Master's Thesis. The University of New Orleans. "Corporal Punishment and Its Association with Anxiety in Youth" by Allison Brown Marks (uno.edu)

[32]Norris, G., Brookes, A., & Dowell, D. (2019). The psychology of internet fraud victimisation: A systematic review. *Journal of Police and Criminal Psychology, 34*(3), 231–245.

[33]Shadel, D., & Pak, K. B. S. (2007). *The psychology of consumer fraud* (Doctoral dissertation, Universiteit van Tilburg).

[34]Being persuasion literate means a person can spot when someone is trying to influence them—whether through logic, emotion, or credibility—and respond thoughtfully. Persuasion literacy also means knowing how to use those same techniques to make one's own arguments more convincing, without being manipulative.

[35]Pellegrino, A. (2024). Online Persuasive Communication and Its Applications. In *Decoding Digital Consumer Behavior: Bridging Theory and Practice* (pp. 95–112). Springer Nature Singapore.

[36]Dove, M. (2020). *The psychology of fraud, persuasion and scam techniques: Understanding what makes us vulnerable*. Routledge.

[37]Howard, D. J., Shu, S. B., & Kerin, R. A. (2007). Reference price and scarcity appeals and the use of multiple influence strategies in retail newspaper advertising. *Social Influence, 2*(1), 18–28.

[38]Ridho, W. F. (2024). Unmasking online fake job group financial scams: a thematic examination of victim exploitation from perspective of financial behavior. *Journal of Financial Crime, 31*(3), 748–758.

[39]The "Ask Before You Answer" campaign is inspired by real-world fraud prevention efforts. For example, the United Kingdom has a campaign called "Take Five to Stop Fraud," which encourages individuals to "Stop. Think. Challenge." before responding to financial solicitations. In the United States, the National Crime Prevention Council (NCPC) and AT&T have launched the "Don't Take the Bait – Validate!" initiative, which urges consumers to verify the legitimacy of unsolicited calls before sharing any personal information. The "Ask Before You Answer" campaign aims to help

consumers pause, question, and confirm the legitimacy of an offer, rather than reacting immediately to urgent or persuasive requests.

[40]Daigle, R. J., Morris, P. W., & Hayes, D. C. (2009). Small businesses: Know thy enemy and their methods. *CPA Journal*, *79*(10).

[41]Hansen, J. D., & Buckhoff, T. A. (2000). To catch a thief. *Journal of Accountancy*, *189*(3), 43–48.

[42]Egiyi, M. A., & Chindengwike, J. D. (2023). The psychology behind financial fraud: Unmasking motives and warning signs. *Contemporary Journal of Psychology and Behavioral Science*, *4*(1), 16–24.

[43]Fisher, K. (2015). The psychology of fraud: What motivates fraudsters to commit crime? *Available at SSRN 2596825*.

[44]Wells, J. (2013). *Corporate fraud handbook: Prevention and detection*. John Wiley & Sons, Inc.

[45]KPMG. (2025). Global profiles of the fraudster. https://assets.kpmg.com/content/dam/kpmg/ar/pdf/2025/profiles-of-a-fraudster.pdf

[46]Cognitive dissonance is the mental discomfort experienced when a person holds two or more conflicting beliefs, values, or attitudes, or when their behavior contradicts their beliefs, often motivating them to resolve the inconsistency.

5 Regulatory Frameworks in the Financial Services Profession

Chapter Outcomes

This chapter focuses on helping learners develop the ability to:

1. Understand the role of financial services regulations in ensuring integrity, transparency, and fairness within financial markets.
2. Identify key regulatory standards relevant to financial services professionals, including requirements to act in a client's best interests, maintain transparent fee structures, and adhere to high standards of professional conduct.
3. Explain how regulations promote consumer well-being by fostering trust and accountability in financial advisory practices.
4. Describe the roles and functions of regulatory bodies such as the Securities and Exchange Commission (SEC), the Financial Industry Regulatory Authority (FINRA), and certification organizations like the Certified Financial Planner Board of Standards, Inc. (CFP Board) in overseeing compliance and enforcing rules.
5. Evaluate the impact of regulatory frameworks on building professional integrity and fostering long-lasting, trust-based client relationships in the financial services profession.

Note: This chapter was copyedited using Grammarly™ and generative AI tools to enhance clarity, grammar, and overall readability. While these tools provided suggestions and assistance in refining the text, the ideas, content, and arguments presented remain the sole work and responsibility of the authors. Any errors or inaccuracies in the final version are also the authors' responsibility.

W. Heo, J. E. Grable, *Ethics and Compliance in Financial Services*,
https://doi.org/10.1007/978-3-032-14449-2_5

Introduction

Financial services professionals operate within a complex and ever-changing regulatory environment. Regulations are in place to ensure (a) market stability, (b) consumer protection, and (c) economic growth. Regulatory frameworks create the structural foundation for financial systems by setting the rules, standards, and oversight mechanisms that govern the behavior of institutions and individuals. Understanding the regulatory landscape is essential for optimizing financial advice, especially for those who advise clients for a fee, commission, or other forms of compensation.

One of the primary reasons for studying regulatory frameworks is their role in reducing systemic economic and market risks. Financial crises, such as the 2008 Global Financial Crisis, highlight how inadequate regulation and enforcement can result in significant economic and societal consequences. As will be described in this chapter, regulatory structures require financial institutions to maintain sufficient capital buffers, implement effective risk management practices, and uphold ethical standards. All of these measures contribute to preventing market failures.

Equally important is the role of regulations in protecting consumers. Financial professionals are entrusted with safeguarding client assets and providing advice that aligns with each client's financial goal(s), time horizon(s), risk-taking ability, risk-taking need, and willingness to take financial risks. Regulatory agencies, such as the Securities and Exchange Commission (SEC) in the United States and the Financial Conduct Authority (FCA) in the United Kingdom, enforce rules that mandate transparency, accountability, and fair practices.[1] For instance, regulations like the European Union's (EU) MiFID II require enhanced disclosure and alignment of investment advice with the best interests of clients.

Studying regulatory frameworks also prepares financial advisors to adapt to dynamic regulatory changes that are often driven by technological advancements, geopolitical shifts, and emerging risks. The rise of financial technology (fintech) and innovations such as blockchain models, cryptocurrencies, and artificial intelligence (AI) continue to prompt new regulations that address data privacy, cybersecurity, and money laundering concerns. Understanding these evolving standards is essential for professionals seeking to remain compliant when offering advice while leveraging new technologies to serve clients more effectively.

Furthermore, regulatory compliance is a legal obligation that can be used to gain a strategic advantage in the marketplace (particularly at the enterprise level). Organizations that demonstrate a proactive approach to compliance can gain a competitive edge in the marketplace. Regulatory compliance enhances a financial advisory firm's reputation and fosters the development of long-term client relationships. For financial advisors, exhibiting expertise in regulatory matters signifies a commitment to ethical standards. Doing so also positions a financial advisor as a client's trusted advisor, which is important in an increasingly scrutinized and competitive market sector.

Perspective

Regulations, procedures, and guidelines are sometimes viewed as obstacles to conducting business efficiently and effectively. However, as the following cases illustrate, financial services regulations should not be seen as operational hurdles. Instead, regulations should be conceptualized as providing a foundation for establishing client relationships that enhance client outcomes. Regulatory guidelines also provide a mechanism to identify wrongdoing and punish those who put their own interests above those of their clients.

In the first case, the Securities and Exchange Commission (SEC) charged Morgan Stanley Smith Barney LLC (MSSB) for failing to reasonably supervise four financial advisors who misappropriated millions of dollars from advisory clients and brokerage customers.[2] MSSB's policies and procedures were insufficient to prevent unauthorized third-party disbursements through Automated Clearing House (ACH) payments and cash wire transfers.[3] MSSB's lack of oversight allowed employees to transfer funds from client accounts to themselves. These transfers occurred over several years, with hundreds of unauthorized ACH transfers from 2015 to 2022. MSSB's lack of a procedure to screen ACH payment instructions led to the firm missing these fraudulent transfers. In response, MSSB agreed to pay a $15 million penalty and undertake measures to review its policies, including retaining a compliance consultant. Additionally, MSSB was required to compensate affected clients. Here is what the SEC discovered:

- MSSB failed to adopt and implement policies and procedures reasonably designed to prevent its financial advisors from making unauthorized transfers from customers' or clients' accounts to themselves or for their own benefit.
- MSSB did not have a policy or procedure to screen externally initiated payment instructions, which violated Section 206(4) and Rule 206(4)-7 of the Investment Advisers Act of 1940[4]; these sections of the Act require firms to supervise investment advisors and registered representatives.[5]
- MSSB also violated the meaning of Section 203(e)(6) of the Advisers Act and Section 15(b)(4)(E) of the Securities Exchange Act of 1934.

Unfortunately, the actions of the MSSB brokers in this case are an all-too-familiar story. In another case, MSSB also faced penalties for failing to prevent an advisor from misappropriating approximately $7 million from four clients through unauthorized transactions. In this case, the firm paid a $3.6 million penalty and reimbursed the affected clients. The advisor was criminally charged. Hundreds of similar cases occur each year across large and small firms.

Implications for Financial Services Professionals

The MSSB cases highlight the SEC's role in enforcing professional standards within the financial services profession. These cases illustrate how compliance failures can lead to significant penalties and harm to clients and society. Additionally, the cases demonstrate the SEC's commitment to ensuring that clients (and other stakeholders) are treated fairly, protecting investors, and maintaining market integrity. The cases emphasize the need for financial institutions to establish and uphold comprehensive compliance systems that can effectively detect and prevent unauthorized activities. Lastly, the cases introduce two concepts that will be discussed later in this chapter: the fiduciary and best-interest standards.

Regulatory Frameworks

A financial service regulatory framework is a comprehensive system of rules, regulations, policies, and supervisory structures designed to govern the behavior of financial institutions, service providers, and markets.[6] Regulatory frameworks are established to maintain the stability, integrity, and efficiency of financial systems, protect consumers, ensure fair competition, and prevent financial crimes such as fraud, money laundering, and market manipulation.[7]

In the United States, there is no single regulatory framework. Regulations, rules, procedures, and guidelines originate at the national, state, self-regulatory, certification, and organizational membership levels. When viewed broadly, regulatory frameworks operate through a combination of laws established by governments and regulatory bodies responsible for firm and advisor enforcement and oversight.[8] These bodies include national regulators (e.g., SEC in the United States and the Financial Conduct Authority [FCA] in the United Kingdom), self-regulatory organizations (e.g., Financial Industry Regulatory Authority [FINRA]), and international entities (e.g., the International Organization of Securities Commissions).

In general, regulatory frameworks share the following commonalities:

1. Licensing and Registration: Financial institutions and professionals generally must obtain authorization to provide services to clients. Regulations ensure that those who offer advice to others for compensation meet minimum required standards for financial strength, expertise, conduct, and competence.
2. Conduct of Business Rules: Regulations are often written to describe how financial institutions should interact with clients. Rules emphasize transparency, fairness, and disclosure. Conduct of business rules also include regulations related to product suitability, risk disclosure, and the prevention of conflicts of interest.
3. Capital and Liquidity Requirements: Regulations outline how financial service firms, particularly banks, must perform when maintaining sufficient reserves and liquidity.
4. Risk Management and Compliance: Regulatory frameworks provide explicit procedures firms must implement and follow when building internal controls, compliance programs, and risk management systems. Regulations are used to prevent illegal activities and reduce potential financial risks to clients and the broader economic system.

5. Market Integrity and Transparency: Regulations are designed to ensure that financial markets function efficiently. Regulators promote accurate and timely reporting through regulatory enforcement, which helps prevent market abuse while fostering investor confidence.
6. Consumer Protection: Regulations are designed to protect investors from misleading marketing and sales practices, fraudulent behavior, and undue risk exposure.
7. Enforcement and Sanctions: Regulatory bodies have the power to investigate and penalize firms or individuals who violate the rules, ensuring accountability within the financial services industry.

The overarching goal of any financial services regulatory framework is to foster trust and stability in the financial system, ensuring that the markets function in a manner that benefits market participants and stakeholders operating in the broader economy.

Key Regulations

The following laws and policies represent some of the most critical regulatory frameworks that impact the delivery of financial advice[9]:

- The **Securities Act of 1933**, also known as the "Truth in Securities Act," ensures transparency in the public offering of securities and protects investors from fraud. The Act mandates that companies provide full disclosures through registration statements and prospectuses, requiring financial advisors to prioritize full disclosure and verify the accuracy of the information supplied by issuers.[10]
- The **Securities Exchange Act of 1934** established the SEC. The SEC oversees securities trading and prevents fraudulent practices in the secondary market. Financial advisors must comply with SEC reporting standards and maintain ethical processes when executing transactions.[11]
- The **Investment Company Act of 1940** regulates mutual funds and other investment companies to ensure transparency and protect investors through operational restrictions. The Act is important because it requires full disclosure of fees and management practices.[12]
- The **Investment Advisers Act of 1940** requires advisors managing over $100 million in assets for a fee (rather than commission) to register with the SEC, adhere to a fiduciary standard, and disclose any conflicts of interest. Under the Act, financial advisors must always act in the best interests of their clients and provide clear disclosures. Those who manage less than $100 million are instead regulated at the state level.[13]
- The **Banking Act of 1933** (Glass-Steagall Act) separated commercial and investment banking to reduce conflicts of interest.[14] The Act also established the **Federal Deposit Insurance Corporation** (FDIC), which provides some protections for cash and other assets held at banks.[15]

- The **Gramm-Leach-Bliley Act of 1999** (GLBA) allowed financial institutions to merge operations across banking, securities, and insurance sectors while prescribing and enforcing data privacy requirements.[16] Today, financial advisors must protect a client's privacy and notify them of how their personal financial information is handled.
- The **Dodd-Frank Wall Street Reform and Consumer Protection Act of 2010** introduced comprehensive reforms and enhanced firm oversight.[17] The Act also established the **Consumer Financial Protection Bureau** (CFPB). Under the Act, advisors must comply with stricter transparency, risk disclosure, and suitability regulations, especially when recommending complex financial products to non-institutional clients.[18]
- The **Sarbanes-Oxley Act of 2002 (SOX)** was enacted to restore investor confidence following numerous corporate scandals at the turn of the millennium.[19] While primarily targeting corporations, SOX affects financial advisors working with clients investing in publicly traded companies by indirectly influencing corporate accountability and transparency.
- **Anti-Money Laundering (AML)** laws require financial institutions to detect and report suspicious client deposit and withdrawal activities.[20] Advisors must monitor transactions for red flags, conduct due diligence, and comply with reporting obligations for high-risk transactions.
- **Know Your Customer (KYC)** regulations require financial institutions to verify client identities and assess the risk profile of clients.[21] KYC rules require financial advisors to gather relevant client information to ensure investment recommendations align with each client's unique financial goal(s), risk tolerance, and personal circumstances. Key assessment data points include a client's income, wealth status, investment objectives, risk tolerance, time horizon, and market knowledge or experience.
- The **Payment Card Industry Data Security Standard (PCI DSS)** sets guidelines for securing card information.[22] Advisors involved in payment transactions must follow PCI DSS standards to protect client data.
- The **Markets in Financial Instruments Directive (MiFID II)** governs EU investment services, ensuring transparency, investor protection, and market integrity for European firms and advisors. Advisors in the EU must provide detailed fee disclosures, ensure the suitability of advice, and record client communications.[23]
- **Basel III** is a global regulatory framework that strengthens banks' capital requirements and market liquidity standards.[24] Financial advisors working with banks must consider risk-weighted capital standards and liquidity constraints when providing advice.
- **Solvency II** is a comprehensive European Union regulatory framework for insurance companies. Implemented in 2016, Solvency II was designed to ensure the financial stability of insurance companies and that companies can meet policyholder obligations.[25] Countries worldwide have since adopted aspects of the regulation to enhance risk-based capital, governance, and disclosure requirements.

- The **National Banking and Securities Commission (CNBV)** regulates financial markets and institutions in Mexico.[26] Commission rules require strict reporting and compliance with anti-corruption standards. Financial advisors who conduct business in Mexico must comply with these regulations.
- The **Australian Securities and Investments Commission Act (ASIC)** governs Australia's financial services and markets, setting licensing, reporting, and conduct standards.[27] Advisors working in Australia must prioritize consumer protection and comply with all aspects of the ASIC Act.
- The **Financial Consumer Agency of Canada (FCAC)** protects Canadian consumers, ensuring that advisors treat clients fairly and provide clear, accurate information about financial products.[28]
- **Office of the Superintendent of Financial Institutions (OSFI) Regulations** oversee federally regulated financial institutions in Canada, focusing on risk management and firm-level solvency.[29] Financial advisors must adhere to these guidelines when developing client portfolios for Canadian citizens.
- The **Bank Act of Canada** regulates the operation of banks in Canada. The Act emphasizes financial stability and consumer protection.[30] Advisors affiliated with banks must comply with strict conduct rules to prioritize client interests.
- The **Insurance Companies Act of Canada** governs insurance companies operating in Canada. The Act requires financial advisors to disclose relevant terms and align recommendations with client needs.[31]
- The **Trust and Loan Companies Act of Canada** regulates trust and loan companies in Canada.[32] Under the Act, financial advisors are required to follow fiduciary standards and avoid conflicts of interest.
- Finally, Canada's **Securities Act** and related provincial laws regulate Canadian securities markets.[33] The Act (and provincial policies) promotes transparency and investor protection. Financial advisors must comply with the Act to ensure fair dealings and suitable investment recommendations for clients.

The Big Six Regulations

Six core regulatory frameworks have primary importance in governing the practice of financial advisors who advise non-exempt clients in the United States. The following frameworks work jointly to shape a financial advisor's responsibilities and practices. These six frameworks are designed to protect clients, ensure transparency, and maintain the financial system's integrity.

Investment Advisers Act of 1940

The Investment Advisers Act of 1940 is a foundational framework for financial advisors. The Act requires those managing over $100 million in assets to register with the SEC, with those managing less registering at the state level. The Act imposes fiduciary obligations on financial advisors, compelling them to act in their client's best interests by avoiding conflicts of interest and providing comprehensive disclosures about fees and compensation structures.[34] Under the Act, advisors must also ensure compliance with its prohibitions on fraudulent practices and false advertising. The following case illustrates how the Act has been enforced.

> In 2024, the SEC charged Obra Capital Management, LLC with violating the SEC's pay-to-play rule for investment advisors.[35] This rule prohibits investment advisors from providing advisory services for compensation to government entities within two years of a campaign contribution made by the firm or its associates to candidates or officials who can influence advisor selection. Obra Capital continued providing advisory services to a government entity after such a contribution was made, violating Section 206(4) and Rule 206(4)-5 of the Investment Advisers Act of 1940. The firm consented to a cease-and-desist order, a censure, and a $95,000 penalty without admitting or denying the SEC's findings.

Actions taken by Obra Capital Management highlight the complex interplay of systematic issues, including inadequate training, misaligned incentives, and a cultural acceptance of unethical practices. Why did the advisors at Obra Capital Management break the law? Several factors may have contributed to this behavior. For instance, making political contributions to secure contracts is a normalized practice in some market sectors. If such actions are culturally accepted or tacitly approved within a firm's environment, advisors might feel justified in bending the rules.

The campaign contributions created apparent conflicts of interest, compromising the objectivity of the government entity's selection process for financial advisors. The firm's leadership, either implicitly or explicitly, condoned these practices to gain a competitive advantage, fostering a culture where violations are viewed as strategic moves rather than ethical breaches.

Moreover, the firm's advisors may not have received adequate education regarding the pay-to-play rule or the broader ethical implications of these contributions. This knowledge gap could have led to unintentional or willful misconduct. The potential financial gains from securing lucrative advisory contracts with government entities might have outweighed the perceived risks of regulatory penalties, thereby incentivizing risky behavior. If individuals within the firm believed that violations would not be traced back to them or would entail minimal consequences, they might have been more inclined to break the rules. Additionally, the firm's pressure to meet revenue or growth objectives may have driven the decision to retain the government contract at all costs, including violating regulations.

Securities Act of 1933

The Securities Act of 1933 mandates transparency in securities offerings.[36] The Act's purpose is to protect investors. The Act requires companies to file a registration statement with the SEC and provide risk disclosures to clients through prospectuses. Advisors recommending new securities must ensure their clients understand the risks associated with particular offerings. Advisors must also verify the credibility of the information provided by issuers. The following case describes an enforcement procedure under the Act.

> A landmark case under the 1933 Act occurred in 1974.[37] The case is known as the Escott vs. BarChris Construction Corporation litigation. Investors who purchased bonds from the BarChris company claimed that the registration statement included false and misleading information. They also claimed that the company's balance sheet, contracts, and prospectus were inaccurate. Regulators found in favor of the investors under Section 11 of the Act. Section 11 allows purchasers of securities to sue issuers of securities for false or misleading information. In this case, the court found that BarChris's officers and directors failed to exercise necessary due diligence, leading to liability for the inaccuracies.

This case underscores how inadequate ethical training, conflicts of interest, and cultural acceptance of misconduct can lead to securities law violations. There are several reasons why officers at the firm may have engaged in deceitful practices, including an ability to exploit the trust of investors who were not able, through information asymmetry, to understand that they were being manipulated through false statements. It is most likely that a corporate culture existed that tolerated or encouraged aggressive securities marketing strategies existed. Unethical practice standards were normalized. This might have occurred due to inadequate ethical training, weak enforcement mechanisms, or compensation structures that rewarded short-term financial performance.

Securities Exchange Act of 1934

The Securities Exchange Act of 1934 regulates secondary securities markets.[38] The Act created the SEC, which sets rules for financial advisors, broker-dealers, exchanges, and market participants. SEC rules prohibit manipulative securities trading practices while also mandating periodic financial reporting for publicly traded companies. Under the Act, financial advisors must ensure fair trading practices and avoid insider trading violations when recommending securities. The following cases illustrate how the Act has been used to deal with insider trading cases.[39] These cases highlight the SEC's ongoing efforts to maintain a level playing field in the securities markets by targeting illegal trading based on material nonpublic information.

- A senior IT professional at Wilson Sonsini Goodrich & Rosati profited by leveraging access to sensitive information and trading ahead of mergers involving the firm's clients. This person breached trust in a high-security environment and gained more than $300,000 in the process.
- A group of golfing friends used inside information shared by an executive at their country club to earn over $554,000 in illicit profits. This represents the casual and brazen misuse of relationships for financial gain.
- Two attorneys collaborated to generate $5.6 million in illegal profits by using nonpublic information accessed through confidential documents in a law firm.

- Business associates in Chile traded on confidential information obtained while serving on the board of a pharmaceutical company. The SEC used its enforcement tools to stop this form of cross-border insider trading.
- A California-based attorney and his wife traded on confidential client information, blatantly violating professional fiduciary duties. The SEC took action to bring charges against the couple.
- During the Deepwater Horizon oil spill, a senior British Petroleum (BP) responder sold family securities based on confidential knowledge of the spill's severity. The SEC found that this person exploited the crisis for personal gain, violating public trust.
- Two individuals traded ahead of the announcement that hedge fund Pershing Square Management had taken a short position of $1 billion in Herbalife Ltd.

Each of these cases involved corporate insiders, attorneys, executives, accountants, and IT personnel using nonpublic information for personal gain. Violations included trading on nonpublic information, trading ahead of acquisitions, and exploiting confidential corporate knowledge. Each person involved in these transactions earned substantial illicit profits, ranging from tens of thousands to millions of dollars. Motivations for engaging in insider trading vary, but at its core, those listed here exhibited a blatant disregard for fairness. Perpetrators were greedy and generally believed that they would not be caught.

Dodd-Frank Wall Street Reform and Consumer Protection Act of 2010

The Dodd-Frank Wall Street Reform and Consumer Protection Act of 2010 introduced sweeping reforms to increase financial transparency and consumer protections.[40] The 2008 global financial crisis prompted policymakers to write the Act, which created the Consumer Financial Protection Bureau (CFPB). The Act also imposed stricter fiduciary standards on financial advisors. Advisors dealing with complex financial products, such as derivatives or alternative investments, must now comply with enhanced disclosure and reporting requirements. Consider the following hypothetical case:

> A financial advisor working at a mid-sized brokerage firm recommends a complex proprietary investment product to retired clients. The advisor promises high returns while downplaying or failing to disclose the significant risks involved with the investment. After receiving a complaint, the advisor and firm are investigated by the SEC and CFPB. The regulators will likely find that the advisor earned excessive commissions while clients suffered significant losses.

Regardless of the investment's performance, the broker in this case violated the Act's fiduciary clause. Under Section 913 of the Dodd-Frank Act, the advisor violated fiduciary duty requirements by prioritizing commissions and firm profits over the best interests of clients. The advisor also violated disclosure and transparency rules by not disclosing that they would receive significant kickbacks through revenue-sharing agreements by promoting the proprietary investment. The advisor could be charged with artificially inflating the performance metrics of the investment. At a minimum, the financial advisor misrepresented the product's actual risk profile, which violates Sections 747 and 753 of the Dodd-Frank Act. As a result, the advisor and firm are subject to civil penalties and increased oversight from regulators. The advisor may also be barred from practicing as a financial advisor.

Numerous reasons explain why this financial advisor might have engaged in this behavior. To begin with, the advisor's clients were vulnerable to the sales pitch because of information asymmetry.[41] They were being manipulated primarily so the broker could earn a higher commission. It is possible that the firm's sales culture encouraged the broker to hide information from clients either through a lax regulatory compliance system or an implicit encouragement to meet sales quotas.

Gramm-Leach-Bliley Act of 1999

The Gramm-Leach-Bliley Act of 1999 (GLBA) allows financial institutions to offer combined banking, securities, and insurance services while enforcing strict privacy protections.[42] Under the Act, financial advisors must provide clients with annual privacy notices. The Act also requires firms to implement cybersecurity measures to protect client data from unauthorized access or breaches. The following case highlights how firms can be held liable for deceptive practices targeting service members and their families.

> In 2023, the Federal Trade Commission (FTC) proposed a $43.5 million settlement with Career Step, an online education company. The FTC charged Career Step with deceptive marketing practices by targeting servicemembers and their families.[43] Career Step promoted its healthcare-related training programs with exaggerated claims, stating that "most learners" and "84% of graduates" found jobs in their field. However, the FTC found that the company lacked substantiated evidence to support these claims, as most students did not complete their programs, and those who did often took significantly longer than advertised to find employment. Additionally, Career Step misrepresented its job placement and externship services, falsely claiming partnerships with employers and guaranteeing employment.
>
> The FTC discovered that the company incentivized fake positive reviews by offering students extensions on their training in exchange for reviews without adequately disclosing the incentives. As part of the proposed settlement, Career Step agreed to pay $15.7 million in consumer redress, canceled $27.8 million in student debt, and implemented other corrective actions, including removing misleading reviews and ensuring more truthful marketing.

This case highlights the importance of substantiating claims and maintaining transparency in advertising, especially when targeting vulnerable groups like military families. Career Step may have engaged in these deceptive marketing practices for various reasons. The company sought to boost enrollment and generate higher revenues by attracting more students. The sales team may have been motivated by pressure to meet enrollment goals. By making exaggerated claims about job placement rates, program completion times, and externship opportunities, Career Step presented an overly optimistic view of its services to convince prospective students to enroll despite the less favorable reality. Deceptive marketing practices, such as promoting misleading employment outcomes and incentivizing reviews, were used as shortcuts to create a false sense of credibility and attract a larger customer base, particularly among those unfamiliar with the industry and those who were susceptible to false promises. While this strategy may have been potentially profitable in the short term, it ultimately resulted in legal consequences and damage to the company's reputation once the truth was revealed.

Anti-Money Laundering (AML) and Know Your Customer (KYC) Policies

The final framework integrates Anti-Money Laundering (AML) and Know Your Customer (KYC) policies that are designed to safeguard individuals and households (as well as the macroeconomic financial system) from illegal business activities, including money laundering, fraud, and terrorist financing. AML and KYC regulations mandate that financial firms and advisors implement vigorous processes to verify client identities, assess risk profiles, and maintain accurate records. These policies ensure transparency and accountability when a financial advisor works with clients. AML and KYC rules require advisors to report suspicious transactions, monitor client activities, and maintain vigilance in identifying potential red flag behaviors. A core component of these regulations is risk-based monitoring, which requires financial advisory firms to determine the risk tolerance of clients and then match recommendations to a client's willingness to take risks.

Failure to comply with AML and KYC requirements can lead to severe consequences, including substantial financial penalties, loss of licenses, operational disruptions, and long-term reputational harm. These risks illustrate the necessity for financial firms and advisors to establish comprehensive compliance programs, regularly update training, and leverage technological tools to enhance the effectiveness of AML and KYC practices.[44] Although regulatory policies vary globally, most regulations require firms to develop a vigorous and flexible process to ensure that investment recommendations are suitable based on each customer's investment objectives, financial situation, and risk tolerance, as well as their knowledge and experience.

In the European Union, the European Securities and Markets Authority (ESMA) governs these practices under the Markets in Financial Instruments Directive II (MiFID II)[45] and the Financial Services Act's (FinSA) Appropriateness Test.[46] According to published standards, any financial service provider offering individual investment advice must consider a client's overall portfolio. The financial advisor must inquire about a client's knowledge and experience and confirm whether financial instruments are suitable before making recommendations. Additionally, FinSA suitability test mandates that advisors take a client's entire portfolio into account, as well as the client's financial situation, investment objectives, and knowledge, rather than simply individual transactions, when making recommendations.[47]

In the United States, the SEC and FINRA have established rules requiring financial advisors to evaluate a client's financial knowledge, educational background, investment experience, and risk tolerance before making recommendations. These regulations ensure that any recommendations provided are suitable and cater to the best interests of a client.[48] The assessment process typically involves using questionnaires and direct consultations with clients. Under the SEC's Regulation Best Interest (Reg BI), effective since June 2020, broker-dealers must act in their client's best interests when making recommendations, considering a client's financial knowledge and risk tolerance. FINRA Rule 2111, known as the Suitability Requirement, similarly obliges broker-dealers to assess a client's investment profile, including their financial situation, investment objectives, and risk tolerance. Financial advisors[49] must have a reasonable basis for recommending products that align with a client's needs. Both the SEC and FINRA also require financial services professionals to gauge a client's capacity to manage investment risks, factoring in their preferences and financial ability to endure market volatility and potential losses. These regulations are designed to protect investors by ensuring they receive tailored advice suited to their financial capacity and goals, with non-compliance potentially resulting in penalties or sanctions against the advisors involved. Consider the following case example:

> A financial advisor recommends high-risk, highly volatile investments to a client without properly assessing or documenting the client's risk tolerance (essentially, their willingness to engage in behavior where the outcomes are uncertain and potentially negative). The advisor suggests that the client invest a sizable portion of their portfolio in speculative, high-risk stocks without realizing that the client actually prefers safer, income-generating investments. In this case, the advisor is in violation of SEC and FINRA rules for failing to adequately assess the client's risk tolerance and making unsuitable recommendations.

Why might the advisor have skipped the risk-tolerance assessment? One possibility is inadequate training. Another is that the advisor may have had an undisclosed conflict of interest that favored personal or firm gains over the client's well-being. Often, such situations stem from a culture of lax regulatory oversight within a firm that normalizes misconduct. Regardless of the reason, the advisor has placed the client in a difficult situation that could lead to penalties, sanctions, and reputational damage for the advisor.

As described above, the Big Six regulations require financial advisors to prioritize legal compliance, fiduciary duty, transparency, data protection, and vigilance against financial crimes. By adhering to these regulations, financial advisors can avoid penalties (including jail time) and build trust and long-lasting relationships with their clients. Compliance also ensures that a financial advisory practice aligns with professional standards and client expectations.

Two Practice Standard Approaches

The fiduciary and best-interest standards represent two foundational frameworks guiding financial professionals in delivering client advice and services. While both are designed to protect consumers, their scope, obligations, and regulatory enforcement differ. The following discussion highlights the similarities and differences between these two standards of practice.

The fiduciary standard imposes the highest duty of care on a financial advisor. The fiduciary standard requires a financial advisor to prioritize the needs of a client above personal or firm interests. This standard demands absolute loyalty and prudence, obligating financial advisors to avoid conflicts of interest or, where unavoidable, fully disclose and mitigate conflicts. The standard commonly applies to Registered Investment Advisers (RIAs) under the Investment Advisers Act of 1940 and to CFP® and CFA® professionals. For instance, fiduciaries must recommend the most cost-effective investment option, even if it results in lower compensation. They must also ensure all advice strictly aligns with a client's objectives and risk tolerance. The fiduciary standard is enforced by federal, state, and certification regulators such as the SEC, with violations potentially resulting in fines, suspensions, or legal action.

In contrast, the best-interest standard requires financial professionals to act in a client's best interest when making recommendations. The standard does not impose as stringent a duty on the advisor as the fiduciary standard. This standard expects a financial advisor to make recommendations that are suitable and reasonable, even if conflicts of interest exist. Unlike the fiduciary standard, best-interest rules mandate the disclosure of conflicts but not necessarily their elimination. The best-interest standard applies primarily to broker-dealers and insurance agents under frameworks such as the SEC's Regulation Best Interest (Reg BI), the NAIC Suitability in Annuity Transactions Model Regulation, and FINRA's Rule 2111. For example, a broker-dealer might recommend an annuity with higher fees if the annuity's features align with the client's financial needs. Enforcement is carried out by the SEC for Reg BI, FINRA for Rule 2111, and state insurance regulators for annuity and insurance recommendations, with penalties for non-compliance.

While both standards aim to protect clients, the fiduciary standard imposes stricter obligations on financial professionals. The best-interest standard, while consumer-focused, provides more flexibility in handling conflicts of interest and compensation. Under both standards, financial professionals must clearly communicate their obligations to clients. Together, these standards shape the regulatory landscape, balancing consumer protection with the practical realities of delivering financial services. Table 5.1 showcases the primary differences between the fiduciary and best-interest standards.

Know the Regulators

Federal and state regulators are tasked with writing and enforcing laws and rules that govern the conduct of financial advisors. Through enforcement, regulators ensure that firms and financial advisors prioritize client interests, operate transparently, and maintain high ethical standards. Dual oversight by federal and state regulators protects investors and fosters trust between advisors and their clients. Regulatory oversight enhances client trust by reassuring clients and related stakeholders that their advisors are acting ethically and transparently. Oversight also increases accountability, as financial advisors are held responsible for their actions

Table 5.1 Key differences in standards of practice

Aspect	Fiduciary standard	Best-interest standard
Primary duty	Act solely in the client's best interest at all times	Act in the client's best interest while considering firm and professional interests
Conflict of interest	Must avoid conflicts or disclose and mitigate them	Disclose conflicts but not necessarily eliminate them
Scope of coverage	Applies to RIAs, CFP® and CFA® professionals, and ERISA fiduciaries	Applies to broker-dealers and insurance agents under specific regulations
Compensation practices	Fee-only or fee-based models are favored to reduce conflicts	Commission-based compensation is allowed if disclosed
Client-first focus	Strict alignment with the client's goals and risk tolerance	Recommendations must align with client needs
Level of accountability	Higher standard, with greater liability for breaches	Moderate standard, with less stringent enforcement
Regulators	SEC (RIAs), DOL (ERISA fiduciaries), CFP board	SEC (Reg BI), FINRA, and state insurance regulators
Investment recommendation example	Recommends the lowest-cost mutual fund that meets the client's goals	May recommend a higher-cost fund if it offers additional benefits that justify the cost
Handling conflicts of interest	Avoids any investment with a potential conflict or mitigates it through complete transparency	Discloses conflicts but may proceed with a recommendation if it is deemed to be in the client's best interest
Product selection	Selects from a broad array of products and selects the best one without compensation-driven bias	May recommend a product that offers a higher compensation payout if it meets the client's needs

and face penalties for non-compliance. Moreover, many federal and state regulations include continuing education requirements. Continuing education ensures advisors remain knowledgeable about evolving professional standards and regulatory changes.

Federal Regulators

The following discussion highlights the federal agencies that most significantly interact with the daily operations of financial services professionals (see Table 5.3 for a comparison of federal and state regulators).

The Securities and Exchange Commission (SEC) oversees the activities of investment advisors managing over $100 million in assets under the Investment Advisers Act of 1940. The SEC enforces fiduciary standards, disclosure rules, and anti-fraud provisions to ensure that advisors act in their clients' best interests. The SEC requires advisors to assess, evaluate, and use a client's financial goals, time horizons, financial capacity, risk tolerance, and other factors when developing, recommending, and implementing recommendations. The SEC mandates that those who are regulated provide clear communication about fees and conflicts of interest and disclose all associated risks with clients. The SEC also investigates and penalizes fraudulent activities, providing clients with assurance that their advisors act ethically.

The Financial Industry Regulatory Authority (FINRA) is a self-regulatory organization. FINRA oversees broker-dealers and registered representatives, enforcing rules under the Securities Exchange Act of 1934. FINRA rules mandate stockbrokers recommend investments that are suitable for each client's financial situation, objectives, and experience. FINRA also offers arbitration and mediation services to resolve client-advisor disputes. FINRA rules also mandate continuing education for advisors to stay updated on industry and regulatory changes. Of particular importance is FINRA's role in licensing financial services professionals. Table 5.2 lists and describes the primary licenses offered by FINRA.

The Department of Labor (DOL) regulates financial advisors managing retirement accounts under the Employee Retirement Income Security Act (ERISA). The DOL imposes a fiduciary standard on financial advisors who provide retirement plan or retirement product advice, regardless of how the advisor might be compensated. Under DOL rules, advisors must act in a fiduciary capacity when working

Table 5.2 FINRA securities licenses

FINRA license	Description
SIE exam	The Securities Industry Essentials (SIE) exam is an entry-level exam administered by FINRA. The exam assesses a candidate's knowledge of fundamental securities industry concepts. Passing the exam is a prerequisite for many FINRA licenses and is designed for individuals interested in beginning a career in the securities profession
Series 24	Allows individuals to supervise and manage broker-dealer operations and compliance
Series 3	Authorizes individuals to sell commodity futures contracts and options
Series 4	Permits supervision of options sales and activities at a firm
Series 6	Allows an advisor to sell mutual funds, variable annuities, and other packaged investment products
Series 7	Authorizes an advisor to sell a broad range of securities, including stocks, bonds, options, and ETFs
Series 63	Provides evidence that an advisor is proficient in state-specific securities laws, which is a requirement to sell securities within a state
Series 65	Permits an advisor to provide investment advice for a fee as an Investment Advisor Representative
Series 66	Combines the Series 63 and Series 65 licenses, tailored for investment advisors and securities agents
Series 79	Allows an advisor to specialize in investment banking activities, such as mergers, acquisitions, and capital raising
Series 99	Covers a broker-dealer's operations and administrative aspects, such as recordkeeping and compliance

Note: Adapted from: https://www.finra.org/registration-exams-ce/qualification-exams

Table 5.3 Similarities and differences between federal and state regulators

Aspect	Federal regulators	State regulators
Scope of oversight	Advisors managing $100 M+ (SEC), brokers (FINRA), and retirement (DOL)	Advisors managing <$100 M and state-level securities
Standards applied	Fiduciary standards (SEC/DOL), AML laws (FinCEN)	Suitability standards, fraud prevention (blue sky laws)
Client protection	Enforces federal anti-fraud and disclosure laws	Localized oversight and enforcement of ethical practices

with retirement plan participants and beneficiaries, providing transparent disclosures about fees and avoiding conflicts of interest that could influence retirement investment advice.

The Financial Crimes Enforcement Network (FinCEN) is used to enforce anti-money laundering (AML) laws and know your customer (KYC) regulations that are designed to prevent financial crimes.[50] Under FinCEN rules, advisors must verify client identities and report suspicious transactions to ensure ethical and lawful client relationships.[51] Firms and advisors must also maintain detailed transaction records to comply with AML regulations.[52]

The Consumer Financial Protection Bureau (CFPB) ensures transparency, fairness, and consumer protection in financial products and services. Per CFPB rules, financial advisors must educate clients about complex financial products and the associated risks with products and services offered to clients. CFPB rules also require that firms and financial advisors provide clear and transparent communication regarding fees, terms, and risks.

Finally, the Uniform Securities Act provides a model for state-level regulation.[53] The Act promotes consistency across regulatory jurisdictions. Under the Act, state regulators conduct periodic audits to ensure advisors are adhering to regulatory standards such as avoiding false or misleading advertising in client communications. This comprehensive regulatory framework protects clients and upholds the integrity of the financial advisory profession (Table 5.3).

State Regulators

State securities regulators, who operate under the North American Securities Administrators Association (NASAA), are responsible for registering financial advisors, conducting audits, and investigating fraud or unethical conduct. State insurance departments, which are part of the National Association of Insurance Commissioners (NAIC), oversee the licensing, education, and behavior of insurance agents and brokers. State regulators ensure compliance with state-specific insurance laws and consumer protection rules. Both sets of regulators work closely with federal agencies like the SEC and FINRA to address cross-jurisdictional violations and ensure enforcement consistency.

State-level regulations for financial advisors, financial planners, and insurance salespeople play a critical role in safeguarding consumer interests and ensuring ethical practices and compliance with non-federal standards. These regulations often complement federal rules but also focus on areas specific to each state, such as licensing, supervision, and enforcement of professional conduct. State-level securities regulators, which often operate under state attorney general and financial institutions offices, oversee fee-earning advisors managing less than $100 million in assets. These regulators also enforce "blue sky laws" that govern the offering and selling of securities within their jurisdiction.[54] At the state level, financial advisors must register with state regulators and meet licensing requirements. They must also recommend investments that align with their client's goals and risk tolerance. State regulators also investigate and prosecute fraud and unethical behavior to protect the public.

As noted above, financial advisors with less than $100 million in assets under management (AUM) must register with their state securities regulator. The registration process typically involves passing FINRA exams like the Series 65 or Series 66, submitting Form U4 through the Investment Adviser Registration Depository (IARD), and complying with state-specific securities laws. These laws are designed to protect investors by requiring advisors to disclose material information about securities and investment strategies. Advisors must also provide clients with Form ADV Part 2 (brochure) that details services, fees, and potential conflicts of interest. Many states also impose suitability standards, ensuring investment recommendations align with each client's goals and risk tolerance. State regulators conduct audits and reviews, ensuring that advisors maintain accurate records and comply with ethical standards, including prohibitions against false or misleading advertising. Violations typically result in disciplinary actions, such as fines or the loss of one or more securities licenses.

In the context of regulatory oversight, it is worth considering that financial advisors (this includes financial planners, financial counselors, financial therapists, and similar service providers) are not universally regulated as a distinct profession at the state level. Multi-level regulations create inconsistencies in oversight across jurisdictions. Regulation typically comes through indirect means, such as licensing requirements for providing investment advice (Series 65/66) or certifications (e.g., CFP®), which impose fiduciary duties and ethical guidelines. States may also require financial planners to disclose their fee structures, compensation models, and any potential conflicts of interest. However, those offering specific investment or insurance advice must comply with state securities or insurance regulations.

Insurance agents and brokers must obtain a state-specific insurance license to sell life, health, property, or casualty insurance. The licensing process generally involves completing pre-licensing education, passing one or more state exams, and submitting an application to the National Insurance Producer Registry (NIPR) or the state insurance department. States often impose suitability standards, requiring insurance agents to recommend products that suit a client's financial situation and needs. In recent years, some states have adopted best-interest standards for annuities and life insurance sales. These rules are influenced by the National Association of Insurance Commissioners (NAIC) Suitability in Annuity Transactions Model Regulation. Insurance agents must complete periodic continuing education to maintain their licenses and stay informed about changes in legal, ethical, and product knowledge. Insurance salespeople are also subject to state regulations regarding advertising and disclosure to prevent misleading claims. Violations of these standards can lead to fines and/or the suspension or revocation of a license.

Key distinctions across states include variations in licensing exams, continuing education requirements, and ethical standards. Some states impose stricter rules on advertising and disclosures, while others focus more on suitability standards, particularly for insurance products. Financial advisors and insurance salespeople working in multiple states must stay informed of the varying state-specific requirements to ensure compliance. The following case example illustrates how state regulators work to protect the interests of consumers:

> In 2021, the State of Massachusetts filed a case against Robinhood, alleging that the platform violated state "Blue Sky" laws by failing to protect inexperienced investors through the gamification of trading.[55] Robinhood employed gamification strategies, such as push notifications, confetti animations for completed trades, and an intuitive interface that made investing feel more like a game than a serious financial decision. The State of Massachusetts argued that Robinhood's practices encouraged novice investors to engage in frequent trading through game-like features that failed to ensure that products and services aligned with each investor's best interests. The state claimed that Robinhood breached its legal obligations to act responsibly and transparently. While Robinhood contested some of the allegations, it ultimately agreed to implement enhanced investor protections.

This case demonstrates the powers state regulators can use to enforce laws designed to protect consumers and ensure that financial advisory firms practice ethically to safeguard trust in the financial system. Why might have Robinhood encouraged excessive trading behavior? Robinhood encouraged excessive trading behavior on its platform because the firm's primary source of income came from payments for order flow (PFOF). Under PFOF arrangements, Robinhood received compensation from market makers by routing investor trades through market maker systems. PFOFs created an incentive for Robinhood to promote higher trading volumes, as more trades generated greater PFOF revenue. Robinhood's business approach prioritized platform profitability over investor protection.

The Role of Non-governmental Certification and Regulatory Organizations

While hundreds of professional designations and certifications serve the financial services profession, the following discussion highlights the leading role of some of the most prominent certification organizations. These organizations help to uphold rigorous standards that shape financial advisors' and planners' professional conduct, ethical obligations, and client-centric practices. Furthermore, the organizations described in this section help establish rules that ensure competence, integrity, and transparency in client interactions, which helps foster client trust through the delivery of high-quality advice.

The Certified Financial Planner Board of Standards, Inc. (CFP Board) administers the Certified Financial Planner™ (CFP®) certification. CFP® professionals are held to a fiduciary duty, requiring them to act in their client's best interests and prioritize client needs over personal or institutional gains. Bound by a Code of Ethics and Standards of Conduct, CFP® professionals agree to follow the Board's Code of Ethics and Standards of Conduct, which require a commitment to integrity, diligence, and fairness in client relationships.[56] Certificants must adhere to a comprehensive seven-step financial planning process that includes understanding a client's financial circumstances, formulating tailored recommendations, and providing ongoing plan monitoring. Additional requirements include safeguarding client confidentiality, providing transparent fee disclosures, and completing 30 hours of continuing education every 2 years, including ethics training. CFP Board standards are intended to ensure clients receive ethical, comprehensive, and customized financial guidance.

Keep in mind that the role of certification bodies and membership organizations in regulating the work of financial advisors does not carry the same weight as federal and state enforcement. For example, a financial advisor who holds a certification such as the Certified Financial Planner mark may lose their right to use the mark due to an ethical or standards of practice behavioral breach. However, this does not mean that the financial advisor will necessarily lose one or more securities licenses or be subject to additional regulatory oversight. On the other hand, nearly all certification boards will revoke a financial advisor's right to use the organization's marks if the advisor loses a license or is found guilty of a felony by a court.

The Chartered Financial Analyst (CFA) Institute confers the designation of the Chartered Financial Analyst (CFA®). The CFA® certification emphasizes rigorous ethical and professional conduct standards. CFA® charterholders are bound by a Code of Ethics and Standards of Professional Conduct that mandate integrity, competence, and diligence when working with clients. When managing client assets or providing investment advice, a CFA® professional must act as a fiduciary. The CFA Institute also enforces fair dealing among clients by mandating strict advisor confidentiality and accurate communication regarding financial risks and performance. The CFA Institute's standards ensure a disciplined, ethical, and analytical approach to investment management and client advisory services.

The National Association of Personal Financial Advisors (NAPFA) oversees the work of fee-only financial advisors who join the organization.[57] NAPFA prohibits advisor members from receiving commissions or compensation tied to product sales. Members must complete 60 hours of continuing education every 2 years. NAPFA emphasizes ethics and holistic financial planning across investments, taxes, retirement, insurance, and estate strategies.

The Investments & Wealth Institute certifies professionals through the Certified Investment Management Analyst® (CIMA®) designation. CIMA® advisors adhere to fiduciary standards by focusing on managing portfolios with advanced tools and strategies to meet a client's risk and return objectives. The Code of Professional Responsibility binds CIMA® advisors to provide services with honesty, integrity, and competency in all interactions.

The American College of Financial Services offers the Chartered Financial Consultant® (ChFC®) and the Chartered Life Underwriter® (CLU®) designations. The ChFC® emphasizes comprehensive financial planning. ChFC® professionals integrate estate, tax, and retirement planning into client strategies while adhering to a strict code of ethics grounded in honesty and diligence. The CLU® designation is a professional certification for individuals specializing in life insurance and estate planning. CLU® professionals are expected to demonstrate expertise in helping clients with life insurance needs, wealth transfer strategies, and financial protection plans.

Lastly, the **American Institute of CPAs** (AICPA) awards the Personal Financial Specialist (PFS®) designation to CPAs with advanced financial planning expertise. PFS® designees integrate tax knowledge with financial strategies, offering clients tax-efficient, customized solutions. Those holding this certification must adhere to the AICPA's strict ethical standards of integrity and objectivity while fulfilling fiduciary obligations.

Although previously discussed, it is important to re-review the role of the Financial Industry Regulatory Authority (FINRA). FINRA oversees advisors holding Series licenses, such as the Series 7 or Series 65.[58] FINRA also mandates adherence to a suitability standard of care.[59] Advisors must ensure that investment recommendations align with their client's financial objectives, risk tolerance, and investment experience. Through its "Know Your Customer" (KYC) rule, FINRA requires advisors to collect and analyze detailed client information before making recommendations. Transparency regarding fees, risks, and conflicts of interest is mandatory. FINRA enforces strict prohibitions against fraud, misrepresentation, and unsuitable practices. Financial advisors are subject to firm-specific supervisory guidelines, periodic audits, and ongoing training.

These types of certification and membership organizations serve as the foundation for establishing ethical and professional standards. By enforcing fiduciary and best-interest transparency and continuing education requirements, certification boards and member organizations provide a necessary regulatory framework that helps financial advisors deliver advice that is ethical, client-centric, and grounded in specialized expertise.

The Role of Regulations in Enhancing Client Trust and Market Stability

As noted throughout this chapter, regulations in the financial services profession are essential for fostering trust, ensuring market stability, and mitigating financial crises and fraud risks. When financial professionals and institutions adhere to robust regulatory guidelines, they create an environment of transparency, accountability, and confidence that benefits clients, markets, and stakeholders within the broader economy. The following discussion examines how regulatory compliance delivers long-term advantages for all stakeholders.

Building Client Trust

Regulations serve as the cornerstone of client trust. Complying with regulatory requirements allows a financial advisor to self-enforce ethical behavior, transparency, and accountability. In a profession where clients often lack the expertise to assess financial decisions thoroughly, regulatory standards build confidence and security. Key regulation mechanisms include the fiduciary duty and best-interest standards, such as those under the Investment Advisers Act of 1940 and Regulation Best Interest (Reg BI), which compel professionals to prioritize client goals and minimize conflicts of interest. Disclosure requirements further enhance trust by mandating transparent communication about fees, risks, and conflicts. Consumer protection laws, such as the Dodd-Frank Act and state-level Blue Sky Laws, protect against predatory practices and fraud.[60] Long-term benefits of these regulations include increased client loyalty and enhanced reputational standing for firms that prioritize ethical practices.

Promoting Market Stability

Regulations act as safeguards for the broader financial system by mandating fair practices, maintaining orderly markets, and mitigating systemic risks. Measures such as Basel III ensure financial institutions maintain sufficient capital buffers and manage liquidity risks, which reduce the likelihood of insolvency.[61] Anti-money laundering (AML) laws and know your customer (KYC) requirements protect market integrity by minimizing illicit activities. Stress testing, mandated under the Dodd-Frank Act, helps guarantee the resilience of financial institutions. Over the long term, such regulations enhance market resilience, support efficient capital allocation, and preserve investor confidence.

Mitigating Financial Crises and Fraud

Another central role of financial regulations is to address the root causes of financial crises and prevent fraudulent practices that erode market confidence. Post-crisis reforms, such as the Sarbanes-Oxley Act (SOX) and Dodd-Frank Act, provide comprehensive corporate governance and risk management oversight.[62] Regulations mandating strict recordkeeping, audit trails, and reporting standards aid in detecting and addressing fraudulent activities and investing schemes. Whistleblower protections under SOX and the SEC Whistleblower Program further bolster enforcement efforts by encouraging the reporting of misconduct. By mitigating risks and addressing systemic vulnerabilities, regulators play a vital role in reducing the frequency and severity of financial crises, which ultimately increases investor confidence.

Compliance as a Strategic Advantage

Complying with regulatory requirements allows financial firms and advisors to establish a competitive edge in the marketplace by aligning ethical practices with strategic goals. Emphasizing an ethical corporate culture enhances a firm's reputation, attracts top-tier talent, and fosters client trust and loyalty. Leveraging advanced technologies, such as automated AML and KYC systems, enables firms to streamline compliance processes, improve accuracy, and minimize risks associated with human error. Firm-level compliance processes allow organizations to monitor regulatory obligations in real time, ensuring swift adaptation to changes and reducing the burden of manual compliance tasks.

Firms that approach compliance as an element of their business strategy are often viewed as agile and forward-thinking in relation to the ever-evolving regulatory and market environment. Adopting a proactive mindset supports innovation and positions firms as industry leaders based on a commitment to transparency and integrity. The long-term advantages of such an approach include avoiding bad publicity and reputational harm. Benefits include cost savings through the minimization of fines, legal disputes, and reputational crises. Additionally, establishing stable and resilient operational frameworks contributes to sustainable growth, fostering a business model that is compliant and adaptable to future challenges and opportunities.

Challenges and Trends in Regulatory Compliance

The financial services sector is currently facing significant challenges and transformative trends related to regulatory compliance. One major compliance factor is an increasing emphasis on Environmental, Social, and Governance (ESG) reporting, which is leading some policymakers to change how they frame regulations. Regulators around the world now require greater transparency and accountability in sustainability practices. As a result, firms are being compelled to integrate ESG considerations into their investment decisions and disclose non-financial performance metrics, which creates new compliance obligations.[63]

Additionally, the rapid rise of cryptocurrencies has led to a surge in regulatory initiatives aimed at mitigating risks such as fraud, money laundering, and systemic instability. Asset innovations are forcing financial institutions to adapt to new and emerging regulatory frameworks.

Globalization has intensified these challenges, as financial professionals must now manage the complexities of cross-border regulations, often balancing conflicting requirements from different jurisdictions. For example, firms operating in multiple markets must navigate the nuances of varying AML and data protection laws, such as the General Data Protection Regulation (GDPR) in the European Union and local privacy laws in other regions.[64] The lack of harmonized standards exacerbates compliance risks, increasing operational and legal burdens for firms.

Technology plays a pivotal role in addressing these challenges.[65] Regulatory Technology (RegTech) solutions are transforming compliance processes by leveraging advanced tools such as artificial intelligence (AI), machine learning, and blockchain models to automate regulatory reporting, enhance risk monitoring, and improve efficiency.[66] These technologies reduce human error and enable firms to manage compliance at scale. However, reliance on technology introduces its own challenges, particularly concerning data privacy and cybersecurity compliance. As regulators continue to impose stringent requirements to protect sensitive information, financial firms must ensure their systems are resilient against cyber threats while meeting privacy standards. Striking a balance between innovation and regulatory adherence remains critical for financial institutions as they attempt to maintain trust and achieve long-term financial viability.

Chapter Summary

Regulatory frameworks are vital for ensuring trust, transparency, and stability in the financial services profession. Regulations are designed to protect clients, maintain the integrity of markets, and help reduce systemic risks that can lead to financial crises or fraud. Important regulations, such as the Investment Advisers Act of 1940, the Dodd-Frank Act, Regulation Best Interest (Reg BI), and Basel III, are in place to guide financial professionals and institutions, shape ethical conduct, and ensure accountability.

Regulatory bodies like the SEC, FINRA, and state-level agencies play a crucial role in enforcing regulatory standards, monitoring market participants, and addressing ethics violations. Together, these regulators create the foundation for a resilient and trustworthy financial ecosystem.

To succeed in a regulated and competitive environment, financial services professionals must commit to ongoing education and ethical practice. Continuous learning is essential for keeping up with regulatory changes, market developments, and evolving best practices. Financial services professionals should also strive to adopt a strong ethical framework that prioritizes the best interests of clients, transparency, and fairness in interactions. Proactive regulatory compliance, utilizing advanced technologies, and implementing robust internal controls are ways to ensure adherence to regulations while promoting innovation and operational efficiency.

Chapter Resources

- Australian Securities and Investments Commission: ASIC.gov.au
- Basel Committee on Banking Supervision: https://www.bis.org/bcbs
- Basel III Implementation: Bank for International Settlements (https://www.bis.org/)
- Canadian Securities Administrators: https://www.securities-administrators.ca/
- Consumer Financial Protection Bureau: consumerfinance.org

- European Securities and Market Authority: https://www.esma.europa.eu/
- Federal Reserve: https://www.federalreserve.gov/
- Federal Trade Commission: https://www.ftc.gov/
- Financial Consumer Agency of Canada: FCAC.gc.ca
- Financial Industry Regulatory Authority (FINRA): https://www.finra.org/
- International Organization of Securities Commissions (IOSCO): https://www.iosco.org
- Office of the Superintendent of Financial Institutions: osfi-bsif.gc.ca
- Overview of Regulation Best Interest: https://www.sec.gov/
- PCI Security Council: https://www.pcisecuritystandards.org/
- Securities and Exchange Commission (SEC): https://www.sec.gov/
- Securities Regulations for Mexico: cnbv.gob.mx

Notes

[1]https://www.centralbank.ie/news/article/press-release-warning-unauthorised-firm-quick-lends-18-july-2019

[2]Case Information

- https://www.sec.gov/newsroom/press-releases/2024-193
- https://www.msn.com/en-us/money/companies/sec-fines-morgan-stanley-15-million-over-failure-to-protect-client-accounts/ar-AA1vCcOi

[3]Automated Clearing House (ACH) payments are electronic transfers of funds between bank accounts, often used for direct deposits, bill payments, and recurring transfers. Cash wire transfers are immediate electronic transfers of funds from one bank or financial institution to another, typically used for urgent or large-value payments.

[4]Although the Investment Advisers Act of 1940 refers to a regulated financial professional as an adviser, for clarity, this chapter uses the term advisor.

[5]Oaker, W. (2018). *A critical analysis of the legal environment in respect of the private equity industry in South Africa*. https://core.ac.uk/download/188223901.pdf

[6]Aljarallah, M. (2021). *The structure and operations of financial regulatory and supervisory authorities* (Doctoral dissertation, Kingston University).

[7]Al-Shebli, A., & Alhajri, T. M. (2024). What is the international best practice for regulation of financial markets? From a legal and practical perspective. *Journal of Ecohumanism*, *3*(4), 1143–1154.

[8]Understanding the Basics: A Beginner's Guide to Payments—IPP Europe. https://www.ippeurope.com/understanding-the-basics-a-beginners-guide-to-payments/

[9]Elgadeh, M. (2011). Morrison v. National Australia Bank: Life after Dodd-Frank. *Fordham Journal of Corporate & Financial Law*. https://ir.lawnet.fordham.edu/cgi/viewcontent.cgi?article=1288&context=jcfl

[10]https://www.investor.gov/introduction-investing/investing-basics/role-sec/laws-govern-securities-industry#secact1933

[11]Ibid.

[12]Ibid.

[13]Ibid.

[14]https://www.federalreservehistory.org/essays/glass-steagall-act

[15]https://www.fdic.gov/

[16]https://www.ftc.gov/business-guidance/privacy-security/gramm-leach-bliley-act

[17]https://www.cftc.gov/LawRegulation/DoddFrankAct/index.htm

[18]https://www.consumerfinance.gov/rules-policy/

[19]https://www.congress.gov/bill/107th-congress/house-bill/3763

[20]https://www.fincen.gov/anti-money-laundering-act-2020

[21]https://www.finra.org/rules-guidance/rulebooks/finra-rules/2090

[22]https://www.pcisecuritystandards.org/

[23]https://eur-lex.europa.eu/eli/dir/2014/65/oj/eng

[24]https://www.bis.org/bcbs/basel3.htm

[25]https://www.eiopa.europa.eu/browse/regulation-and-policy/solvency-ii_en

[26]https://www.cnbv.gob.mx/en/Paginas/default.aspx/

[27]https://www.asic.gov.au/

[28]https://www.canada.ca/en/financial-consumer-agency.html

[29]https://www.osfi-bsif.gc.ca/en

[30]https://laws-lois.justice.gc.ca/ENG/ACTS/B-1.01/index.html

[31]https://laws-lois.justice.gc.ca/eng/acts/I-11.8/

[32]https://laws-lois.justice.gc.ca/eng/acts/T-19.8/

[33]https://laws-lois.justice.gc.ca/eng/acts/T-19.8/

[34]The Importance of Transparency in Investment Customer Relations. https://thecsaedge.com/the-importance-of-transparency-in-investment-customer-relations/

[35]https://www.sec.gov/enforcement-litigation/administrative-proceedings/ia-6662-s?utm_source=chatgpt.com

[36]https://www.investor.gov/introduction-investing/investing-basics/role-sec/laws-govern-securities-industry#secact1933

[37]Speech: A Commission Dilemma: Directors' Guidelines Revisited, May 7, 1974.

[38]https://www.investor.gov/introduction-investing/investing-basics/role-sec/laws-govern-securities-industry#secexact1934

[39]SEC Enforcement Actions: Insider Trading Cases.

[40]https://www.cftc.gov/LawRegulation/DoddFrankAct/index.htm

[41]Information asymmetry occurs when one party in a transaction (e.g., financial advisor) has more or better information than the other (e.g., client). This information advantage gives the advisor a potential advantage that can lead to market inefficiencies or unfair outcomes.

[42]https://www.ftc.gov/business-guidance/privacy-security/gramm-leach-bliley-act

[43]About $43.5 million in redress and debt cancellation to service members, military spouses, and other consumers due to multiple missteps by education provider Career Step | Federal Trade Commission.

[44]https://www.osc.ca/sites/default/files/2021-02/iap_20151112_risk-profiling-report.pdf

[45]https://www.esma.europa.eu/sites/default/files/library/esma35-43-3172_final_report_on_mifid_ii_guidelines_on_suitability.pdf

[46]https://www.handbook.fca.org.uk/handbook/COBS/9/2.html

[47]https://www.esma.europa.eu/sites/default/files/library/esma35-43-2938_gls_appropriateness_ex-only.pdf

[48]OCIE Risk Alert - IA Best Execution.pdf

[49]Although the North American Securities Administrators Association (NASAA) adopted a model rule in 2025 that prohibits broker-dealer agents from using the titles "advisor" or "adviser" unless they are also registered as investment adviser representatives, in this book, a broad definition of financial advisor is retained. A financial advisor advises clients on managing their finances to help them achieve specific financial goals. This advice can cover many areas, including investment

management, retirement planning, estate planning, tax planning, insurance needs, debt management, and wealth building.

[50]Regulations Governing Cross-Border Payments. https://www.fablefintech.com/blogs/post/regulations-governing-cross-border-payments

[51]Al-Zubaidie, M. (2024). Providing security for flash loan system using cryptocurrency wallets supported by XSalsa20 in a blockchain environment. *Applied Sciences, 14*(14), 6361.

[52]Strategies for Preventing First Party Fraud in Your Business. https://www.urbansplatter.com/2023/04/strategies-for-preventing-first-party-fraud-in-your-business/

[53]https://www.nasaa.org/industry-resources/uniform-securities-acts/

[54]Blue sky laws are state-level regulations in the United States that govern the offering and sale of securities to protect investors from fraud and deceptive practices.

[55]https://www.mass.gov/doc/robinhood-financial-llc-v-william-galvin-et-al-sjc-13381/download

[56]CFP Board Warns Unqualified Advisors to Limit Crypto Advice. https://www.wealthprofessional.ca/news/industry-news/cfp-board-warns-unqualified-advisors-to-limit-crypto-advice/372203

[57]Ohashi-Sides, J. (2020). Ethical standard for stockbrokers in the United States: An ethical analysis of the suitability and fiduciary standards. https://core.ac.uk/download/352161859.pdf

[58]What is the Role of the Financial Industry Regulatory Authority (FINRA) as it Relates to Investment Crowdfunding? https://www.crowdfundingecosystem.com/listing/crowdfunding-professional-association/ask/what-is-the-role-of-the-financial-industry-regulatory-authority-finra-as-it-relates-to-investment-crowdfunding

[59]Tennyson, S. (2009). Analyzing the role for a Consumer Financial Protection Agency. https://doi.org/10.2139/ssrn.1525603

[60]Elgadeh, M. (2011). Morrison v. National Australia Bank: Life After Dodd-Frank. *Fordham Journal of Corporate & Financial Law*. https://ir.lawnet.fordham.edu/cgi/viewcontent.cgi?article=1288&context=jcfl

[61]Basel III: A Crucial Framework for Preventing Future Banking Crises. https://economymiddleeast.com/news/basel-iii-a-crucial-framework-for-preventing-future-banking-crises/

[62]Huber, W. D. (2013). Audit fees, PCAOB sanctions, sanction risk, sanction risk premiums, and public policy: Theoretical framework and a call for research. Social Science Research Network. https://papers.ssrn.com/sol3/Delivery.cfm/SSRN_ID2307559_code2139.pdf?abstractid=2307559&mirid=1&type=2

[63]As ESG faces criticism, institutions are shifting to sustainability, responsible investing, and impact investing. These focal points emphasize measurable outcomes over reputational goals. New frameworks like the Ecological Benefits Framework aim for holistic value assessments. Others advocate for corporate accountability, standardized metrics, and binding standards. Regulatory mandates such as the EU's CSRD further formalize disclosures. Increasingly, emphasis is placed on materiality and financial relevance to align sustainability with performance.

[64]Idoko, I. P., Igbede, M. A., Manuel, H. N. N., Adeoye, T. O., Akpa, F. A., & Ukaegbu, C. (2024). Big data and AI in employment: The dual challenge of workforce replacement and protecting customer privacy in biometric data usage. *Global Journal of Engineering and Technology Advances*. https://doi.org/10.30574/gjeta.2024.19.2.0080

[65]Empowering Education: How Technology Addresses Overcrowded School Challenges for Parents. https://overcrowdednycschools.org/empowering-education-how-technology-addresses-overcrowded-school-challenges-for-parents

[66]Enalito and Mason together for AI-powered Growth in e-Commerce Business. https://www.enalito.com/blogs/enalito-and-mason-together-for-ai-powered-growth-in-e-commerce-business

From Misconduct to Oversight: A History of Financial Wrongdoing and Regulation

6

Chapter Outcomes

This chapter focuses on helping learners develop the ability to:

1. Understand the historical development of financial regulations and the significance of regulations in driving ethical and compliant practices.
2. Analyze the evolution of regulatory frameworks behind current rules and anticipate potential future regulatory changes.
3. Identify landmark cases and regulatory milestones that have shaped the financial services profession.
4. Evaluate lessons from regulatory breakdowns and describe the catastrophic consequences of oversight failures and ethical misconduct.
5. Apply insights from historical cases to foster a culture of proactive compliance and continuous risk assessment.
6. Describe the roles of regulatory bodies, such as the Securities and Exchange Commission (SEC) and the Financial Industry Regulatory Authority (FINRA), in maintaining professional standards and accountability.
7. Develop a principled approach to financial advising, grounded in historical awareness, regulatory understanding, and ethical integrity.

Note: This chapter was copyedited using Grammarly™ and generative AI tools to enhance clarity, grammar, and overall readability. While these tools provided suggestions and assistance in refining the text, the ideas, content, and arguments presented remain the sole work and responsibility of the authors. Any errors or inaccuracies in the final version are also the authors' responsibility.

W. Heo, J. E. Grable, *Ethics and Compliance in Financial Services*,
https://doi.org/10.1007/978-3-032-14449-2_6

Introduction

Financial regulations have evolved over centuries, shaped by economic crises, market innovations, and societal demands for fairness and accountability. From the stock market crash of 1929 to the 2008 global financial crisis to the COVID-19 pandemic market correction, historical events have exposed vulnerabilities in financial systems, prompting regulators to establish frameworks that safeguard consumers, stabilize markets, and enforce ethical conduct. For financial services professionals, understanding this regulatory history is not merely an academic exercise; regulatory knowledge is a critical foundation for navigating the complex compliance landscape and upholding ethical standards in client interactions.

This chapter explores the evolution of financial regulations, focusing on pivotal moments that transformed the financial services profession. By examining landmark regulatory cases, such as the creation of the Securities and Exchange Commission (SEC) and the fallout from corporate scandals, this chapter uncovers the drivers behind regulatory reforms. This chapter also analyzes lessons learned from regulatory failures, which highlight the devastating consequences of inadequate oversight and unethical behavior. Finally, this chapter assesses how these historical developments continue to influence modern compliance practices, equipping financial professionals with the tools to build trust, mitigate risks, and foster long-term client relationships.

As a precursor to the chapter discussion, it is worth noting that the study of regulatory history reveals a recurring theme: robust regulations are essential for balancing innovation with accountability. As financial markets become increasingly globalized and technology-driven, the lessons of the past remain vital for addressing emerging challenges, from cryptocurrency regulation and artificial intelligence (AI) protocols to Environmental, Social, and Governance compliance issues. By tracing the arc of regulatory change, this chapter prepares financial professionals to anticipate future trends, adhere to ethical standards, and contribute to a resilient financial ecosystem.

Perspective

This chapter challenges the perception that regulations are bureaucratic obstacles. Instead, the chapter frames regulations as tools for ethical practice and market stability. Regulations are often perceived as constraints that hinder financial innovation or burden professionals with compliance tasks. However, this view overlooks the fundamental role regulations play in protecting consumers and ensuring market integrity. Historical regulatory changes, driven by crises and misconduct, demonstrate that regulations are not mere hurdles but essential safeguards that enable ethical behavior and sustain public trust. Consider the case of the 1929 stock market crash, which exposed rampant unregulated speculation and inadequate market oversight, leading to the creation of the Securities and Exchange Commission (SEC) and other foundational securities laws. This transformative moment in the history of the securities markets underscores that regulations arise from necessity, addressing systemic failures to prevent harm and promote fairness.

The stock market crash of 1929 serves as a powerful example of how regulations often emerge in response to market failures. This crash was driven by a combination of speculative investing, excessive use of margin (borrowing money to buy stocks), a lack of financial regulation, and widespread investor overconfidence. In the years leading up to the crash, stock prices soared far beyond their actual value, fueled by the belief that the market would continue to rise indefinitely. However, when confidence faltered in October 1929, panic selling erupted, triggering a dramatic collapse in stock prices.

The consequences of the crash were devastating. The market meltdown contributed to the onset of the Great Depression, a global economic downturn marked by massive unemployment, widespread bank failures, and significant declines in industrial production and consumer spending.[1] The fragility of the financial system was exposed, leading to sweeping reforms in the 1930s. For financial advisors, the 1929 crash serves as a crucial historical lesson about the dangers of speculation and the importance of regulatory safeguards. This landmark event underscores the need for ethical client guidance, emphasizing the responsibility to promote sound investment practices, ensure portfolio diversification, and help clients avoid emotionally driven decisions. Furthermore, it acts as a reminder of the critical role regulation plays in maintaining market stability and protecting investors.

Regulatory history offers a lens through which financial services professionals can gain a better understanding of the consequences of ethical lapses and the importance of regulatory compliance. By learning from past failures, such as landmark Ponzi schemes of the early twentieth century or accounting fraud scandals of the early 2000s, financial services professionals can better appreciate the role of regulators in enforcing accountability. This perspective encourages a proactive approach to compliance, where regulations are seen as partners in building a trustworthy and sustainable financial services profession.

Evolution of Financial Regulations

Regulation of the financial markets and financial advisors has evolved over time. The evolution of rules and regulations has arisen in alignment with economic, political, and technological changes. Understanding this evolution offers insights into why regulations exist, how they function, and what ethical and practical challenges financial services professionals must anticipate. The following discussion provides an historical overview of the development of regulatory frameworks.

Early Foundations (Pre-twentieth Century)

Financial oversight in the seventeenth to nineteenth centuries was basic, somewhat volatile, and far from uniform. Early European regulatory systems relied on common law, usury restrictions, and self-regulation by banks. Stock exchanges operated with minimal oversight. The result is that fraud was common because of the prevalence of information asymmetry and speculative behavior. An investing craze commonly known as "Tulip Mania" is the most well-known example of the way investments were made and regulated in the seventeenth century. Tulip Mania happened in the Netherlands during the 1630s. As tulip bulbs became a symbol of wealth, demand from wealthy households increased, and with rising demand, prices surged. As a result, tulip bulbs lost their original purpose (flowers) and became merely a vehicle for speculation. Consequently, tulip bulb contract prices skyrocketed due to unchecked speculation in informal tavern-based trading, with limited enforceability of contracts and biased information sources. At the height of the mania, people were trading homes, estates, and other hard assets for tulip bulbs. Things came to an end in 1637 when the price bubble burst. The general public quickly lost confidence not only in the tulip market but also in the broader financial system.[2] It took decades for the Netherlands to recover.

Similarly, the South Sea Bubble in England in 1720 highlights how widespread market manipulation can alter the course of wealth accumulation at the national and household level. The South Sea Company was a British joint-stock company founded in 1711. The firm was initially created to consolidate and reduce the national debt of England through a scheme that involved trade with South America. This trade was largely speculative and limited in reality. In 1720, the company's stock became the center of a financial frenzy known as the South Sea Bubble. The South Sea Company's stock price was artificially inflated through various unethical activities such as insider trading, bribery, and false promises of high returns amid weak regulatory controls.[3] Investors speculated wildly on the company's potential profits, driving stock prices to unsustainable heights. When confidence collapsed, the bubble burst, leading to a dramatic market crash that ruined many investors and shook public trust in financial markets. The crash resulted in investor ruin and heightened demands for parliamentary investigations. As a result, the public began to demand greater transparency and legal accountability, as seen in post-bubble measures like the Bubble Act of 1720 in England, which restricted unauthorized joint-stock companies as a way to prevent future crises.

The Great Depression and the Birth of Modern Regulation (1929–1934)

Although introduced earlier in the chapter, it is worth reviewing again what many consider to be the greatest speculative bubble in recent history—a bubble that included insider trading and widespread investor misinformation: the 1929 stock market crash. The crash triggered the Great Depression and exposed systemic vulnerabilities in the U.S. financial system.[4] The events of 1929 led to an unprecedented worldwide economic collapse, characterized by massive bank failures. Over 5000 banks collapsed between 1929 and 1933 in the United States. In addition, there was widespread unemployment, which prompted the U.S. government to introduce sweeping regulatory reforms to restore trust and integrity in the U.S. financial system.[5] The Pecora Commission hearings (1932–1934) played a pivotal role in bringing stability to the markets by uncovering Wall Street abuses such as unethical tax practices, insider trading, and manipulative stock practices that fueled the crash. The Commission's work laid the groundwork for future reforms. Some key reforms included the following, which institutionalized fiduciary responsibility and market accountability:

- Securities Act of 1933: Mandated registration and disclosure of securities offerings to address the misinformation and fraud revealed in the 1929 crash and Pecora hearings.
- Securities Exchange Act of 1934: Established the Securities and Exchange Commission (SEC) to enforce transparency and prevent fraud, directly responding to the manipulative practices exposed by the Pecora Investigation.
- Banking Act of 1933 (Glass-Steagall): Separated commercial and investment banking to avoid conflicts of interest. The Act also created the Federal Deposit Insurance Corporation (FDIC) to protect deposits, as a reaction to the bank runs and failures during the early Great Depression.

Post-WWII Expansion and Institutional Development (1940–1980)

After WWII, and building on lessons from the Great Depression and wartime financial strains, financial regulation expanded to address challenges associated with rapid economic growth, the internationalization of capital markets, and increasing investor sophistication.[6] This period saw heightened regulatory efforts to prevent market abuses exposed by earlier crises such as the investment trust scandals of the 1930s. The following regulatory developments shaped U.S. financial markets in the mid-twentieth century:

- Investment Advisers Act of 1940: Enacted after a five-year SEC study revealed widespread market abuses, including excessive fees, conflicts of interest, and fraud, the Act imposed fiduciary duties on investment advisors[7] and expanded SEC oversight.[8]
- Expansion of FDIC and Federal Reserve powers: Building on the Banking Act of 1935, which centralized the Fed's authority during the Great Depression, postwar reforms raised FDIC deposit insurance to $10,000 in 1950.[9] This move was intended to strengthen public confidence during economic expansion and heavy wartime lending. Today, the FDIC limit is $250,000.
- SEC rules on market manipulation and insider trading: Rule 10b-5, introduced in 1942, targeted insider abuses and became the foundation for later enforcement. Landmark cases such as *SEC v. Texas Gulf Sulphur* in 1968 expanded the definition of insider trading as markets grew more complex.[10]

By the 1970s, however, momentum shifted toward deregulation. Pressures from inflation, technology, and calls for efficiency led to the end of fixed brokerage commissions on "May Day" in 1975 under SEC Rule 19b-3. While this reform increased competition, it also introduced new risks, including higher volatility, underscoring the challenge of balancing innovation, market access, and accountability.[11]

Deregulation and Financial Crises (1980–2000)

In the United States, the Reagan and Clinton administrations introduced numerous market deregulation reforms under the belief that markets could self-correct if freed from the burdens of heavy regulatory oversight. The loosening of regulations across the economy was driven by neoliberal economic policies, emphasizing reduced government intervention, tax cuts, and financial liberalization as a way to spur growth amid inflation and global competition in the 1980s and 1990s.[12] This era began with the Depository Institutions Deregulation and Monetary Control Act of 1980, which phased out interest rate ceilings and expanded thrift powers, setting the stage for increased risk-taking in the financial sector.[13] Shortly after the Act went into effect, the savings and loan (S&L) crisis occurred. This crisis resulted from aggressive lending and insufficient oversight triggered by deregulations. As an example, the Germain Depository Institutions Act of 1982 permitted thrifts to invest in high-risk ventures such as commercial real estate. Provisions of the Act worked well until interest rates and oil prices contracted. The crisis culminated in widespread fraud, insolvencies, and a taxpayer bailout exceeding $124 billion.[10] In the end, over 1000 savings and loan institutions collapsed.

As with other regulator frameworks, Congress reacted to the savings and loan crisis by passing the Financial Institutions Reform, Recovery, and Enforcement Act (FIRREA) of 1989. FIRREA strengthened federal oversight of thrifts and restructured thrift regulations. The Act established the Resolution Trust Corporation (RTC) to liquidate failed institutions, recapitalizing the deposit insurance fund, and imposing harsher civil and criminal penalties for financial misconduct to prevent future abuses.

Deregulation continued through the 1990s. Unintended consequences arose, such as increased systemic market risks and growing conflicts of interest.[14] Near the end of the twentieth century and based on the belief that markets could nonetheless self-correct with minimal levels of federal and state oversight, the Gramm-Leach-Bliley Act (1999) was enacted. This Act repealed parts of Glass-Steagall that had prohibited certain mergers in the banking, insurance, and securities sectors. Many critics of the Act have argued that the 2008 financial crisis was a direct result of the Act by exacerbating systemic risks in the banking and financial services industries.[15]

Post-2000 Reforms and Global Integration (2000–Present)

The early 2000s saw numerous corporate and financial market scandals that stemmed from ethical violations and a lack of regulatory enforcement. The case of Enron in 2001 exemplifies one of the most egregious examples of fraud in American history. Executives at Enron hid billions in debt, resulting in massive investor losses.[16] Similarly, in 2002, WorldCom scandalized the markets when it was learned that executives had inflated asset values by nearly $11 billion through improper expense capitalization. This led to bankruptcy and eroded market trust. These were precursors to the 2008 financial crisis, which accelerated global regulatory transformation. The 2008 financial crisis resulted in widespread bank failures, government bailouts totaling trillions of dollars, and a severe recession that exposed households to substantial losses in real estate values and security holdings. The crisis also made visible the vulnerabilities associated with a lack of regulatory oversight.[17] In reaction to the crisis, Congress passed several bills that have implications for the way financial service firms operate today. The most important of these laws are described below:

- Sarbanes-Oxley Act (2002): Strengthened audit independence and corporate accountability, enacted as a direct response to the Enron and WorldCom scandals that highlighted failures in financial reporting, auditor conflicts, and executive misconduct. The Act imposed stricter penalties for fraud and required CEO/CFO certifications of financial statements.[18]
- Dodd-Frank Act (2010): Created the Consumer Financial Protection Bureau (CFPB), mandated stress testing, and imposed higher transparency requirements of financial services firm. Passed under President Obama to rectify the causes of the 2008 Great Recession, the Act was intended to deal with derivatives trading, predatory lending, and the "too big to fail" problem that necessitated bailouts for institutions like AIG.[19]
- Basel III: Set global standards for bank capital and liquidity risk management. The standards were introduced by the Basel Committee on Banking Supervision in 2010–2011 to address the banking sector's undercapitalization and liquidity shortages revealed during the 2008 crisis.[20]
- MiFID II (EU): Enhanced investor protection and disclosure in financial markets. The policies were implemented in January 2018 as a revision to the original 2007 MiFID directive, which was influenced by the 2008 Great Recession, high-frequency trading risks, and cross-border regulatory gaps in the EU. Regulators hoped that MiFID would foster fairer competition and reduce systemic market threats.[21]

Table 6.1 provides a summary of some of the most important regulatory trends that have occurred in reaction to market events and crises. The unifying theme of these laws is the focus on ethical practice, risk management, and market stability.

Table 6.1 Historical regulatory phases and laws

Period	Key regulatory actions	Ethical focus
Pre-twentieth century	Usury laws, informal banking regulation	Need for formal oversight
1929–1934	SEC formation, Glass-Steagall	Transparency, market integrity
1940–1980	Investment Advisers Act, FDIC expansion	Fiduciary duty, access vs. oversight
1980–2000	Gramm-Leach-Bliley, S&L crisis	Conflict of interest, risk containment
2000–Present	SOX, Dodd-Frank, Basel III, MiFID II	Ethical accountability, global standards

Representative Regulatory Cases

The following series of case narratives presents a curated set of significant events and the regulatory responses that have profoundly shaped the financial services profession. Each case provides insight into how financial misconduct, regulatory oversights, and institutional or cultural failures can cause considerable harm, not only to individual investors and firms but also to the integrity of entire financial systems.

Charles Ponzi and the Postal Coupon Scheme (1920)

This example is often cited as the "classic" financial services fraud.[22] The case is so famous that the term "Ponzi scheme" was coined to describe all similar activities. Charles Ponzi was a Boston-based entrepreneur. He was charismatic and promised investors an astonishing 50% return in just 45 days by exploiting price differences in international postal reply coupons. The idea was theoretically feasible. However, Ponzi never executed the arbitrage. Instead, he used funds from new investors to pay earlier investors. This method of robbing one investor to pay another investor resulted in a rapidly ballooning investor base. At the height of the fraud, Ponzi had tens of thousands of investors. As suspicions mounted and withdrawals surged, the scheme unraveled. Ponzi did not have enough new money coming in to pay off earlier investors. Finally, it was revealed that only a fraction of the money invested had been used for legitimate business purposes. The scandal shocked the nation, especially since many victims were working-class families who had entrusted Ponzi with their savings.

Regulators lacked a comprehensive framework to prosecute Charles Ponzi. Regulators were caught flat-footed. The fallout from Ponzi's fraud played a crucial role in shaping U.S. securities laws. The scheme contributed directly to the passage of the Securities Act of 1933 and the Securities Exchange Act of 1934. These laws laid the groundwork for modern disclosure requirements, anti-fraud measures, and the creation of the Securities and Exchange Commission (SEC).[23] As an ethical illustration, the Ponzi case highlights the dangers of unchecked optimism, asymmetric information, and the absence of third-party validation. The Ponzi case also shows the importance of due diligence and investor education.

Enron Scandal and the Collapse of Corporate Trust (2001)

Given the importance of Enron in the development of market regulations, it is worth reviewing this unique historical event. Enron Corporation's fall from grace in 2001 became a global symbol of corporate fraud.[24] Although Enron was originally hailed as an innovator in the energy sector, corporate executives used complex off-balance-sheet entities and accounting loopholes to hide debt and inflate earnings. These deceptive actions misled investors and regulators alike. The deception involved collusion between executives and Enron's auditing firm, Arthur Andersen, which was complicit in approving questionable financial statements and later destroying related audit documents.

The consequence of Enron's deceptive actions was the company's bankruptcy. At the time, Enron was the seventh largest company in the U.S. financial market. The firm's bankruptcy led to massive shareholder losses, the dissolution of Arthur Andersen, and the loss of thousands of jobs and pensions. In response, Congress passed the Sarbanes-Oxley Act of 2002 (SOX), which overhauled corporate governance standards. SOX created the Public Company Accounting Oversight Board (PCAOB), required executives to certify financial reports, and imposed criminal penalties for falsified disclosures.[25]

The ethical lessons from the Enron situation have implications for the way financial services firms operate today. The Enron fiasco highlights the perils of greed and underscores the consequences of fostering a corporate culture that prioritizes stock price over transparency. Additionally, the scandal exposed the critical failure of regulators and auditors to protect public trust. For financial professionals, the Enron saga reinforces the need for robust internal controls, audit independence, and the courage to confront unethical practices.

Bernie Madoff and the Largest Ponzi Scheme in History (2008)

In 2008, it was disclosed that Bernie Madoff, a former NASDAQ chairperson and highly respected investment advisor, was running a $65 billion Ponzi scheme (the largest in history). Madoff's firm offered consistently high returns, but it was all a fraud. Instead of executing trades, Madoff used money from new investors to pay off previous investors. He fabricated account statements and claimed trades that never occurred. Despite repeated warnings from whistleblowers like Harry Markopolos, the SEC failed to act for years.[26]

The scandal's exposure during the global financial crisis stimulated public outrage. In response, the Dodd-Frank Wall Street Reform and Consumer Protection Act was passed in 2010. The SEC created the Office of the Whistleblower, offering protections and financial incentives for reporting fraud.[27] Madoff's downfall reminds financial professionals that reputation and regulatory status are not substitutes for data verification. The case illustrates the moral hazard of investing primarily on trust. The case also highlights the need for rigorous due diligence, robust anti-money laundering (AML) and know your customer (KYC) protocols when ethically managing assets.[28]

Wells Fargo Account Fraud Scandal (2016)

The Wells Fargo scandal is a prototypical compliance failure. In 2016, Wells Fargo was found to have opened over 3.5 million unauthorized bank and credit card accounts on behalf of customers without their consent. Unrealistic sales goals and incentive-based performance metrics pressured employees to act unethically. Those employees engaged in widespread unethical behavior to meet sales targets. As a result of the unauthorized actions, customers were being charged fees and incurring reputational damage via damaged credit scores, and, in some cases, bank customers faced legal action.[29] The Consumer Financial Protection Bureau (CFPB), the Office of the Comptroller of the Currency (OCC), and the Los Angeles City Attorney levied a $185 million fine against the bank. The fraud led to firm resignations at the highest levels, public hearings, and reforms in corporate governance and incentive structures.[30] The Wells Fargo case prompted nearly all other financial institutions to reevaluate their compensation models, internal controls, and ethics training programs. The case also reinforced the notion that a firm's values and culture are integral to acting ethically and complying with laws, standards, and regulations.

Lessons Learned from Regulatory Failures

The historical failures discussed in this chapter created a legacy of insights that shape today's regulatory frameworks and ethical standards. The following lessons offer practical guidance for financial professionals and institutions seeking to improve trust, compliance, and accountability. These lessons reflect the moral foundations of sound financial practice and call on professionals to be proactive stewards of public trust. Adopting a preventative, rather than reactive, mindset ensures the continued integrity and resilience of the financial services industry.

Inadequate Oversight as a Catalyst for Market Harm

Throughout financial history, inadequate regulatory oversight has repeatedly proven to be a root cause of widespread investor harm and economic destabilization. Iconic examples, such as the 1929 stock market crash and the collapse of major Ponzi schemes, most notably the massive fraud perpetrated by Bernard Madoff, underscore how weak supervision, insufficient auditor checks, and unchallenged trust in financial actors can open the door to systemic abuse and collapse.

The 1929 stock market crash revealed the perils of unregulated speculation, opaque financial practices, and rampant conflicts of interest. The crash ultimately plunged the nation into the Great Depression. In response, the U.S. government created the Securities and Exchange Commission (SEC) and enacted foundational legislation, including the Securities Act of 1933 and the Securities Exchange Act of 1934, to enforce transparency, promote fair dealing, and curb fraud in capital markets. Decades later, the unraveling of Madoff's multi-billion-dollar Ponzi scheme exposed similar regulatory blind spots, including weak regulatory enforcement, failure to act on whistleblower tips, and an overreliance on trust without verification.

These events highlight a consistent and vital lesson for modern financial professionals: internal confidence is no substitute for independent oversight. Robust governance frameworks featuring regular audits, external reviews, and rigorous third-party verification are essential to maintaining ethical integrity and safeguarding both clients and markets. Frameworks serve not only to detect and deter misconduct but also to prevent internal misjudgments or cultural complacency from metastasizing into large-scale crises.

Ethical Lapses Undermine Trust and Threaten Institutional Stability

The financial services profession depends fundamentally on trust—trust between clients and advisors, institutions and regulators, and markets and the public. When that trust is broken, the consequences can be far-reaching and deeply damaging. The Enron and Wells Fargo scandals offer stark and instructive examples of how ethical failures, particularly those driven by a short-sighted pursuit of profit or performance metrics, can dismantle even the most established institutions.

Enron, once hailed as a symbol of innovation and corporate success, collapsed spectacularly in 2001 after revelations of widespread accounting fraud. Through deceptive practices such as off-balance-sheet entities and manipulated earnings reports, the company misled investors and regulators for years. The fallout not only bankrupted Enron but also led to the dissolution of Arthur Andersen, one of the world's largest accounting firms, and ultimately gave rise to the Sarbanes-Oxley Act—a significant overhaul of corporate governance and financial transparency regulations.

Similarly, the Wells Fargo scandal exposed systemic ethical failures within one of the nation's largest banks. Driven by an aggressive internal sales culture, employees opened millions of unauthorized accounts to meet unrealistic performance quotas. This misconduct resulted in massive reputational harm, billions in regulatory fines, and long-term damage to customer relationships and employee morale.

These cases highlight a critical truth: when ethics are subordinated to profit motives or operational targets, the cost is not merely financial, but it is existential. The erosion of stakeholder trust can dismantle brand value, attract severe regulatory scrutiny, and destabilize internal culture.

To avoid such outcomes, financial services firms must treat ethics not as a compliance obligation but as a strategic imperative. This means investing in comprehensive ethical training, embedding values-based decision-making into daily operations, and fostering leadership that consistently models integrity, accountability, and client-first principles. Ethical leadership should promote transparency, support whistleblowing, and reward long-term value creation over short-term gains. In the long run, sustained success in the financial services profession requires more than technical competence or regulatory adherence, demands a deep and visible commitment to doing what is right, even when it is not easy or immediately profitable.

Deregulation Without Safeguards Can Amplify Risk and Destabilize Markets

While deregulation is often championed as a way to foster innovation, enhance market efficiency, and reduce bureaucratic barriers, history shows that when deregulation occurs without corresponding safeguards, it can lead to unchecked risk-taking, systemic vulnerabilities, and widespread financial harm. Two of the most consequential financial crises in U.S. history—the savings and loan (S&L) crisis of the 1980s and the global financial crisis of 2008—demonstrate the perils of deregulation in the absence of effective oversight and compliance infrastructure.

In the 1980s, legislative changes allowed savings and loan institutions to engage in a broader range of lending activities with less regulatory scrutiny and fewer capital requirements. Many institutions, previously limited to low-risk residential lending, rapidly expanded into speculative real estate and high-yield investments. With inadequate risk controls and poor regulatory supervision, the result was catastrophic: more than a thousand S&Ls failed, costing taxpayers hundreds of billions of dollars and prompting the creation of FIRREA (the Financial Institutions Reform, Recovery, and Enforcement Act of 1989) to restructure and tighten regulatory oversight.

Similarly, the 2008 financial crisis was preceded by years of financial deregulation that allowed for the proliferation of complex derivatives, subprime mortgage lending, and excessive leverage within the banking system. Financial institutions operated in an environment that prioritized profit maximization and innovation, often at the expense of risk management and consumer protection. The dismantling of safeguards, such as the repeal of the Glass-Steagall Act and weak oversight of emerging financial products, contributed to the build-up of systemic risk that ultimately triggered a global economic meltdown.

These historical episodes make clear that deregulation, when not balanced with robust compliance frameworks and institutional accountability, does not eliminate risk; it merely obscures and redistributes risk, often to the detriment of consumers, taxpayers, and market stability. For policymakers and financial professionals, the lesson is not that regulation stifles innovation but that sustainable and ethical innovation depends on a strong foundation of regulatory checks, transparency, and internal controls. A well-regulated environment can provide the clarity, consistency, and trust necessary for new financial tools and services to flourish. On balance, thoughtful regulation and compliance are not barriers to progress; they are essential enablers of long-term integrity, resilience, and ethical advancement in the financial system.

Consumer Protection Is Paramount

Across financial history, one pattern remains tragically consistent: when regulatory systems fail or ethical standards are compromised, it is consumers who suffer the most. From the thousands defrauded in Charles Ponzi's infamous early twentieth-century investment scam to the more recent Wells Fargo scandal (where customers were unknowingly enrolled in unauthorized accounts), individuals often bear the direct and disproportionate consequences of institutional misconduct and oversight breakdowns.

These events serve as powerful reminders that consumer protection must be the highest priority in the financial services profession. Consumer protection is not simply a regulatory requirement. It is a moral and professional duty that upholds the very foundation of trust upon which the financial system depends. To safeguard clients effectively, financial institutions must implement and rigorously enforce compliance protocols, foremost among them, know your customer (KYC), anti-money laundering (AML) procedures, and suitability assessments. These mechanisms are designed not only to detect and prevent criminal activity but also to ensure that financial products and advice are genuinely aligned with each client's financial goals, needs, and risk tolerance. Specifically:

- KYC protocols go beyond identity verification; these practices are essential for understanding a client's financial background, risk profile, and investment experience, which helps financial advisors provide appropriate, personalized recommendations.
- AML frameworks play a critical role in identifying and stopping illicit financial flows, including money laundering and terrorist financing. Effective AML systems protect firms, advisors, and the financial ecosystem as a whole, by reducing systemic vulnerabilities and reputational risk.
- Suitability assessments ensure that investment strategies and financial products are matched to a client's specific financial situation, objectives, and risk appetite. Without this ethical alignment, clients may unknowingly be placed in harm's way through overly aggressive or inappropriate financial solutions.

Institutions that fail to prioritize consumer protection face more than just legal and financial penalties. Compliance failures risk eroding public trust, losing client loyalty, and damaging the credibility of the profession at large. Conversely, firms that embrace a client-first philosophy, supported by strong compliance systems, clear communication, and a culture of transparency, position themselves as ethical leaders in an increasingly complex and scrutinized marketplace.

Whistleblower Protections Enhance Accountability

One of the most sobering lessons from high-profile financial scandals, such as the Bernard Madoff Ponzi scheme, is that early warning signs are often present, yet ignored or inadequately investigated by regulators and internal stakeholders. In the Madoff case, credible concerns were raised for years, including detailed reports from financial analyst Harry Markopolos. Still, due to institutional inertia, regulatory fragmentation, and lack of internal accountability, those warnings went unheeded. The result was one of the largest financial frauds in history, with devastating consequences for investors, charitable organizations, and public confidence in regulatory systems.

This pattern of oversight failure reveals a critical vulnerability in financial institutions: without strong internal reporting channels and protections, misconduct can remain hidden until it reaches a catastrophic scale. Whistleblower protections serve as a vital safeguard against this risk by empowering employees and insiders to come forward with concerns without fear of retaliation, professional harm, or personal loss.

When effectively designed and enforced, whistleblower systems provide a confidential and secure mechanism for identifying unethical or illegal activity early, often before external stakeholders or regulators are aware. These mechanisms act as a critical "internal audit" function, supplementing formal compliance systems and offering a direct line of defense against fraud, abuse, and systemic failure.

The Dodd-Frank Wall Street Reform and Consumer Protection Act, passed in the wake of the 2008 financial crisis, marked a significant advancement in this area. Its whistleblower provision, administered by the U.S. Securities and Exchange Commission (SEC), offers protections for individuals who report securities violations. In addition to confidentiality and legal safeguards against retaliation, the law also introduced monetary incentives, awarding eligible whistleblowers a percentage of fines collected in successful enforcement actions. This model has proven effective, resulting in numerous high-impact cases being brought to light and billions of dollars in penalties and recoveries.

For financial professionals and institutions, accountability issues underscore the need to foster a culture of transparency and ethical courage. Beyond compliance with legal mandates, organizations should actively encourage internal reporting, train employees on how to recognize and report red flags and support leadership that treats whistleblower input as a constructive part of the risk management process rather than a threat to be silenced. In today's complex and fast-paced financial environment, whistleblower protections are not merely an ethical add-on. These protections are a cornerstone of modern accountability frameworks. When institutions empower individuals to speak up and respond thoughtfully to internal concerns, they strengthen their ability to detect misconduct early, preserve trust, and uphold the integrity of the financial system.

Behavioral Insights

The historical trajectory of financial scandals in the United States has profoundly influenced the evolution of compliance practices, embedding ethical vigilance, consumer protection, and systemic stability into the delivery of financial services. From early twentieth-century frauds to more recent crises, each episode of large-scale misconduct has catalyzed regulatory reform, deepened professional accountability, and redefined the role of compliance in financial institutions.

However, beyond structural and regulatory outcomes, it is increasingly vital to integrate behavioral insights into the analysis of persistent ethical failures. Many financial scandals are not solely the result of technical non-compliance or regulatory loopholes but also of cognitive distortions, groupthink, overconfidence, and moral disengagement—psychological factors that drive individuals and institutions to take outsized risks or ignore warning signs.

Recent high-profile cases, such as the collapse of FTX in 2022 and the failure of Archegos Capital Management in 2021, exemplify this convergence of behavioral vulnerabilities and compliance breakdowns.[31] In both cases, unchecked optimism, distorted risk perception, and a culture of opacity fueled decision-making that ultimately triggered massive financial damage. These failures mirror earlier crises that exposed the inadequacy of rule-based compliance approaches in addressing deeper ethical and psychological risks.

As a result, there has been a significant shift in regulatory thinking. Compliance is no longer viewed as a passive, box-checking exercise, but rather as a proactive, behaviorally informed action that seeks to anticipate and mitigate misconduct before it escalates. This shift in regulatory focus recognizes that effective oversight must account not only for what individuals do but why they do it. Modern-day frameworks emphasize cultural dynamics, incentive structures, and the cognitive biases that influence ethical judgment.

By integrating behavioral psychology (as introduced in Chap. 4) with the structural frameworks of compliance (outlined in Chap. 5), financial institutions can create more resilient systems, ones that are capable of detecting early warning signs, curbing irrational decision-making, and reinforcing ethical conduct in real time. The following discussion explores how the lessons learned from past scandals, when reinterpreted through the lens of behavioral finance and ethics, inform the ongoing transformation of compliance in the U.S. financial services profession.

Countering Overconfidence with the Fiduciary and Best-Interest Standards

Overconfidence and self-interest biases sometimes lead advisors to prioritize personal gain over client welfare. Consider again the case of Bernie Madoff. No one better exhibited an exaggerated belief in their ability to sustain a fraud indefinitely than did Madoff. His ability to continuously attract new investors to pay returns to earlier investors fed Madoff's overconfidence. His ability to attract new capital also led regulators to underestimate the systemic risks inherent in his fraudulent strategies. Overconfidence, common among professional advisors, leads to irrational judgments where someone overestimates their control and predictive accuracy, escalating minor ethical lapses into large-scale fraud through a "slippery slope" of rationalizations. Complementing this is a self-interest bias. Many unethical people, like Madoff, focus on personal ambition and financial benefits at the expense of client interests. They do this by exploiting regulatory gaps and client trust to perpetuate a scheme.[32] Academic research in behavioral finance underscores how these intertwined biases contribute to distorted decision-making, where self-serving motivations override ethical considerations, ultimately eroding market integrity and necessitating stronger oversight mechanisms.

The Investment Advisers Act of 1940 established what is known as the fiduciary duty, later reinforced by the Dodd-Frank Act (2010) and Regulation Best Interest (Reg BI) (2020).[33] The fiduciary standard compels advisors who charge a fee for services to always place a client's interests above their own. Alternatively, broker-dealers and broker representatives must act in the best interests of clients. Both rules work to counter the overconfidence bias by mandating structured decision-making that emphasizes stringent forecasting procedures, external information gathering, and transparent communication to mitigate irrational self-assurance. For example, many large brokerage firms follow stringent know your customer (KYC) systems with behavioral nudges, such as prompts for portfolio reviews and stop orders to protect against losses. KYC helps counter overconfidence by encouraging more deliberate and evidence-based recommendations based on client goals rather than impulsive judgments. Practice standards today require advisors to document suitability for complex products and use client relationship summaries (CRS) to mitigate the self-interest bias and offset self-attribution bias, where individuals attribute successes to personal skills and failures to external factors.

Combating Ethical Fading Through Transparency and Disclosure

Ethical fading is a psychological process involving self-deception where individuals subconsciously suppress the ethical implications of their actions. By suppressing subjective outcome assessments, people allow themselves to behave unethically while maintaining a positive self-image. Ethical fading may have driven Enron's accounting fraud in 2001, where executives rationalized manipulative practices like off-balance-sheet entities as mere business strategies, obscuring the moral dimensions of misleading shareholders and other stakeholders. Similarly, in the FTX collapse that happened in 2022, ethical fading was compounded by a self-serving bias.[34] In the case of FTX, self-serving led to the misappropriation of $10 billion in customer funds.

Regulatory systems can be used to address ethical fading. The Securities Act of 1933 and the Sarbanes-Oxley Act (SOX) of 2002 require certified financial statements to counteract biases. The regulatory frameworks impose strict disclosure standards that highlight ethical considerations and help prevent the subconscious erosion of moral accountability in corporate reporting. Additionally, post-FTX cryptocurrency disclosure rules enhance financial transparency and regulatory inspections, which help disrupt self-deceptive rationalizations and address biases, such as overconfidence, in unregulated environments.[35]

Today, for advisors who are regulated by the SEC or at the state level are required to file Form ADV Part 2, which outlines their fees and any conflicts of interest.[36] The filing process aims to reduce ethical fading by explicitly acknowledging material conflicts and encouraging advisors to address potential self-serving biases that may result in prioritizing their personal benefits over client welfare. Nearly all brokerage firms utilize digital dashboards to highlight these disclosures. Dashboards combat ethical fading by incorporating behavioral nudges that provide visible, real-time reminders of conflicts. This approach promotes accountability and decreases the likelihood of subconscious ethical oversights.

Behavioral nudges (i.e., subtle interventions that guide decision-making without restricting choice) have become an increasingly used tool in promoting ethical financial behavior, particularly in environments where complex or high-risk products are involved. One prominent example is the use of mandatory risk warnings for highly volatile assets. These disclosures are more than regulatory formalities. When designed effectively, disclosures function as behavioral guardrails that prompt reflection, reduce impulsivity, and enhance client understanding.

Behavioral nudges are rooted in psychology and are specifically tailored to counteract cognitive biases that frequently undermine sound judgment. For instance, optimism bias can lead individuals to underestimate the likelihood of negative outcomes. Similarly, self-serving bias allows investors to interpret ambiguous information in ways that reinforce their existing beliefs or desired outcomes, often leading them to minimize potential risks or overestimate their ability to manage them.

By clearly framing risks through plain language, visual cues, and comparative data, cognitive, behavioral, and psychological nudges help disrupt common biases. Rather than allowing clients to rely solely on emotional intuition or selective interpretation, regulatory interventions can be used to reframe decision contexts in a way that focuses on potential consequences. In doing so, regulatory nudges enhance financial literacy, promote realistic expectations, and reduce susceptibility to misinformation or manipulative marketing.

Importantly, regulatory nudges also protect financial professionals by aligning transparency with ethical duty. When nudges are embedded into client communications and product disclosures, they reduce the risk of misrepresentation (whether intentional or unintentional) and support an advisor's fiduciary responsibility to act in the client's best interest.

In this sense, behavioral nudges transform transparency from a passive requirement into an active component of ethical financial planning. Nudges empower clients to make informed decisions while reinforcing a compliance culture that prioritizes clarity, honesty, and psychological insight. As financial products grow more complex and investor behavior becomes increasingly shaped by emotion and cognitive shortcuts, the strategic use of behavioral nudges will remain a critical element of modern, client-centered financial practice.

Disrupting Herd Behavior Through Anti-fraud and AML/KYC Measures

Herd behavior and psychological rationalization are powerful drivers of financial misconduct. These cognitive and social biases enable schemes to persist well beyond what rational analysis would justify. The Madoff Ponzi scheme is a striking example. Despite numerous red flags—most notably, improbably consistent returns over decades—advisors and investors continued to participate. This persistence was primarily due to herd behavior, where individuals conformed to what appeared to be socially validated choices. Madoff's reputation, bolstered by endorsements within trusted affinity groups and perceived institutional legitimacy, fueled a false sense of security. Investors took comfort in the widespread participation of others—an effect rooted in social proof—rather than conducting independent due diligence.

Compounding this was rationalization, a psychological mechanism where individuals reduce cognitive dissonance by justifying questionable decisions. Many investors convinced themselves that Madoff's strategy was legitimate simply because so many others, including sophisticated institutions, had invested. The herding effect created an echo chamber of misplaced trust and perceived low risk, despite warning signs. These dynamics illustrate how collective irrationality, amplified by emotional reasoning and status quo reinforcement, can override both regulatory vigilance and ethical judgment.

To counter these behaviors, modern compliance systems increasingly integrate robust anti-money laundering (AML) and know your customer (KYC) protocols. Following the Patriot Act of 2001, regulatory oversight expanded significantly, particularly through enforcement of the Bank Secrecy Act (BSA) and the work of the Financial Crimes Enforcement Network (FinCEN). These frameworks compel financial institutions to implement stringent client identification, transaction monitoring, and suspicious activity reporting standards. These are essential tools in uncovering hidden financial networks and preventing illicit transactions from slipping through regulatory loopholes.

The collapse of Archegos Capital Management in 2021 illustrates the consequences of unchecked psychological biases, particularly confirmation bias and overconfidence. Archegos founder Bill Hwang used total return swaps to build highly leveraged positions without triggering standard disclosure requirements. As losses mounted, Hwang selectively interpreted favorable market signals to reinforce his strategies while dismissing contrary evidence. His overreliance on a narrow set of convictions, combined with opaque derivative exposures, led to a rapid and costly unwinding that caught central counterparties off guard and exposed significant gaps in risk surveillance.

In response to these types of risks, financial services firms are increasingly adopting AI-driven compliance systems that detect behavioral patterns and anomalies at scale. These tools analyze large volumes of transaction data to identify suspicious spikes in activity, deviations from typical trading behaviors, and signs of collective irrationality. For example, sudden surges in coordinated investments or rapid asset reallocations may signal herd-driven decision-making. At the same time, repeated patterns inconsistent with known market indicators can reveal overconfidence bias or fraudulent intent.

Technological enhancements not only strengthen compliance but also serve as early warning systems by disrupting herd behavior and behavioral biases before they escalate into systemic risks. By embedding behavioral analysis into AML/KYC systems, financial institutions can move from reactive enforcement to proactive prevention, countering the psychological forces that often enable fraud, misconduct, and market instability.[37] Furthermore, these measures deter illicit financial behavior by making accountability unavoidable. Non-compliance, as in Robinhood's $70 million FINRA fine in 2021 for lax KYC, often stems from optimism bias and overconfidence in platform scalability, where executives underestimated regulatory risks and prioritized rapid user growth over thorough due diligence, leading to inadequate customer verification and heightened vulnerability to fraud.[38]

Overcoming Groupthink Through Ethical Culture and Governance

Groupthink is a psychological phenomenon where the desire for consensus and harmony within a cohesive group overrides realistic appraisal of alternatives, leading to flawed decision-making.[39] Groupthink combined with pressure to exceed sales targets was evident in the Wells Fargo fake accounts scandal of 2016. Wells Fargo established aggressive sales quotas that fostered an environment of conformity bias, demonstrating how individuals yield to majority opinions even when incorrect.[40] Modern governance counters groupthink by requiring ongoing ethics training and encouraging whistleblower programs that promote critical thinking and dissent to disrupt groupthink dynamics.[41] For example, Dodd-Frank's whistleblower protections have resulted in hundreds of millions of dollars being distributed to ethical employees every year.[42] Additionally, social incentives that encourage reporting by providing anonymity and rewards work to counter groupthink's illusion of unanimity and self-censorship (i.e., a collective denial of perpetuated violations). Behavioral strategies, like anonymous hotlines and independent compliance officers, make ethical culture a measurable asset by facilitating safe channels for voicing concerns, thus reducing conformity biases, such as the tendency to align with perceived group standards to avoid conflict. Regulatory frameworks enhance client trust through proactive mitigation of collective irrationality.

Mitigating Complacency in Global and Technological Integration

It is important to note that overreliance on technology can foster ethical complacency, as seen in Citadel Securities' $7 million fine in 2023 for algorithm-trading errors stemming from a coding flaw in its automated system.[43] In the Citadel Securities case, automation bias may have led traders to excessively trust the system's outputs without sufficient verification. By ignoring potential discrepancies and underestimating error risks in high-speed executions, traders at the firm became complacent. This complacency ultimately cost clients and the firm millions of dollars.

In response to repeated financial crises and market failures, global reforms such as Basel III, MiFID II, and recent U.S. cryptocurrency oversight following the collapse of FTX have emerged to establish more consistent, cross-border regulatory standards. These initiatives are not only structural, but they are also grounded in behavioral finance, with the primary aim being to reduce the presence of psychological biases that often drive reckless decision-making.[44]

Basel III tackles overconfidence bias within the banking sector by requiring higher capital buffers and stricter leverage ratios. The Basel III measures are designed to prevent excessive risk-taking, particularly during economic booms when institutions tend to underestimate potential downturns. By enforcing more conservative financial cushions, Basel III seeks to temper the overly optimistic risk assessments that contributed to past banking crises.[45]

Meanwhile, MiFID II (the Markets in Financial Instruments Directive II) addresses behavioral distortions in investment decision-making, specifically herd behavior and confirmation bias. Through enhanced transparency requirements and stricter investor protection rules, MiFID II reduces the likelihood that market participants will unthinkingly follow crowd behavior or selectively interpret data that aligns with dominant market narratives. The directive promotes a more disciplined, evidence-based approach to trading and investment analysis.

Advancements in regulatory technology (RegTech) have further strengthened compliance efforts by embedding behavioral nudges into automated systems. For instance, Nasdaq's Verafin (a leading anti-money laundering [AML] platform) monitors transaction data in real time to detect anomalies. The system helps combat complacency bias, which occurs when firms become overly reliant on routine processes and fail to notice emerging fraud patterns. Verafin's alerts prompt immediate investigation, maintaining vigilance where human attention may lapse. Similarly, Bloomberg's ESG Terminal supports accurate Environmental, Social, and Governance (ESG) reporting by offering robust, real-time data tracking. This system combats confirmation bias by presenting users with a full spectrum of performance metrics (both positive and negative), which encourages objective analysis rather than the selective acceptance of only favorable data.

However, the growing reliance on automation comes with its own risks. Most notably, automation bias, where users defer uncritically to algorithmic outputs and ignore their own judgment or oversight responsibilities. This overdependence can lead to blind spots, particularly when systems are assumed to be infallible.[46] To prevent this, human oversight must remain central to any compliance or investment framework. For example, advisors managing portfolios should go beyond system-generated ratings and conduct independent ethical evaluations to ensure that sustainability claims are valid and meaningful. Doing so helps counter status quo bias, which can lead firms to maintain outdated investment practices simply because they are familiar or widely accepted, rather than actively reevaluating their ethical and financial relevance.

Challenges and Trends in the Regulatory Environment

The evolution of financial regulations faces ongoing challenges influenced by technological advancements, globalization, and societal expectations. Drawing from historical lessons learned from previous crises and scandals, regulators and financial services firms strive to maintain strong and ethical standards. The following discussion examines some challenges and trends in the regulatory environment with the goal of providing practical insights for financial professionals when navigating an ever-changing regulatory environment.

Adapting to technological innovation requires learning from historical events, such as the 1929 stock market crash, where a lack of oversight led to significant risks and negative global outcomes. Today, the rise of fintech, including cryptocurrencies and artificial intelligence, poses similar challenges, as these innovations can outpace existing regulations. In response, regulators are developing frameworks such as the SEC's guidelines for digital assets and new rules for AI-driven trading as a way to balance innovation with consumer protection. For financial advisors, this means staying informed about fintech regulations and utilizing RegTech standards to ensure compliance (see Chaps 14 and 15 for more details about RegTech and cross-national regulatory frameworks).

Global regulatory harmonization continues to be a priority across regulatory jurisdictions. The dangers and outcomes associated with the global financial crisis, which was driven in part by uncoordinated regulatory systems, led to initiatives like Basel III. Currently, financial advisors must navigate conflicting regulations across borders such as the differences between GDPR in Europe and CCPA in the United States.[47] Today, firms need to implement global compliance systems, drawing from insights shared in Chap. 5 on global frameworks. The expected outcome is ensuring fair treatment across all jurisdictions as a way to build client trust (see Chap. 11 for more details about cross-border regulations).

Environmental, Social, and Governance (ESG) initiatives, although not as highly followed in today's investing environment, have created compliance issues and regulatory actions to protect investors. Regulators are increasingly mandating ESG-type disclosures and imposing new duties on advisors who incorporate sustainability into client portfolios. Increasing regulatory oversight necessitates aligning investments with ESG standards while reflecting lessons on transparency from history.

Finally, cybersecurity and data privacy concerns resonate with historical wrongdoing. Modern data breaches pose similar threats to advisors, firms, and the economy. Firms must now invest in secure systems, echoing past needs for consumer protection as discussed in Chap. 10. Doing so safeguards privacy and fulfills fiduciary obligations. Finally, behavioral and cultural shifts point to lessons learned from scandals like Wells Fargo's fake account fiasco, where an unethical corporate culture undermined compliance. Today, firms must foster ethical environments despite profit pressures through training and committed leadership. Financial advisors play a crucial role in promoting these practices.

Chapter Summary

The history of financial regulation is a dynamic response to market failures, systemic market crises, and ethical breaches. Regulations are designed to safeguard consumers, enhance market stability, and uphold professional integrity in financial services. The establishment of the U.S. Securities and Exchange Commission (SEC) in the 1930s, following the 1929 market crash, marked a foundational step in formalizing oversight to ensure transparency and protect investors. Subsequent crises, such as Charles Ponzi's infamous scheme in the 1920s, Enron's accounting fraud in 2001, Bernard Madoff's multi-billion-dollar Ponzi scheme uncovered in 2008, and Wells Fargo's unauthorized account scandal in 2016, exposed persistent vulnerabilities stemming from ethical lapses and inadequate regulatory frameworks. These events catalyzed significant legislative reforms, including the Sarbanes-Oxley Act of 2002, which strengthened corporate governance and financial reporting standards, and the Dodd-Frank Wall Street Reform and Consumer Protection Act of 2010, which introduced robust consumer protections and systemic risk oversight. More recently, Regulation Best Interest (Reg BI), implemented in 2020, elevated the standard of care for broker-dealers, mandating that client interests supersede financial incentives.

Historical regulatory and compliance failures underscore recurring themes, such as the critical need for transparency, rigorous oversight, and a culture of ethical accountability. Regulatory frameworks have driven the adoption of modern compliance mechanisms, such as the fiduciary and best-interest standards, anti-money laundering (AML) and know your customer (KYC) protocols, and enhanced whistleblower protections, which empower stakeholders to report misconduct without fear of retaliation. As financial markets evolve with the rise of fintech, ESG considerations, and global interconnectedness, these lessons remain vital. Financial professionals must navigate an increasingly complex regulatory landscape by committing to continuous education, ethical decision-making, and proactive regulatory compliance. By internalizing these principles, financial services firms and professionals can not only mitigate risks but also foster trust, promote market stability, and advance the profession's ethical mandate, which aligns with the broader objectives of integrity and accountability in financial services.

Chapter Resources

- Bank Secrecy Act (BSA): https://www.fincen.gov/resources/statutes-and-regulations/bank-secrecy-act
- Banking Act of 1933 (Glass-Steagall): https://www.federalreservehistory.org/essays/glass-steagall-act
- Basel III: https://www.bis.org/bcbs/basel3.htm
- CCPA (State of California): https://www.oag.ca.gov/privacy/ccpa
- Dodd-Frank Wall Street Reform and Consumer Protection Act: https://www.fdic.gov/system/files/2024-07/ar10doddfrank.pdf
- Financial Crimes Enforcement Network (FinCEN): https://www.fincen.gov/

- Financial Institutions Reform, Recovery, and Enforcement Act of 1989: https://www.congress.gov/bill/101st-congress/house-bill/1278
- GDPR in Europe: https://gdpr.eu/what-is-gdpr/
- Investment Advisers Act of 1940: https://www.govinfo.gov/content/pkg/COMPS-1878/pdf/COMPS-1878.pdf
- Markets in Financial Instruments Directive II (MiFID II): https://business.bofa.com/en-us/content/mifid-ii-regulation-summary-requirements.html
- Patriot Act of 2001: https://www.justice.gov/archive/ll/what_is_the_patriot_act.pdf
- Sarbanes-Oxley Act (2002): https://www.dol.gov/agencies/oalj/PUBLIC/WHISTLEBLOWER/REFERENCES/STATUTES/SARBANES_OXLEY_ACT_OF_2002
- Securities Act of 1933: https://www.sec.gov/rules-regulations/statutes-regulations#secact1933
- Securities Exchange Act of 1934: https://www.sec.gov/rules-regulations/statutes-regulations#secexact1934

Notes

[1]Bilginsoy, C. (2014). A history of financial crises: Dreams and follies of expectations. Routledge.

[2]Shiller, R. J. (2005). *Irrational Exuberance*: (Second Edition). Princeton University Press. http://www.jstor.org/stable/j.ctt7st4s

[3]https://www.historic-uk.com/HistoryUK/HistoryofEngland/South-Sea-Bubble/

[4]National Archives. Congress Investigates: The Senate Investigation of the Stock Exchange during the Great Depression (Pecora Investigation). https://www.archives.gov/legislative/resources/education/pecora

[5]Maues, J. Banking Act of 1933 (Glass-Steagall). Federal Reserve History. https://www.federalreservehistory.org/essays/glass-steagall-act

[6]Rose, T. A. (1997). 11B. Report from the Federal Deposit Insurance Corporation: National Deposit Insurance Has Worked to Promote Banking Stability. IMF eLibrary. https://www.elibrary.imf.org/display/book/9781557755032/ch016.xml

[7]Although the North American Securities Administrators Association (NASAA) adopted a model rule in 2025 that prohibits broker-dealer agents from using the titles "advisor" or "adviser" unless they are also registered as investment adviser representatives, in this book, a broad definition of financial advisor is retained. A financial advisor advises clients on managing their finances to help them achieve specific financial goals. This advice can cover many areas, including investment management, retirement planning, estate planning, tax planning, insurance needs, debt management, and wealth building.

[8]Securities and Exchange Commission Historical Society. *Timeline 1940s*. https://www.sechistorical.org/museum/timeline/1940-timeline.php

[9]Maues, J. Banking Act of 1933 (Glass-Steagall). Federal Reserve History. https://www.federalreservehistory.org/essays/glass-steagall-act

[10]Pitchard, A. C., & Thompson, R. (2023). *A History of Securities Law in the Supreme Court,* A History of Securities Law in the Supreme Court. https://corpgov.law.harvard.edu/

[11]Securities and Exchange Commission Historical Society. *In the Midst of Revolution: The SEC, 1973–1981. Foundation for Renewal.* https://www.sechistorical.org/museum/galleries/rev/rev02e.php

[12]Sherman, M. (2009). *A Short History of Financial Deregulation in the United States.* Center for Economic and Policy Research. https://cepr.net/publications/a-short-history-of-financial-deregulation-in-the-united-states/

[13]FDIC. (2023). *History of the Eighties - Lessons for the Future - Volume 1*, FDIC. https://www.fdic.gov/publications/history-eighties-lessons-future-volume-1

[14]Shepherd, J. (1992). *The Liability of Officers and Directors Under the Financial Institutions Reform, Recovery and Enforcement Act of 1989*, 90 MICH. L. REV. 1119. https://repository.law.umich.edu/mlr/vol90/iss5/7

[15]Wilmarth, A. E. (2017). *The Road to Repeal of the Glass-Steagall Act*. GWWU Law School Public Law Research Paper No. 2017–61. https://scholarship.law.gwu.edu/cgi/viewcontent.cgi?article=2556&context=faculty_publications

[16]Partnoy, F. (2009). *Infectious Greed: How Deceit and Risk Corrupted the Financial Markets*. PublicAffairs

[17]Avgouleas, E. (2012). *Governance of Global Financial Markets: The Law, the Economics, the Politics*. Cambridge University Press.

[18]Peregrine, M. W., & Elson, C. W. (2022). The Important Legacy of the Sarbanes-Oxley Act. Harvard Law School Forum on Corporate Governance. https://corpgov.law.harvard.edu/

[19]Berman, N. (2023). What Is the Dodd-Frank Act? Council on Foreign Relations. https://www.cfr.org/backgrounder/what-dodd-frank-act

[20]BIS. *History of the Basel Committee*. https://www.bis.org/bcbs/history.htm

[21]Moloney, N. (2023). EU financial market regulation a decade from the financial-crisis-era reforms: crisis, uncertainty, and capacity. *Yearbook of European Law, 42*, 169–209, https://doi.org/10.1093/yel/yead008

[22]Zuckoff, M. (2005). *Ponzi's Scheme: The True Story of a Financial Legend*. Random House.

[23]SEC (2013). *The Laws That Govern the Securities Industry*. https://www.sec.gov/about/laws.shtml

[24]McLean, B., & Elkind, P. (2003). *The Smartest Guys in the Room: The Amazing Rise and Scandalous Fall of Enron*. Portfolio.

[25]U.S. Congress (2002). *Sarbanes-Oxley Act of 2002*. Public Law 107–204.

[26]Markopolos, H. (2010). *No One Would Listen: A True Financial Thriller*. Wiley.

[27]SEC (2025). *Whistleblower Protections*. https://www.sec.gov/enforcement-litigation/whistleblower-program/whistleblower-protections

[28]AML/KYC protocols refer to key compliance procedures in the financial industry designed to prevent financial crimes, such as money laundering, fraud, and terrorist financing. These two frameworks work together to ensure that financial institutions understand who their clients are and monitor their activities appropriately.

[29]CFPB (2016). *Consumer Financial Protection Bureau Fines Wells Fargo $100 Million for Widespread Illegal Practice of Secretly Opening Unauthorized Accounts*. https://www.consumerfinance.gov/about-us/newsroom/consumer-financial-protection-bureau-fines-wells-fargo-100-million-widespread-illegal-practice-secretly-opening-unauthorized-accounts/

[30]U.S. House of Representatives (2020). *The Real Wells Fargo: Board & Management Failures, Consumer Abuses, and Ineffective Regulatory Oversight*. https://www.congress.gov/116/meeting/house/110719/documents/HHRG-116-BA00-20200311-SD003.pdf

[31]FTX, once a leading cryptocurrency exchange, collapsed in November 2022 after it was revealed that the company had misused customer funds. FTX's founder, Sam Bankman-Fried, allegedly diverted billions of dollars in client assets to his trading firm, Alameda Research, to cover losses and fund risky bets. The company lacked basic financial controls and governance, and when concerns about solvency emerged, a sudden wave of customer withdrawals triggered a liquidity crisis. FTX filed for bankruptcy, wiping out billions in customer and investor funds. The collapse led to criminal charges against Bankman-Fried and intensified global calls for stricter crypto regulation. Similarly, Archegos Capital Management, a family office run by Bill Hwang, imploded in March 2021 after highly leveraged bets on a few concentrated stocks unraveled. Archegos used total

return swaps—derivatives that allowed it to take massive positions with borrowed money—without triggering public disclosure requirements. When stock prices fell and margin calls were unmet, major banks rapidly sold off Archegos' holdings, resulting in more than $10 billion in losses across global financial institutions. The failure exposed significant lapses in risk management and highlighted the dangers of opacity and leverage in loosely regulated investment entities.

[32]Nobel C. (2016). *Bernie Madoff Explains Himself.* Working Knowledge, Harvard Business School. https://www.library.hbs.edu/working-knowledge/bernie-madoff-explains-himself

[33]FINRA/SEC Regulation Best Interest (Reg BI). FINRA https://www.finra.org/rules-guidance/key-topics/regulation-best-interest

[34]Self-serving biases occur when decision-makers interpret information in ways that favor their own interests such as prioritizing personal gains over fiduciary duties.

[35]McDeviott, A. (2025). *The rise, fall, and rise of crypto: Lessons from FTX amidst a changing regulatory landscape.* International Compliance Association. https://www.int-comp.org/insight/the-rise-fall-and-rise-of-crypto-lessons-from-ftx-amidst-a-changing-regulatory-landscape/

[36]https://www.sec.gov/about/forms/formadv-part2.pdf

[37]FinCEN. (2023). *FinCEN Year in Review for Fiscal Year 2023* https://www.fincen.gov/news/news-releases/fincen-year-review-fiscal-year-2023

[38]https://democrats-financialservices.house.gov/news/documentsingle.aspx?DocumentID=409578

[39]Janis, I. L., (1982). *Groupthink: Psychological Studies of Policy Decisions and Fiascoes*, Second Edition, New York: Houghton Mifflin.

[40]CFPB. (2016). Consumer Financial Protection Bureau Fines Wells Fargo $100 Million for Widespread Illegal Practice of Secretly Opening Unauthorized Accounts. https://www.consumerfinance.gov/about-us/newsroom/consumer-financial-protection-bureau-fines-wells-fargo-100-million-widespread-illegal-practice-secretly-opening-unauthorized-accounts/

[41]Morgan Stanley (2025). Code of Conduct 2025. https://www.morganstanley.com/about-us-governance/code-of-conduct

[42]U.S. SEC. Whistleblower Program. https://www.sec.gov/enforcement-litigation/whistleblower-program

[43]U.S. SEC. SEC Charges Citadel Securities for Violating Order Marking Requirements of Short Sale Regulations. https://www.sec.gov/newsroom/press-releases/2023-192

[44]https://www.bis.org/publ/work591.htm

[45]https://verafin.com/

[46]Krokidam, S., Makrychoriti, P., & Spyrou, S. (2020). Monetary policy and herd behavior: International evidence. *Journal of Economic Behavior & Organization, 170*, 386–417. https://doi.org/10.1016/j.jebo.2019.12.018

[47]The General Data Protection Regulation (GDPR) and the California Consumer Privacy Act (CCPA) are landmark data privacy laws designed to protect individuals' personal information. GDPR, enacted by the European Union in 2018, sets strict rules for how organizations collect, process, and store personal data of EU residents, emphasizing user consent, transparency, and rights like data access and deletion. It applies globally to entities handling EU data, with hefty fines for non-compliance. The CCPA, effective in California since 2020, grants state residents similar rights, including the ability to know what personal data businesses collect, opt out of data sales, and request data deletion. While GDPR is broader and applies across industries, CCPA focuses on consumer-facing businesses with specific revenue or data-processing thresholds. Both laws aim to enhance user control over personal data, though they differ in scope, jurisdiction, and enforcement mechanisms.

7 Risk Mitigation as a Foundation for Compliance

Chapter Outcomes
This chapter focuses on helping learners develop the ability to:

1. Identify and assess potential compliance risks that could impact the operations, reputation, or legal standing of financial services firms and organizations.
2. Implement targeted mitigation strategies to reduce exposure to compliance risks and strengthen organizational safeguards.
3. Integrate risk management with compliance functions to create a cohesive framework that aligns regulatory requirements with strategic objectives.
4. Evaluate the importance of a holistic approach to risk management, understanding that it should not be treated as a stand-alone process but as an integral part of organizational compliance.

Introduction

Traditionally, financial services firms, regardless of size, treated risk management and regulatory compliance as separate functions. Risk management focused on financial or operational risks, while compliance dealt with regulatory obligations and ensuring that financial advisors were compiling with state and federal regulations. Today, these two areas are deeply interconnected with non-compliance itself being a major risk. Organizations that fail at compliance expose themselves to substantial risks, while organizations that fail at risk management struggle to remain compliant, which can be costly in terms of dollar fines and strikes to firm and

Note: This chapter was copyedited using Grammarly™ and generative AI tools to enhance clarity, grammar, and overall readability. While these tools provided suggestions and assistance in refining the text, the ideas, content, and arguments presented remain the sole work and responsibility of the authors. Any errors or inaccuracies in the final version are also the authors' responsibility.

W. Heo, J. E. Grable, *Ethics and Compliance in Financial Services*,
https://doi.org/10.1007/978-3-032-14449-2_7

advisor reputations. The most resilient companies create an integrated framework where compliance is part of the broader risk strategy.

This chapter explores the critical functions of risk management and regulatory compliance within financial services firms, focusing on how these tasks are carried out at the organizational level. Risk management is the structured process by which firms identify, assess, and respond to threats that could interfere with achieving strategic objectives. Compliance, by contrast, ensures that the firm operates within applicable laws, regulations, professional standards, and internal policies. Throughout this chapter, the discussion will illustrate these concepts with real-world examples, provide guidance on how firms integrate risk and compliance practices, and offer practical steps firms can use to increase the effectiveness of their risk management and compliance obligations. This includes describing risk registers, designing mitigation strategies, and evaluating the effectiveness of integrated compliance frameworks.

What Is Risk Management?

Risk management is the process of identifying, assessing, and responding to threats that could disrupt an organization's goals.[1] These threats, often called *risks*, can take many forms, but most commonly, risks manifest as financial losses, legal penalties, operational breakdowns, reputational damage, or strategic missteps. Effective risk management does not eliminate risks entirely; instead, risk management equips organizations to anticipate problems and minimize negative consequences.

What Is Compliance?

Alternatively, compliance is the process of ensuring that a financial services firm follows the laws, regulations, professional standards, and internal policies that govern its operations.[2] While risk management focuses on anticipating and controlling uncertainty, compliance ensures that organizations operate within established rules.

Perspective

As the following case narrative illustrates, risk management and compliance are two sides of the same coin. In this well-known case (one that is described in greater detail in other chapters), the U.S. Securities and Exchange Commission (SEC) charged Wells Fargo & Co. with materially misleading investors regarding the efficacy of its core business strategy, specifically its Community Bank's cross-selling model.[3] This enforcement action stemmed from a period during which the bank engaged in widespread misconduct, including the creation of millions of unauthorized accounts and the aggressive sale of superfluous financial products to unsuspecting customers. As part of a broader $3 billion resolution with both the SEC and the

Department of Justice, Wells Fargo consented to a $500 million civil penalty, which will be allocated to compensate defrauded investors.

According to the SEC's findings, between 2012 and 2016, Wells Fargo made repeated public assertions about the success of its cross-sell strategy (the sale of additional financial products to existing customers). Cross-selling became a central driver of revenue and earnings growth for the firm. However, the SEC determined that this metric was artificially inflated by accounts and services that were either unused, unnecessary, or fraudulently opened. The bank's internal sales practices, which spanned from 2002 to 2016, were found to be fundamentally inconsistent with its public representations of a needs-based selling approach.

The SEC emphasized that Wells Fargo's use of deceptive performance metrics misled investors about the integrity and sustainability of the firm's business model. The SEC concluded that the bank violated the anti-fraud provisions of the Securities Exchange Act of 1934. The SEC ordered Wells Fargo to cease and desist from future violations. A $500 million penalty was distributed to affected customers through the SEC's Fair Fund mechanism. The total cost to Wells Fargo was approximately $3 billion.

The Wells Fargo scandal serves as a prime example of how deficiencies in risk management and compliance can lead to severe reputational, financial, and legal consequences for financial institutions and their advisors. In terms of risk management, the case exposed significant operational risks stemming from aggressive sales targets and incentive structures that fostered a high-risk environment for misconduct. These operational failures were inadequately monitored, amplifying the damage. The scandal also inflicted substantial reputational harm, eroding customer trust, fueling investor skepticism, and triggering long-term financial impacts like customer attrition and heightened regulatory scrutiny.

Strategically, Wells Fargo's cross-selling strategy, once a celebrated growth driver, became a liability when fraudulent activities inflated its success. The case shows the dangers of misaligning strategic goals with ethical execution. On the compliance front, the firm's misleading disclosures about its cross-selling strategy violated anti-fraud provisions, highlighting the critical need for transparent communication in investor relations and regulatory filings. Weak internal controls failed to detect or prevent fraudulent account openings and unethical sales practices, while a culture of non-compliance, driven by unrealistic sales goals, normalized unethical behavior.

The case has important lessons for financial advisors and financial services firms. For example, a lesson learned is the importance of thorough due diligence when evaluating institutional practices. Due diligence ensures compensation structures do not incentivize misconduct. Other lessons include the implementation of oversight through audits, whistleblower protections, compliance training, and prioritizing transparency and fiduciary responsibility to maintain client trust. Ultimately, the Wells Fargo debacle underscores the notion that risk management and regulatory compliance are not mere regulatory requirements but foundational pillars of sustainable and ethical financial practices.

A Firm-Level Risk Management and Compliance Structure

In a medium to large financial services company, the risk management and compliance department or office is typically structured as part of a broader Governance, Risk, and Compliance (GRC) framework,[4] often operating as interconnected but distinct functions to ensure comprehensive oversight of risks, regulatory adherence, and ethical practices.[5] This setup promotes a centralized approach to identifying, assessing, mitigating, and reporting on various risks, such as operational, credit, market, liquidity, and reputational, while ensuring compliance with laws, regulations, and internal policies.[6]

The department usually reports to senior leadership, including the Chief Executive Officer (CEO) or Board of Directors. The department may employ dozens to hundreds of professionals depending on the firm's size, complexity, and regulatory environment. The risk management and compliance office often follows models like the "four lines of defense," where business units form the first line (owning day-to-day risks), risk and compliance teams serve as the second line (monitoring and challenging), internal auditing acts as the third line (independent assurance), and external auditors or regulators provide the fourth line (external oversight).[7] The office fosters a culture of proactive risk awareness and ethical behavior, integrating technology for data analytics, reporting, and monitoring to support decision-making.

The risk management side of a risk management and compliance department is commonly led by the Chief Risk Officer (CRO), who oversees enterprise-wide risk strategy, ensures alignment with business objectives, and chairs risk committees to facilitate cross-functional coordination.[8] Reporting directly to the CRO are specialized teams, including Risk Assessment Analysts, who research and evaluate current and emerging risks (e.g., market volatility, cybersecurity threats, or geopolitical factors) using tools like stress testing and scenario analysis to quantify potential impacts and recommend mitigation strategies.[9] Market Risk Analysts focus on assessing and modeling exposures to financial market fluctuations, such as interest rate changes or asset price volatility, while Credit Risk Analysts evaluate borrower default risks and set credit limits. Operational Risk Managers handle risks from internal processes, systems, or human errors, often developing indicative measures like error rates or downtime metrics to track and report issues. Risk Reporting Specialists compile data into comprehensive reports on risk profiles, sales changes, and framework performance, distributing them to management, regulators, and stakeholders to support informed decisions. Additionally, Internal Auditors, who may operate independently but collaborate with the risk team, conduct periodic evaluations of controls, processes, and adherence to policies, recommending improvements to enhance efficiency and mitigate vulnerabilities.

On the compliance side, the Chief Compliance Officer (CCO) heads the function, focusing on regulatory changes and internal policy enforcement. The CCO serves as the ultimate authority on compliance matters, often with direct access to the board for independence.[10] Compliance Managers oversee specific areas, such as anti-money laundering (AML) or know your customer (KYC) protocols, ensuring teams align activities with legal requirements and industry standards. Compliance Analysts or Officers monitor day-to-day operations, conduct risk assessments, review transactions for irregularities, and support audits to detect non-compliance, while also developing training programs to educate employees on ethical standards and regulations. Ethics and Compliance Coordinators handle investigations into misconduct, manage whistleblower programs, and promote a culture of integrity by reviewing policies for ethical alignment and providing guidance on conflicts of interest. Legal Counsel or Regulatory Specialists advise on legal risks, interpret regulations, and engage with external regulators, while IT Security Officers focus on cybersecurity compliance, implementing data protection measures and ensuring adherence to standards like General Date Protection Regulation (GDPR) or the Sarbanes-Oxley Act (SOX).[11] In integrated operations, roles like GRC Analysts support both risk and compliance by managing software tools for data collection, reporting, and assessments, bridging the two functions to enhance cohesive oversight.[12]

Table 7.1 illustrates the structure of a typical risk management and compliance department in a medium to large financial services firm. The table highlights the key people involved in the process, their primary responsibilities, and their focus areas. Overall, the table captures the hierarchy and functions described, including both risk management and compliance teams, and highlights their integration within a GRC framework.

The diversity of roles and responsibilities shown in Table 7.1 illustrates the importance of risk management and compliance across the financial services sector. With this information in mind, the following discussion reviews some of the most common compliance risks faced by financial services firms and financial professionals. This is followed by a review of risk mitigation strategies and an overview of compliance issues.

Identifying and Assessing Compliance Risks

Compliance risks represent scenarios where an organization may fail to adhere to applicable laws, regulations, or internal policies, potentially leading to severe consequences such as financial penalties, operational disruptions, or reputational harm.[13] These risks manifest in various forms, each with distinct implications. Here are common examples:

- Legal and regulatory risks arise from non-compliance with industry-specific mandates, such as the Sarbanes-Oxley Act for financial reporting in publicly traded companies or the Health Insurance Portability and Accountability Act (HIPAA) for healthcare data protection, where violations can result in fines or legal action.
- Operational risks stem from inadequate adherence to internal processes, such as failing to implement proper data security protocols, which could lead to data breaches.

Table 7.1 Risk management and compliance department overview

Role	Primary responsibilities	Focus area
Chief Risk Officer (CRO)	Oversees enterprise-wide risk strategy, chairs risk committees, aligns risk with business goals	Risk strategy, governance, board reporting
Risk assessment analysts	Research and evaluate current/emerging risks, conduct stress tests and scenario analyses	Operational, market, credit, geopolitical risks
Market risk analysts	Assess and model exposures to market fluctuations (e.g., interest rates and asset prices)	Financial market volatility, hedging strategies
Credit risk analysts	Evaluate borrower default risks, set credit limits, monitor credit portfolios	Credit exposure, loan quality
Operational risk managers	Manage risks from internal processes, systems, or human errors, develop risk metrics	Process failures, system downtimes
Risk reporting specialists	Compile and distribute risk profile reports to management, regulators, and stakeholders	Risk data aggregation, reporting
Internal auditors	Conduct independent evaluations of controls and processes and recommend improvements	Assurance, control effectiveness
Chief Compliance Officer (CCO)	Oversees regulatory compliance, enforces policies, serves as board-level authority	Regulatory adherence, ethical oversight
Compliance managers	Oversee specific compliance areas (e.g., AML, KYC) and aligns operations with regulations	AML, KYC, regulatory standards
Compliance analysts/officers	Monitor operations, review transactions, support audits, and develop training programs	Transaction monitoring, training, audits
Ethics and compliance coordinators	Investigate misconduct, manage whistleblower programs, and ensure ethical policy alignment	Ethics, whistleblower support, investigations
Legal counsel/ regulatory specialists	Advise on legal risks, interpret regulations, and liaise with external regulators	Legal compliance, regulatory engagement
IT security officers	Implement cybersecurity measures and ensure compliance with data protection standards (e.g., GDPR, SOX)	Cybersecurity, data protection
GRC analysts	Manage GRC software tools; support data collection, reporting, and assessments for risk management and compliance	Integrated GRC oversight, analytics

- Financial and reporting risks involve inaccuracies in financial statements that could potentially trigger an audit or shareholder distrust.
- Reputational risks emerge when public perception of non-compliance, even without legal violation, damages stakeholder trust.

The following case example illustrates the importance of monitoring and compliance systems:

In 2012, JPMorgan Chase experienced a significant trading loss, widely known as the "London Whale" incident. The incident stemmed from highly leveraged derivatives positions taken by the bank's Chief Investment Office in London.[14] *The trades, intended to hedge credit risk, became so large and complex that they distorted market prices, attracting com-*

petitor and regulatory scrutiny. The incident resulted in losses exceeding $6 billion. While the positions were legal under regulatory frameworks at the time, the magnitude of the exposure highlighted critical deficiencies in the bank's risk identification and monitoring processes. A more robust risk management system—capable of tracking unusual trading patterns, aggregating exposures across desks, and escalating emerging anomalies to senior management (e.g., *a heat map)—might have detected the growing risk earlier, potentially mitigating or even preventing financial and reputational damage.*

This case underscores the importance of integrating sophisticated risk monitoring tools with governance and compliance frameworks to ensure that both regulatory and operational risks are actively managed in real time. The compliance lesson from the "London Whale" case is that robust monitoring and reporting systems are essential to ensure that trading activities comply with internal policies and regulatory requirements. Even legal trades can create enormous risks if they exceed limits or are not properly overseen. Integrating compliance with risk management allows firms to detect unusual or high-risk activity early, escalate it appropriately, and prevent both financial losses and regulatory breaches.

Identifying compliance risks requires a proactive and systematic approach. A risk register can be used as a centralized repository to catalog potential issues across departments in a firm. A register can be used to track GDPR compliance gaps in a multinational corporation's data handling practices.[15] Process mapping involves a detailed examination of operational workflows to identify potential compliance and risk vulnerabilities. For example, insufficient oversight in client onboarding or transaction approvals could expose institutions to violations of anti-money laundering (AML) regulations or the U.S. Foreign Corrupt Practices Act (FCPA). Engaging front-line staff in risk management activities is essential, as they are often the first to encounter emerging risks. Relationship managers or call center teams, for instance, may notice patterns in customer complaints related to data privacy or suspicious account activity, which are issues that, if unaddressed, could trigger regulatory investigations or reputational damage.

Assessing these (and other similar) risks involves qualitative and quantitative methods to prioritize mitigation efforts. A risk register should be updated to document risks, their sources, and potential impacts. Qualitative assessments rank risks as high, medium, or low based on their likelihood and potential impact. For instance, a bank might classify non-compliance with know your customer (KYC) protocols as high risk due to the potential for regulatory fines and reputational damage stemming from money laundering exposure. Quantitative assessments are used to assign numerical values to risks, enabling more precise forecasting. For example, a financial institution might estimate a $10 million potential loss from a cybersecurity breach, drawing on industry benchmarks like IBM's Cost of a Data Breach report.[16] Heat maps can also be used. These are visualization tools that plot risk likelihood against impact, helping firms focus on critical areas such as high-likelihood, high-impact risks like insider trading, data breaches, or system outages in high-frequency trading environments.[17] Figure 7.1 shows a hypothetical heat map.

In Fig. 7.1, the risk categories are cybersecurity, insider trading, system outages, and regulatory non-compliance. Scores are based on likelihood and impact. A scale from 1 (low) to 10 (high) might be used. Risks are then plotted on a grid with

		Likelihood				
Impact	Very High		Insider Trading			Cybersecurity
	High					
	Medium				System Outages	
	Low					
	Very Low				Non-compliance	
		Very Low	Low	Medium	High	Very High

Fig. 7.1 Hypothetical firm heat map

Likelihood on the x-axis and Impact on the y-axis. In this way, risk can be visualized from green (low risk) to red (high risk).

Risk Mitigation Strategies in Compliance

Effective risk mitigation in compliance demands a multifaceted strategy encompassing preventive, detective, and corrective controls, each tailored to an organization's regulatory compliance landscape and operational complexity. Preventive controls begin with well-designed policies and procedures that clearly delineate acceptable conduct, conflict of interest boundaries, and protocols for handling sensitive data. These documents must be meticulously maintained, regularly reviewed, and aligned with evolving regulatory requirements. Complementing documentation are comprehensive training programs, which should be mandatory for all personnel and intensified for high-risk roles such as traders and IT professionals. Technological interventions further strengthen prevention through automated monitoring systems, including real-time transaction surveillance and AI-driven anomaly detection, which integrate seamlessly into existing workflows and offer customizable alert thresholds to preemptively flag potential risks.

Detective controls act as a second line of defense, helping to identify and assess compliance breaches through systematic reviews. Internal audits, conducted by independent teams, should focus on high-risk areas such as financial reporting, trade execution, and data access. These audits need to follow a risk-based schedule and include follow-up reviews to ensure that remediation efforts are effective.

Whistleblower hotlines offer a vital channel for reporting misconduct, providing secure, anonymous, and multilingual access 24/7, supported by a firm policy against retaliation. Additionally, advanced data analytics tools can be used to enhance detection capabilities by monitoring behavioral and transactional metrics, like login patterns and data access logs, to reveal anomalies and generate actionable insights, often visualized through heat maps that highlight areas of risk.

Corrective actions close the loop by addressing identified breaches with precision and accountability. Remediation plans must be structured and comprehensive, incorporating root cause analysis, immediate corrective steps, and long-term process enhancements, with clearly assigned responsibilities and timelines. Policy revisions and disciplinary measures must then follow, ensuring that gaps are closed and lessons learned are institutionalized. With this approach, disciplinary actions should be proportionate to the severity of the infraction and legally vetted. Finally, regulatory reporting is essential when breaches meet disclosure thresholds, requiring timely, jurisdiction-specific submissions, such as SEC filings or GDPR notifications. Reporting is needed to document incidents and corrective actions undertaken. Together, these strategies form a resilient compliance framework capable of anticipating, detecting, and resolving risk with rigor and agility. The following case narrative illustrates these concepts:

HSBC, a global banking giant, faced significant regulatory penalties due to deficiencies in its anti-money laundering (AML) compliance systems, most notably a $1.9 billion fine in 2012 from U.S. authorities for violations of the Bank Secrecy Act (BSA), the International Emergency Economic Powers Act (IEEPA), and the Trading with the Enemy Act (TWEA).[18] *These violations stemmed from HSBC's failure to maintain an effective AML program, particularly in monitoring transactions involving its Mexican affiliate, which facilitated the laundering of over $881 million for drug cartels like Mexico's Sinaloa and Colombia's Norte del Valle gangs. The bank's inadequate due diligence on foreign correspondent accounts and understaffed compliance function from 2006 to 2010 allowed over $670 billion in wire transfers and $9.4 billion in U.S. dollar purchases to go unmonitored, enabling illicit activities like the Black Market Peso Exchange. In 2012, HSBC entered a deferred prosecution agreement (DPA) with the U.S. Department of Justice, committing to extensive remediation, including replacing senior management, clawing back bonuses, and restructuring its AML compliance framework.*

Despite these efforts, HSBC faced further scrutiny, with the U.K.'s Financial Conduct Authority (FCA) imposing a £63.9 million ($84.3 million) fine in 2021 for "serious weaknesses" in its automated transaction monitoring systems from 2010 to 2018. The FCA identified failures such as inadequate risk assessments, untested monitoring scenarios, and inaccurate data inputs, which missed suspicious activities, including transactions linked to VAT fraud and cigarette smuggling.

In response, HSBC invested heavily in remediation, tripling personnel dedicated to transaction monitoring, adopting AI-based AML systems, and enhancing employee training to bolster compliance. By 2023, HSBC's AI-driven transaction monitoring improved suspicious activity detection by two to four times while reducing false positives by 60%, enabling faster identification of criminal networks. These efforts culminated in the U.S. Federal Reserve terminating its decade-long enforcement action against HSBC in 2022, acknowledging significant improvements in its financial crime risk management.

The HSBC AML violations and subsequent investments in automated monitoring and training highlight the necessity of implementing robust, proactive compliance frameworks. Using this case as an example, financial institutions must integrate advanced technology, comprehensive training, and systematic risk assessments to mitigate legal, operational, financial, and reputational risks. The case serves as a cautionary tale, emphasizing that compliance is not a one-time fix but an ongoing commitment requiring cultural and structural transformation to withstand regulatory and public scrutiny.

Integrating Risk Management with Compliance

Traditionally, financial services organizations have treated risk management and compliance as distinct, siloed functions, with risk teams focused on operational and financial exposures, and compliance teams focused on adhering to laws, regulations, and internal policies. However, this separation sometimes failed in closing gaps in oversight, which increased the possibility that problems remained undetected. The siloed approach also increased the likelihood of financial, operational, or reputational loss. Today, nearly all firms operating in the financial services domain have integrated risk management with compliance (see Table 7.1). Firms have done this to ensure that regulatory obligations are embedded into every stage of risk assessment. Doing so creates a cohesive system in which all potential threats are evaluated not only for operational impact but also for legal and regulatory consequences.

Organizations use several structured approaches to manage risk and ensure compliance across their operations. One widely adopted method is Enterprise Risk Management (ERM), which takes a broad, company-wide view of risk.[19] ERM helps businesses identify, evaluate, and address potential risks at every level of operations.

Another helpful framework is Governance-Risk-Compliance (GRC), which brings together policies, risk assessments, and compliance efforts into one coordinated system.[20] GRC integration ensures that following regulations is not just a box-checking exercise. Instead, the process is directly tied to how the company understands and manages risk. For example, large companies dealing with GDPR (Europe's data privacy law) often include data protection concerns within their overall risk strategy.[21] By doing so, they are better equipped to avoid fines, prevent disruptions, and protect their reputation. This kind of unified oversight shows how strategic coordination can make compliance more effective and less reactive.

Leadership and organizational culture are also of critical importance to successful risk management and compliance integration. Ethical and engaged leadership sets the tone from the top, signaling that compliance and risk management are strategic priorities rather than administrative tasks.[22] A strong moral culture encourages employees to report risks, follow procedures, and escalate concerns, whereas a weak ethical culture can lead to deliberate bypassing of controls, which creates risk exposures that may escalate into significant, and costly, incidents.

Finally, technology plays an increasingly vital role in the integration of risk management and compliance.[23] Compliance management systems enable firms to track policies, document policy adherence, and generate automated reports for oversight and auditing purposes. Advanced AI and data analytics tools can identify unusual data use patterns, detect sales anomalies, and flag potential violations in near real time, allowing risk and compliance teams to respond proactively rather than reactively.[24] Together, leadership, culture, and technology form a comprehensive environment in which risk management and compliance are fully integrated, which enhances organizational resilience and safeguards regulatory and strategic objectives. The following case study illustrates how integration of risk management and compliance can be done in practice at the smaller-firm level.

Facing the challenges of managing enterprise risk, regulatory compliance, third-party risk, and business continuity, Bankers' Bank of Kansas implemented a comprehensive solution using a third party suite of interconnected tools.[25] *Given the size of the bank, it was not feasible to combine risk management functions with compliance operations. Instead, the bank used customizable Enterprise Risk Management (ERM) software that enabled the bank to continuously evaluate, measure, and report on risk in real time. Adopting ERM systems allowed the bank to streamline its risk assessment processes, ensuring that compliance obligations were considered in all risk evaluations. By centralizing risk data and automating workflows, the bank improved its ability to monitor and mitigate risks, aligning with internal policies and external regulatory requirements.*

This case illustrates how financial institutions, even those with limited technology budgets, can enhance their resilience and compliance posture by integrating risk management and compliance functions, thereby safeguarding against potential financial and reputational damages.

Future Trends in Risk Management and Compliance

The landscape of risk management and compliance is undergoing a significant transformation as organizations confront an evolving array of challenges and opportunities. Among the emerging risks, cybersecurity stands out as a pressing concern, with an escalating frequency and sophistication of attacks targeting sensitive data and critical infrastructure.[26] These threats, ranging from ransomware to state-sponsored espionage, necessitate robust defenses and proactive monitoring to safeguard organizational assets.

Equally critical are the risks associated with the ethical development and use of artificial intelligence (AI), where the deployment of AI introduces potential pitfalls such as algorithmic biases, privacy violations, and errors that can undermine trust and regulatory compliance.[27] As AI becomes integral to decision-making processes, financial services organizations must (either by choice or through regulatory nudging) establish rigorous governance frameworks to ensure transparency and fairness, addressing issues like disparate impact in automated lending or hiring systems.[28]

Additionally, Environmental, Social, and Governance (ESG) standards and compliance—although deemphasized in the United States—continue to rapidly transition from voluntary corporate codes to mandated regulatory requirements across global jurisdictions. In some regulatory jurisdictions, firms are compelled to integrate sustainability metrics, diversity policies, and governance disclosures into their operational strategies. This is true in Europe under regulatory frameworks like the EU's Sustainable Finance Disclosure Regulation (SFDR) and the Task Force on Climate-related Financial Disclosures (TCFD). The regulatory standards are used to mitigate legal and reputational risks.[29]

The complexity of global harmonization[30] further complicates the risk management landscape for organizations operating across borders. Banks, brokerages, and other financial institutions must now navigate a patchwork of regulatory regimes, each with distinct requirements, such as the U.S. Dodd-Frank Act, the EU's General Data Protection Regulation (GDPR), and Asia-Pacific data protection laws. This regulatory fragmentation can lead to compliance fatigue and inconsistent risk profiles. To address this, harmonized frameworks like ISO 31000[31] are helping to provide a standardized approach to risk management. ISO 31000 offers a universal language and methodology that enables organizations to align their risk management and compliance practices with global best practices.[32] By adopting such frameworks, firms can streamline compliance efforts, reduce redundancy, and enhance their ability to respond to cross-border risks, though they must still tailor implementations to meet local legal nuances.

The role of compliance officers in strategy development and management also continues to evolve. Today, compliance officers have advanced from rule enforcers to strategic partners at the highest levels of firms. Compliance officers today are increasingly involved in shaping organizational strategy, leveraging their deep understanding of the risk environment to inform long-term planning. By integrating risk insights, such as those derived from cybersecurity threat assessments or ESG performance metrics, into business decisions, compliance officers enhance organizational resilience and foster a competitive advantage.[33] Strategically integrating compliance teams at the highest organizational levels is one way for firms to anticipate regulatory shifts, adapt to emerging risks, and position themselves as leaders in ethical and sustainable business practices. For example, a compliance officer might advocate for investments in AI governance tools or ESG-aligned initial public offerings, ensuring that risk management not only protects but also moves the organization forward in an increasingly complex global market.

Risk Management Compliance Strategies

Firms can strengthen their compliance cultures by embedding integrity and accountability protocols into every level of the organization, starting with committed leadership that exhibits ethical behavior and empowers compliance officers to oversee initiatives effectively.[34] For instance, creating dedicated chief compliance officer roles with direct access to the board ensures that compliance is treated as a strategic priority rather than a mere checkbox function. This fosters a top-down culture where employees feel supported in adhering to regulations.[35] Regular compliance training programs, tailored to specific roles and risks, can be used to help educate staff on ethical standards and legal obligations while incorporating real-world scenarios to make learning engaging and applicable. Implementing whistleblower hotlines or anonymous reporting mechanisms can be used to encourage employees to voice concerns without fear of retaliation. Whistleblower policies can help uncover potential issues early and reinforce a speak-up environment. Additionally, conducting culture surveys and analyzing existing data sources, such as employee feedback or incident reports, allow firms to gauge the effectiveness of their compliance efforts and identify areas for improvement. Proactive assessment measures like regular audits, compliance ambassadors programs, and clear goal-setting further normalize ethical practices, turning compliance into a shared responsibility that aligns with business objectives and enhances customer trust.[36]

To design more effective risk management and regulatory compliance frameworks, financial institutions should adopt a structured, integrated approach that begins with clearly defining objectives, such as identifying operational, credit, and market exposure risks, and aligning them with the firm's strategic goals.[37] Best practices include:

- Establishing a comprehensive governance structure that promotes risk ownership across departments, with centralized oversight to avoid silos and ensure consistent application of policies.
- Leveraging technology, such as data analytics and automated monitoring systems, to enable real-time risk detection and mitigation.

Incorporating emerging factors like ESG and geopolitical risks into risk management and compliance frameworks prepares firms for evolving threats.[38] A risk-aware culture can be cultivated through ongoing training, scenario planning, and minimum viable product testing for new initiatives. Engaging in these steps allows for iterative improvements and proactive adaptation.[39] Regular assessments, including internal audits and stress testing, help validate the framework's resilience, while clear communication channels ensure that risk insights are promptly shared with stakeholders for informed decision-making. An effective framework is adaptable, data-driven, and integrated with compliance efforts to minimize vulnerabilities and support sustainable growth.

Drawing lessons from the Wells Fargo scandal discussed earlier in the chapter, firms must prioritize and strengthen centralized risk management and compliance functions to prevent decentralized structures from impeding oversight.[40] Firms should focus on creating integrated risk management systems that cover all key operational areas, including cultural alignment between business units and audit teams. This approach is one way to avoid risk management failures that erode credibility and lead to reputational damage.[41] Proactive risk evaluation by senior management, coupled with ethical incentive structures that do not pressure employees into misconduct, can mitigate failures like those seen in Wells Fargo's aggressive cross-selling strategy. By learning from such cascades of compliance breakdowns, institutions can implement strong internal controls, foster a genuine culture of integrity, and conduct thorough reviews of sales practices to rebuild trust and prevent recurrence.

Chapter Summary

The intersection of risk management and compliance forms a critical foundation for organizational resilience. Organizations that falter in compliance inevitably expose themselves to heightened risks, while weak risk management practices erode the effectiveness of compliance efforts, creating a vicious cycle of vulnerability. To preempt potential issues, proactive identification of risks is paramount. Leveraging sophisticated tools such as risk registers, process mapping, and heat maps are ways to reduce the likelihood of insider trading, data breaches, and system outages in high-frequency trading environments. These tools enable companies to detect compliance failures early, allowing for timely intervention. Effective mitigation demands a layered approach, integrating preventive controls, such as clearly documented policies, regular training workshops, and automated monitoring systems, alongside detective controls like internal audits, whistleblower hotlines, and data analytics to identify irregularities, and corrective actions including remediation plans, policy updates, and regulatory reporting. This multi-tiered strategy reduces both the likelihood and impact of breaches, ensuring a robust defense mechanism.

The integration of risk and compliance processes through frameworks like Enterprise Risk Management (ERM) and Governance-Risk-Compliance (GRC) is essential for creating a cohesive strategy that aligns organizational objectives with regulatory requirements. These frameworks can be used to facilitate a unified risk management and regulatory compliance approach, embedding risk considerations into strategic planning and enhancing overall governance. Central to this is the role of leadership and organizational culture, where ethical leaders and a strong compliance culture foster an environment where employees are encouraged to act responsibly and report misconduct without fear of retaliation. As the risk landscape evolves, emerging threats such as cybersecurity attacks, ethical dilemmas in AI deployment, bias and privacy violations, ESG standards and mandates necessitate adaptability. Organizations must anticipate these challenges, integrating insights from global harmonization efforts like ISO 31000 and positioning compliance officers as strategic partners to leverage risk insights for competitive advantage, thereby fortifying their resilience in an increasingly complex global market.

Chapter Resources

- Committee of Sponsoring Organizations (COSO): https://www.coso.org/internal-control
- Institute of Internal Auditors: https://www.theiia.org/globalassets/site/content/guidance/recommended/supplemental/practice-guides/global-practice-guide-assessing-the-risk-management-process/gpg_assessing_the_risk_management_process_2nd_ed.pdf
- OCEG Red Book: *Principled Performance and GRC Capability Model.*
- U.S. Department of Justice (DOJ) "Evaluation of Corporate Compliance Programs": https://www.justice.gov/criminal/criminal-fraud/page/file/937501/dl
- U.S. Securities and Exchange Commission (SEC) enforcement actions database: https://www.sec.gov/divisions/enforce/enforceactions.shtml

Notes

[1]https://www.rit.edu/fa/compliance/sites/rit.edu.fa.compliance/files/files/docs/ERM_Guide_to_Risk_Assessment_and_Response.pdf

[2]https://www.gao.gov/products/gao-24-106206

[3]Securities and Exchange Commission: https://www.sec.gov/newsroom/press-releases/2020-38

[4]Frigo, M. L., & Anderson, R. J. (2009). A strategic framework for governance, risk, and compliance. *Strategic Finance*, 90(8), 20–61.

[5]Price, Waterhouse, Coopers: https://www.pwc.com.tr/en/assets/about/svcs/abas/frm/operational-risk/articles/pwc_enterprisewiderisk.pdf

[6]U.S. Treasury, *Comptroller's Handbook*: https://www.pwc.com.tr/en/assets/about/svcs/abas/frm/operationalrisk/articles/pwc_enterprisewiderisk.pdf

[7]Arndorfer, I., & Minto, A. (2015). Occasional paper No. 11: The "four lines of defense model" for financial institutions. Bank for International Settlements. https://www.bis.org/fsi/fsipapers11.pdf

[8]Definitions sourced from Diligent.com: https://www.diligent.com/resources/guides/grc

[9]Karanja, E., & Rosso, M. A. (2017). The Chief Risk Officer: a study of roles and responsibilities. *Risk Management*, *19*(2), 103–130.

[10]Freeman, E. H. (2007). Regulatory compliance and the chief compliance officer. *Information Systems Security*, *16*(6), 357–361.

[11]The following table compares and contrasts GDPR and SOX:

Feature	GDPR	SOX
Region	EU (global impact)	The United States
Focus	Data privacy	Financial integrity
Applies to	Any org handling EU data	U.S. public companies
Enforcement	EU regulators	SEC and PCAOB
Penalties	Up to €20M or 4% global revenue	Fines, imprisonment for fraud

[12]U.S. Department of Treasury: https://home.treasury.gov/system/files/216/Financial-Services-Sector-Risk-Management-Plan.pdf

[13]https://www.occ.gov/publications-and-resources/publications/comptrollers-handbook/files/compliance-mgmt-systems/pub-ch-compliance-management-systems.pdf

[14]Securities and Exchange Commission: s71418-4531827-176081.pdf

[15]FERMA. (2025). Risk Register, Risk Matrix, Risk Profile, Risk Map. In *Essentials and Assessment of Risk Management* (pp. 217–233). Emerald Publishing Limited.

[16]https://www.ibm.com/reports/data-breach

[17]Dickson, J., & Einstein, A. (2010). On measures for illustrating credit risk assessments: the case of heat maps, risk matrices and cubes. *IFC Bulletin*, *25*, 365–374.

[18]U.S.DepartmentofJustice:https://www.justice.gov/archives/opa/pr/hsbc-holdings-plc-and-hsbc-bank-usa-na-admit-anti-money-laundering-and-sanctions-violations

[19]Bromiley, P., McShane, M., Nair, A., & Rustambekov, E. (2015). Enterprise risk management: Review, critique, and research directions. *Long range planning*, *48*(4), 265–276.

[20]Racz, N., Weippl, E., & Seufert, A. (2010, May). A frame of reference for research of integrated governance, risk and compliance (GRC). In *IFIP International Conference on Communications and Multimedia Security* (pp. 106–117). Berlin, Heidelberg: Springer Berlin Heidelberg.

[21]Goddard, M. (2017). The EU General Data Protection Regulation (GDPR): European regulation that has a global impact. *International Journal of Market Research*, *59*(6), 703–705.

[22]Schwartz, M. S., Dunfee, T. W., & Kline, M. J. (2005). Tone at the top: An ethics code for directors? *Journal of Business Ethics*, *58*(1), 79–100.

[23]Friday, S. C., Lawal, C. I., Ayodeji, D. C., & Sobowale, A. (2022). Advances in digital technologies for ensuring compliance, risk management, and transparency in development finance operations. *International Journal of Multidisciplinary Research and Growth Evaluation*, *3*(1), 955–966.

[24]Aziz, L. A. R., & Andriansyah, Y. (2023). The role artificial intelligence in modern banking: an exploration of AI-driven approaches for enhanced fraud prevention, risk management, and regulatory compliance. *Reviews of Contemporary Business Analytics*, *6*(1), 110–132.

[25]https://www.ncontracts.com/case-study/bankers-bank-of-kansas-risk-and-compliance?utm_source=chatgpt.com

[26]Thummala, V. R., & Bindewari, S. (2024). Optimizing Cybersecurity Practices through Compliance and Risk Assessment. *International Journal of Research Radicals in Multidisciplinary Fields, ISSN*, 910–930.

[27]Deshpande, A. (2024, April). Regulatory compliance and AI: navigating the legal and regulatory challenges of AI in finance. In *2024 International Conference on Knowledge Engineering and Communication Systems (ICKECS)* (Vol. 1, pp. 1–5). IEEE.

[28]Lau, D., Samy, G. N., Rahim, F. A., Maarop, N., & Hassan, N. H. (2023). Review of the governance, risk and compliance approaches for artificial intelligence. *Open International Journal of Informatics*, *11*(2), 25–35.

[29]Busch, D. (2023). EU sustainable finance disclosure regulation. *Capital Markets Law Journal*, *18*(3), 303–328.

[30]Global harmonization refers to the process of creating common standards and practices across countries or regions to ensure consistency and compatibility.

[31]ISO 31000 is an international standard that provides guidelines for effective risk management across all types of organizations. It offers a structured approach to identifying, assessing, and treating risks, with the goal of improving decision-making, enhancing resilience, and achieving strategic objectives.

[32]Purdy, G. (2010). ISO 31000: 2009—setting a new standard for risk management. *Risk Analysis: An International Journal*, *30*(6), 881–886.

[33]PWC Middle East Banking Study, 2024: Evolution of Risk Management in Banking. https://www.pwc.com/m1/en/publications/evolution-of-risk-management-in-banking.html

[34]BAI: https://www.bai.org/banking-strategies/lifting-your-compliance-culture/

[35]Thomson Reuters: https://legal.thomsonreuters.com/en/insights/articles/creating-a-culture-of-compliance

[36]Adeniran, I. A., Abhulimen, A. O., Obiki-Osafiele, A. N., Osundare, O. S., Agu, E. E., & Efunniyi, C. P. (2024). Strategic risk management in financial institutions: Ensuring robust regulatory compliance. *Finance & Accounting Research Journal*, *6*(8), 1582–1596.

[37]Benson, K. (2025). Enhancing your compliance training program. Federal Reserve. https://www.consumercomplianceoutlook.org/2019/first-issue/enhancing-your-compliance-training-program/

[38]OnBoardBlogPost(2025):https://www.mvsi-onboard.com/blog/risk-management-in-banking-best-practices

[39]Zainudin, Z., Samad, S. A., & Altounjy, R. (2019). The determinants factors of an effective risk-aware culture of firms in implementing and maintaining risk management program. *International Journal of Financial Research*, *11*(5), 459–465.

[40]Verschoor, C. C. (2016). Lessons from the Wells Fargo Scandal. *Strategic Finance*. https://www.sfmagazine.com/articles/2016/november/lessons-from-the-wells-fargo-scandal/

[41]Karp, B. S., & Gonzalez, R. J. (2017). Lessons learned from the Wells Fargo practice investigation report. *Harvard Law School Forum on Corporate Governance*. https://corpgov.law.harvard.edu/2017/04/22/lessons-learned-from-the-wells-fargo-sales-practices-investigation-report/

Ethics in Client-Facing Roles

8

Chapter Outcomes
This chapter focuses on helping learners develop the ability to:

1. Define the concepts of integrity, fairness, accountability, and transparency as they apply to financial services engagements.
2. Demonstrate ways to incorporate integrity, fairness, accountability, and transparency into interactions with clients to foster trust and ethical decision-making.
3. Identify potential conflicts of interest, cultural sensitivities, and moral dilemmas that may arise in financial advisory relationships among clients, firms, and advisors.
4. Apply a structured model to anticipate, analyze, and address conflicts in financial services engagements.
5. Develop an understanding of ethical practice standards to enhance a financial advisor's ability to navigate complex client relationships.

Introduction

Financial services professionals who work in direct client-facing roles regularly encounter conflicts of interest. Conflicts can happen at any stage of the client-advisor relationship due primarily to the intimate and trust-dependent nature of the relationship. Think about how financial advisors handle sensitive client information, navigate diverse cultural expectations, and balance their organization's objectives. Often, the lines separating obligations to clients, employers, and regulators get

Note: This chapter was copyedited using Grammarly™ and generative AI tools to enhance clarity, grammar, and overall readability. While these tools provided suggestions and assistance in refining the text, the ideas, content, and arguments presented remain the sole work and responsibility of the authors. Any errors or inaccuracies in the final version are also the authors' responsibility.

W. Heo, J. E. Grable, *Ethics and Compliance in Financial Services*,
https://doi.org/10.1007/978-3-032-14449-2_8

blurred, leading to difficult behavioral choices. While ethical considerations including confidentiality, transparency, and avoiding conflicts of interest should always drive a financial advisor's approach when working with clients, it is not always clear how to ensure that this occurs.

Additionally, financial services professionals face challenges in managing client and employer expectations. For example, a client may have a capital preservation investment goal, whereas the advisor's employer may set sales benchmarks for investments that exhibit price volatility. How the financial advisor acts when faced with these competing priorities depends on how they frame trust, professionalism, and integrity. Acting ethically is a pathway to addressing these issues. Upholding ethical standards ensures that decisions and actions are legally compliant and aligned with moral principles. The following discussion presents three case scenarios that illustrate how determining what is ethical when engaging with clients can range from apparent to very blurred.

Perspective

The first case highlights a serious ethical violation that went beyond simply "selling away." Steven Pagartanis, a registered representative of a broker-dealer, solicited clients to invest in unapproved real estate ventures outside his firm's supervision while simultaneously operating a Ponzi scheme.[1] He promised guaranteed returns but instead diverted funds to pay earlier investors and cover his own expenses. Pagartanis' misconduct violated his duty to act in the best interests of his clients and placed clients and the firm at risk. Although unaware of the scheme, the firm was still held liable because its compliance team failed to detect and prevent the misconduct. This case underscores two key conflicts. First, the tension between an advisor's duty to clients and an obligation to follow firm policies. Second, the risks created when compliance safeguards are bypassed. Selling away not only circumvents a firm's oversight but also exposes clients to hidden dangers such as fraud, unsuitable investments, and significant financial harm.

The second case exemplifies a situation that is not quite as clear of an ethical violation. In 2022, the Securities and Exchange Commission (SEC) charged HighPoint Advisor Group, LLC, a registered investment advisor, with breaching its fiduciary duties to clients by failing to disclose conflicts of interest, neglecting best execution practices, and violating its duty of care.[2] From 2014 to 2019, HighPoint invested wrap program clients in higher-cost mutual fund share classes when lower-cost alternatives of the same funds were available. While HighPoint avoided transaction fees by recommending no-transaction-fee mutual funds offered by its clearing firm, these funds often carried higher 12b-1 fees. Although neither HighPoint nor its representatives received the 12b-1 fees directly, the firm's practices prioritized revenue production for itself over securing the most cost-effective investments for clients. The SEC found that HighPoint failed to provide full and fair disclosure about these practices and violated fiduciary obligations under the Investment Advisers Act of 1940. HighPoint consented to a cease-and-desist order, censure, and financial penalties, including $508,995 in payments to victims, $130,742 in prejudgment interest, and a $125,000 civil penalty. This case highlights how financial advisors can sometimes inadvertently cross into unethical behavior through a lack of transparency, best execution, and operational convenience.

The third case demonstrates how a financial advisor's fiduciary duty depends on the context of their role and the regulatory framework governing activities. Brokers owe special duties to clients, particularly when providing personalized investment advice. These duties include acting in the client's best interest, avoiding conflicts of interest, providing full disclosure of material facts, and ensuring that investment recommendations align with the client's financial goals and risk tolerance. These responsibilities are reinforced by regulatory frameworks such as the Investment Advisers Act of 1940 and regulatory standards established by FINRA and independent certification boards. It is important to note that financial advisors also owe a duty of loyalty and compliance to their employer. For brokers, this duty (a fiduciary obligation) is to the broker-dealer firm. An advisor's duties include adhering to firm policies, disclosing outside business activities, avoiding unauthorized transactions ("selling away"), and upholding the firm's reputation. When a conflict arises between a client's best interest and the advisor's obligations to their employer, regulatory standards such as Regulation Best Interest (Reg BI) (discussed in more detail later in the chapter) mandate that financial advisors prioritize their client's interest over the firm's or their own financial gain. However, this prioritization does not remove a financial advisor's full fiduciary duty to their employer.

In this context, consider a situation involving a broker who is engaged in recommending and facilitating investments in annuity products that have not been approved by the employing firm. As noted above, this is known as "selling away." In this case, imagine that the annuity investments result in financial gains for the advisor's clients. Even though client outcomes are positive, under state and federal law, the advisor will be deemed to have engaged in unethical and illegal behavior. What might happen? It is likely that the advisor will be fired by the firm, barred by FINRA, and prosecuted by the SEC and the brokerage firm. Federal penitentiaries are filled with former financial advisors who have engaged in the behavior described above.

This case illustrates a critical ethical dilemma where a financial advisor's failure to comply with regulatory requirements and firm policies will be seen as a breach of fiduciary and professional duty even when clients benefit financially. Selling away compromises a firm's ability to supervise transactions, assess the suitability of investments, and ensure compliance with securities laws.[3] This behavior also reduces firm profits. By circumventing firm and regulatory safeguards, financial advisors who engage in behavior, even with good intentions, which exposes one or more clients and their firm to potential risks, including fraud, lack of due diligence, and reputational harm, will face severe punishment.

The key takeaway from this discussion is that financial advisors must balance their duty to clients with fiduciary obligations to their employers. Doing so requires a financial advisor to act transparently, disclose conflicts of interest, and prioritize a client's interests to ensure compliance with ethical standards and legal requirements.

Standards of Practice for Financial Services Professionals in Client-Facing Roles

The guiding principles of Regulation Best Interest (Reg BI) and the fiduciary standard under the Investment Advisers Act (IA fiduciary standard) play a central role when it comes to ensuring that financial advisors and broker-dealers meet their obligations to clients.[4] While the precise applications of Reg BI and the IA fiduciary standard vary and are triggered at different times, their overarching goal is the same: to uphold responsibilities owed to non-institutional clients. The following discussion provides insights into how financial services professionals can meet their obligations when recommending accounts, securities, products, and services.

Reg BI was adopted by the SEC in 2019 as a reform of the obligations of broker-dealers under the Securities Exchange Act of 1934.[5] Reg BI requires broker-dealers to act in the best interest of clients when making investment recommendations to retail clients while deprioritizing their own financial interests. The rule includes guidance on addressing conflicts of interest that may affect recommendations. Reg BI marks a departure from the traditional "suitability standard," which only requires that recommendations align with a client's general financial situation. Instead, Reg BI moves broker-dealers closer to the fiduciary standard traditionally applied to investment professionals as defined by the SEC.

The SEC's Investment Adviser (IA) fiduciary standard is a legal requirement that governs the conduct of investment advisers (those registered with the SEC), ensuring they act in the best interests of their clients at all times.[6] Based on the Investment Advisers Act of 1940, the standard applies to individuals and firms who provide advice on securities for compensation (not a commission). Fiduciary standards encompass several key principles. The first is loyalty, which requires advisors to prioritize their clients' interests over their own and avoid conflicts of interest. If disputes arise, an advisor must disclose relevant information and take steps to mitigate the impact of any conflicts. Second, the duty of care mandates that advisors offer prudent, informed advice backed by thorough research tailored to a client's financial situation and investment objectives. Duty of care also ensures that a financial advisor manages client assets with competence and diligence. Third is disclosure, which requires financial advisors to provide clients with detailed information about services, fees, forms of compensation, and potential conflicts of interest. The fiduciary standard also imposes a duty of ongoing monitoring that is intended to guarantee that implemented products and services continue to align with a client's needs and goals. The fiduciary standard also prohibits self-dealing by prohibiting transactions that benefit an advisor at the expense of a client. Finally, financial advisors are required to maintain accurate records of their advice, recommendations, and disclosures. The SEC's fiduciary standard is stricter than the Reg BI standard.

Understanding Which Standard Applies

Financial services professionals must consider the capacity in which they act, be it as a broker-dealer, investment advisor registered with the SEC or their state, or through multiple channels when making recommendations. Both Reg BI and the IA fiduciary standard require a thorough evaluation of a client's circumstances to ensure that recommendations align with a client's best interests. In instances where roles overlap, as is common in dually licensed situations, a financial services professional should operate under the assumption that both standards apply until it becomes clear which standard should be followed. Answers to the following questions can help determine which standard applies:

1. Does the financial services professional earn a commission based on the sale of products and services? If yes, Reg BI applies.
2. Does the financial services professional charge clients a fee for services? If yes, the IA fiduciary standard applies.

Disclosing Capacity and Considering Alternatives

Clear communication about the capacity in which a financial services professional operates is critically important. When working with a client, Reg BI requires a broker-dealer representative to disclose all material facts about the relationship's scope and terms. Similarly, investment advisors must disclose material facts under duty of loyalty standards. At the firm level, policies must be in place to guide effective disclosures.

Both standards also mandate the consideration of reasonably available alternatives when recommending accounts, products, and services. Financial services professionals must evaluate a spectrum of account options while avoiding recommendations based solely on a firm's limited offerings or licensing restrictions. Limitations and associated material facts, such as fees and services, should always be disclosed to clients.

Evaluating Investor Profiles and Account Characteristics

Thorough knowledge of a retail investor's financial profile is essential whenever a financial advisor makes recommendations to clients. Factors to consider include a client's financial situation, risk tolerance, investment goals, tax status, and investment time horizon. These factors fall under "Know Your Client" (KYC) rules. Standards of practice require that account characteristics, including services, fees, and investment options, align with a client's goals and situational factors. It is not only imprudent, but it is also against the law for a financial advisor to move forward, making recommendations with insufficient information. Regulatory frameworks make it clear that a financial services professional cannot form a reasonable belief that their recommendations are in a client's best interest without thoroughly assessing and utilizing the client's financial profile.

Costs and Other Considerations

Cost is a fundamental consideration whenever an account, product, or service recommendation is made. While neither Reg BI nor the IA fiduciary standard requires a financial services professional to recommend the least expensive option at all times, standards of practice require that an advisor ensures that additional factors justify higher-cost recommendations. Costs to consider include account fees, transaction costs, tax implications, and indirect costs like payment for order flow or fund management fees.

Special Considerations for Rollovers

Account and retirement plan rollovers present additional complexities. Financial services professionals must assess the benefits and costs of transferring assets compared to leaving them in an existing account or employer plan. Relevant factors to consider include investment options, creditor protections, and fees. In retirement plan rollover scenarios, regulators have clearly stated that it is essential for a financial advisor to document the basis for recommendations and demonstrate compliance with regulatory standards.

Addressing Conflicts of Interest

Mitigating conflicts of interest is of paramount importance when working with clients. Disclosure regulations place some of the conflict disclosure burden on firms. Firms should avoid practices that incentivize recommendations that create a misalignment with a client's best interests. Examples of practices that should be avoided include compensation structures tied to specific account types and inadequate oversight of retirement plan rollover recommendations. Firm policies should be designed to eliminate or minimize conflicts of interest as a way to ensure that firm employees act ethically.

Documentation and Compliance

Under current regulatory standards, financial firms and advisors are required to document the rationale behind account recommendations. The reason behind this standard of practice is that it ensures products and services meet the needs of clients. The rule facilitates the ongoing evaluation of the effectiveness of implemented recommendations. Proper documentation is particularly critical when a client's decisions contradict a financial advisor's recommendation.

Other Standards of Practice

An important standard of practice went into effect in 2024. The Department of Labor's Retirement Security Rule and associated amendments redefined fiduciary responsibilities under the Employee Retirement Income Security Act of 1974 (ERISA). Under current rules, financial advisors who provide advice on retirement plan assets must act as fiduciaries when providing advice. This places many financial advisors who might be generally obligated to follow Reg BI to higher practice standards of care and loyalty.[7] Under Department of Labor (DOL) rules, financial advisors who provide advice, regardless of the way they are paid, on retirement plan products must avoid conflicts of interest and disclose information about fees and real or potential Department of Labor Retirement Security Rule conflicts of interest. This means that advice as simple as recommending that retirement assets be rolled over into a new account requires a financial advisor to provide services as a fiduciary.

It is important for client-facing financial advisors to understand how the rule redefines who qualifies as an investment advice fiduciary. The rule centers on the advisor-client relationship and aims to ensure that financial services professionals offering retirement advice are held to fiduciary standards when their recommendations are provided for compensation. Specifically, the rule stipulates that fiduciary status applies if an advisor (1) makes investment recommendations, (2) receives fees or commissions, and (3) positions themselves as a trusted advisor acting in the investor's best interest.[8]

While much of the discussion thus far has involved standards of practice for those engaged in investment planning, it is important to note that insurance agents and brokers must also adhere to additional standards of practice. These standards are governed by federal, state, and industry regulators. The cornerstone of these regulations are provisions under the National Association of Insurance Commissioners (NAIC) model laws, although individual states also have specific requirements.[9] An important component of these standards is the duty of disclosure and honesty, which mandates that insurance agents provide full transparency about the terms, conditions, costs, exclusions, and benefits of the insurance products they offer.

Under current practice standards, insurance agents are required to recommend products that are suitable for a client's needs, financial situation, and goal(s) (i.e., a suitability standard). In some states, best-interest rules have been enacted. These rules require insurance professionals to always act in a client's best interest. Best-interest rules are particularly relevant when an agent sells complex products like variable annuities and life insurance.[10] Equally important are the principles of fair treatment and anti-discrimination. Insurance agents are prohibited from engaging in discriminatory practices based on race, gender, religion, or other protected categories.

Ethical Decision-Making When Working with Clients

The discussion to this point has been focused on relatively high-level concepts. The remainder of this chapter aims to describe how the principles of integrity, fairness, accountability, and transparency can be put into practice. Similar to the way attorneys, physicians, and accountants provide professional services, financial services professionals are expected to (a) care for their clients and do no harm, (b) act fairly and never cheat or lie, (c) avoid dominating or bullying clients, (d) be loyal, (e) be helpful, and (f) follow the rules.[11] How is one supposed to do these things when client, firm, and regulatory frameworks are framed by complexity?

An answer to this question can be found in the counseling literature. Similar to financial advisors, counselors frequently encounter situations that demand strong ethical decision-making skills. Counselors and financial advisors are called upon to determine the best course of action in difficult environments. Ethical decision-making in counseling is grounded in several foundational principles that are central to effective practice.[12] These principles, first identified by Beauchamp and Childress,[13] include autonomy, justice, beneficence, nonmaleficence, and fidelity, which together form the foundation for providing services guided by the highest ethical standards. Autonomy emphasizes respecting an individual's independence and self-determination. Autonomy ensures clients are allowed to make their own decisions within a framework that considers personal competency. Justice requires a financial advisor to be fair. Fairness means that a financial advisor treats all clients (and colleagues) equally. Beneficence prompts financial advisors to proactively contribute to the well-being of clients, whereas nonmaleficence mandates avoiding harm, both intentional and unintentional. Fidelity focuses on maintaining trust and loyalty and honoring commitments within the client-advisor relationship. If a financial advisor were to engage every client encounter through the lens of these five principles, it would be possible to mitigate nearly all claims of wrongdoing.

There are times, however, when these principles are not enough to guide a financial advisor when working with clients. Rather than rely on general concepts to guide practice, decision-making experts recommend the use of ethical engagement models. The one model that is most often cited as effective was developed by James Rest.[14] The model, called the Four-Component Model of moral development, highlights the most important aspects of ethical decision-making: moral sensitivity, moral judgment, moral motivation, and moral character. Moral sensitivity involves understanding a situation and recognizing how different actions might affect others. Moral judgment is the ability to evaluate which action is ethically correct. Judgment requires knowledge of ethical principles and codes of conduct. Moral motivation refers to the internal drive to take the appropriate action, while moral character is the courage to follow through on those actions. Figure 8.1 illustrates the model.

The four-component model provides a structured framework for understanding and navigating ethical situations and improving overall decision-making. A precursor to utilizing the model in practice involves recognizing when an ethical dilemma exists. This involves identifying situations where moral principles may be at stake. The concept of empathy is important to consider. Empathy requires one person to attempt to understand an issue or concern from another person's perspective and then connect more fully to the other person's point of view.[15] This contrasts with sympathy, which is one's expression of pity or sorrow for another person's circumstances or experience. Consider the following example: a client indicates that their parent recently died.

A sympathetic response would be:

- "I am so sorry for your loss. This must be really hard for you. Let me know how to help."

An empathetic response would be:

- "I can't imagine the pain you must be feeling right now. Losing someone you love is never easy. Please know that I am here anytime you want to talk about this or need support."

An empathetic financial advisor is one who genuinely attempts to better understand a client's concerns, thoughts, and emotions.[16] Empathizing involves "walking in someone else's shoes" and attempting to experience how the other person thinks and feels. A sympathetic response does not include appreciating the other person's true feelings. To express sympathy is simply to voice pity or sorrow.

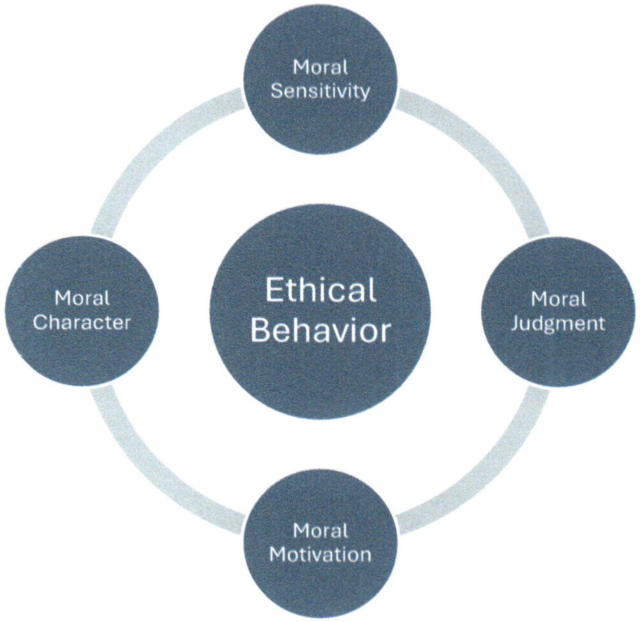

Fig. 8.1 James Rest's four-component model of moral development

Being empathetic requires moral awareness and the ability to distinguish between complex and competing interests. To be morally sensitive (the model's first element) is to be empathetic. The second component of the model involves making moral judgments. This involves focusing on an evaluation of the ethical dimensions of possible actions. This is where applying fairness, justice, and integrity comes into play. The third model element, moral motivation, entails resolving conflicts between competing values and determining which course of action should be pursued. The last model component is acting morally (ethically). This translates into making judgments that are based on integrity, fairness, accountability, and transparency. At this point in the model, a financial advisor takes action, which may require overcoming barriers such as fear of repercussions or social pressure.

A financial advisor often needs to exhibit courage when navigating real-world situations. The following scenario walks through how the four-component model can be applied in practice.

Haley, a 45-year-old professional, has worked with her financial advisor (Josway) for six months. In today's meeting, Haley explains that she recently inherited a large sum of money from her father. She also indicates feeling overwhelmed by the loss of her father and the decision-making process about how to invest the inheritance. Here is how Josway can apply the four-component model.

To begin with, Josway listens to Haley and endeavors to connect with her in an empathetic way. To do so, Josway listens intently to Haley's concerns about the inheritance. He acknowledges that while Haley is grateful for the financial legacy, she is grieving the loss of her father. Josway recognizes that Haley's emotional state may make a series of well-thought-out decisions difficult. Josway is careful not to push Haley into making quick financial decisions. Josway is systematic in his approach and is attuned to Haley's emotions. Rather than view Haley's scenario as an opportunity to make a sale, Josway demonstrates empathy, showing moral sensitivity and patience.

In the context of listening, Josway reflects on a potential course of action for Haley. Josway considers the complexity of Haley's feelings. He recognizes that Haley's state of mind is likely causing confusion about the best investment approach. She may also feel guilt, fear, apprehension, and uncertainty about her future. Josway recognizes that engaging Haley in a purely financial discussion will be counterproductive. Instead, he strives to be supportive and thoughtful in his approach.

Josway methodically moves to the next stage of the four-component model. After thinking about Haley's emotional and financial situation, he begins evaluating the ethical dimensions related to the inheritance. Thinking about her financial situation, Josway asks himself if Haley should prioritize paying off her debts to ease her financial burdens, invest the money for retirement, or perhaps set aside a portion of the proceeds for charitable purposes in her father's memory. He understands that two of these alternatives will generate no income for him or the firm, but he dismisses these thoughts and thinks about what would be in Haley's long-term best interests. When thinking about investments, he immediately considers whether there might be investments that would be in conflict with Haley's moral values. His intuitive response is to balance what is best for Haley's financial situation while remaining sensitive to her emotional state.

Josway moves easily to the next step in the four-component model. He feels a strong moral responsibility to help Haley navigate her emotional and financial situation. He resolves to prioritize Haley's peace of mind and long-term security over making what would likely be a very easy product sale, even if the product might benefit Haley financially. He decides that allowing her time to grieve and reflect is more important than pushing a product or service. His motivation is to help Haley make a decision that is ethical, fair, and aligned with her values.

Although walking through the four-component model has taken some time, Josway knows there are some concrete steps he needs to take to help Haley move forward in a way that respects her emotional needs and financial goals. He suggests a phased approach to investing the inheritance, advising Haley to keep a portion in cash and to take time for reflection. He also recommends speaking with an estate attorney to ensure that her father's legacy is honored in a way that will reflect his wishes. Importantly, he explains all the recommendations transparently and clearly, ensuring Haley fully understands the rationale behind each recommendation. Additionally, Josway recognizes that his advice might not be immediately implemented. He acknowledges that it could take time for Haley to move from intending to take action to implementing recommendations. Nonetheless, Josway stands firm in his commitment to fairness, transparency, and integrity. His approach, though measured, is ultimately designed to protect Haley's interests, and he is willing to address any concerns or doubts she might have. Josway is motivated to do what is right for Haley, even if it requires courage to stand by his approach because others in the firm are nudging him to do something different.

As this case illustrates, by following the four-component model, Josway was able to help Haley make sound financial choices while creating a safe, client-centered space for Haley to make future decisions. Josway's approach shows how it is possible to foster trust between a client and advisor, maintain the highest degree of ethical practice, and ensure that recommendations align with a client's immediate emotional needs and long-term financial situation.

The Role of Ethical Codes and Practice Standards

Adhering to a code of ethics and professional standards of practice is one way to help a financial services professional navigate the complexities associated with providing financial advice for compensation. A code of ethics helps establish trust, integrity, and accountability when working with clients. The foundation of a code of ethics underpins client relationships and the overall reputation of the profession.

Practice standards are necessary because they help ensure that products and services are offered with honesty, transparency, and integrity. Rather than being mandated by a federal or state agency, nearly all codes of ethics and standards of practice are enforced by membership organizations or certification bodies. The following list, while not exhaustive, provides a sample of organizations that publish and enforce stringent codes of ethics and practice standards:

1. Certified Financial Planner Board of Standards (CFP Board)
   - Certification: Certified Financial Planner™ (CFP®)
   - Ethics: CFP Board Code of Ethics and Standards of Conduct
2. Financial Planning Association (FPA)
   - Membership: Financial planners, educators, and allied professionals
   - Ethics: FPA Code of Ethics

3. National Association of Personal Financial Advisors (NAPFA)
   - Membership: Fee-only financial advisors
   - Ethics: NAPFA Fiduciary Oath and Code of Ethics
4. Society of Financial Services Professionals (FSP)
   - Membership: Professionals in financial planning, insurance, law, and accounting
   - Ethics: FSP Code of Professional Responsibility
5. Chartered Financial Analyst Institute (CFA Institute)
   - Certification: Chartered Financial Analyst (CFA®)
   - Ethics: CFA Institute Code of Ethics and Standards of Professional Conduct
6. Investment Management Consultants Association (IMCA) (Now the Investments & Wealth Institute)
   - Certifications: Certified Investment Management Analyst® (CIMA®), Certified Private Wealth Advisor® (CPWA®)
   - Ethics: Code of Professional Responsibility
7. Global Association of Risk Professionals (GARP)
   - Certifications: Financial Risk Manager (FRM®), Energy Risk Professional (ERP®)
   - Ethics: GARP Code of Conduct
8. Alternative Investment Management Association (AIMA)
   - Membership: Hedge fund and alternative investment managers
   - Ethics: AIMA Guide to Sound Practices
9. Chartered Alternative Investment Analyst Association (CAIA Association)
   - Certification: Chartered Alternative Investment Analyst (CAIA®)
   - Ethics: Code of Ethics and Professional Conduct
10. American College of Financial Services
    - Certifications: ChFC®, CLU®, RICP®
    - Ethics: Code of Ethics for Financial Professionals
11. International Association for Quantitative Finance (IAQF)
    - Membership: Quantitative finance professionals
    - Ethics: Promotes professional integrity and ethical practices
12. Financial Industry Regulatory Authority (FINRA)
    - Membership: Securities brokers and firms
    - Ethics: FINRA Rules and Regulations
13. National Association of Insurance and Financial Advisors (NAIFA)

- Membership: Insurance agents and financial advisors
- Ethics: NAIFA Code of Ethics

14. Financial Services Institute (FSI)

    - Membership: Independent financial services firms and advisors
    - Ethics: Standards of Conduct

15. Association for Financial Professionals (AFP)

    - Certifications: Certified Treasury Professional (CTP), Certified Corporate FP&A Professional (FPAC)
    - Ethics: AFP Code of Ethical Conduct

16. European Financial Planning Association (EFPA)

    - Membership: Financial planning professionals across Europe
    - Ethics: EFPA Code of Ethics

17. Institute of Financial Planning (IFP) (Now merged with the CISI)

    - Certifications: Various financial planning credentials
    - Ethics: Principles of Integrity and Professionalism

18. Chartered Insurance Institute (CII)

    - Certifications: DipPFS, ACII, FCII
    - Ethics: Code of Ethics

19. Asia Pacific Financial Services Association (APFinSA)

    - Membership: Financial advisors in the Asia-Pacific region
    - Ethics: Professional Code of Conduct

20. Accredited Investment Fiduciary (AIF®)

    - Organization: Fi360 (A Broadridge Company)
    - Ethics: AIF Code of Ethics

21. Certified Trust and Fiduciary Advisor (CTFA)

    - Organization: American Bankers Association (ABA)
    - Ethics: ABA Code of Ethics

22. Personal Financial Specialist (PFS)

    - Organization: American Institute of CPAs (AICPA)
    - Ethics: AICPA Code of Professional Conduct

Adhering to a code of ethics and related practice standards also enhances the credibility and respectability of the financial services profession. A code of ethics and practice standards also guides how claims against a financial advisor should be handled. Codes and standards can assist firms in managing conflicts of interest, ensuring that decisions made at the enterprise and advisor levels align with the principles of fairness and integrity. Stated another way, professional codes and standards establish accountability and consistency by establishing uniform professional expectations. These shared expectations reduce the risk of unethical behavior. Moreover, practice standards encourage professional development as a way to increase the role of ethical behavior when working with clients, ultimately enhancing the quality of service provided to clients. As an example, consider the following summary of the CFP Board's Duties Owed to Clients under the Board's Standards of Practice:[17]

> *A CFP® professional owes clients a fiduciary duty, requiring the professional to act in the client's best interests at all times when providing financial advice. This fiduciary obligation encompasses several key responsibilities. The duty of loyalty mandates prioritizing the client's interests above all else, avoiding or fully disclosing material conflicts of interest, and managing such conflicts to ensure the client's informed consent while maintaining their best interests. The duty of care requires advisors to act with prudence, skill, and diligence, aligning their recommendations with the client's goals, risk tolerance, and circumstances. Additionally, they must adhere to the client's instructions, objectives, and restrictions within the scope of the engagement.*
>
> *CFP® professionals must perform services with integrity, upholding honesty and candor without subordinating ethical principles to personal or professional gain. Competence is crucial, requiring professionals to possess or acquire the necessary knowledge and skills for the services provided. They must also diligently deliver services, responding to client inquiries promptly and thoroughly. Transparency is vital in managing conflicts of interest; full disclosure of material conflicts must be specific and comprehensive enough for a client to make an informed decision.*
>
> *CFP® professionals must exercise sound and objective judgment free from undue influence or financial incentives that could compromise their objectivity. They are expected to demonstrate professionalism, treat all stakeholders with respect and dignity, and adhere to all relevant laws and regulations. Confidentiality is paramount, with strict safeguards in place to protect clients' non-public personal information. Clients must be provided with clear, accurate, and timely disclosures about services, costs, compensation methods, and other material details impacting their decisions. Advisors must accurately represent their compensation structure, avoiding misleading statements about fee-only or commission-based models.*
>
> *When recommending or collaborating with additional service providers, CFP® professionals must ensure the providers' qualifications, disclose any compensatory arrangements, and protect the client's interests throughout the process. When using or recommending technology, they must exercise reasonable care to ensure its reliability and appropriateness. Lastly, CFP® professionals must refrain from borrowing or lending money to clients (except under strict conditions) and avoid commingling client assets with their own or their firm's assets, ensuring the utmost integrity and accountability in their professional conduct.*

Identifying Situations Where Clients May Be More Susceptible to Making Poor Decisions or Taking Unethical Financial Advice

Research highlights the critical role of numeracy, cognitive abilities, and contextual factors in describing who may be more susceptible to poor decision-making and unethical financial advice.[18] Numeracy (an ability to understand and use data), distinct from exhibiting basic calculation skills, influences comprehension of, engagement with, and the ability to make sense of financial information.[19] Lower numeracy is a particular problem in the older adult community. Whether due to lifelong challenges or age-related cognitive decline, low numeracy has been linked to worse financial decisions and increased susceptibility to financial exploitation. Studies show that individuals with higher numeracy are better equipped to manage financial decisions, reduce risks of exploitation, and demonstrate stronger financial planning skills.[20] Cognitive decline, including mild cognitive impairment (MCI) and dementia, exacerbates vulnerabilities.[21]

Deficits in memory, judgment, and executive functioning are known to significantly impair financial capacity. This can manifest as exploitation through the undue influence of a financial advisor who uses coercive dynamics to benefit from client vulnerabilities. Social isolation is another factor that can lead to poor decision-making and exploitation. Social isolation can increase vulnerability by limiting access to external advice or support, leaving clients open to manipulation by those they view as trusted advisors.[22]

Being aware of these factors is one way for a financial services professional to recognize when a client may need additional support or protection when making financial decisions. These factors also underscore legal frameworks that are designed to protect consumers from unscrupulous, unethical, and exploitative behavior, particularly for those experiencing cognitive decline.[23] Having an appreciation of these factors is also a way to protect oneself from accusations of deception and unethical behavior. For example, rather than move forward in a client relationship when low numeracy, cognitive ability, and contextual factors are present, a financial advisor should take steps to document that the client fully understands the financial implications of their decisions. This goes beyond disclosure. In this case, documentation can include having a client or the client's representative acknowledge in writing their agreement with the reasoning behind a given strategy. Doing so will reduce the likelihood that the outcome of a decision will be flagged as exploitative. By proactively identifying these types of vulnerabilities, financial advisors can act in their client's best interest and demonstrate due diligence in protecting themselves from potential accusations of unethical behavior. This proactive approach aligns with professional ethical standards and can provide a clear defense against claims of unethical behavior.

Chapter Summary

Professional codes of ethics and practice standards play a vital role in guiding the delivery of financial advice in a principled way.[24] Despite the presence of ethical codes, practice standards, firm procedures, and regulatory frameworks, ethical breaches still occur, often involving financial services professionals who are unaware of their ethical obligations. As noted in this chapter, it is crucial to go beyond knowledge of professional codes and standards to foster ethical behavior among those with a client-facing role. This chapter described ways a financial advisor can apply the principles of integrity, fairness, accountability, and transparency in their daily work with clients. Expanding on the concepts of autonomy, justice, beneficence, nonmaleficence, and fidelity, the four-component model of moral development was introduced. This model illustrates how ethical decision-making can be enhanced through the application of moral sensitivity, moral judgment, moral motivation, and moral character. This chapter also showed how financial advisors can identify and mitigate risks in their practice by understanding behavioral factors that govern ethical and unethical actions, ensuring a higher standard of professionalism and integrity.

Chapter Resources

- Certified Financial Planner Board of Standards, Inc.: https://www.cfp.net/ethics/code-of-ethics-and-standards-of-conduct
- Department of Labor Retirement Security Rule: https://www.dol.gov/agencies/ebsa/about-ebsa/our-activities/resource-center/fact-sheets/retirement-security-rule-and-amendments-to-class-pte-for-investment-advice-fiduciaries
- National Association of Insurance Commissioners: https://content.naic.org/
- Regulation Best Interest: https://www.sec.gov/resources-small-businesses/small-business-compliance-guides/regulation-best-interest
- SEC IA Fiduciary Standard: https://www.sec.gov/about/divisions-offices/division-trading-markets/broker-dealers/staff-bulletin-standards-conduct-broker-dealers-investment-advisers-account-recommendations-retail
- U.S. Department of Justice: https://www.justice.gov/elderjustice/prosecutors/statutes

Notes

[1] https://www.sec.gov/files/litigation/admin/2021/34-91149.pdf

[2] https://www.sec.gov/enforcement-litigation/administrative-proceedings/ia-6003-s

[3] https://crsreports.congress.gov/product/pdf/R/R46115/1

[4] https://www.sec.gov/about/divisions-offices/division-trading-markets/broker-dealers/staff-bulletin-standards-conduct-broker-dealers-investment-advisers-account-recommendations-retail

[5] https://crsreports.congress.gov/product/pdf/R/R46115/1

[6] Although the Investment Advisers Act of 1940 refers to a regulated financial professional as an adviser, for clarity, this chapter uses the term advisor.

[7] https://www.dol.gov/sites/dolgov/files/ebsa/about-ebsa/our-activities/resource-center/fact-sheets/retirement-security-rule-and-amendments-to-class-pte-for-investment-advice-fiduciaries.pdf

[8] https://investmentadviser.org/wp-content/uploads/2024/03/14.b.DOL-Fiduciary-Rule-and-Exemption-Developments.pdf

[9] https://content.naic.org/model-laws

[10] An insurance agent who recommends or sells variable annuities or certain types of life insurance with an investment component must hold a FINRA license and an insurance license. To sell and recommend these products, an insurance professional must hold a FINRA Series 6 or Series 7,

depending on the specific products they intend to sell. A separate license is not needed to sell fixed annuities or fixed life insurance policies.

[11]Vozzola, E. C. (2016). The case for the four component model vs. moral foundations theory: A perspective from moral psychology. *Mercer L. Rev., 68*, 633–648.

[12]Forester-Miller, H., & Davis, T. E. (2016). *Practitioners' guide to ethical decision making*. The Center for Counseling Practice, Policy, and Research. https://www.counseling.org/docs/default-source/ethics/practioner-39-s-guide-to-ethical-decision-making.pdf

[13]Beauchamp, T. L., & Childress, J. F. (2012). *Principles of biomedical ethics* (7th ed.). Oxford University Press.

[14]Rest, J. R. (Ed.). (1994). *Moral development in the professions: Psychology and applied ethics*. Psychology Press.

[15]Grable, J. E., & Goetz, J. W. (2017). *Communication essentials for financial planners: Strategies and techniques*. John Wiley & Sons.

[16]Ibid.

[17]https://www.cfp.net/ethics/code-of-ethics-and-standards-of-conduct

[18]Wood, S., & Lichtenberg, P. A. (2017). Financial capacity and financial exploitation of older adults: Research findings, policy recommendations, and clinical implications. *Clinical Gerontologist, 40*(1), 3–13.

[19]Schwartz, L. M., Woloshin, S., Black, W. C., & Welch, H. G. (1997). The role of numeracy in understanding the benefit of screening mammography. *Annals of Internal Medicine, 127*(11), 966–972.

[20]Reyna, V. F., Nelson, W. L., Han, P. K., & Dieckmann, N. F. (2009). How numeracy influences risk comprehension and medical decision making. *Psychological Bulletin, 135*(6), 943.

[21]Duke Han, S., Boyle, P. A., Yu, L., Arfanakis, K., James, B. D., Fleischman, D. A., & Bennett, D. A. (2016). Grey matter correlates of susceptibility to scams in community-dwelling older adults. *Brain Imaging and Behavior, 10*, 524–532.

[22]Lichtenberg, P. A., Sugarman, M. A., Paulson, D., Ficker, L. J., & Rahman-Filipiak, A. (2016). Psychological and functional vulnerability predicts fraud cases in older adults: Results of a longitudinal study. *Clinical Gerontologist, 39*(1), 48–63.

[23]Peisah, C., Finkel, S., Shulman, K., Melding, P., Luxenberg, J., Heinik, J., ... & Bennett, H. (2009). The wills of older people: risk factors for undue influence. *International Psychogeriatrics, 21*(1), 7–15.

[24]Cicero, F. R. (2021). Behavioral ethics: Ethical practice is more than memorizing compliance codes. *Behavior Analysis in Practice, 14*(4), 1169–1178.

9 Insider Trading and Market Manipulation

Chapter Outcomes

This chapter focuses on helping learners develop the ability to:

1. Articulate the definitions, forms, and common characteristics of insider trading and market manipulation, and explain their detrimental effects on financial markets and public trust.
2. Describe the legal frameworks, key enforcement actions, and roles of oversight agencies responsible for preventing and addressing insider trading and market manipulation.
3. Analyze how insider trading and market manipulation undermine fairness, transparency, and integrity in financial markets and client relationships.
4. Interpret real-world case studies of insider trading and market manipulation to extract practical lessons as a way to enhance ethical awareness and professional judgment in financial decision-making.
5. Identify the psychological and behavioral factors that contribute to insider trading and market manipulation.
6. Explain the importance of a proactive compliance culture in preventing insider trading.

Note: This chapter was copyedited using Grammarly™ and generative AI tools to enhance clarity, grammar, and overall readability. While these tools provided suggestions and assistance in refining the text, the ideas, content, and arguments presented remain the sole work and responsibility of the authors. Any errors or inaccuracies in the final version are also the authors' responsibility.

W. Heo, J. E. Grable, *Ethics and Compliance in Financial Services*,
https://doi.org/10.1007/978-3-032-14449-2_9

Introduction

Insider trading and market manipulation strike at the heart of financial market integrity. These behaviors erode public trust and undermine the principles of fairness and transparency that define the delivery of ethical financial services. When individuals exploit nonpublic information or manipulate market prices for personal gain, they not only violate laws but also betray the confidence of investors who rely on a level playing field. Trading on nonpublic information, often fueled by greed or pressure to outperform others, has led to some high-profile financial scandals. These scandals range from historical insider trading schemes to modern cases involving cryptocurrencies and social media-driven market manipulations.

This chapter explores the definitions, consequences, and prevention of insider trading and market manipulation, offering financial services professionals a roadmap to navigate challenges associated with using nonpublic information for personal (or client) gain. The chapter begins by defining insider trading and market manipulation practices and providing examples to illustrate their forms and impacts. The chapter then analyzes the ethical implications associated with engaging in these behaviors, emphasizing the importance of integrity and accountability in client interactions. The discussion uncovers lessons from high-profile scandals through real-world case studies. Finally, this chapter draws on psychological and behavioral insights to understand the motivations behind these unethical acts and propose strategies to foster compliance. By becoming skilled at identifying insider trading and market manipulation, financial services professionals can better uphold ethical standards, protect market integrity, and build lasting trust with clients in an increasingly complex financial landscape.

Perspective

Insider trading and market manipulation are often dismissed as victimless acts or savvy financial strategies. Unfortunately, this view ignores the negative impact these actions can have on market fairness and investor confidence. When a corporate executive trades on confidential merger information or a trader manipulates stock prices, they gain an unfair advantage, leaving other investors at a disadvantage. Consider the following case:

In 1999, James McDermott Jr., a highly compensated and well-respected investment banker, became entangled in an insider trading scandal that ultimately ended his career. McDermott, then CEO of Keefe, Bruyette & Woods, abused his access to confidential, nonpublic information regarding at least five upcoming bank mergers. He leaked this information to his mistress, Kathryn Gannon—a Canadian adult film actress known professionally as Marilyn Star—who used the tips to trade stocks and options. Over several months, Gannon executed well-timed trades that netted her roughly $80,000 in illegal profits. The tips were often shared during private moments, underscoring the role personal relationships can play in compromising market integrity.

The scheme unraveled when the Securities and Exchange Commission (SEC) and federal investigators detected suspicious trading patterns in stocks linked to the mergers. Upon closer examination, authorities identified a strong correlation between McDermott's access to confidential information and Gannon's trades. This discovery led to the disclosure of their relationship and the flow of illicit information. While the case lacked the massive profits or celebrity status of other scandals such as those involving Martha Stewart or Ivan Boesky, it drew attention for its salacious elements, involving an influential banker and an adult film star.

The legal consequences were swift. McDermott was arrested and pleaded guilty to one count of insider trading. He was sentenced to 8 months in prison, 2 years of supervised release, and fined $25,000. Gannon, who cooperated with the investigation, received a lighter sentence of 3 months in jail and a $5000 fine. Though the financial penalties were modest compared to larger cases, the fallout was professionally devastating. McDermott's conviction abruptly ended his career, damaged the reputation of his firm, and served as a cautionary tale about the blurred lines between personal relationships and professional responsibilities.

Although the case did not trigger sweeping regulatory reforms, it highlighted critical issues in compliance and oversight. Specifically, the case underscored the importance of monitoring the personal conduct of financial professionals who have access to market-moving information. The SEC's decision to pursue a relatively small case emphasized the SEC's broader commitment to enforcing insider trading laws, regardless of the monetary scale. In terms of market and public perceptions, the McDermott-Gannon case had a limited financial impact, as the companies involved were not major players and the trades were relatively small. However, the situation added to the public's skepticism about Wall Street's ethical standards, reinforcing concerns about how easily personal motives can distort market fairness. Though not widely remembered, the case serves as an enduring example of how insider trading can occur in unexpected ways and why vigilance remains essential to preserving trust in the financial system.

Definition and Examples of Insider Trading and Market Manipulation

Insider Trading

Insider trading is the act of buying or selling securities by someone who possesses material nonpublic information (MNPI) about the securities.[1] Financial professionals violate their duty of trust and confidence when they use nonpublic information to buy or sell securities.[2] While insider trading can technically refer to any trading by insiders (e.g., corporate officers or directors), the term often includes illegal activity when the trade is made based on MNPI. U.S. law prohibits such trades under Section 10(b) and Rule 10b-5[3] of the Securities Exchange Act of 1934.[4]

Insider trading laws in the United States has been shaped by a series of landmark court cases, most notably SEC v. Texas Gulf Sulphur Co.[5] and Dirks v. SEC.[6] These cases clarified the legal boundaries between permissible and impermissible trading based on material nonpublic information. The Texas Gulf Sulphur case established the precedent that anyone in possession of insider information must either disclose it publicly or abstain from trading, while *Dirks* addressed the concept of "tipper-tippee" liability, ruling that recipients of insider information (tippees) can also be held liable if they know the tip was provided in breach of a fiduciary duty.

As noted above, illegal insider trading occurs when individuals trade securities based on material nonpublic information, thereby gaining an unfair advantage over other market participants. This practice undermines market integrity and violates legal and ethical standards. However, not all insider trading is unlawful. Legal insider trading refers to corporate insiders, such as executives, directors, and employees, buying or selling shares of their own company, provided the transactions are properly disclosed to the SEC. Disclosure occurs through Form 4 filings under Rule 10b5-1 trading plans.[7]

Insider trading arises in various forms and can involve a range of actors with access to privileged information. For example, in 2022, the SEC charged a Chief Information Officer (CIO) of a technology company who purchased large quantities of company stock shortly before the announcement of a confidential acquisition. The CIO realized substantial profits when the stock price surged following the public disclosure. The suspicious timing of the trades triggered regulatory scrutiny, ultimately leading to enforcement action.[8]

In another prominent case, United States v. Newman, hedge fund managers received insider information about upcoming earnings reports from a network of corporate insiders.[9] The information was passed through several intermediaries. The courts ultimately found sufficient grounds to hold the recipients accountable for millions of dollars in illegal profits. The case raised complex questions about the standards of knowledge and intent required for conviction.

Similarly, a 2020 case involved an associate at a multinational law firm who misused confidential information about pending mergers and acquisitions.[10] The individual shared the information with friends who then traded on the information. This resulted in securities fraud charges.

These examples underscore the diverse pathways through which insider trading occurs, from corporate boardrooms and IT departments to legal offices and social circles. At its core, insider trading compromises the fundamental principles that underpin fair and efficient financial markets. It perpetuates information asymmetry, allowing a privileged few to profit at the expense of uninformed investors. Beyond its legal consequences, insider trading erodes public confidence in the markets and violates ethical norms of transparency, fairness, and fiduciary responsibility.[11] Preventing such misconduct requires not only robust regulatory enforcement but also a deep organizational commitment to ethical conduct and compliance culture.

Market Manipulation

Market manipulation occurs when an individual, firm, or other entity intentionally distorts the free and fair operation of financial markets.[12] Market manipulation typically involves creating false or misleading appearances of market activity, including artificial price movements or fabricated trading volumes. These practices are strictly prohibited under Sections 9(a) and 10(b) of the Securities Exchange Act of 1934.[13] Market manipulation is also controlled under international regulations such as the European Union's Market Abuse Regulation.[14] Regulatory bodies, including the U.S. Securities and Exchange Commission (SEC), the Commodity Futures Trading Commission (CFTC), and global counterparts, enforce market manipulation prohibitions as a way to maintain market integrity.

Market manipulation encompasses a range of deceptive practices designed to distort the true value or activity of financial instruments for personal or institutional gain. Typical forms of manipulation include pump-and-dump schemes, spoofing, wash trading, and quote stuffing. Each undermines the integrity of capital markets in distinct but harmful ways.

One high-profile example of a pump-and-dump scheme occurred in 2018, when the SEC charged a network of individuals who exploited social media to disseminate false and misleading information about thinly traded microcap stocks. These individuals created the illusion of firm credibility and stock price momentum, driving up stock prices before offloading their holdings at a profit. The group collectively generated over $100 million in illicit gains. The case revealed how digital platforms can be weaponized to manipulate retail sentiment on a large scale.[15]

Spoofing involves submitting large orders with the intent of cancelling them before execution, thereby giving a false impression of market demand or supply. This tactic distorts the order books of dealers that can then trigger algorithmic or human responses that manipulators exploit. In a landmark case, high-frequency trader Navinder Sarao was charged in 2015 with spoofing activities that contributed to the 2010 "Flash Crash." Sarao's strategic placement and rapid cancellation of large S&P 500 E-mini futures orders sent misleading signals that destabilized the market and highlighted systemic vulnerabilities in the market's electronic trading infrastructure.[16]

Wash trading, which includes the simultaneous buying and selling of the same asset to create artificial trading volume, continues to plague traditional and digital markets. Wash trading falsely signals liquidity and investor interest, luring legitimate traders into manipulated price movements. In 2022, the Commodity Futures Trading Commission (CFTC) penalized several cryptocurrency exchanges for failing to detect and prevent wash trading activity occurring on their platforms. These enforcement actions reinforced concerns about lax compliance frameworks in emerging financial ecosystems.

Quote stuffing is another manipulative strategy in which traders rapidly submit and cancel large volumes of orders to slow down the trading systems of other traders and manipulate price feeds. Though harder to detect, quote stuffing can significantly impact market efficiency by creating data congestion that misleads market participants.

The ethical implications of market manipulation are profound. Such practices erode investor confidence, distort price discovery mechanisms, and exploit less-informed market participants who depend on the accuracy and transparency of market data. Manipulation violates fundamental ethical standards, including fairness, honesty, integrity, and professional responsibility. Market manipulation not only harms individual investors but also destabilizes the broader financial system by undermining the credibility of market institutions and regulatory frameworks. Preventing such behavior requires coordinated efforts from regulators, firms, and market participants to strengthen surveillance systems, improve enforcement, and cultivate a culture of ethical decision-making across the financial industry.

Regulatory Responses and Enforcement Actions

Regulatory authorities have responded to insider trading and market manipulation by developing robust legal frameworks and enforcement strategies. In the United States, the Securities Exchange Act of 1934 remains the principal legislation prohibiting fraudulent practices, including insider trading and manipulation, through Section 10(b) and Rule 10b-5.[17] The 1934 Act established the SEC, granting the Agency the authority to investigate and prosecute violations.[18] The Insider Trading Sanctions Act of 1984 further strengthened the Agency's ability to deal with insider trading and market manipulation by allowing civil penalties up to three times the profit gained or loss avoided in illegal insider trading cases.[19]

Regulatory developments have continued in the wake of recent financial crises and technological changes. The Dodd-Frank Wall Street Reform and Consumer Protection Act of 2010 introduced significant whistleblower protections, incentivizing market participants to report insider trading and market manipulation.[20] As a result, the SEC's Whistleblower Program has awarded more than $2 billion to individual whistleblowers since its inception. The Whistleblower program distributed over $255 million in awards in fiscal year 2024 alone.[21] Self-regulatory bodies also act in cases of insider trading and market manipulation. In the United States, FINRA Rule 2020 prohibits manipulative or fraudulent devices, while Rule 3110 mandates that financial firms supervise to detect and prevent violations.[22] In Europe, the Market Abuse Regulation (MAR), effective since 2016, standardized rules across European Union member states, requiring enhanced transparency and ongoing surveillance of trading activities.[23]

Over the past quarter-century, enforcement actions by regulatory bodies have increased in scope and sophistication. The SEC filed 583 enforcement actions in fiscal year 2024,[24] obtaining orders for $8.2 billion in financial remedies—the highest in its history—with a marked rise in cases involving cryptocurrency, AI-related misstatements, and social media–driven manipulation. Notable actions include charges against a former Lumentum executive for insider trading, resulting in substantial fines and permanent injunctions.[25] The SEC has also targeted "pump-and-dump" schemes perpetrated via online platforms. An example of this regulatory enforcement is a case involving misleading promotion and coordinated trading of

China Liberal Education Holdings shares. Enforcement of pump-and-dump regulations led to the company forfeiting $214 million in proceeds.[26] Additionally, the SEC is increasingly leveraging data analytics and machine learning to identify suspicious trading patterns and possible trading collusion.

FINRA is also engaged in addressing regulatory lapses. FINRA plays a role in disciplining broker-dealers who fail to supervise employees or detect manipulation, imposing fines and suspensions.[27] FINRA reported 552 disciplinary actions in 2024, reflecting a 22% increase from the previous year.[28] For example, TradeZero America was fined for inadequate oversight of social media influencers who misled retail investors.[29] In the futures and commodities markets, the Commodity Futures Trading Commission (CFTC) prosecutes pricing manipulation.[30] The CFTC's landmark case against Navinder Sarao, who contributed to the 2010 Flash Crash by spoofing S&P 500 futures, illustrates the use of criminal and civil enforcement to deter abuse.[15]

Given the increasingly global nature of financial misconduct, cross-border cooperation has become essential to deal with market abuses. The International Organization of Securities Commissions (IOSCO) coordinates regulatory responses to address global schemes and harmonize enforcement across jurisdictions.[31] Recent trends include enhanced scrutiny of technology-driven violations such as crypto pump-and-dump schemes, greater reliance on AI and surveillance tools, and the imposition of stricter penalties, including public bans and reputational sanctions.

Ethical Implications and Prevention Strategies

Insider trading and market manipulation present significant ethical challenges for those who provide financial advice. Ethical violations have profound practical consequences for financial markets and institutions. At their core, insider trading and market manipulation undermine foundational values such as fairness, transparency, and trust. When individuals or organizations exploit material nonpublic information or distort market activity, they gain an unfair trading advantage. This erodes the confidence of market participants, clients, other stakeholders, and the broader public.[32] Any perception (and possible reality) of unfairness can discourage market participation and investment, particularly among retail investors. The result, ultimately, is a reduction in market liquidity and efficiency.[33]

Investors and financial advisory clients are directly harmed by market manipulation and insider trading. Manipulated markets expose clients to unjust losses and mispricing, subverting the fiduciary and best-interest standards that form the ethical foundation of financial advice. When prices do not reflect genuine supply and demand, informed and uninformed investors alike face distorted investment outcomes.

The legal profession is aware of these outcomes. Each year, numerous class action lawsuits, typically following major market abuse scandals, result in billions of dollars in client restitution and legal penalties for financial institutions.[34] Consider the LIBOR scandal. This case involved a series of fraudulent manipulations by major banks of the London Interbank Offered Rate (LIBOR), a benchmark interest rate used globally for loans, derivatives, and financial products. Between 2005 and 2011, traders at institutions like Barclays, UBS, and Deutsche Bank colluded to submit false borrowing rates to influence LIBOR, either to boost trading profits or make their banks appear more stable during the 2008 financial crisis. The scandal, uncovered in 2012, led to billions of dollars in fines, criminal convictions, and the eventual phase-out of LIBOR in 2023 in favor of alternatives like the Secured Overnight Financing Rate (SOFR).[35]

The consequences for jeopardizing market integrity can also be severe. Widespread manipulation or repeated insider trading can lead to systemic reputational harm, driving volatility and undermining the reliability of price signals. If left unchecked, manipulative behaviors can escalate into broader crises of confidence, with negative spillovers for market stability and economic growth. From a financial advice standpoint, ethical lapses tarnish individual and institutional reputations, making it more challenging to build and sustain client relationships. Financial advisors and firms implicated for misconduct frequently face long-term regulatory restrictions, loss of licensure, and significant outflows of client assets.

In response to the risks and consequences associated with insider trading and other forms of market abuse, financial institutions and regulators have developed increasingly sophisticated prevention strategies that align with both regulatory mandates and industry best practices. At the core of these efforts are complex compliance programs, which serve as the first line of defense against unethical behavior. These programs typically include strict pre-clearance procedures for employee trades, real-time surveillance systems to detect anomalous activity, and formal escalation protocols for investigating and addressing suspected violations.

Technological advancements have played a critical role in enhancing these capabilities. Many firms now deploy machine learning algorithms and pattern recognition tools to identify unusual trading behaviors, such as timing irregularities or potential collusion, especially in fast-moving markets like cryptocurrency and high-frequency trading. These tools can sift through vast volumes of transactional data to proactively flag red flags that might otherwise go unnoticed.

In addition to surveillance, ongoing ethics and compliance training remains a key component of prevention. When tailored to specific roles within an organization, such training helps employees understand their duties. Training also equips them to recognize and resist unethical pressures. The most effective programs incorporate real-world case studies, offer guidance on navigating ethical gray areas, such as the use of alternative data or influencer interactions, and provide practical steps for escalating concerns.

Confidential whistleblower channels further strengthen prevention frameworks. Internal hotlines and secure digital portals make it easier for employees and third parties to report suspected misconduct without fear of retaliation. These mechanisms are not merely symbolic; they have proven highly effective. The SEC Whistleblower Program, for example, continues to generate a record number of credible tips, many of which have led to substantial enforcement actions.

An often overlooked but vital prevention strategy is client education. Firms and financial advisors that proactively communicate with clients about market risks, trading mechanics, and the warning signs of potential manipulation help reduce the likelihood of client exploitation. Transparency builds trust and creates an informed client base that is better equipped to avoid becoming a victim of unethical behavior.

In the end, organizational culture is one of the most powerful deterrents to misconduct. Firms with strong ethical cultures, visible executive commitment to compliance, and well-defined consequences for unethical actions consistently report fewer violations. Cultural reinforcement strategies may include mandatory ethics pledges, executive participation in compliance events, frequent ethics communications from senior leadership, and the integration of ethical behavior into performance reviews and incentive compensation. For example, some leading investment banks require that all employee trades involving sensitive securities be pre-approved by compliance officers and logged in electronic systems, subject to real-time audits. Others have gone further by linking executive bonuses to ethical culture metrics and compliance outcomes.

Together, these layered prevention strategies, which span technology, training, reporting, client education, and cultural reform, represent a comprehensive approach to safeguarding market integrity and restoring trust in the financial system.[36]

Case Studies on Trading and Market Manipulation

The following discussion presents a series of case studies that illustrate how insider trading and market manipulation have unfolded in the past. By examining actual enforcement actions and regulatory responses, these examples provide insights into the tactics used to exploit financial markets, the consequences for those involved, and the broader implications for market integrity. Each case highlights not only the legal and financial outcomes but also the ethical challenges and compliance failures that allowed the misconduct to occur.

Martha Stewart and ImClone Insider Trading (2001)

In 2001, Martha Stewart—an American businessperson, writer, television personality, and lifestyle icon known for transforming domestic arts into a media empire—sold nearly 4000 shares of ImClone Systems. She acted after receiving a tip from her broker that the company's CEO was selling his holdings. Stewart received this information ahead of a public announcement that the Food and Drug Administration (FDA) had rejected ImClone's new drug application. By acting on this nonpublic information, Stewart avoided approximately $45,000 in losses.[37] Although Stewart was acquitted of insider trading itself, she was found guilty of obstruction of justice and making false statements during the investigation. The SEC imposed fines and a five-year ban from serving as a director or officer of any public company.[38]

Martha Stewart's case offers the following ethical lesson: even seemingly minor acts of insider trading breach fundamental principles of fairness and fiduciary duty. The case underscores how attempts to conceal misconduct, regardless of the financial scale, can lead to serious legal consequences and lasting reputational harm. From a behavioral standpoint, Stewart's actions were influenced by a fervent desire to avoid personal monetary loss, illustrating how loss aversion can drive individuals toward unethical decisions. This incident highlights the critical need for firms to implement and rigorously enforce controls over material nonpublic information (MNPI), ensuring that impulsive or biased choices by employees and clients are effectively mitigated.

Raj Rajaratnam and the Galleon Group Insider Trading Scandal (2009)

Raj Rajaratnam, founder of the Galleon Group hedge fund, orchestrated one of the largest insider trading networks in U.S. history. From 2003 to 2009, Rajaratnam received confidential information from corporate insiders at major companies, including Intel and Goldman Sachs, which allowed him to generate over $63 million in illegal trading profits.[39] Law enforcement authorities used wiretaps for the first time in an insider trading case to record conversations that provided direct evidence of wrongdoing. Rajaratnam was convicted of securities fraud and conspiracy and sentenced to 11 years in prison.[40]

The case of Raj Rajaratnam highlights a critical ethical lesson: collusion and systemic breaches of trust can severely undermine market integrity. Large-scale insider trading not only distorts the fair allocation of capital but also erodes investor confidence in financial systems. Behaviorally, Rajaratnam's actions were fueled by a relentless pursuit of competitive advantage and an overconfidence in his ability to avoid detection. These are traits that often accompany high-stakes misconduct. This case underscores the importance of robust surveillance mechanisms and strong inter-agency cooperation, including tools like wiretaps and whistleblower programs, which are vital for uncovering and dismantling complex networks of unethical behavior.

GameStop Short Squeeze and Social Media–Driven Market Volatility (2021)

In January 2021, retail investors organized on the Reddit forum (*r/WallStreetBets*) to coordinate in purchasing large volumes of GameStop shares, driving the price from under $20 to over $480 within weeks.[41] The coordinated buying created a "short squeeze," forcing institutional short sellers to cover their positions at significant losses. While some observers alleged market manipulation, regulatory investigations concluded that no traditional market manipulation occurred, but the episode highlighted gaps in oversight related to social media influence and collective action.

The GameStop trading frenzy reveals an important ethical lesson: while mass coordination by retail investors may not be technically illegal, it can disrupt market fairness and raise serious concerns about the influence of herd behavior and information cascades on price formation. This event was primarily driven by herd mentality, with social media amplifying group behavior and leading to extreme price volatility. Such dynamics pose significant risks, particularly to less sophisticated investors who may not fully grasp the consequences of speculative surges. In response, regulators and financial professionals must evolve their approaches to education and oversight, tailoring them to the realities of online communities and ensuring that clients understand the risks inherent in collective speculation.

Navinder Sarao and the 2010 Flash Crash (2010–2016)

On May 6, 2010, U.S. stock markets experienced a rapid crash and recovery, with the Dow Jones Industrial Average plummeting nearly 1000 points within a few minutes. Subsequent investigation found that Navinder Singh Sarao, a British trader, used spoofing tactics—placing, then canceling, large orders in S&P 500 futures contracts to create false market signals and manipulate prices.[42] Sarao's actions contributed to the instability that triggered the "Flash Crash." Sarao was arrested in 2015 and extradited to the United States, where he pleaded guilty to wire fraud and market manipulation. He was ordered to forfeit over $12 million.

The case involving Navinder Sarao underscores a vital ethical lesson: market manipulation, especially when facilitated by algorithmic and high-frequency trading, threatens financial stability and undermines trust in the fairness of markets. Sarao's actions reveal behavioral patterns often seen in financial misconduct, including overconfidence and a disregard for ethical accountability, which drove his high-risk and isolated decision-making. To counter such threats, financial institutions must implement real-time monitoring systems and automated controls designed to detect and prevent manipulative trading strategies, particularly within the fast-paced environment of electronic markets.

Psychological and Behavioral Insights

Exhibiting a deeper understanding of the psychological and behavioral forces behind insider trading and market manipulation allows someone to obtain a deeper understanding of the causes of these behaviors. In nearly all the cases described in this chapter, people engage in these unethical behaviors because of a complex mix of cognitive biases, situational pressures, and shifting market conditions. Traditional motivators like greed, overconfidence, and herd mentality also played a significant role in shaping behavior. However, recent research and enforcement cases point to other influential factors, including digital disinhibition,[43] moral disengagement,[44] and the normalization of unethical behavior within certain organizational cultures.

The following discussion provides insight into these causes of insider trading and market manipulation.

Digital Disinhibition and Anonymity

The rise of online trading communities and social media has introduced new psychological dynamics that contribute to market manipulation, with digital disinhibition emerging as a particularly influential factor. Digital platforms, by offering a degree of anonymity and distance, reduce a user's sense of personal accountability and social restraint. As a result, individuals may engage in behaviors online, such as aggressive trading tactics or the spread of misleading information, that they would likely avoid in face-to-face environments.

A prominent example of this phenomenon occurred during the 2021 GameStop trading frenzy, which unfolded on Reddit's *WallStreetBets* forum. This historical episode demonstrates how online communities can foster collective digital identities through shared narratives, memes, and viral content. Rapid information sharing accelerated risk-taking behavior among retail investors, who engaged in coordinated buying of GameStop shares to drive up the price. This collective action was fueled by social proof bias, as participants increasingly conformed to the group's sentiment, believing that the sheer number of supporters validated the strategy.

The result was a surge in irrational exuberance, where emotional momentum overtook rational analysis. Many investors disregarded the company's financial fundamentals, diminishing the perceived ethical weight of their actions. This behavior was further reinforced by overconfidence bias, with users overestimating their ability to challenge institutional short sellers and control market outcomes.[45] Memes and online commentary gave some investors a false sense of mastery over complex financial dynamics, leading them to underestimate the risks of volatility and loss.

Additionally, confirmation bias played a critical role in the case. Traders actively sought and amplified information that supported their anti-establishment narrative. They positioned themselves as underdog retail investors battling Wall Street elites. They also ignored data that contradicted their beliefs. This created a self-reinforcing echo chamber that sustained manipulative momentum and reduced critical engagement with reality.[46]

Moral Disengagement and Ethical Fading

Studies show that people who engage in unethical trading often use mental tricks to ignore the wrongness of their actions. One key tactic is called moral disengagement.[47] Moral disengagement refers to a set of psychological strategies that allow individuals to commit unethical acts without feeling guilt. These strategies include eight interconnected mechanisms. For instance, moral justification reframes harmful behavior as serving a noble purpose, such as claiming, "This is for the company's survival." Euphemistic labeling softens the language around misconduct, turning a scam into "a smart business move." Advantageous comparison makes unethical actions seem acceptable by contrasting them with worse behavior, like thinking, "Others do much worse." Displacement and diffusion of responsibility shift blame to authority figures or groups, with excuses like "My boss told me to" or "Everyone was doing it." Distortion of consequences minimizes the perceived harm, such as believing, "No one really gets hurt." Finally, dehumanization reduces empathy by viewing victims as faceless or merely numbers. These mechanisms collectively suppress moral self-regulation, enabling individuals to act unethically without remorse.

In addition to these mental tactics, rationalizations like "everyone does it" or "no one is directly harmed" contribute to ethical fading, which is a process where the moral aspects of decisions become obscured. This fading is often fueled by self-deception biases, such as motivated blindness (ignoring unethical elements when they serve personal interests) and bounded ethicality (cognitive limitations that hinder ethical awareness despite good intentions). These biases shift focus toward financial, technical, or procedural concerns, allowing harmful actions to occur unintentionally.

Interviews with convicted insider traders reveal that many did not view their actions as criminal.[48,49] Instead, insider traders cited competitive pressure or industry norms as justification for their actions. Common self-serving biases included harm minimization (downplaying the impact on victims as indirect or diffuse) and conformity bias (adopting peer behavior to rationalize rule-breaking as standard practice). In their testimonies, traders often described insider tips as "opportunistic exchanges" rather than fraudulent acts, illustrating how psychological mechanisms can normalize misconduct in high-pressure environments.

Normalization of Deviance in High-Pressure Environments

Within organizations, repeated exposure to boundary-pushing behavior can lead to the normalization of deviance, where initially unacceptable practices become routine. Consider the case of the Galleon Group. As discussed earlier in the chapter, the Galleon Group case was a major insider trading scandal centered around hedge fund manager Raj Rajaratnam. In 2019, Rajaratnam was arrested and later convicted on 14 counts of securities fraud and conspiracy for trading on nonpublic information obtained from a network of corporate insiders at firms like Intel, IBM, and Goldman Sachs. The Galleon case exposed deep ethical lapses in the financial industry and highlighted how competitive pressure and personal networks can facilitate large-scale financial misconduct.

The Galleon Group case also revealed the existence of collusive insider networks. These networks were sustained by implicit company approval and weak regulatory oversight. Over time, this environment led to widespread violations of financial regulations. Rajaratnam exhibited obvious signs of overconfidence bias.[50] Specifically, he overestimated his ability to avoid detection through sophisticated trading strategies. He also exhibited a self-serving bias by prioritizing personal profit over duties owed to others. Falling prey to cognitive biases distorted Rajaratnam's judgment. As a result, he rationalized the illegal sharing of insider information.

Similar dynamics were evident in the Wells Fargo sales scandal, which was also discussed earlier in the chapter.[51] Incentive structures and management expectations encouraged ethically questionable behaviors among employees. Conformity bias played a significant role in advancing fraudulent behavior, as staff aligned with perceived group norms to meet aggressive sales targets. Rationalization bias was further contributed to by allowing employees to justify the creation of fake accounts as necessary for job security. These biases suppressed ethical concerns and normalized fraudulent practices within the organization.

Temporal Discounting and Short-Termism

Financial misconduct is frequently driven by temporal discounting. This bias, often modeled as hyperbolic discounting, reflects the tendency of individuals to apply steep and inconsistent discount rates over time. Here's how temporal discounting works:

> *Imagine a stockbroker who learns confidential information that a company's stock will soon drop. Selling the stock now based on that insider knowledge could earn the broker a quick $10,000. They know it is illegal and could have severe consequences, like losing their job or going to prison. But because those consequences feel distant and uncertain, they prioritize the immediate reward.*

This is temporal discounting. The broker heavily discounts future risks and overvalues short-term gains. The decision reflects hyperbolic discounting, where the urgency of the present overwhelms rational long-term thinking, making unethical behavior more tempting. When engaged in temporal discounting, future outcomes are disproportionately devalued compared to immediate rewards. Such intertemporal inconsistencies can lead to preference reversals, whereby individuals prioritize short-term gratification at the expense of long-term welfare. This mechanism helps explain why some actors engage in unethical or risky financial behavior despite foreseeable negative consequences.[52,53]

Although temporal discounting is common, there are effective strategies to counteract this bias. Research in behavioral finance shows that emphasizing long-term concerns, such as professional reputation and legacy, can help reduce a present bias. One helpful approach is the planner-doer framework, where the reflective "planner" sets up commitment devices to guide the impulsive "doer" self. These devices, like pre-set rules, accountability systems, or delayed decision mechanisms, strengthen self-control and encourage choices that align with long-term ethical and financial goals. Academic studies in corporate environments support this strategy, showing that when reputation is made salient, individuals are less likely to engage in short-sighted or risky behavior.[54] In other words, reminding people of their future image and impact can help them make better decisions today.

Behavioral Interventions and Prevention

Effective prevention of insider trading and market manipulation increasingly relies on behavioral insights to influence decision-making and reduce misconduct. One approach involves the use of "pre-commitment" tools, which prompt traders to affirm their adherence to ethical guidelines before executing sensitive transactions.[55] Similarly, firms are implementing "just-in-time" ethics prompts. These are real-time alerts that appear when trading behavior triggers risk indicators. These interventions serve as cognitive nudges, encouraging individuals to pause and reflect before acting unethically.

Research from controlled studies in banking and investment settings supports the value of these strategies. Regular feedback on ethical performance, when combined with real-time monitoring, has been shown to lower the incidence of rule violations significantly. By making ethical expectations more visible and immediate, these behavioral mechanisms help mitigate impulsive or self-serving decisions.

Changing organizational and industry-wide social norms is another preventive tool. The publicization of enforcement actions, such as the conviction of Raj Rajaratnam for insider trading or regulatory scrutiny following the GameStop short squeeze, has deterrent and educational effects. These high-profile cases reinforce the message that unethical behavior carries real and lasting consequences, thereby reshaping what is seen as acceptable within professional communities.

As the examples described in this chapter illustrate, the psychology behind insider trading and market manipulation cannot be reduced to simple greed or rational calculation. A complex interplay of technological environments, cultural norms, and organizational structures influences these behaviors. As such, sustainable prevention requires a holistic approach, one that blends behavioral science with robust regulatory frameworks, visible leadership commitment, and adaptive compliance systems capable of evolving in response to emerging risks.

Challenges and Trends in Addressing Insider Trading and Market Manipulation

Efforts to combat insider trading and market manipulation have become increasingly complex due to rapid advancements in financial technology, the globalization of markets, and changing organizational behaviors. These factors have transformed the economic landscape, presenting regulators with a dynamic and challenging set of issues. High-profile incidents, such as the social media-driven GameStop stock surge in 2021 and the rise of cryptocurrencies, have already compelled regulatory bodies to adapt their risk management and compliance strategies. Additionally, several emerging and nuanced challenges continue to reshape the enforcement environment. The following discussion examines some of these challenges in greater detail, highlighting their implications and the evolving strategies that regulators are using to address them. This discussion focuses on some of the trends and challenges related to insider trading and market manipulation.

Rise of Decentralized Finance (DeFi) and "Anonymity Laundering"

A significant emerging challenge facing financial regulators stems from the rapid growth of decentralized finance (DeFi) platforms and decentralized exchanges (DEXs), which enable users to trade digital assets without the oversight of a centralized authority.[56] Unlike traditional financial systems, DeFi platforms often rely on blockchain-based protocols and cryptographic tools that conceal user identities, which significantly weakens established surveillance and compliance mechanisms.

This anonymity has made DeFi an attractive tool for illicit actors, including cybercriminals, ransomware operators, and state-sponsored entities, to launder illicit proceeds. The U.S. Department of the Treasury's 2023 *Illicit Finance Risk Assessment* report highlighted this concern, noting that DeFi is increasingly being used to obscure the origins of unlawfully obtained funds.[57] Common tactics include cross-chain asset transfers (which move funds between different blockchains), mixing services (which blend multiple transactions to hide individual sources), and liquidity pool layering (which fragments transactions across decentralized trading pools). Together, these techniques enable what regulators and analysts call "anonymity laundering," making it extremely difficult to trace the flow of illicit funds. Both academic research and regulatory reports emphasize the growing urgency of addressing these vulnerabilities. As DeFi continues to evolve, it presents a significant challenge for policymakers and enforcement agencies seeking to maintain market transparency, enforce anti-money laundering (AML) standards, and preserve the integrity of global financial systems.

Meme Stocks, "Crowdsourced" Manipulation, and Disinformation

The meme-stock phenomenon revealed a significant shift in how market manipulation can occur. This trading approach demonstrates that market manipulation is no longer limited to institutional actors. Instead, large-scale coordination among retail investors, often fueled by viral narratives, online forums, and misinformation, has shown the capacity to distort price discovery and overwhelm traditional market risk controls. This shift became particularly evident during the 2021 meme-stock surge, when the SEC observed a rapid escalation in retail trading activity. The SEC noted that this surge exposed structural vulnerabilities in equity and options markets, challenging long-standing assumptions about market behavior and oversight effectiveness.[58] Empirical studies of Reddit's *r/Wallstreetbets* forum show that coordinated discussions not only predicted but actively drove dramatic increases in trading volume and stock prices for companies such as GameStop, AMC, and other heavily shorted securities. This bottom-up collective action disrupted conventional market surveillance systems, which were not designed to detect or manage manipulation emerging from decentralized, digital communities.

Further complicating the issue is the use of coordinated manipulation strategies like "pump-and-dump" and "short-and-distort" campaigns. These tactics have been amplified by automated bots and the spread of disinformation, making it even more difficult for regulators to detect misconduct or trace its origin. As a result, attribution and enforcement have become increasingly complex in an environment where digital coordination and anonymity often shield manipulators from accountability. Overall, the meme-stock episode highlights the evolving nature of market manipulation in the digital age where social media, technology, and retail mobilization can create market distortions once thought to be the domain of large institutional players. This new landscape demands updated surveillance tools, cross-disciplinary regulatory approaches, and a deeper understanding of the social and behavioral forces shaping modern trading behavior.

AI-Driven Evasion Tactics and Regulatory Arms Race

Regulators have increasingly adopted artificial intelligence and machine learning (e.g., PCA-RF models[59]) to conduct advanced market surveillance and to detect collusive trading and other manipulative behaviors. For example, FINRA has invested in machine learning tools and enhanced surveillance patterns to identify complex misconduct in equity, options, and fixed-income markets. However, malicious actors have retaliated by leveraging similar technologies to create adaptive trading algorithms designed to evade detection. In this context, adversarial machine learning presents notable risks not only to regulatory frameworks but also to the integrity of the markets.

In response to increasingly sophisticated forms of market manipulation, researchers have developed conceptual frameworks to better understand the ongoing interaction between regulatory surveillance systems and evasive market manipulators. One such approach is known as "adversarial learning," which models this dynamic as a continuous, adaptive struggle. In this framework, regulators train advanced detection algorithms to identify suspicious trading behavior, while manipulators intentionally modify their tactics to mimic legitimate market activity and avoid detection. The give-and-take of market actors and regulators creates an evolving cat-and-mouse dynamic, where both sides are constantly learning and adapting in response to each other's strategies. Such models highlight the need for flexible, AI-driven surveillance tools that can evolve alongside increasingly complex manipulation techniques.

Insider Trading via Alternative Data and Non-traditional Channels

New forms of insider trading are emerging that utilize alternative data sources. Alternative data includes non-traditional datasets that provide insights into company activities, such as satellite imagery, geolocation tracking, and supply chain analytics, to gain material nonpublic information outside traditional corporate channels.[60] Although often legally accessible, these datasets can reveal material nonpublic information when analyzed with insider knowledge. These methods allow bad actors to exploit publicly available data to infer sensitive insights about a company's performance, while encrypted messaging platforms and global data brokers complicate regulatory efforts.

Traders sometimes combine alternative data with insider tips to predict corporate events, such as earnings surprises or mergers. For instance, increased factory activity captured by satellite imagery could signal an upcoming production ramp-up. The legality of alternative data usage is ambiguous, complicating the proof of insider trading due to the lack of regulatory guidelines. The use of alternative data has prompted regulators to rethink insider trading enforcement.[61] The SEC and other agencies are investing in advanced technologies to detect suspicious trading patterns, but the rapid evolution of tools often outpaces regulatory frameworks. More precise definitions of material nonpublic information and stronger international cooperation are needed to tackle these challenges. Looking forward, proactive regulatory measures, including enhanced corporate data security and public education on data misuse risks, will become increasingly important for maintaining market integrity as technology reshapes financial markets.

Blurring Lines Between Market Manipulation and Political/Geopolitical Influence

In recent years, there have been instances where market manipulation is linked to geopolitical or state-sponsored campaigns. Investigations by the U.S. Department of Justice (DOJ) and European Union agencies have uncovered cases of state-affiliated actors who have intentionally sought to create market volatility as a form of economic coercion or to undermine confidence in Western financial systems. The U.S. Department of Homeland Security's 2025 Homeland Threat Assessment documents that adversaries, including state-linked actors, actively attempt to manipulate markets, engage in economic espionage, and use coercive economic tools to weaken the competitiveness and stability of U.S. and European industries and consumers.[62]

Additionally, the U.S. Department of Justice's Office of Inspector General (DOJ OIG) has reported on the covert use of economic coercion, including manipulation through media placement, to gain an advantage or exert undue influence to destabilize financial markets. These cases challenge existing legal frameworks and cross-border cooperation, necessitating intelligence sharing and coordinated regulatory responses that extend beyond just financial authorities.[63]

Whistleblower Retaliation and Underreporting

Despite the existence of strong statutory protections for whistleblowers, such as those provided under the Dodd-Frank Act and reinforced by SEC enforcement, high-profile cases continue to reveal the ongoing risk of retaliation, particularly within multinational corporations or firms operating in loosely regulated environments. These cases underscore the challenges whistleblowers face, even when legal safeguards are in place.

Reports from the SEC and Transparency International highlight a troubling trend: namely, the persistent underreporting of misconduct, often driven by a fear of professional retaliation. Financial advisors and employees of financial services firms may worry about career setbacks, damaged reputations, or even termination if their identity is exposed. These fears are especially acute in organizational cultures where whistleblower protections are poorly implemented or where reporting mechanisms lack anonymity, transparency, or follow-through.

Moreover, in global firms with complex governance structures, jurisdictional inconsistencies in whistleblower laws can further weaken protections. Even when employees report wrongdoing in good faith, they may encounter indirect forms of retaliation, such as exclusion from key projects, stalled promotions, or subtle workplace ostracism. These risks contribute to a chilling effect, discouraging individuals from stepping forward despite the clear ethical and legal imperatives to do so. To address these concerns, organizations must go beyond mere legal compliance. Well-designed, confidential reporting systems, coupled with clear anti-retaliation policies, leadership support, and visible consequences for retaliatory behavior, are critically important to creating a culture where whistleblowers feel safe, heard, and protected.

Erosion of Ethical Norms Through Gig and Contract-Based Finance

The rise of gig-based work, independent financial analysts, and "pay-for-signal" trading communities has significantly reshaped the landscape of market participation and not without consequences. These non-traditional market actors often function outside the formal structures of regulated financial institutions, leading to a diffusion of responsibility and a noticeable erosion of established ethical norms.

Unlike traditionally employed financial services professionals bound by well-defined compliance frameworks, gig and contract-based workers frequently operate under looser accountability standards, with limited oversight, unclear fiduciary obligations, and minimal exposure to ethics training. As a result, their actions may not be subject to the same scrutiny or disciplinary consequences as those working within regulated environments.

This regulatory gray area creates vulnerabilities in the financial system. For instance, contractor-based analysts may produce and distribute market-moving insights without disclosing conflicts of interest. At the same time, "pay-for-signal" platforms—where subscribers pay for trading tips or alerts—can facilitate manipulative behavior or misinformation with little to no transparency. The informal and decentralized nature of these ecosystems makes it difficult to enforce consistent standards of professionalism, fairness, and investor protection.

To address these emerging risks, regulators and firms must consider expanding ethical oversight and developing tailored compliance strategies for non-traditional market participants. Without such efforts, the growing presence of loosely regulated actors threatens to undermine the integrity and fairness of modern financial markets.

Regulatory Arbitrage and Fragmented Oversight

Finally, as financial markets become more globally interconnected, a growing number of market participants are deliberately structuring transactions across multiple jurisdictions to take advantage of inconsistent or weaker regulatory regimes. This practice, often referred to as regulatory arbitrage, creates serious challenges for enforcement agencies, as oversight becomes fragmented and critical information can fall into jurisdictional "blind spots."

These gaps in cross-border coordination are not theoretical. They have been actively exploited in several high-profile market abuse cases, particularly those involving multinational hedge funds and digital asset platforms. For example, firms may route trades through lightly regulated markets to evade stricter surveillance elsewhere or use entities in one country to conceal manipulative practices occurring in another. In digital finance, the decentralized and borderless nature of many crypto platforms has further complicated enforcement, enabling bad actors to move assets across networks that operate outside traditional regulatory frameworks.

The lack of uniform rules and enforcement capacity across jurisdictions undermines the effectiveness of global financial safeguards and hampers efforts to detect and prosecute misconduct. As such, greater international regulatory cooperation, harmonization of compliance standards, and cross-border data-sharing protocols are urgently needed to address these structural vulnerabilities and close the loopholes that enable sophisticated forms of market manipulation.

Chapter Summary

Insider trading and market manipulation pose serious threats to market integrity, fairness, and public trust, creating complex ethical and compliance challenges for financial services professionals. These practices, whether through the misuse of nonpublic information or the distortion of market signals, can harm investors and erode the core principles of transparency and accountability. To address these risks, regulatory frameworks such as the Securities Exchange Act of 1934 and the Dodd-Frank Act, enforced by agencies like the SEC and FINRA, offer powerful tools for enforcement and oversight. Real-world cases—from Martha Stewart's insider trading to the GameStop trading frenzy—illustrate the consequences of unethical behavior and the importance of firm and advisor vigilance. Psychological research sheds light on the behavioral drivers behind misconduct, including greed, overconfidence, and herd mentality, and offers strategies to promote ethical decision-making. Financial professionals can reduce violations by implementing strong compliance programs, providing ethics training, and fostering a culture of integrity. As technology and globalization continue to reshape financial markets, ongoing education and proactive compliance efforts are essential to uphold professional standards and protect market trust.

Chapter Resources

- Department of the Treasury, 2023 Illicit Financial Risk Assessment: https://home.treasury.gov/news/press-releases/jy1391
- EU Market Abuse Regulation (MAR): https://eur-lex.europa.eu/eli/reg/2014/596/oj/eng
- FINRA Rule 2020: https://www.finra.org/rules-guidance/rulebooks/finra-rules/2020
- Insider Trading Regulations: https://www.sec.gov/resources-small-businesses/small-business-compliance-guides/insider-trading-arrangements-and-related-disclosures
- Securities and Exchange Act of 1934: https://www.nyse.com/publicdocs/nyse/regulation/nyse/sea34.pdf

Notes

[1]Securities Exchange Act of 1934, 15 U.S.C. § 78a et seq.

[2]Langevoort, D.C. (2025). *Insider Trading: Regulation, Enforcement, and Prevention*. Clark Boardman Callaghan.

[3]SEC Rule 10b-5, 17 C.F.R. §240.10b-5.

[4]Securities Exchange Act of 1934, §10(b), 15 U.S.C. §78j(b).

[5]*SEC v. Texas Gulf Sulphur Co.*, 401 F.2d 833 (2d Cir. 1968).

[6]*Dirks v. SEC*, 463 U.S. 646 (1983).

[7]U.S. Securities and Exchange Commission. (2022). *Form 4 - Statement of Changes in Beneficial Ownership of Securities*. https://www.sec.gov/files/form4.pdf

[8]U.S. Securities and Exchange Commission. (2022). *Litigation Release No. 25391: SEC Charges Tech Executive with Insider Trading Ahead of Merger*. https://www.sec.gov/litigation/litreleases/2022/lr25391.htm

[9]*United States v. Newman*, 773 F.3d 438 (2d Cir. 2014).

[10]U.S. Securities and Exchange Commission. (2020). *Litigation Release No. 23697: SEC Charges Attorney and Friends with Insider Trading in M&A Deals*. https://www.sec.gov/litigation/litreleases/2020/lr23697.htm

[11]Boatright, J.R. (2014). *Ethics in Finance* (3rd ed.). Wiley-Blackwell.

[12]https://www.financestrategists.com/financial-advisor/business-ethics/market-manipulation/

[13]U.S. Congress. (1934). *Securities Exchange Act of 1934*, 15 U.S.C. §§ 78a–78qq. https://www.govinfo.gov/content/pkg/USCODE-2022-title15/html/USCODE-2022-title15-chap2B.htm

[14]European Union. (2016). *Regulation (EU) No 596/2014 of the European Parliament and of the Council of 16 April 2014 on market abuse (Market Abuse Regulation) and repealing Directive 2003/6/EC*. Official Journal of the European Union, L 173, 1–61. https://eur-lex.europa.eu/legal-content/EN/TXT/?uri=CELEX%3A32014R0596

[15]SEC v. Honig et al., Litigation Release No. 24395, 2018. https://www.sec.gov/litigation/litreleases/2018/lr24395.htm

[16]*CFTC v. Sarao*, No. 15-cv-3398 (N.D. Ill. 2015).

[17]https://www.sec.gov/rules-regulations/statutes-regulations

[18]https://www.sec.gov/newsroom/press-releases/2024-186

[19]https://www.congress.gov/bill/98th-congress/house-bill/559

[20]https://www.congress.gov/bill/111th-congress/house-bill/4173/text

[21]https://www.sec.gov/files/fy24-annual-whistleblower-report.pdf

[22]https://www.finra.org/rules-guidance/rulebooks/finra-rules/3110

[23]https://www.esma.europa.eu/

[24]https://www.sec.gov/newsroom/press-releases/2024-186

[25]https://corpgov.law.harvard.edu/2025/07/27/insider-trading-disclosure-updates/

[26]https://www.justice.gov/usao-ndil/pr/us-attorneys-office-chicago-obtains-forfeiture-214-million-proceeds-alleged-pump-and

[27]https://www.finra.org/rules-guidance/rulebooks/finra-rules

[28]https://www.advisorhub.com/finra-enforcement-actions-increased-in-2024-for-first-time-in-eight-years-report/

[29]https://www.finra.org/rules-guidance/oversight-enforcement/finra-disciplinary-actions-online

[30]https://www.cftc.gov/LawRegulation/EnforcementActions/index.htm

[31]https://www.iosco.org

[32]https://www.cfainstitute.org/standards/professionals/code-ethics-standards

[33]Langevoort, D.C. (2014). *Insider Trading: Regulation, Enforcement, and Prevention.* Wolters Kluwer.

[34]https://www.cfr.org/backgrounder/understanding-libor-scandal

[35]https://www.newyorkfed.org/markets/reference-rates/sofr

[36]https://www.sec.gov/reports?aId=edit-field-article-sub-type-secart-value&year=All&field_article_sub_type_secart_value=Reports%20and%20Publications-AnnualReports&tid=All

[37]United States v. Stewart, 433 F.3d 273 [2d Cir. 2006].

[38]https://www.cftc.gov/LawRegulation/EnforcementActions/index.htm

[39]https://www.sec.gov/news/press/2009/2009-221.htm

[40]https://www.justice.gov/usao-sdny/pr/former-galleon-group-employee-and-hedge-fund-founder-ali-far-sentenced-manhattan

[41]https://www.sec.gov/newsroom/press-releases/2021-212

[42]https://www.justice.gov/criminal/criminal-vns/united-states-v-navinder-singh-sarao

[43]Digital disinhibition is the tendency for people to behave more openly, aggressively, or impulsively online than they would in face-to-face settings. Anonymity, invisibility, and a reduced sense of accountability contribute to disinhibition.

[44]Moral disengagement is the psychological process by which people justify or rationalize unethical behavior. Disengagement allows people to act against their own moral standards without feeling guilt or remorse.

[45]Mancini, A., Desiderio, A., Clemente, R. D., & Climini, G. (2022). Self-induced consensus of Reddit users to characterise the GameStop short squeeze. *Scientific Reports, 12*, 13780. https://doi.org/10.1038/s41598-022-17925-2

[46] Verdear, D., Johnson, N.F., & Wuchty, S. Influence of Twitter social network graph topologies on traditional and meme stocks during the 2021 GameStop short squeeze. *npj Complex 2*, 18. https://doi.org/10.1038/s44260-025-00042-2

[47] Detert, J. R., Treviño, L. K., & Sweitzer, V. L. (2008). Moral disengagement in ethical decision making: A study of antecedents and outcomes. *Journal of Applied Psychology, 93*(2), 374–391. https://doi.org/10.1037/0021-9010.93.2.374

[48] Langevoort, D. C. (2023). *What Were They Thinking? State of Mind Puzzles in Insider Trading.* Georgetown Law Faculty Publications and Other Works. 2496. https://scholarship.law.georgetown.edu/cgi/viewcontent.cgi?article=3514&context=facpub

[49] https://ethicsunwrapped.utexas.edu/video/raj-rajaratnam-insider-trader

[50] Ibid.

[51] https://ethicsunwrapped.utexas.edu/video/wells-fargo-fraud

[52] Thaler, R. H., & Shefrin, H. M. (1981). An economic theory of self-control. *Journal of Political Economy, 89*(2), 392–406.

[53] Klimczak, K.M., Sison, A.J.G., Prats, M. & Torres, M. B. (2022). How to Deter Financial Misconduct if Crime Pays? *Journal of Business Ethics, 179*, 205–222. https://doi.org/10.1007/s10551-021-04817-0

[54] https://www.researchgate.net/profile/Owen-Parker-2/publication/356929487_Reputation_belongs_in_more_strategic_decision_models_and_some_data_to_measure_it/links/61fd60d6007fb50447363984/Reputation-belongs-in-more-strategic-decision-models-and-some-data-to-measure-it.pdf

[55] CFA Institute. (2023). *Standards of Practice Handbook* (12th ed.).

[56] Schuler, K., Cloots, A. S., & Schär, F. (2024). On DeFi and On-Chain CeFi: How (Not) to Regulate Decentralized Finance, *Journal of Financial Regulation, 10*(2), 213–242, https://doi.org/10.1093/jfr/fjad014

[57] https://home.treasury.gov/news/press-releases/jy1391?utm_source=chatgpt.com

[58] https://www.sec.gov/newsroom/press-releases/2021-212

[59] PCA-RF models combine Principal Component Analysis (PCA) and Random Forest (RF) statistical techniques. PCA is first used to reduce the dimensionality of a dataset by transforming correlated variables into a smaller set of uncorrelated components. These components are then used as inputs for a Random Forest prediction model. Random Forest is used to classify variables. PCA-RF models help handle high-dimensional data, reduce noise, and improve model performance and interpretability.

[60] Bergemann, D., Bonatti, A., & Gan, T. (2022). The Economics of Social Data. *RAND Journal of Economics, 53*(1), 5–38.

[61] https://www.cftc.gov/LawRegulation/EnforcementActions/index.htm

[62] https://www.dhs.gov/publication/homeland-threat-assessment

[63] https://oig.justice.gov/reports/evaluation-us-department-justices-efforts-coordinate-information-sharing-about-foreign

Data Privacy and Cybersecurity

10

Chapter Outcomes

This chapter focuses on helping learners develop the ability to:

1. Explain the core requirements of major data protection regulations, such as the General Data Protection Regulation (GDPR) and the California Consumer Privacy Act (CCPA), and their impact on financial institutions.
2. Describe the elements of robust data governance frameworks, including secure data handling practices, explicit consent mechanisms, and consumer rights protection.
3. Analyze the ethical considerations financial services professionals must address to ensure confidentiality, integrity, and availability of sensitive client information.
4. Demonstrate knowledge of advanced cybersecurity measures, such as encryption, multi-factor authentication (MFA), and intrusion detection systems, to mitigate data privacy threats.
5. Articulate the role of compliance with data privacy standards in maintaining trust, operational integrity, and strategic risk management within the financial services profession.

Introduction

In today's hyperconnected digital economy, data can be viewed as an invaluable asset and a profound liability. The ability to collect, store, analyze, and share vast amounts of personal client and organizational information underpins innovation,

---

Note: This chapter was copyedited using Grammarly™ and generative AI tools to enhance clarity, grammar, and overall readability. While these tools provided suggestions and assistance in refining the text, the ideas, content, and arguments presented remain the sole work and responsibility of the authors. Any errors or inaccuracies in the final version are also the authors' responsibility.

W. Heo, J. E. Grable, *Ethics and Compliance in Financial Services*, https://doi.org/10.1007/978-3-032-14449-2_10

drives decision-making, and enables unprecedented levels of efficiency. Yet, this same data is increasingly vulnerable to misuse, exploitation, and theft. As organizations across the financial services profession grapple with digital transformation, the twin imperatives of data privacy and cybersecurity have emerged as cornerstones of strategic resilience and trust.[1]

Data privacy concerns the rights of individuals and organizations to control how their information is collected, processed, and shared.[2] Data privacy intersects with legal frameworks, ethical responsibilities, and consumer expectations that vary across jurisdictions but share a common emphasis on transparency, consent, and accountability. Cybersecurity, by contrast, represents the set of practices, technologies, and governance mechanisms designed to protect data and systems from unauthorized access, disruption, or destruction.[3] Here is another way of thinking about cybersecurity: it is the organization and collection of resources, processes, and structures used to protect cyberspace and cyberspace-enabled systems from occurrences that misalign de jure from de facto property rights.[4] While data privacy and cybersecurity are distinct concepts, the two are inseparable. Privacy without security is an illusion, and security without privacy erodes the very trust it seeks to preserve.[5]

The stakes for firms, financial advisors, and clients have never been higher. Cyberattacks are escalating in frequency, sophistication, and cost, with global damages projected in the billions of dollars.[6] Regulatory regimes such as the EU's General Data Protection Regulation (GDPR), the California Consumer Privacy Act (CCPA), and sector-specific frameworks like HIPAA in healthcare reflect the growing insistence on robust data governance. Beyond compliance, organizations must contend with reputational risks, consumer distrust, and operational disruptions that accompany privacy violations and security breaches.

The remainder of this chapter explores the evolving landscape of data privacy and cybersecurity, examining the regulatory frameworks supporting data privacy and organizational practices. The chapter highlights the ethical tensions between innovation and data protection, the strategic trade-offs between access and control, and emerging technologies reshaping the field.

Perspective

For financial services organizations (regardless of the firm's size), safeguarding data is no longer just an IT responsibility, it is a strategic business imperative. Data protection is also a regulatory requirement. Every customer interaction, financial transaction, and operational decision produces digital footprints that, if mishandled or exposed, can undermine trust, damage reputation, and trigger regulatory and financial penalties. Data privacy and cybersecurity are therefore not isolated technical issues, but organizational-wide priorities that affect governance, culture, and long-term firm competitiveness.

As noted previously, data privacy centers on an organization's ability to responsibly manage information about customers, employees, and partners. This means not only adhering to legal requirements but also going beyond compliance to build transparent practices around data collection, consent, and usage. Customers and stakeholders increasingly judge organizations based on how well their privacy expectations are respected, making it a core driver of brand reputation and loyalty.

Alternatively, cybersecurity encompasses the tools, processes, and governance frameworks that protect systems and data from unauthorized access, misuse, or disruption. In practice, cybersecurity involves more than firewalls and encryption. Cybersecurity requires a comprehensive risk management approach that includes employee training, vendor oversight, incident response planning, and board-level engagement. Without strong cybersecurity practices, even the most well-designed privacy policies cannot be upheld.

The interdependence of privacy and security creates challenges and opportunities for organizations. Firm executives must strike a balance between enabling data-driven innovation and mitigating risks. They need to also recognize that compliance alone is not enough to reduce monetary and reputational risks. Regulators may set a minimum standard, but clients expect absolute protection and ethical stewardship of their personal information. Data privacy and cybersecurity programs serve as a signal to clients that one of a firm's competitive advantages is trustworthiness and resilience in an uncertain digital environment.

A notable cautionary case in the financial services profession where lack of data privacy created havoc is the Capital One data breach of 2019, which exposed the personal information of more than 100 million customers across the United States and Canada.[7] The case shows the reality that even well-resourced financial institutions remain vulnerable to cyberattacks. The case also highlights the importance of maintaining rigorous cybersecurity defenses alongside compliance with data protection regulations.

The data breach occurred in March 2019, when Paige Thompson, a former Amazon Web Services (AWS) employee, exploited a misconfigured firewall within Capital One's cloud infrastructure. Thompson gained unauthorized access to data stored on AWS servers. Through this vulnerability, Thompson accessed approximately 106 million customer records containing highly sensitive information, including names, addresses, dates of birth, phone numbers, email addresses, credit scores, credit limits, balances, and payment histories. Particularly concerning was the exposure of 140,000 Social Security numbers, 80,000 bank account numbers, and one million Canadian Social Insurance numbers, as well as income data from credit card applications. The breach, enabled by a preventable server misconfiguration, revealed serious deficiencies in Capital One's configuration management and oversight of its cloud environment.

The consequences of the data breach were far-reaching. Financially, Capital One faced immediate costs of roughly $100–150 million to notify customers, provide credit monitoring, and pay legal fees. In addition, the Office of the Comptroller of the Currency (OCC) levied an $80 million fine in 2020, citing failures in risk assessment processes and internal controls.[8] Legal and regulatory repercussions followed. Investigations were launched by the OCC, the Consumer Financial Protection Bureau (CFPB), and several state attorneys general, while class-action lawsuits from consumers alleged negligence in safeguarding personal data.[9] The reputational damage to Capital One was equally severe, as customer trust eroded and the institution's credibility as a steward of sensitive financial information came under scrutiny.

Four lessons for other firms and financial advisors emerged from this case. First, the case illustrates the necessity of rigorous configuration management in cloud environments, including regular auditing, testing, and monitoring. Second, the case demonstrates the importance of compliance with sector-specific regulations. Capital One failed in this regard. Third, the data breach revealed gaps in Capital One's cybersecurity architecture, particularly in its detection and monitoring systems. The situation showed that firms of all sizes need advanced tools such as anomaly detection, encryption, and multi-factor authentication to ensure data privacy.[10] Finally, the case reinforces the ethical imperative for financial institutions to treat data stewardship as a fiduciary responsibility, ensuring transparency, accountability, and proactive protection of consumer information.[11]

Regulatory and Compliance Landscape

The global regulatory landscape governing data privacy and cybersecurity in financial services is complex and rapidly evolving, reflecting the strategic importance of safeguarding sensitive client data. In the United States, regulations remain fragmented across federal and state levels, with the Gramm-Leach-Bliley Act (GLBA) imposing safeguards on financial institutions and requiring transparency through privacy notices and opt-out options.[12] More recent frameworks, such as the California Consumer Privacy Act (CCPA) and its amendment and the California Privacy Rights Act (CPRA), grant consumers rights to access, delete, and restrict the sale of their data, setting a higher bar for data governance nationwide. At the same time, the Consumer Financial Protection Bureau's proposed open banking rule is expected to reshape the field by mandating secure data-sharing practices between banks and fintech firms. In the United States, penalties for violating regulatory guidelines vary widely. With the GLBA, fines can be up to $100,000 per violation. At the state level, fines tend to be in the thousands of dollars per infraction. For firms, the biggest obstacle faced in relation to data risk management lies in navigating the patchwork of overlapping regulations in the absence of a comprehensive federal privacy law.[13] The following case illustrates how state-level enforcement can sometimes happen before federal action takes place.

In 2020, a group of prominent e-commerce companies found themselves out of compliance with data privacy laws when the California Attorney General's Office launched an enforcement sweep to investigate compliance with the California Consumer Privacy Act (CCPA).[14] *The AG probe revealed that some retailers were leveraging sophisticated web tracking technologies and sharing the personal information of consumers* (e.g., *browsing habits, purchase histories, and demographic details) with third parties for advertising and analytics purposes. The AG found that these firms failed to provide a clear mechanism for consumers to opt out of these data sales practice, which was a clear violation of the CCPA, which states consumers Global Privacy Control (GPC) signals—a browser-based feature that allows users to automatically signal their preference to opt out of data sharing—must be followed. Upon receiving notices of non-compliance, the retailers scrambled to rectify their practices. They updated their service-provider contracts to align with legal requirements and integrated technology to detect and honor GPC signals. Firms also implemented safeguards to block unauthorized data transfers when GPC was activated. This case gained particular significance with the introduction of the California Privacy Rights Act (CPRA) on January 1, 2023, which eliminated the 30-day cure period previously allowed under the CCPA, signaling a new era of stricter enforcement. The incident serves as a stark reminder that ensuring consumer privacy is non-negotiable.*

Whereas the regulatory frameworks in the United States are fragmented, the European Union has one of the most mature and stringent regulatory data protection regimes. The General Data Protection Regulation (GDPR) remains the gold standard, with its extraterritorial scope, stringent consent requirements, and steep penalties of up to 4% of global turnover.[15] Complementing GDPR, the Digital Operational Resilience Act (DORA), which went into effect January 2025, standardizes ICT risk management and incident reporting[16] across financial institutions, while the NIS2 Directive expands cybersecurity obligations to critical sectors.[17] Together, these frameworks unify data protection and cyber resilience expectations, making the EU a model of regulatory coherence.

Other jurisdictions are following the European Union in implementing similar regulatory frameworks. In Australia, the Privacy Act 1988 was strengthened in 2024 by raising maximum penalties to AU$50 million or more, while the Notifiable Data Breaches (NDB) scheme enforces prompt disclosure of incidents.[18] The Australian Critical Infrastructure Protection Act further underscores the financial sector's designation as critical infrastructure, with associated obligations. New Zealand's Privacy Act 2020 also emphasizes transparency, data minimization, and breach notification, while a proposed Cybersecurity Bill is expected to align with international standards, enhancing protections for critical financial systems.[19]

In Canada, the forthcoming Consumer Privacy Protection Act (CPPA) signals a move toward GDPR-style rigor, including stronger consent requirements, portability rights, and higher penalties (up to CA$25 million or 5% of global turnover).[20] This evolution in data privacy oversight aligns with the GDPR, which eases cross-border data flows with the European Union.

In Asia, regulatory regimes vary but are increasingly stringent. China enforces one of the most restrictive environments under its Personal Information Protection Law (PIPL), Cybersecurity Law (CSL), and Data Security Law (DSL).[21] Together, these laws mandate explicit consent, enforce strict data localization, and regulate cross-border transfers, with fines reaching 5% of annual turnover or business suspension for serious violations. Japan's APPI, by contrast, aligns closely with GDPR. The Japanese framework emphasizes client consent in a way that allows for data transfers with the European Union.[22] Singapore's Personal Data Protection Act (PDPA) and Cybersecurity Act adopt a flexible, innovation-friendly model while imposing strict obligations on critical infrastructure, including mandatory breach reporting and significant fines for failures.[23]

Taken together, these frameworks illustrate the global trend toward heightened data regulatory scrutiny, with an emphasis on making cross-border data transfers as safe as possible. While each country/region is unique (e.g., the U.S. model is fragmented, whereas the EU framework is integrated) the regulatory future is clear. Financial institutions must take steps to improve data privacy and cybersecurity protocols. Organizational success will depend on adopting and managing a holistic risk management approach that integrates regulatory compliance, technological safeguards, cultural awareness, and ethical responsibility. Only in this way can firms and financial advisors ensure that client trust and organizational resilience are maintained.[24]

Table 10.1 provides a side-by-side comparison of some of the most important data privacy and cybersecurity laws that relate directly to financial services firms and financial advisors operating in the United States, the European Union, Australia, New Zealand, Canada, and prominent Asian countries. The table highlights specific regulations, their scope, compliance requirements, penalties, and unique features relevant to financial institutions as of 2025.

As noted above, U.S. regulatory frameworks are fragmented across state and federal lines. In addition to the regulatory models described in Table 10.1, financial firms operating in the United States may encounter additional regulations designed to safeguard client data and mitigate cyber threats.[25] The following are examples of some of these regulatory frameworks:

- Federal Financial Institutions Examination Council (FFIEC) Guidelines: The FFIEC offers detailed guidance on managing cybersecurity risks. Its Cybersecurity Assessment Tool enables institutions to evaluate their preparedness and identify areas for improvement.
- Federal Reserve System Guidance: The Federal Reserve provides cybersecurity recommendations focused on governance, risk management, and coordination with regulatory bodies to strengthen institutional resilience.
- Payment Card Industry Data Security Standard (PCI-DSS): Though not exclusive to banking, PCI-DSS is essential for institutions handling credit card transactions. The standard sets forth stringent requirements to protect cardholder data and prevent unauthorized access.
- NIST Cybersecurity Framework: Widely adopted as a best practice, the NIST Framework offers a flexible model for assessing and enhancing cybersecurity posture. The framework emphasizes risk management and continuous improvement, though it is not legally mandated.
- State Data Breach Notification Laws: Individual states have enacted laws requiring financial institutions to notify affected customers following a data breach. These laws typically define specific timelines and procedures for disclosure.

Table 10.1 Key worldwide data privacy and cybersecurity regulations

Jurisdiction	Key regulations	Scope	Compliance requirements	Penalties for non-compliance	Unique features
United States	– Gramm-Leach-Bliley Act (GLBA) – California Consumer Privacy Act (CCPA)/ California Privacy Rights Act (CPRA) – State Privacy Laws (e.g., Delaware, Iowa, Minnesota, effective 2025) – CFPB Open Banking Rule	– Applies to banks, insurance companies, investment firms, and third-party service providers handling financial data – CCPA/CPRA applies to businesses processing California residents' data, including financial firms – State laws cover consumer data broadly – CFPB rule promotes consumer data access and portability	– Implement safeguards for personal financial data (e.g., encryption, access controls) – Provide privacy notices and opt-out options (GLBA) – CCPA/CPRA: Grant consumer rights (access, deletion, opt-out of data sales) – Conduct risk assessments and vendor oversight – CFPB: Develop consumer interfaces for data sharing, comply by 2026 for large institutions	– GLBA: Fines up to \$100,000 per violation for institutions, \$10,000 for officers/directors; up to 5 years imprisonment for willful violations – CCPA/CPRA: Fines up to \$7500 per intentional violation – State laws: Vary, e.g., \$7500 per violation in some states – CFPB: Potential fines, corrective actions, or loss of charter	– Fragmented regulatory landscape with no comprehensive federal privacy law – State laws (e.g., CCPA) set stricter standards, influencing national practices – CFPB's open banking rule (2024) drives secure data sharing with financial technology firms

(continued)

Table 10.1 (continued)

Jurisdiction	Key regulations	Scope	Compliance requirements	Penalties for non-compliance	Unique features
European Union	– General Data Protection Regulation (GDPR) – Digital Operational Resilience Act (DORA) (effective January 17, 2025) – Network and Information Security Directive (NIS2)	– GDPR: Applies to all organizations processing EU residents' personal data, including financial firms – DORA: Covers financial entities (banks, insurers, investment firms) and ICT third-party providers – NIS2: Targets critical infrastructure, including financial services	– GDPR: Obtain explicit consent, ensure data subject rights (access, rectification, erasure), appoint Data Protection Officers (DPOs), report breaches within 72 hours – DORA: Implement ICT risk management, cyber threat assessments, incident reporting, and vendor oversight – NIS2: Enhance cybersecurity controls, report incidents, and ensure supply chain security	– GDPR: Fines up to €20M or 4% of global annual turnover, whichever is higher – DORA: Fines up to 1% of daily global turnover, public reprimands, or withdrawal of authorization – NIS2: Fines vary by member state, up to €10M or 2% of global turnover	– GDPR's extraterritorial reach impacts global firms – DORA unifies cybersecurity standards for financial entities, complementing GDPR – NIS2 expands cybersecurity obligations for critical sectors
Australia	– Privacy Act 1988 (amended 2024) – Notifiable Data Breaches (NDB) Scheme – Critical Infrastructure Protection Act	– Applies to financial institutions and businesses handling personal data – NDB Scheme mandates breach notifications – Critical Infrastructure Act covers financial services as critical infrastructure	– Implement Australian Privacy Principles (APPs) for data handling, consent, and transparency – Notify breaches likely to cause serious harm within 30 days – Conduct privacy impact assessments and maintain data security measures – Critical Infrastructure Act: Comply with cybersecurity standards for critical systems	– Privacy Act: Fines up to AU$50M, 30% of annual turnover, or three times the benefit gained from breach – NDB non-compliance: Similar fines – Critical Infrastructure Act: Fines up to AU$11M for non-compliance	– Recent Privacy Act reforms (2024) increase penalties and strengthen enforcement – Proposed cybersecurity laws (2025) may align with EU/UK frameworks – Emphasis on consumer data rights and open banking

New Zealand	– Privacy Act 2020 – Proposed Cybersecurity Bill (pending 2025)	– Applies to organizations overseeing personal data, including financial firms – Cybersecurity Bill aims to enhance protections for critical infrastructure, including finance	– Comply with Information Privacy Principles (IPPs), including data minimization and security – Notify serious data breaches within 72 hours – Obtain consent for data processing and ensure transparency – Proposed Cybersecurity Bill: Likely to mandate incident reporting and critical system protections	– Privacy Act: Fines up to NZ$10,000 per breach; compensation for harm – Proposed Cybersecurity Bill: Penalties TBD, but likely aligned with international standards (e.g., fines, corrective actions)	– Privacy Act exemptions for non-prejudicial non-compliance (effective post-June 2025) – Cybersecurity Bill may borrow from EU/Australian frameworks, focusing on critical infrastructure
Canada	– Personal Information Protection and Electronic Documents Act (PIPEDA) – Consumer Privacy Protection Act (CPPA) (proposed, pending 2025)	– PIPEDA: Applies to commercial organizations, including financial institutions, managing personal data – CPPA: Will replace PIPEDA, enhancing consumer rights and enforcement	– PIPEDA: Obtain consent, ensure data security, and provide access/correction rights – Report breaches causing significant harm to the Office of the Privacy Commissioner – CPPA: Proposes stricter consent rules, data portability, and mandatory breach notifications	– PIPEDA: Fines up to CA$100,000 per violation – CPPA: Proposed fines up to 5% of global revenue or CA$25M, whichever is higher – Regulatory orders and reputational damage	– CPPA aligns with GDPR, emphasizing consumer rights and hefty penalties – Canada's adequacy status under GDPR facilitates EU data transfers – Open banking framework (2025) enhances secure data sharing

(continued)

Table 10.1 (continued)

Jurisdiction	Key regulations	Scope	Compliance requirements	Penalties for non-compliance	Unique features
Asia (China)	– Personal Information Protection Law (PIPL) – Cybersecurity Law (CSL) – Data Security Law (DSL)	– PIPL: Applies to all entities processing personal data of Chinese citizens – CSL/DSL: Covers financial institutions, mandating cybersecurity and data localization	– PIPL: Obtain explicit consent, conduct data protection impact assessments, appoint DPOs – CSL: Implement cybersecurity measures, store critical data locally – DSL: Classify data by sensitivity, restrict cross-border transfers without approval	– PIPL: Fines up to CNY 50M or 5% of annual turnover; potential business suspension – CSL/DSL: Fines up to CNY 10M, license revocation, or criminal penalties	– Strict data localization requirements – Cross-border data transfers require security assessments – Heavy government oversight of financial data
Asia (Japan)	– Act on the Protection of Personal Information (APPI)	– Applies to businesses handling personal data, including financial institutions	– Obtain consent, ensure data security, and restrict third-party data sharing – Notify breaches promptly to the Personal Information Protection Commission – Conduct risk assessments for sensitive data (e.g., financial information)	– Fines up to JPY 100M for serious violations – Reputational damage and regulatory orders	– Aligns closely with GDPR, with adequacy agreement for EU data transfers – Emphasis on consumer consent and transparency

Asia (Singapore)	– Personal Data Protection Act (PDPA) – Cybersecurity Act 2018	– PDPA: Applies to organizations handling personal data, including financial firms – Cybersecurity Act: Covers critical information infrastructure, including finance	– PDPA: Obtain consent, implement reasonable security measures, notify breaches – Cybersecurity Act: Mandate incident reporting, cybersecurity audits, and critical system protections	– PDPA: Fines up to S$1M per breach – Cybersecurity Act: Fines up to S$100,000, imprisonment up to 7 years for critical infrastructure failures	– Flexible framework balancing innovation and security – Aligns with global standards like GDPR for cross-border data flows

Notes:

- United States: The lack of a federal privacy law creates a complex compliance landscape, with state laws like CCPA/CPRA setting high standards. Financial firms must navigate sector-specific regulations (e.g., GLBA) alongside emerging state laws
- European Union: GDPR and DORA set global benchmarks, with DORA specifically targeting financial sector resilience. NIS2 broadens cybersecurity obligations, impacting financial firms as critical infrastructure
- Australia: Recent reforms strengthen penalties and align with global trends, with open banking frameworks driving secure data sharing
- New Zealand: The Privacy Act 2020 is comprehensive, but the proposed Cybersecurity Bill (2025) may introduce stricter requirements for financial firms
- Canada: PIPEDA's replacement with CPPA (pending) signals a shift toward GDPR-like protections, with open banking enhancing consumer control
- Asia: China's PIPL and CSL impose stringent localization and oversight, contrasting with Japan and Singapore's more flexible, GDPR-aligned frameworks

Cybersecurity Risks Facing the Financial Services Profession

Financial institutions operating in the United States face a complex and evolving landscape of cybersecurity risks that threaten operational integrity and the confidentiality of client information.[26] Consider the following cyberattack that occurred in 2014:

In one of the most significant data breaches in U.S. banking history, JPMorgan Chase fell victim to a sophisticated cyberattack that compromised the personal information of over 83 million accounts, affecting 76 million households and 7 million small businesses.[27] The breach, which exposed sensitive data including names, email addresses, phone numbers, and physical addresses, occurred when hackers exploited vulnerabilities in JPMorgan's systems. By gaining access to a list of applications used by the bank, the attackers were able to infiltrate the network and extract personal information. Fortunately, critical financial details such as account passwords, Social Security numbers, and banking data were reportedly not accessed, limiting the potential for immediate financial harm. The scope of the attack extended beyond JPMorgan, targeting other major financial institutions, though JPMorgan suffered the most severe impact. In the aftermath, four individuals, including international hackers, were indicted for their roles in the breach. The incident sent shockwaves through the financial sector, raising alarm about the vulnerabilities in even the most robust banking systems. The case prompted heightened regulatory scrutiny and spurred calls for stronger cybersecurity measures to protect consumer data in an increasingly digital financial landscape.

Among the most persistent cybersecurity threats are malware attacks, where malicious software, such as viruses, worms, and Trojans, compromises computer systems to gain unauthorized access and steal sensitive data. Equally pervasive are phishing schemes and other social engineering tactics. These schemes exploit human vulnerabilities through fraudulent communications designed to deceive employees can clients into revealing confidential information or authorizing illegitimate transactions. Institutions are also frequently targeted by distributed denial-of-service (DDoS) attacks, in which cybercriminals deploy botnets to overwhelm networks and disrupt customer access to financial services. Additionally, insider threats (whether intentional misconduct or inadvertent disclosure by employees or contractors with privileged access) pose a significant internal risk to data security.

The consequences of these cyberattacks can be severe and multifaceted.[28] Data breaches expose the personal and financial information of clients, which creates opportunities for identity theft and unauthorized account takeovers. Criminals leverage these vulnerabilities to commit financial fraud, including fraudulent transfers, account manipulation, and unauthorized transactions. Fraud results in direct monetary losses at the firm, advisor, and client levels. Beyond the immediate monetary impact, cybersecurity incidents undermine public trust in financial institutions, causing reputational damage that can erode customer confidence, reduce client retention, and affect long-term profitability. Moreover, regulatory and legal consequences can be significant. Failure to adequately safeguard client data can result in substantial fines, legal liabilities, and ongoing compliance challenges, underscoring the imperative for robust cybersecurity strategies that anticipate and counter emerging threats. The following list summarizes the most common cybersecurity threats faced by organizations operating in the financial services sector.

- Malware Attacks: Malware remains one of the most significant threats to the banking and financial services sectors. Malicious software, including viruses, worms, and Trojans, can infiltrate financial systems to gain unauthorized access and extract sensitive data. Once deployed, malware can disrupt operations, identify login credentials, and compromise customer accounts.
- Phishing and Social Engineering: Phishing is a widespread cyber threat in which attackers use fraudulent emails, text messages, or websites to trick bank employees or customers into divulging confidential information. These schemes often impersonate trusted entities, making them highly effective in obtaining login credentials or authorizing unauthorized transactions. Broader social engineering tactics, such as impersonation, manipulation, or pretexting, exploit human trust and error, bypassing technical safeguards to access sensitive data.
- Distributed Denial-of-Service (DDoS) Attacks: DDoS attacks aim to disrupt banking operations by overwhelming networks with massive amounts of traffic, rendering online services inaccessible to customers. Attackers often employ botnets (networks of compromised computers) to generate this traffic, making it difficult to detect and mitigate in real time. While DDoS attacks may not always involve direct data theft, they can cause significant reputational and operational damage by denying clients access to essential financial services. Consider the following situation that occurred in 2012:

In 2012, a series of sophisticated and coordinated Distributed Denial-of-Service (DDoS) attacks targeted several major U.S. financial institutions, including Bank of America, Wells Fargo, and JPMorgan Chase, significantly disrupting their online services.[29] *The attackers, later identified as the Izz ad-Din al-Qassam Cyber Fighters, a group reportedly linked to politically motivated cyber operations, flooded each bank's servers with overwhelming volumes of internet traffic. This barrage caused widespread outages and delays, preventing customers from accessing online banking services, including account management, bill payments, and other critical functions. The attacks exploited vulnerabilities in each bank's digital infrastructure, revealing the fragility of even the most prominent financial institutions to such disruptive cyber threats. Unlike data breaches that aim to steal sensitive information, these DDoS attacks were designed to cripple service availability, creating inconvenience and eroding customer trust. The scale and coordination of the attacks raised alarms across the financial sector, highlighting the need for enhanced cybersecurity measures. In response, banks and regulators began prioritizing the development of better digital defenses, including advanced traffic filtering, load balancing, and incident response protocols to mitigate future disruptions. The 2012 attacks served as a wake-up call, underscoring the growing sophistication of cyber adversaries and prompting a broader industry push toward resilience against evolving digital threats.*

- Insider Threats: Insider threats stem from employees, contractors, or other individuals with legitimate access to financial systems. These risks may be intentional (e.g., data theft or fraud) or unintentional (e.g., accidental disclosures or mishandling of sensitive information). Given the privileged access insiders hold,

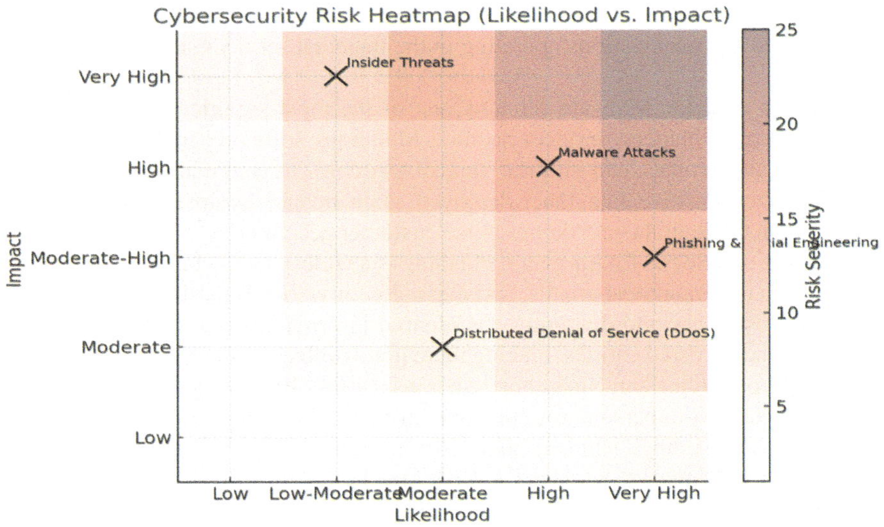

Fig. 10.1 Cybersecurity heatmap

these threats can bypass external security defenses and result in substantial harm, ranging from compromised customer data to regulatory violations.

The heatmap shown in Fig. 10.1 illustrates the risk severity of these cybersecurity threats. Darker areas represent a higher combined likelihood and impact. The plotted risks show that phishing and social engineering tend to be highly likely and impactful. Malware attacks are also in the high-risk zone. DDoS attacks sit in the mid-range, whereas insider threats are positioned lower in likelihood but extremely high in impact.

Data Privacy and Cybersecurity Best Practices

In the financial services profession, implementing robust security controls and measures at the enterprise level is a cornerstone activity used to safeguarding sensitive information against evolving cyber threats.[30] The following discussion outlines some of the most important best practices used by firms and other organizations when anticipating and dealing with cybersecurity threats.

At the top of this list is implementing access controls, such as role-based access and privileged account management, which helps ensure that only authorized individuals can access sensitive systems and data, which reduces the risk of internal security breaches. Encryption protocols can also be used to convert data into an unreadable format through cryptographic algorithms. Encryption protects data held on in-house servers and while data is being shared. Today, Transport Layer Security (TLS) and Secure Sockets Layer (SSL) are routinely used to protect data during network transmission. These systems prevent data interception and tampering. To strengthen security further, multi-factor authentication (MFA) is strongly encouraged as a way to confirm a client's identity through multiple forms of validation.

To minimize the impact of cybersecurity incidents, financial institutions need to implement and maintain strong incident response and recovery procedures. Procedures should include forming a specialized response team, establishing clear escalation protocols, and maintaining a detailed plan to ensure quick containment and data recovery. Given increasing regulatory oversight, investment in these procedures is becoming even more important. Other cybersecurity protocols include hosting regular data security workshops, responding to simulated phishing tests, and promoting open lines of communication to help advisory staff understand cybersecurity risks, follow best practices, and actively contribute to a firm's data protection systems.

It is also important for firms to implement vigorous data classification and handling procedures. Organizations need ways to categorize data by sensitivity and criticality while establishing guidelines for access, storage, sharing, and disposal. Secure storage solutions, such as encrypted databases or cloud platforms, can be used to protect data on in-house computers, while secure transmission protocols like TLS can be used to maintain confidentiality and integrity during data transfers. Tokenization is another way to strengthen client data protection.[31] Tokenization substitutes sensitive information with non-sensitive equivalents, reducing exposure during processing and transmission.

Advanced fraud detection and prevention techniques are increasingly being used to counter cybersecurity risks. Anomaly detection identifies deviations from normal patterns, while machine learning and artificial intelligence enhance accuracy by analyzing vast datasets to flag suspicious activities with fewer false positives.[32] Behavioral analytics is also an important risk management too. Behavioral analytics can be used to scrutinize transaction trends and user interactions to uncover irregularities indicative of fraud, enabling proactive intervention and asset protection.[33]

Anti-money laundering (AML) strategies, including Know Your Customer (KYC) protocols, customer due diligence, and enhanced transaction monitoring are additional tools that can be used to ensure regulatory compliance and detect illicit activities. Transaction monitoring systems scrutinize patterns for signs of laundering or fraud, while employee screening and background checks to mitigate insider threats.[34]

As noted above, emerging technologies are transforming the way cybersecurity is conceptualized and managed at the firm level. Artificial intelligence (AI) and machine learning (ML) have revolutionized threat detection by allowing compliance teams to analyze large data volumes for anomalies. AI enables compliance staff to identify malicious patterns in user and network activities and automating responses.[35] Additionally, blockchain technology is being used to secure data transactions and data integrity through decentralized, immutable data structures.

Given the growing complexity of cybersecurity threats, many firms are adopting real-time monitoring and threat intelligence sharing as core defense strategies. Tools such as Security Information and Event Management (SIEM) systems enable continuous monitoring and rapid detection of potential incidents. At the same time, collaborative intelligence exchanges serve as a form of collective defense, allowing organizations to share insights and strengthen resilience. Initiatives like the Financial Services Information Sharing and Analysis Center (FS-ISAC), public–private partnerships with agencies such as the FBI and DHS, and sector-specific forums including BITS and the Financial Services Sector Coordinating Council (FSSCC) play a critical role in facilitating the exchange of threat data and best practices to enable faster mitigation of data breaches. For small and mid-sized firms in particular, partnerships with cybersecurity vendors often provide the most effective path to advanced protections. Vendors offer access to specialized services such as threat intelligence platforms, incident response capabilities, and managed Security Operations Centers (SOCs) that deliver 24/7 monitoring and expertise.

A best practice for enhancing cybersecurity involves adhering to well-established standards and frameworks, which provide a structured approach to managing and mitigating risks. The NIST Cybersecurity Framework, for instance, offers a comprehensive blueprint with five core functions:

- Identify
- Protect
- Detect
- Respond
- Recover[36]

The "Identify" function helps organizations assess and catalog their assets, risks, and vulnerabilities, enabling a clear understanding of their security posture. The "Protect" function focuses on implementing safeguards such as access controls, data encryption, and employee training to prevent incidents. The "Detect" function emphasizes continuous monitoring and anomaly detection to identify threats early, while the "Respond" function outlines incident response plans, including containment and eradication strategies. Finally, the "Recover" function supports restoration efforts, ensuring business continuity through backup systems and recovery protocols. Similarly, ISO 27001, an internationally recognized standard for information security management systems, provides a systematic framework for establishing, implementing, maintaining, and continually improving security controls.[37] ISO 27001 includes detailed policies for risk assessment, incident management, and employee awareness programs, tailored to protect sensitive data across various industries. The Payment Card Industry Data Security Standard (PCI DSS) complements these models by setting specific, actionable requirements for organizations handling payment card information, such as regular security testing, strong access controls, and encryption of cardholder data to prevent fraud and ensure compliance.[38]

By integrating existing security frameworks with collaborative strategies (e.g., participating in information-sharing initiatives and forging partnerships with cybersecurity vendors), financial services firms can enhance their cybersecurity defenses. Taking a holistic approach enables firms to adapt to evolving threats, maintain operational integrity, and enhance resilience in an increasingly complex and dynamic cybersecurity landscape. Table 10.2 summarizes the strategies firms can use to address data privacy and cybersecurity concerns.

Table 10.2 Data privacy and cybersecurity best practices

Category	Measure	Description
Access control	Role-based access and privileged account management	Restricts access to sensitive systems/data to authorized individuals, reducing internal breach risks
Data protection	Encryption (TLS/SSL)	Converts data into unreadable format to protect it during storage and transmission, preventing interception
Authentication	Multi-factor authentication (MFA)	Verifies user identity through multiple validation methods to enhance security
Incident response	Response team and escalation protocols	Specialized team and clear protocols ensure quick containment and recovery from cybersecurity incidents
Training and awareness	Data security workshops and phishing tests	Educates staff on risks, best practices, and promotes open communication to strengthen data protection
Data management	Data classification and handling procedures	Categorizes data by sensitivity, sets guidelines for access, storage, sharing, and disposal
Data protection	Tokenization	Substitutes sensitive data with non-sensitive equivalents to reduce exposure during processing/transmission
Fraud detection	Anomaly detection and behavioral analytics	Identifies deviations from normal patterns and analyzes transaction/user trends to detect fraud proactively
Regulatory compliance	AML, KYC, and customer due diligence, transaction monitoring	Ensures compliance and detects illicit activities through monitoring and employee screening
Emerging technologies	AI and machine learning	Analyzes large datasets to detect anomalies, malicious patterns, and automate threat responses
Emerging technologies	Blockchain	Secures data transactions and integrity through decentralized, immutable structures
Monitoring and intelligence	SIEM systems and threat intelligence sharing (e.g., FS-ISAC)	Enables real-time monitoring, rapid incident detection, and collective defense through shared insights
Cybersecurity frameworks	NIST cybersecurity framework	Provides a blueprint with identify, protect, detect, respond, and recover functions for comprehensive security
Cybersecurity frameworks	ISO 27001	Offers a systematic framework for risk assessment, incident management, and security control improvement
Cybersecurity frameworks	PCI DSS	Sets requirements for securing payment card data through testing, access controls, and encryption

The Human Factor: Cognition, Behavior, and Culture

While organizations often invest heavily in technical safeguards, human cognition and behavior remain two of the most significant sources of vulnerability in the context of data privacy and cybersecurity. Cognitive, behavioral, and psychological biases, such as exhibiting overconfidence in one's ability to recognize phishing attempts and optimism bias that underestimates the likelihood of being targeted, shape how employees perceive and respond to risks. These psychological blind spots make firms more susceptible to breaches caused by insider threats and simple human error. Addressing data privacy and cybersecurity challenges requires more than a compliance checklist. Dealing with threats at the firm level demands sustained training, awareness, and the cultivation of a culture where data protection is understood as a shared responsibility across all levels of the organization. Table 10.3 shows common cognitive, behavioral, and psychological biases (see Chap. 4 for a more detailed description of these cognitive biases) that can increase firm threats.

Financial services firms can mitigate the effects of cognitive, behavioral, and psychological biases as they relate to vulnerabilities in data privacy and cybersecurity by integrating behavioral science principles into employee training and awareness programs. For instance, overconfidence and optimism biases, which lead some employees to underestimate personal or institutional risks that increase phishing susceptibility or the likelihood of detection in unauthorized data access, can be countered through scenario-based simulations that demonstrate real-world data breach consequences.[39] This can include anonymized case studies from peer institutions. Training programs should employ debiasing techniques like pre-mortems (where teams anticipate failure modes in advance) and regular feedback loops via gamified quizzes that highlight knowledge gaps, addressing anchoring bias by challenging reliance on outdated security protocols.[40]

Confirmation bias, often manifesting in selective attention to non-alarming audit results, can be disrupted by assigning someone to make counter arguments (i.e., play devil's advocate) during training sessions, encouraging participants to actively seek disconfirming evidence. Moreover, incorporating nudges such as personalized risk dashboards that visualize individual contributions to firm-wide security metrics can counteract availability bias, which overemphasizes recent high-profile external hacks while ignoring insidious internal threats. This is one way to ensure training evolves with threat landscapes through adaptive, AI-driven modules that refresh content based on emerging vulnerabilities.[41]

Insider threats and human error, recognized as primary determinants of data breaches in financial ecosystems, accounting for up to 74% of incidents according to industry reports, demand targeted interventions that directly confront biases that amplify these risks.[42] Herding behavior, where employees mimic lax security practices observed in colleagues, such as sharing credentials or bypassing multi-factor authentication, can be defended by implementing anonymous reporting mechanisms and peer accountability frameworks that reward vigilance rather than conformity. To address the endowment effect, which causes employees to overvalue their

Table 10.3 Cognitive, behavioral, and psychological biases associated with firm-level data privacy and cybersecurity threats

Cognitive bias	Definition	Relevance to financial firm's vulnerability to data privacy and cybersecurity threats
Overconfidence bias	Overconfidence bias occurs when an employee overestimates their knowledge, skills, or control over client outcomes[a]	Employees or advisors may overestimate their ability to manage cybersecurity risks, leading to inadequate implementation of security measures, such as skipping updates or ignoring best practices, increasing the risk of data breaches
Anchoring bias	Anchoring bias can occur when an employee fixates on past performance benchmarks, compensation targets, or previously successful schemes[b]	Decision-makers might fixate on outdated security benchmarks or initial threat assessments, failing to adapt to evolving cyber threats, which can leave systems vulnerable to new attack vectors in handling sensitive financial data
Confirmation bias	Confirmation bias prompts some employees to selectively seek information that justifies unethical behavior while ignoring red flags or regulatory warnings[c]	Security teams may selectively focus on information that downplays threats, ignoring warnings or evidence of vulnerabilities, resulting in overlooked risks to data privacy and delayed responses to potential breaches
Herding behavior	Herding behavior can influence employees to emulate peers who have engaged in questionable or fraudulent practices[d]	Firms may follow industry peers in adopting minimal security practices without assessing their own needs, normalizing insufficient protections and exposing client data to common threats if peers are also underprepared
Availability bias	Availability bias may cause some employees to overestimate the likelihood of success in committing fraud based on recent cases of "successful" misconduct they have read or heard about[e]	Overemphasis on recent or highly publicized cyber incidents may lead to disproportionate focus on certain threats (e.g., ransomware) while neglecting others like insider data leaks, creating gaps in comprehensive privacy safeguards
Endowment effect	The endowment effect can lead some employees to overvalue their control over client accounts or investment products[f]	Organizations might overvalue their existing in-house security systems, resisting upgrades or external audits, which can perpetuate vulnerabilities in data storage and transmission, heightening privacy breach risks
Optimism bias	Optimism bias can make employees occasionally underestimate the likelihood of criminal detection, assuming that audits, client complaints, or regulators will not uncover their misconduct[g]	Leaders may underestimate the likelihood of cyberattacks on their firm, assuming robust defenses without evidence, leading to underinvestment in privacy tools and incident response, amplifying exposure to data theft or fraud

[a] Ul Abdin, S. Z., Qureshi, F., Iqbal, J., & Sultana, S. (2022). Overconfidence bias and investment performance: A mediating effect of risk propensity. *Borsa Istanbul Review*, *22*(4), 780–793

[b] Furnham, A., & Boo, H. C. (2011). A literature review of the anchoring effect. *The Journal of Socio-economics*, *40*(1), 35–42

[c] Nickerson, R. S. (1998). Confirmation bias: A ubiquitous phenomenon in many guises. *Review of general psychology*, *2*(2), 175–220

[d] Raafat, R. M., Chater, N., & Frith, C. (2009). Herding in humans. *Trends in Cognitive Sciences*, *13*(10), 420–428

[e] Tversky, A., & Kahneman, D. (1973). Availability: A heuristic for judging frequency and probability. *Cognitive psychology*, *5*(2), 207–232

[f] Thaler, R. (1980). Toward a positive theory of consumer choice. *Journal of Economic Behavior & Organization*, *1*(1), 39–60.

[g] Marks, A. B. (2009). *Corporal punishment and its association with anxiety in youth*. Unpublished Master's Thesis. The University of New Orleans. "Corporal Punishment and Its Association with Anxiety in Youth" by Allison Brown Marks (uno.edu)

control over proprietary data systems and resist updates, firms should enforce mandatory rotation of access privileges and conduct bias-awareness audits that quantify the costs of inertia, such as simulated insider attacks revealing how entrenched habits enable data exfiltration.[43] Human error driven by optimism bias, like assuming "it won't happen to me" in handling sensitive client information, necessitates rigorous error-proofing protocols, including just-in-time training prompts embedded in workflows and behavioral analytics tools that flag anomalous actions in real time. By leveraging machine learning to predict and preempt bias-induced errors, such as pattern recognition for repeated minor lapses escalating to major breaches, firms can shift from reactive remediation to proactive prevention, in the end reducing the cost of data breaches.[44]

Building a culture of shared responsibility to protect data and reduce cybersecurity threats requires embedding anti-bias strategies at all organizational levels.[45] Anti-bias strategies transform individual accountability into collective resilience against cybersecurity threats. To combat herd mentality and confirmation bias, firms need to model transparency through events like town halls that promote open discussions about experiences across the firm that could have (or did) result from these biases. The effects of optimism and overconfidence can be reduced by instituting "red team" exercises where diverse groups simulate adversarial perspectives, ensuring that shared responsibility extends to continuous improvement via metrics like breach simulation success rates and employee engagement surveys.[46] Table 10.4 summarizes the types of strategies a firm can use to develop anti-bias strategies.

Finally, to strengthen a firm's cybersecurity culture, senior leadership should take steps to align incentive structures with collective data protection outcomes. For example, tying employee bonuses to team-based security key performance indicators (KPIs) rather than individual performance helps reduce anchoring bias by discouraging reliance on past successes and encouraging ongoing vigilance. This approach supports key regulatory frameworks such as NIST and ISO 27001, which emphasize continuous improvement and risk-based governance. Moreover, aligning

Table 10.4 Anti-bias strategies in practice

Strategy	Description	Cybersecurity impact
Pre-mortems	Teams imagine a future breach and work backward to identify failure points	Reduces overconfidence and promotes proactive thinking
Scenario-based simulations	Realistic exercises that mimic insider threats or phishing attacks	Counters availability bias by making internal risks tangible
Access rotation policies	Regularly changing system access privileges	Disrupts the endowment effect and reduces insider risk
Bias-awareness audits	Assessments that identify behavioral vulnerabilities	Quantifies how habits and assumptions contribute to risk
Gamified feedback loops	Quizzes and dashboards that reveal knowledge gaps	Challenges anchoring bias and keeps training dynamic
AI-driven adaptive training	Personalized modules that evolve with threat landscapes	Ensures learning stays relevant and bias-resistant

incentives with data protection processes fosters psychological safety, empowering employees to report errors or biases without fear of reprisal. By promoting transparency and shared accountability, firms can enhance their adaptive capacity in the face of evolving cyber threats.

A Practice Model

Table 10.5 provides a framework that can be used by financial services firms to address data privacy and cybersecurity threats. This model represents a summary of recommendations from the NIST Cybersecurity Framework (CSF).[47] The model

Table 10.5 A data privacy and cybersecurity threat practice model

Stage	Objective	Key actions	Key enablers applied
Governance and culture building	Establish leadership commitment and a culture of shared responsibility	Form cross-functional teams, set bias-aware policies, align incentives with security KPIs, and model transparency	Mitigate biases via leadership training; enforce anonymous reporting; promote psychological safety
Identify	Assess risks, assets, vulnerabilities, and cognitive biases	Catalog systems, conduct risk assessments, share threat intelligence via FS-ISAC, and identify biases like overconfidence	Use scenario-based training to counter biases; screen employees to reduce insider risks
Protect	Implement safeguards to prevent breaches and mitigate human error	Deploy access controls, encryption, MFA, tokenization, and conduct phishing simulations and bias-focused training	Nudge employees with risk dashboards; implement error-proofing workflows
Detect	Identify threats early through continuous monitoring	Use SIEM systems, AI/ML for anomaly detection, and behavioral analytics to spot insider activities or errors	Apply behavioral analytics to counter biases; monitor for insider threat patterns
Respond	Contain and mitigate breaches effectively	Activate incident response plans, use escalation protocols, employ pre-mortems to counter confirmation bias, and communicate transparently	Use red team exercises to challenge biases; ensure anonymous reporting for rapid response
Recover	Restore operations and address root causes	Use backups for restoration, conduct post-incident reviews, and update training to address biases like optimism or herding	Reinforce shared responsibility via post-incident cultural updates
Continuous improvement	Adapt and enhance defenses based on metrics and regulations	Review framework effectiveness, align with PCI DSS/NYDFS, and track breach reduction and cultural engagement metrics	Update debiasing techniques and error-proofing based on lessons learned

also incorporates elements from the Financial Services Sector Cybersecurity Profile and CRI Profile, which map NIST CSF to sector-specific needs.[48] The model shows strategies that can be used to reduce the impact of employee cognitive, behavioral, and psychological biases, address insider threats and human error, and foster a culture of shared responsibility. Although the framework is presented in a step-by-step way, the model is actually a cyclical process. This means that the steps should be revisited on an ongoing basis as a firm adapts to different threats.

The following hypothetical case narrative provides a detailed example of how this practice model can be implemented within an organizational setting. The narrative highlights key steps, challenges, and results:

Company Background

FinSecure Bank, a mid-sized regional institution headquartered in Los Angeles, manages $50 billion in assets and serves two million customers across retail banking, wealth management, and digital payments. Like many of its competitors, the FinSecure Bank faced escalating cybersecurity threats, including phishing attacks, insider risks, and scrutiny from regulators. Recently, a minor data leak brought cybersecurity to the attention of senior bank management. In response, FinSecure launched a bias-aware cybersecurity program that combined traditional defenses with behavioral frameworks.

The Challenge

Internal audits revealed that 70% of data privacy incidents in the bank stemmed from human error and bias, not technical failures. Employees often ignored red flags because of overconfidence or adopted lax practices through herding behavior. FinSecure's leadership set a bold goal: cut breaches by 50% within two years while maintaining compliance and operational efficiency.

Implementation of the Bias-Aware Framework

The CEO established a cross-functional task force spanning IT, HR, compliance, and frontline staff. New policies encouraged anonymous reporting, tied incentives to security KPIs, and promoted psychological safety. Executives shared personal stories of bias at town halls, signaling transparency. Within six months, employee engagement scores rose 40%, with staff more willing to flag concerns.

The bank cataloged critical assets, analyzed vulnerabilities, and assessed cognitive biases through surveys. It was determined that overconfidence was widespread, with 60% of employees overrating their phishing detection skills. Scenario-based training and insider-risk screenings helped uncover weak points, particularly in legacy systems.

FinSecure Bank tightened access controls, enforced multi-factor authentication (MFA), encrypted sensitive data, and tokenized payments. Employees were required to undergo monthly phishing simulations and bias-focused training, supported by "nudge" dashboards that displayed phishing susceptibility scores. Automated approvals reduced human error, blocking more than 200 simulated attacks in the first year.

Advanced Security Information and Event Management (SIEM) and AI-driven monitoring were also implemented to flag anomalies such as unusual logins or file access. Behavioral analytics helped detect biases. This led to the rapid discovery of an insider attempting to leak data, averting a $5 million loss.

Response plans emphasized bias checks, using pre-mortems and red team drills to challenge assumptions. A near-miss phishing incident illustrated the value of escalation protocols and transparent communication with regulators and clients. Incidents were typically contained in under 24 hours, limiting reputational harm.

Backups restored operations quickly, while post-incident reviews identified optimism and herding biases in recovery assessments. Lessons learned were fed into training programs and shared through "lessons learned" updates. Operations were consistently restored within 48 hours, and related incidents fell by 45%.

FinSecure Bank also began tracking performance outcomes through data breach reduction audits, cultural surveys, and compliance benchmarks. Updates included AI-driven training nudges and refinements to bias-mitigation policies. Within two years, the bank achieved a 55% reduction in incidents, surpassing its target.

Outcomes and Lessons Learned

By embedding debiasing into every stage of the bank's cybersecurity protocols, FinSecure Bank avoided $10 million in potential losses, improved regulatory scores, and boosted customer trust, as reflected in a 25% rise in net promoter scores. This case highlights two core lessons: (1) cross-functional collaboration is critical, and (2) ongoing debiasing can be used to effectively keep pace with evolving threats.

Chapter Summary

Safeguarding customer data and mitigating financial fraud by breaches in cybersecurity in the financial services profession demand a comprehensive and proactive cybersecurity strategy. Financial institutions face persistent and sophisticated threats, ranging from malware and phishing to insider risks and large-scale system disruptions. These threats place a firm's operational integrity and customer trust at risk.[49] The consequences of cyberattacks extend beyond financial loss, encompassing data breaches, fraud, reputational harm, and significant regulatory and legal liabilities. To counter these risks, financial institutions need to implement layered defenses that include risk assessments, security controls, incident response and recovery protocols, and continuous employee awareness programs.

The regulatory framework is something firms and financial advisors need to understand. In the United States, laws such as the Gramm-Leach-Bliley Act, enforced by federal agencies including the OCC and FDIC, establish the foundation for compliance and accountability in cybersecurity practices. Effective data protection requires strong client data privacy policies, secure data classification and handling processes, and advanced protective technologies such as encryption and tokenization. Similarly, fraud prevention requires vigorous detection systems, anomaly monitoring, anti-money laundering controls, and the integration of machine learning techniques capable of identifying suspicious patterns in real time.

Emerging technologies provide new opportunities to enhance cybersecurity measures. Artificial intelligence, blockchain applications, and real-time threat intelligence sharing are increasingly being used to counter data privacy and cybersecurity threats. Equally important are collaborative efforts, such as cross-industry information-sharing initiatives, partnerships with cybersecurity vendors, and adherence to frameworks like the NIST Cybersecurity Framework.

Ultimately, the sustainability of the digital financial ecosystem rests on the ability of financial services firms and financial advisors to anticipate, prevent, and respond to cyber threats. A holistic cybersecurity posture at the firm level that combines regulation, technology, organizational preparedness, and collaboration remains the primary way firm can protect customer data, prevent fraud, and preserve public confidence in the financial system.

Chapter Resources

- NIST (National Institute of Standards and Technology): https://www.nist.gov/
- CISA (Cybersecurity and Infrastructure Security Agency): https://www.cisa.gov/
- FTC (Federal Trade Commission): https://www.ftc.gov/
- ENISA (European Union Agency for Cybersecurity): https://www.enisa.europa.eu/
- ICO (Information Commissioner's Office): https://ico.org.uk/
- Office of the Privacy Commissioner of Canada (OPC): https://www.priv.gc.ca/en/
- Australian Cyber Security Centre (ACSC): https://www.cyber.gov.au/
- Singapore Cyber Security Agency (CSA): https://www.csa.gov.sg/about-csa
- Electronic Frontier Foundation (EFF): https://www.eff.org/
- Center for Democracy & Technology (CDT): https://cdt.org/
- ISACA (Information Systems Audit and Control Association): https://www.isaca.org/
- IAPP (International Association of Privacy Professionals): https://iapp.org/
- CyberPeace Institute: https://cyberpeaceinstitute.org/
- Open Web Application Security Project (OWASP): https://owasp.org/
- MITRE Corporation (Federally Funded R&D Center): https://www.mitre.org/our-impact/rd-centers

Notes

[1]Chui, K. T. (2023). Building digital trust: Challenges and strategies in cybersecurity. *Cyber Security Insights Magazine, Insights2Techinfo, 5*, 15–18.

[2]De Capitani Di Vimercati, S., Foresti, S., Livraga, G., & Samarati, P. (2012). Data privacy: Definitions and techniques. *International Journal of Uncertainty, Fuzziness and Knowledge-Based Systems, 20*(06), 793–817.

[3]Priyadarshini, I. (2019). Introduction on cybersecurity. *Cyber Security in Parallel and Distributed Computing: Concepts, Techniques, Applications and Case Studies*, 1–37.

[4]Craigen, D., Diakun-Thibault, N., & Purse, R. (2014). Defining cybersecurity. *Technology innovation management review, 4*(10). https://www.timreview.ca/article/835

[5]Murphy, Cl. (2020). You can have security without privacy … but you cannot have privacy without security! Cybersecurity Blog. https://community.opentext.com/cybersec/b/cybersecurity-blog/posts/you-can-have-security-without-privacy-but-you-cannot-have-privacy-without-security

[6]Singh, S., & Kumar, S. (2020). The times of cyber attacks. *Acta Technica Corviniensis-Bulletin of Engineering, 13*(3), 133–137.

[7]Khan, S., Kabanov, I., Hua, Y., & Madnick, S. (2022). A systematic analysis of the capital one data breach: Critical lessons learned. *ACM Transactions on Privacy and Security, 26*(1), 1–29.

[8]Office of the Comptroller of the Currency: https://www.occ.gov/news-issuances/news-releases/2020/nr-occ-2020-101.html

[9]Consumer Financial Protection Bureau: https://www.consumerfinance.gov/about-us/newsroom/cfpb-sues-capital-one-for-cheating-consumers-out-of-more-than-2-billion-in-interest-payments-on-savings-accounts/

[10]Novaes Neto, N., Madnick, S., Moraes G de Paula, A., & Malara Borges, N. (2020). A case study of the capital one data breach. *Stuart E. and Moraes G. de Paula, Anchises and Malara Borges, Natasha, A Case Study of the Capital One Data Breach (January 1, 2020).*

[11]Daswani, N., & Elbayadi, M. (2021). The capital one breach. In *Big Breaches: Cybersecurity Lessons for Everyone* (pp. 35–53). Berkeley, CA: Apress.

[12]In the United States, financial services firms are required to provide privacy statements to clients. This obligation comes from the Gramm-Leach-Bliley Act (GLBA) of 1999, specifically its Privacy Rule.

Under the GLBA, (a) covered entities include banks, securities firms, insurance companies, and other financial institutions; (b) firms must provide customers with a clear, conspicuous privacy notice at the start of the customer relationship and annually thereafter; (c) the notice must explain what personal information is collected, how it is used, with whom it is shared, and how it is protected; and (d) clients must also be given the option to opt out of certain data sharing with nonaffiliated third parties. The Federal Trade Commission (FTC) and federal banking regulators enforce these provisions. Non-compliance can result in significant fines and enforcement actions.

[13]The following illustrates a sample GLBA-compliant privacy notice that mirrors what financial institutions are required to distribute to clients. This format is based on the model form issued by U.S. regulators:

Privacy Notice

Facts: What does [Your Firm's Name] do with your personal information?

Why?

Financial companies choose how they share your personal information. Federal law gives consumers the right to limit some but not all sharing. Federal law also requires us to tell you how we collect, share, and protect your personal information. Please read this notice carefully to understand what we do.

What?

The types of personal information we collect and share depend on the product or service you have with us. This information can include:

- Social Security number and income
- Account balances and transaction history
- Credit history and investment experience

When you are no longer our customer, we continue to share your information as described in this notice.

How?

All financial companies need to share customers' personal information to run their everyday business. In the section below, we list the reasons financial companies can share their customers' personal information, whether [Your Firm's Name] chooses to share, and whether you can limit this sharing.

Reasons we can share your personal information	Does [Your Firm] share?	Can you limit this sharing?
For our everyday business purposes—such as to process your transactions, maintain your account(s), respond to court orders and legal investigations	Yes	No
For our marketing purposes—to offer our products and services to you	Yes	No
For joint marketing with other financial companies	Yes	No
For our affiliates' everyday business purposes—information about your transactions and experiences	Yes	No
For our affiliates' everyday business purposes—information about your creditworthiness	No	We don't share
For nonaffiliates to market to you	No	We don't share

Who we are

- **Who is providing this notice?** [Your Firm's Name], a [bank/broker-dealer/investment adviser/ insurance company].

What we do

- **How does [Your Firm] protect my personal information?**
- To protect your personal information from unauthorized access and use, we use security measures that comply with federal law. These measures include computer safeguards, encryption, and secured files and buildings.
- **How does [Your Firm] collect my personal information?**
- We collect your personal information, for example, when you:
  - Open an account or deposit money
  - Apply for insurance or seek financial advice
  - Provide employment or income information
- **Why can't I limit all sharing?**
- Federal law gives you the right to limit only:
  - Sharing for affiliates' everyday business purposes—information about your creditworthiness
  - Affiliates from using your information to market to you
  - Sharing for nonaffiliates to market to you

State laws and individual companies may give you additional rights to limit sharing.
Definitions

- **Affiliates**: Companies related by common ownership or control. They can be financial and non-financial companies.
- **Nonaffiliates**: Companies not related by common ownership or control. They can be financial and non-financial companies.
- **Joint Marketing**: A formal agreement between nonaffiliated financial companies that together market financial products or services to you.

[14]California Attorney General's Office: https://www.oag.ca.gov/privacy/ccpa/enforcement

[15]See: https://gdpr-info.eu/issues/fines-penalties/

[16]The EU ICT (Information and Communication Technology) risk management refers to the process of identifying, assessing, mitigating, and monitoring risks related to an organization's digital infrastructure. In financial services, this includes everything from data breaches and system outages to third-party software vulnerabilities.

[17]See: https://gdprlocal.com/gdpr-fines-understanding-percentages-and-penalties/

[18]Office of the Australian Information Commissioner: https://www.oaic.gov.au/about-the-OAIC/our-regulatory-approach/guide-to-privacy-regulatory-action/chapter-7-privacy-assessments

[19]New Zealand Government: https://docref.digital.govt.nz/nz/pri/181/en/#en1

[20]Parallel 49 AI Canada: In Canada, the transition from PIPEDA to the forthcoming Consumer Privacy Protection Act (CPPA) signals a move toward GDPR-style rigor, including stronger consent requirements, portability rights, and higher penalties—up to CA$25 million or 5% of global turnover.

[21] PWC:https://www.pwc.com/id/en/pwc-publications/services-publications/legal-publications/a-comparison-of-cybersecurity-regulations/china.html

[22] See: https://www.japaneselawtranslation.go.jp/en/laws/view/4241/en

[23] Singapore Government Agency Website: https://www.csa.gov.sg/legislation/cybersecurity-act

[24] Kaufmann & Company. (2024). Holistic ethics and compliance management for multinational companies across industries. White Paper: https://kaufmann-company.com/wp-content/uploads/2025/04/Holistic-Ethics-Compliance-Management-for-Multinational-Companies-Across-Industries_Whitepaper.pdf

[25] The primary regulatory agencies that oversee cybersecurity enforcement in the United States include the Office of the Comptroller of the Currency (OCC), the Federal Deposit Insurance Corporation (FDIC), and the Consumer Financial Protection Bureau (CFPB).

[26] Paul, E., Callistus, O., Somtobe, O., Esther, T., Somto, K., Clement, O., & Ejimofor, I. (2023). Cybersecurity strategies for safeguarding customer's data and preventing financial fraud in the United States financial sectors. *International Journal on Soft Computing, 14*(3), 01–16.

[27] USA Today: https://www.usatoday.com/story/money/business/2014/08/27/reports-jpmorgan-hack-attack/14706545/

[28] Paul, E., Callistus, O., Somtobe, O., Esther, T., Somto, K., Clement, O., & Ejimofor, I. (2023). Cybersecurity strategies for safeguarding customer's data and preventing financial fraud in the United States financial sectors. *International Journal on Soft Computing, 14*(3), 01–16.

[29] Council on Foreign Relations: https://www.cfr.org/cyber-operations/denial-service-attacks-against-us-banks-2012-2013

[30] Paul, E., Callistus, O., Somtobe, O., Esther, T., Somto, K., Clement, O., & Ejimofor, I. (2023). Cybersecurity strategies for safeguarding customer's data and preventing financial fraud in the United States financial sectors. *International Journal on Soft Computing, 14*(3), 01–16.

[31] Ogigau-Neamtiu, F. (2016). Tokenization as a data security technique. *Zeszyty Naukowe AON*, 2 (103), 124–135.

[32] Devineni, S. K., Kathiriya, S., & Shende, A. (2023). Machine learning-powered anomaly detection: Enhancing data security and integrity. *Journal of Artificial Intelligence & Cloud Computing. SRC/JAICC-198. https://doi.org/10.47363/JAICC/2023(2)184*, 2–9.

[33] Zhang, Z., Yin, H., Rao, S. X., Yan, X., Wang, Z., Liang, W., ... & Jiang, J. (2025). Identifying e-commerce fraud through user behavior data: Observations and insights. *Data Science and Engineering, 10*(1), 24–39.

[34] Federal Deposit Insurance Corporation: https://www.fdic.gov/risk-management-manual-examination-policies/insider-fraud-and-abuse

[35] Mohamed, N. (2025). Artificial intelligence and machine learning in cybersecurity: a deep dive into state-of-the-art techniques and future paradigms. *Knowledge and Information Systems*, 1–87.

[36] Shen, L. (2014). The NIST cybersecurity framework: Overview and potential impacts. *Scitech Lawyer, 10*(4), 16–19.

[37] Brenner, J. (2007). ISO 27001 risk management and compliance. *Risk management, 54*(1), 24–29.

[38] See: https://gemserv.com/wp-content/uploads/2019/08/PCI_DSS-3.2-web.pdf

[39] Lei, W., Hu, S., & Hsu, C. (2023). Unveiling the process of phishing precautions taking: The moderating role of optimism bias. *Computers & Security, 129*, 103249.

[40] Carter, W. (2025). Financial Forecasting and Cognitive Biases: A Theoretical Examination of Framing Effects and Predictive Accuracy. https://www.preprints.org/frontend/manuscript/fc3b03485b4a572a020019e64c2a7a21/download_pub

[41] Rana, S., & Chicone, R. (2025). AI-Driven Personalized Learning in Cybersecurity Training. In *Fortifying the Future: Harnessing AI for Transformative Cybersecurity Training* (pp. 25–50). Cham: Springer Nature Switzerland.

[42]Peters, J. (2023). Human error is responsible for 74% of data breaches. *Infosec*. https://www.infosecinstitute.com/resources/security-awareness/human-error-responsible-data-breaches/

[43]Crumbaugh, J. (2024). Endowment effect. *Phishfirewall Blog*. https://www.phishfirewall.com/cognitive-biases/endowment-effect

[44]Wright, V. (2024). The 8 hidden costs of a data breach: Insights from the 2024 IBM report. https://bigid.com/blog/2024-ibm-report-data-breach-insights/ (see: https://www.ibm.com/reports/data-breach).

[45]An anti-bias strategy in cybersecurity refers to intentional methods used to identify, mitigate, and counteract cognitive biases that impair sound judgment and decision-making in digital security environments. These strategies aim to reduce human error, improve threat detection, and foster a more resilient organizational culture (see: Viskovich, Y., & Mohan, V. (2025). Ethical Dilemmas and Human Factors in the Application of AI in Cybersecurity. In AI Ethics in Practice: Navigating Academic Insight, Managerial Expertise, and Philosophical Inquiry (pp. 71–91). Cham: Springer Nature Switzerland.

[46]Glynn, F. (2025). Red teaming exercises: Processes and examples. *Mindgard Blog*. https://mindgard.ai/blog/red-teaming-exercises-processes-examples

[47]See: https://csrc.nist.gov/pubs/cswp/29/the-nist-cybersecurity-framework-csf-20/final

[48]See: https://cyberriskinstitute.org/the-profile/

[49]Paul, E., Callistus, O., Somtobe, O., Esther, T., Somto, K., Clement, O., & Ejimofor, I. (2023). Cybersecurity strategies for safeguarding customer's data and preventing financial fraud in the United States financial sectors. *International Journal on Soft Computing*, *14*(3), 01–16.

11 Fair Treatment of Clients

Chapter Outcomes
This chapter focuses on helping learners develop the ability to:

1. Explain the three core dimensions of fairness in the financial services profession (procedural fairness, interactional fairness, and distributive fairness[1]) and the significance of each when delivery services.
2. Describe the principles of procedural fairness, including neutrality, transparency, and adherence to due process, and how each ensures impartial decision-making processes.
3. Analyze the role of courtesy, respect, attentiveness, and two-way communication to make clients feel valued and understood.
4. Evaluate the equity of outcomes in financial transactions, focusing on the fair allocation of resources, benefits, and costs based on the contributions and needs of all parties.
5. Discuss how relationship marketing, consumer protection laws, and financial services regulatory frameworks contribute to promoting fairness in client interactions.
6. Identify methods to help clients overcome cognitive, behavioral, and psychological biases and decision paralysis that may expose them to potential mistreatment in financial transactions.

Note: This chapter was copyedited using Grammarly™ and generative AI tools to enhance clarity, grammar, and overall readability. While these tools provided suggestions and assistance in refining the text, the ideas, content, and arguments presented remain the sole work and responsibility of the authors. Any errors or inaccuracies in the final version are also the authors' responsibility.

W. Heo, J. E. Grable, *Ethics and Compliance in Financial Services*,
https://doi.org/10.1007/978-3-032-14449-2_11

Introduction

Marketing ethicists study the moral principles that guide the way organizations interact with consumers.[2] Historically, there have been two points of view on the study of ethics in marketing. The first is "buyer beware." From this point of view, the rights of the organization dominate transactions. The second is "seller beware." Using this perspective, organizations are assumed to be immoral, with consumers requiring a maximum amount of consumer protection. Today, the consensus is that neither position is fully correct. The truth lies somewhere in the middle. Non-profit and for-profit organizations are increasingly adopting a middle-ground position that is based on relationship marketing. Relationship marketing involves building meaningful and deeper interactions with clients in an attempt to strengthen long-term client satisfaction and loyalty.[3] The relationship marketing context emphasizes the connection between the service provider and client rather than the sale of a product.

Financial services professionals who adopt a relationship marketing approach need to be aware of ethical standards and codes of acceptable behavior. This means a financial advisor must recognize the viewpoints of three parties: the client, the firm, and the profession. These groups often have unique needs and wants, which can create ethical conflicts. An example is when a financial advisor[4] is required to meet a sales quota. Without a recognized practice standard, the financial professional may choose not to inform a client of the quota. Non-disclosure creates a potential conflict of interest in that the client can never know if the product being offered is in their best interest. In this example, the firm seeks to maximize profits. Profit maximization can create an environment that promotes ethical conflicts for those who engage directly with clients. This is why federal and state regulators and membership and certification groups develop and enforce practice standards. Standards have four functions: (1) to help identify acceptable practices, (2) to foster internal control, (3) to avoid confusion and reduce conflicts, and (4) to facilitate a basis for enforcement.

This chapter describes how relationship marketing, consumer protection laws, and financial services regulatory frameworks work together to increase the likelihood that all clients are treated fairly. The chapter includes detailed case examples and a discussion of ways to help clients overcome cognitive biases and decision paralysis that can make them vulnerable to being mistreated.

Perspective

Fair treatment of clients in the financial services profession is a cornerstone of ethical business practice and regulatory compliance. Treating clients fairly emphasizes the importance of putting a client's needs and interests first at all times. As noted throughout this book, treating clients fairly includes transparency, accountability, respect, accessibility, and proactively using a client-centered perspective.[5] Transparency involves providing clear, concise, and honest information about products and services. Accountability requires a financial advisor to take responsibility for the outcomes of advice or recommendations. Respect recognizes the diverse needs and circumstances of each client. Accessibility ensures that products and services are available and understandable to all clients, whereas client-centricity means that a financial advisor aligns practice goals with the well-being and satisfaction of clients.[6] Together, these principles ensure trust and foster long-term relationships between a financial advisor and their clients. Consider the following case narrative, which illustrates these principles in action.

In this case, a financial advisory firm specializes in offering investment strategies and retirement planning services. A new client, Narang, a single mother and small business owner, approaches the firm seeking guidance on reallocating her retirement savings assets and creating a savings program to fund her children's future educational expenses. Narang's limited experience with these topics requires an approach that integrates education, transparency, and the ethical delivery of services. The following discussion highlights how transparency, accountability, respect, accessibility, and a client-centered perspective can be combined to help Narang.

During the initial consultation, Narang's financial advisor, Steffen, provides Narang with clear and easily accessible information about the firm's services, fees, and potential risks associated with various investment options. During the meeting, Steffen avoids using technical jargon, ensuring Narang fully understands the investment planning process. For example, when explaining an investment strategy involving mutual funds, Steffen discloses potential management fees and market volatility risks in an easy-to-understand way.

During follow-up meetings, Steffen implements firm and certification board practice standards. He commits to meeting measurable benchmarks when managing Narang's assets. For instance, he shows Narang that it is possible to achieve an 8% before-tax rate of return on her retirement assets and that her retirement goal can be accomplished if this average return is achieved. He assures Narang that he will monitor the investment plan, provide regular updates, and adjust holdings in the portfolio as needed based on performance and changing circumstances.

At the core of Steffen's work with Narang is the notion of using concepts from relationship marketing. Steffen tailors his work with Narang in a way that respects her unique circumstances, such as her need for financial stability as a sole provider and her desire to prioritize her children's future. Rather than rely on one or a handful of products that are used across client accounts, Steffen incorporates Narang's risk tolerance, preferences, perceptions, and other factors into analyses that suggest a unique mix of assets with different risk and return characteristics. Additionally, Steffen considers Narang's cultural values, ensuring his recommendations align with her long-term goals and financial priorities.

Throughout the client engagement process, Steffen accounts for Narang's busy schedule and possible concerns regarding information overload. In this regard, Steffen ensures that all documents and forms, including investment statements and required investment disclosures, are accessible. He introduces Narang to an intuitive mobile application that provides real-time updates on her portfolio and offers step-by-step tutorials as needed. Steffen also makes himself available for periodic consultations that accommodate her, rather than his, constraints.

At every stage of the client engagement, Steffen works to align his firm's services with Narang's needs rather than pushing prepackaged solutions, products, or services. Rather than promote a high-commission financial product, Steffen prioritizes more cost-effective, tax-advantaged assets. The key aspect of Steffen's behavior is a genuine concern for Narang rather than doing so because of regulatory requirements. When working with Narang, Steffen evaluates the long-term impact of each recommendation on Narang's financial situation as a pathway to ensuring her satisfaction and trust in the advisory process.

This is not to say that Steffen is blind to his regulatory and firm obligations. Quite the contrary. Steffen ensures Narang's nonpublic personal information (NPI) is securely stored and only shared with third parties when necessary and with Narang's explicit consent. He educates Narang on her rights to opt out of data sharing with nonaffiliated parties, further demonstrating a commitment to her privacy and security.

As this case illustrates, it is possible to adopt a relationship marketing perspective that builds on the concepts of transparency, accountability, respect, accessibility, and holding a client-centered perspective to successfully help clients like Narang meet their immediate and long-term goals while fostering trust and satisfaction.

The following case describes another real-life situation showing how a well-established insurance company decided to focus on ethical relationship marketing rather than aggressive sales tactics to increase sales and build client trust.

Johnathan, a 38-year-old father of two, was considering purchasing a life insurance policy to provide financial security for his family in the event of his premature death. As a middle-income earner, he wanted to protect his family, but he did not want to spend money to purchase more coverage than necessary. High-pressure sales tactics had previously soured Johnathan's experience with life insurance companies. In several prior encounters, salespeople had tried to upsell him large policies without truly understanding his financial situation and needs. He felt uneasy about these interactions and remained hesitant to make a decision, unsure whether he was being sold more than he needed.

This was when Johnathan met Liana. Liana's firm focuses on building relationships with potential clients through ethical marketing practices. Liana's employer emphasizes understanding each client's needs, goals, and financial constraints before recommending a policy. The company's marketing philosophy highlights transparency, trust, and education, with a focus on offering clients products that are in their best interest.

Using the practice model, Liana immediately set a comfortable tone for the conversation during their first meeting. She started by asking Johnathan about his life goals, current financial situation, and concerns about his family's future. Instead of focusing on policy details first, she spent much of the time listening to Johnathan's needs. During the conversation, Liana took notes about (a) how much of his current income his family would need if he were to die, (b) what his family's current financial obligations were, (c) what his desired level of protection was for his children's education, and (d) his budget for life insurance.

After gathering relevant information, Liana provided Johnathan with a clear explanation of different life insurance options, including term life and whole life policies, and how each aligned with his goals. She emphasized that based on his current situation, a 20-year term life policy would best meet his needs at a modest premium. In doing so, Liana knew that she was making a recommendation that would reduce her commission income, but she knew that the recommendation was ethically sound because it matched Johnathan's needs and budget.

Liana's sales and marketing approach emphasized transparency and education. She made it clear that the recommended policy would provide sufficient coverage without costing too much. She also explained how certain riders could be added without inflating the cost dramatically. Throughout the conversation, she was transparent about the features and costs of the policy and avoided any sales pressure, leaving Johnathan time to consider his options. She also provided information on how to review and adjust the policy in the future as his life circumstances changed.

Impressed by Liana's honesty and understanding, Johnathan decided to proceed by purchasing the policy. Unlike previous interactions with other life insurance salespeople, Johnathan felt that he was being treated with respect and that his financial goals were prioritized above the company's sales agenda. Liana followed up regularly after the policy was issued to ensure Johnathan was satisfied with his coverage and that his financial needs had not changed.

Johnathan's situation evolved over the next few years. His salary increased and his children grew older. Liana reached out annually to review his life insurance needs. Johnathan was grateful for these proactive discussions, which reinforced his trust in Liana. As a result, Johnathan became a loyal client. He referred several family members and friends, praising the firm's ethical sales and marketing approach.

At the enterprise level, the firm continued its ethical marketing approach and gained recognition within the insurance industry for its commitment to client-centric practices. The company was awarded several industry accolades for its transparent sales approach. The company's reputation for fairness and integrity attracted many new clients seeking more trustworthy alternatives to traditional insurance sales tactics. In addition to positive word-of-mouth referrals from satisfied clients like Johnathan, the firm also saw a significant increase in customer retention rates, with many clients opting to upgrade their policies over time rather than switching providers. The company's focus on education and suitability in product recommendations helped distinguish it from its competitors.

This case highlights the value of ethical relationship marketing as a way to promote long-term customer loyalty and trust. By focusing on the needs and financial goals of clients, Liana was able to build a lasting relationship based on transparency and mutual respect. Ethical relationship marketing not only benefits clients by ensuring they receive products suited to their needs, but it also results in financial growth and positive industry recognition for companies that commit to the technique.

Treating Clients Fairly: Regulatory Requirements

Numerous federal and state regulatory frameworks have been described throughout this book. These frameworks have one commonality—ensuring that financial services professionals treat clients fairly. Consumer protection laws add an additional layer of protection by safeguarding the rights of clients.[7] Consumer protection laws aim to prevent firms (and advisors) from engaging in unfair practices, fraud, or deceptive behavior. These laws also promote transparency, competition, and accountability.

Consumer protection laws aim to protect privacy by ensuring firms handle a consumer's personal information responsibly. The Gramm-Leach-Bliley Act (GLBA) regulates how financial institutions collect, use, and share personal financial data, while the General Data Protection Regulation (GDPR) offers similar privacy protections in the European Union. Under GLBA, the sharing of nonpublic personal information (NPI) is highly regulated.[8] Privacy laws apply to entities that are "significantly engaged" in financial activities, including those not traditionally viewed as financial institutions, such as lenders, financial advisors, and tax preparers. The GLBA mandates that financial institutions notify consumers of their information-sharing practices and provide an opt-out option for sharing NPI with certain nonaffiliated third parties. Entities receiving NPI from financial institutions face restrictions on data reuse and redisclosure. The Act distinguishes between "consumers," who engage in financial transactions for personal use, and "customers," who maintain ongoing relationships with financial institutions. Institutions must consider the nature and frequency of their financial activities to determine if they are subject to privacy rules. NPI includes identifiable financial data collected during transactions, except for information deemed publicly available after reasonable verification. Lists derived even partially from NPI remain protected under the rule, emphasizing the importance of safeguarding consumer relationships and personal financial information.

Promoting financial literacy is another important function of consumer protection laws. The Dodd-Frank Wall Street Reform and Consumer Protection Act was arguably the most important piece of consumer protection regulation enacted over the past quarter century. The Act created the Consumer Financial Protection Bureau (CFPB), which has a mandate of educating consumers about financial products and services while protecting them from deceptive practices. Finally, laws exist to protect vulnerable consumers, such as the elderly or those with limited financial literacy, from exploitation or fraud. The Older Americans Act (OAA) is one such law. The Act mandates adhering to standards that protect older individuals from financial abuse and scams. Table 11.1 provides a summary of some of the most important consumer protection regulations that have an impact on the financial services profession.[9]

Although the laws described in Table 11.1 serve different purposes, each shares a common goal, namely, to ensure the fair treatment of consumers. Four themes run through each piece of legislation. First, nearly all consumer protection laws have strict disclosure requirements that mandate financial institutions disclose all

Table 11.1 Important consumer protection laws

Act	Description of the Act
Bankruptcy Abuse Prevention and Consumer Protection Act (BAPCPA)	Enacted in 2005, this law provides protections for consumers filing for bankruptcy. This Act ensures that the process is fair and that certain types of debts (e.g., child support) are prioritized[a]. The Act also requires credit counseling before filing for bankruptcy
Community Reinvestment Act of 1977	Encourages financial institutions to help meet the credit needs of their communities, particularly low- and moderate-income neighborhoods
Consumer Leasing Act of 1976	Requires that institutions disclose the cost and terms of consumer leases, including automobile leases
Credit Card Accountability, Responsibility, and Disclosure Act (CARD Act)	The CARD Act was enacted to protect consumers from unfair credit card practices and promote transparency in the credit card market. Signed into law in 2009, the Act prohibits sudden interest rate hikes, excessive penalties, and hidden fees. The Act also mandates that credit card issuers disclose terms and conditions to promote transparency. Additionally, issuers must assess a consumer's ability to pay before extending credit and include special provisions for consumers under the age of 21. The CARD Act limits upfront fees during the first year of an account and restricts back-end penalty fees for late payments or exceeding credit limits. Furthermore, the Act establishes strict regulations for when and how interest rates on credit cards can be increased
Dodd-Frank Wall Street Reform and Consumer Protection Act	Passed in 2010, this law established the Consumer Financial Protection Bureau (CFPB) to oversee and enforce regulations related to consumer financial services. The CFPB is tasked with protecting consumers from unfair, deceptive, or abusive acts and practices within the financial services industry. As part of its mission, the CFPB ensures that American consumers receive clear and accurate information when shopping for financial products. The CFPB also protects consumers from hidden fees, abusive terms, and deceptive practices. The Bureau has the independent authority to create and enforce consumer protection rules applicable to all financial institutions—both banks and non-banks—offering consumer financial products or services
Electronic Fund Transfer Act of 1978	The Act established the basic rights, liabilities, and responsibilities of (1) consumers who use electronic fund transfer services and (2) financial institutions that offer these services. Covers transactions conducted at ATMs, at point-of-sale terminals in stores, and through telephone-bill-payment plans and preauthorized transfers to and from a customer's account, such as direct deposit of salary or Social Security payments
Equal Credit Opportunity Act of 1974 (ECOA)	The Act prohibits discrimination in credit transactions on many grounds, including sex, marital status, age, race, religion, color, national origin, the receipt of public assistance funds, or the exercise of any right under the Consumer Credit Protection Act. The law requires creditors to grant credit to qualified individuals without requiring co-signature by spouses, inform unsuccessful applicants in writing of the reasons credit was denied, and allow married individuals to have credit histories on jointly held accounts maintained in the names of both spouses

(continued)

Table 11.1 (continued)

Act	Description of the Act
Expedited Funds Availability Act of 1987	This Act specifies when depository institutions must make funds deposited by consumers available
Fair and Accurate Credit Transaction Act of 2003	This law enhances a consumer's ability to combat identity theft. The Act increases the accuracy of consumer reports, allows consumers to exercise greater control over the type and amount of marketing solicitations they receive, restricts the use and disclosure of sensitive medical information, and establishes uniform national standards in the regulation of consumer reporting. The Act amended the Fair Credit Reporting Act
Fair Credit and Charge Card Disclosure Act of 1988	The Act requires that applications for credit cards that are sent through the mail, solicited by telephone, or made available to the public (for example, at counters in retail stores or through catalogs) contain information about key terms of the account. The law amended the Truth in Lending Act
Fair Credit Billing Act of 1974	This law specifies how creditors must respond to billing complaints from consumers. The Act imposes requirements to ensure that creditors handle accounts fairly and promptly. The law applies primarily to revolving and credit card accounts (e.g., store card and bank card accounts). The law amended the Truth in Lending Act
Fair Credit Reporting Act of 1970	The Act protects consumers against inaccurate or misleading information in credit files maintained by credit reporting agencies. The law requires credit reporting agencies to allow credit applicants to correct erroneous reports
Fair Credit Reporting Act (FCRA)	The FCRA, enacted in 1970, ensures the accuracy, fairness, and privacy of consumer credit reports[b]. The Act gives consumers the right to access their credit reports, dispute inaccuracies, and be informed if a credit report is used against them in lending decisions
Fair Debt Collection Practices Act of 1977	The law prohibits abusive debt-collection practices. The Act applies to banks that function as debt collectors for other entities
Fair Housing Act of 1968	The Act prohibits discrimination in the extension of housing credit on the basis of race, color, religion, national origin, sex, handicap, or family status
Federal Trade Commission Improvement Act of 1980	It authorizes the Federal Reserve to identify unfair or deceptive acts or practices by banks and to issue regulations to prohibit them. Using this authority, the Federal Reserve has adopted rules substantially similar to those adopted by the FTC that restrict certain practices in the collection of delinquent consumer debt (e.g., practices related to late charges, responsibilities of cosigners, and wage assignments)
Flood Disaster Protection Act of 1973	This law requires flood insurance on property in a flood hazard area that falls under the National Flood Insurance Program
Gramm-Leach-Bliley Act of 1999 (*Regulation P—Privacy of Consumer Financial Information*)	This law describes the conditions under which financial institutions may disclose nonpublic personal information about consumers to nonaffiliated third parties, provides a method for consumers to opt out of information sharing with nonaffiliated third parties and requires financial institutions to notify consumers about their privacy policies and practices

(continued)

Table 11.1 (continued)

Act	Description of the Act
Gramm-Leach-Bliley Act of 1999 (*Regulation H—Consumer Protection in Sales of Insurance*)	The law describes conditions for retail sales, solicitations, advertising, or offers of insurance products or annuities by state member banks or by others at an office of a bank. The Act prohibits coercion and misrepresentations and requires disclosures in connection with the initial purchase of an insurance product or annuity
Home Equity Loan Consumer Protection Act of 1988	The Act requires creditors to provide consumers with detailed information about open-end credit plans secured by the consumer's dwelling, including a general brochure describing home equity loans. The law also regulates advertising of home equity loans and restricts the terms of home equity loan plans
Home Mortgage Disclosure Act of 1975	The Act requires mortgage lenders to annually disclose to the public data about the geographic distribution of their applications, originations, and purchases of home-purchase and home-improvement loans and refinancings. Requires lenders to report data on the ethnicity, race, sex, and income of applicants and borrowers and pricing data on certain loans. The Act also directs the Federal Financial Institutions Examination Council, of which the Federal Reserve is a member, to make summaries of the data available to the public
Home Ownership and Equity Protection Act (HOEPA)	Enacted in 1994 as part of the Truth in Lending Act (TILA), the Act aims to protect consumers from predatory lending practices in the home loan market. Specifically, HOEPA targets abusive practices in refinances and closed-end home equity loans with high interest rates or fees. HOEPA imposes additional disclosure requirements and restrictions on loan terms for high-cost mortgages, often referred to as "HOEPA loans" or "Section 32 loans." Following the Dodd-Frank Wall Street Reform and Consumer Protection Act (Dodd-Frank Act) in 2010, these loans are now commonly called "high-cost mortgages." The Dodd-Frank Act expanded HOEPA's scope to include purchase-money mortgages and home equity lines of credit (HELOCs). The Act also updated the criteria for determining HOEPA coverage and introduced enhanced consumer protections. Among its key provisions, the Act requires consumers to receive homeownership counseling before obtaining a high-cost mortgage. The 2013 HOEPA Rule, issued by the Consumer Financial Protection Bureau (CFPB), implemented these changes and expanded counseling requirements for certain loans under TILA's Regulation Z and the Real Estate Settlement Procedures Act's (RESPA's) Regulation X. Together, these measures are designed to prevent predatory lending practices and ensure that consumers are well-informed and supported before entering into high-cost mortgage agreements
Home Ownership and Equity Protection Act of 1994	The Act provides additional disclosure requirements and substantive limitations on home-equity loans with rates or fees above a certain percentage or amount. The law amended the Truth in Lending Act

(continued)

Table 11.1 (continued)

Act	Description of the Act
Homeowners Protection Act of 1998	The law established rules for automatic termination and borrower cancellation of private mortgage insurance (PMI) on home mortgages
Office of the Comptroller of the Currency (OCC)	Although it is not a specific legislative act, the OCC has rules aimed at ensuring fair access to banking services by large national banks, federal savings associations, and foreign bank agencies[c]. The rules apply to banks with assets exceeding $100 billion, requiring them to offer their chosen products and services to all eligible customers in their service areas based on impartial, risk-based criteria. Rules allow banks to maintain autonomy in product offerings and geographic markets while ensuring decisions are grounded in objective assessments
Real Estate Settlement Procedures Act of 1974	The Act requires that the nature and costs of real estate settlements be disclosed to borrowers. The Act also protects borrowers against abusive practices, such as kickbacks, and limits the use of escrow accounts
Right to Financial Privacy Act of 1978	The law protects bank customers from the unlawful scrutiny of their financial records by federal agencies and specifies procedures that government authorities must follow when they seek information about a customer's records from a financial institution
Truth in Lending Act of 1968 (TILA)	Enacted in 1968, TILA requires lenders to disclose clear and accurate information about credit terms, including interest rates, fees, and payment schedules, so that consumers can make informed decisions about borrowing[d]. TILA also provides the right to cancel certain types of loans within a specific period. The Act authorizes compliance by most non-depository entities. Furthermore, the Act requires creditors who deal with consumers to make certain written disclosures concerning finance charges and related aspects of credit transactions (including disclosing an annual percentage rate (APR)). The Act has been amended on numerous occasions, adding requirements for credit cards and open-end credit; for mortgage credit such as ability to repay standards, loan origination, anti-steering, appraisal independence, and mortgage servicing; and others
Truth in Savings Act of 1991	The Act requires that depository institutions disclose certain information to depositors about their accounts, including the annual percentage yield (APY), which must be calculated in a uniform manner. The Act also prohibits certain methods of calculating interest and regulates advertising of savings accounts
Women's Business Ownership Act of 1988	The Act extends to applicants for business credit certain protections afforded consumer credit applicants, such as the right to an explanation for credit denial and amended the Equal Credit Opportunity Act

Source: Federal Reserve (https://www.federalreserve.gov/pubs/complaints/laws.htm)

[a] https://www.ftc.gov/legal-library/browse/statutes/bankruptcy-abuse-prevention-consumer-protection-act-2005

[b] https://www.consumer.ftc.gov/sites/default/files/articles/pdf/pdf-0096-fair-credit-reporting-act.pdf

[c] https://www.occ.gov/news-issuances/news-releases/2021/nr-occ-2021-8.html

[d] https://www.ftc.gov/legal-library/browse/statutes/truth-lending-act

relevant risks, fees, and potential conflicts of interest. Second, the laws create suitability standards for products and services. Third, each law provides a mechanism for consumers to resolve complaints by providing accessible and efficient dispute resolution methods. Finally, nearly all the laws listed in Table 11.1 create protections for consumer privacy by ensuring that firms safeguard nonpublic personal information.

Ethical Considerations in Product Marketing and Sales Practices

Treating clients fairly in the context of relationship marketing requires firms and financial advisors to use their ethical reputation as a key selling point.[10] Unethical practices at the firm or advisor level can lead to dissatisfied clients, negative publicity, loss of trust, and possible legal action. A first step in treating clients fairly is to confirm that sales and marketing efforts are ethical. This involves avoiding misleading advertising and misrepresenting financial product terms and conditions, focusing on product and service transparency, discouraging excessive consumer debt and account churning, and promoting client well-being. To do otherwise can erode client trust, damage relationships, reduce customer retention, and lower sales. In contrast, ethical marketing practices increase customer satisfaction, trust, confidence, and loyalty, which are vital for building long-term relationships.[11] Ethical practices also create a competitive market advantage. Companies can promote ethical behavior by developing codes of ethics, fostering a moral climate, and designing compensation systems that reward ethical actions while discouraging unethical ones.

Ethics extends beyond regulatory compliance. Ethics encompasses the moral obligations firms and advisors have toward their clients. Fundamental ethical considerations include avoiding misrepresentation,[12] relying on informed consent, using target marketing strategies, and engaging in continuing client monitoring and review. Specifically, marketing materials should accurately reflect the benefits and limitations of products. Additionally, clients should clearly understand what they are purchasing and why they are making a purchase. Products and services should be designed and marketed to those who can benefit from them, avoiding practices like predatory lending or high-pressure sales tactics. Finally, firms and advisors should periodically evaluate products and services to ensure they meet clients' evolving needs and align with regulatory requirements. The following case narrative illustrates how easy it can be for a firm to engage in unethical marketing when these concepts are disregarded:

> *A firm, XYZ Financial Advisors, has a track record of promoting investment products that exaggerate potential returns while downplaying possible risks. One of the firm's most promoted products is a complex, high-risk investment vehicle that promises high returns with a "guaranteed" safety net. However, in the fine print disclosure, it is revealed that the product is highly speculative and not appropriate for the average investor. Figure 11.1 illustrates an example of one of the firm's marketing brochures:*

XYZ Financial Advisors: Your Path to Guaranteed High Returns!*

Looking for a worry-free way to grow your wealth? XYZ Financial Advisors proudly presents our exclusive High-Yield Opportunity Fund. With promises of market-beating returns and a "guaranteed safety net," this revolutionary investment product is tailored for those who dream big!

- **Exceptional Returns**: Unlock the potential of your portfolio with returns that outperform traditional investments.
- **Built-In Safety**: Rest easy knowing your investment is "secure" with our unique risk management strategy.

Don't miss out! This once-in-a-lifetime opportunity is available exclusively through XYZ Financial Advisors. Take control of your financial future today!

Call Today:

Call us today at 1-800-HIGH-RETURNS or visit us online at www.xyzadvisors.com to learn more.

*The "guaranteed safety net" is not a formal guarantee. This investment carries substantial risk of loss. This product involves complex strategies and is highly speculative. Past performance is not indicative of future results. Please consult a professional before investing. This investment is not suitable for average or risk-averse investors. Terms and conditions apply. Investors may lose more than their initial investment.

Fig. 11.1 XYZ Financial Advisors' marketing brochure

The firm's marketing department argues that the product is not being misrepresented because the risk and return characteristics of the product are disclosed in marketing materials. An outside observer would likely disagree and argue that the firm is misrepresenting the product while violating ethical marketing principles. To begin with, not only did the firm distort the nature of the investment, but the firm buried the risk and return characteristics in fine print that unsophisticated clients may not read.

One of the most important issues the firm faces is the claim that it failed to ensure clients fully understood the product they purchased. In line with ethical business practices, informed consent is a requirement in almost all consumer protection legislation. The firm's approach focuses on persuading clients to make a purchase based on product advantages while minimizing risk disclosures. Lack of transparency violates the firm's ethical obligation to ensure informed consent. Informed consent requires that clients be given appropriate information to make a decision. The firm's failure to uphold this principle will ultimately lead to client disputes and investigations by regulatory authorities.

Furthermore, the firm may be subject to claims of inappropriate target marketing. Financial services firms must ensure the products they offer are suitable for the specific needs of their target market. In this case, XYZ Financial Advisors is marketing a high-risk investment vehicle to average investors. These clients may not be in a financial position to absorb the potential losses that can arise from high-risk investments. A regulator might also find the firm is engaged in offering products with high fees and unfavorable terms and targeting individuals with limited financial knowledge.

Given the firm's business practices, it is likely that XYZ Financial Advisors will come up short in providing account reviews and adjusting product offerings to ensure alignment with the interests of clients. Firms like XYZ Financial Advisors often neglect to conduct thorough suitability reviews for existing clients, many of whom have been steered into products that no longer match their evolving financial needs or risk tolerance. The failure to conduct ongoing reviews means that clients are often stuck with investments that no longer meet their needs, which can result in significant losses and/or opportunity costs. The firm's inability to adapt its offerings to better suit the long-term needs of its clients compounds ethical concerns.

As a result, the firm will likely face significant repercussions. Regulators are likely to launch investigations. In addition to financial penalties, the licenses of advisors working in the firm are subject to suspension. Damage to the firm's reputation is potentially substantial. Trust, once lost, is exceedingly difficult to rebuild. To remain competitive, the firm will need to revamp its business practices, implement more stringent compliance procedures, revise its marketing strategies to avoid misleading claims, and improve its client education efforts.

The Fiduciary and Best-Interest Standards

Treating clients fairly involves prioritizing a client's interests and ensuring the client receives transparent, ethical, and professional services throughout the client-advisor relationship. Fairness is built upon several principles. First, financial services professionals must act in their client's best interest by providing advice, products, or services that align with their client's financial goals, needs, attitudes, preferences, and perceptions. Transparency and honesty are also essential, with clear disclosure of relevant information such as fees, charges, and potential conflicts of interest being a cornerstone of treating clients fairly. Additionally, financial advisors must recommend products and services that are suitable for each client's financial situation, rather than promoting options that disproportionately benefit the advisor or the advisor's firm. Accessibility and responsiveness are also important. Treating clients fairly also means avoiding discrimination and offering equal treatment and opportunities to all clients regardless of background or personal characteristics. Moreover, financial services professionals must protect clients from harm by preventing predatory practices, hidden fees, and unnecessarily complex financial products. Lastly, accountability is vital. Financial advisors must take responsibility for any errors or oversights and resolve disputes in a fair and timely manner. Together, these principles help build trust, foster long-term relationships, and ensure compliance with regulatory standards designed to protect consumers.

Federal and state regulations provide guidance to help financial advisors navigate issues related to fairness. Two practice standards directly apply to this issue: The fiduciary and the best-interest standards of care. Both standards aim to ensure that financial services professionals act in the best interests of their clients. The standards differ in scope and rigor. The fiduciary duty imposes the highest standard of care, requiring financial services professionals to prioritize a client's interests above their own. This includes acting with loyalty and care, avoiding conflicts of interest, or fully disclosing relevant information.

In contrast, while still protective, the best-interest standard is less stringent. The best-interest standard requires a financial advisor to recommend products and services that are *suitable* for a client. The following cases describe how the fiduciary duty and the best-interest standard differ in terms of treating clients fairly. The first case illustrates a violation of the fiduciary standard. The second case describes a violation of the best-interest standard.

Case One: The Fiduciary Standard

This case deals with Apex Wealth Advisors (AWA). AWA was a well-known advisory firm in its community. The company marketed itself as a trusted advisory firm that offered comprehensive wealth management services to high-net-worth individuals. However, an investigation revealed that several financial advisors employed by the firm failed to act in their client's best interests. These advisors were found to be recommending high-commission investment products, such as annuities and mutual funds, which provided marginal benefit to clients but generated significant fees for the advisors and the firm.

One situation involved a retired couple, Abed and Susan, who sought financial planning services to help them manage their retirement funds. The couple, whose risk tolerance was low, had limited investment knowledge. They were counseled by their AWA advisor to invest a substantial portion of their retirement savings into an annuity product that was laden with high fees and surrender charges. Based on the advisor's recommendation, Abed and Susan bought the annuity within their 403(b) retirement plan. The higher commission primarily drove the advisor's decision to sell the annuity. The advisor failed to consider the couple's actual financial needs or the fact that placing a tax-deferred product into a tax-deferred account is almost always a problematic action.

Abed and Susan's financial advisor clearly breached their fiduciary duty. The advisor violated several core principles, including the obligation to act with loyalty and care. Instead of prioritizing the couple's financial security and goals, the advisor acted for personal gain. AWA's failure to enforce the Department of Labor's fiduciary standard related to providing advice about retirement assets resulted in significant financial harm to Abed and Susan, who ended up paying thousands of dollars in fees and penalties that they could hardly afford. Additionally, AWA's failure to adequately disclose conflicts of interest to their clients compounded the issue. By hiding potential conflicts, clients like Abed and Susan were left unaware of the financial incentives driving their advisor's recommendations.

Case Two: The Best-Interest Standard

In another case, a middle-aged single mother, Rachel, sought advice from an AWA financial advisor on securing her financial future and saving for a new home. Despite Rachel's clearly stated goals and her documented low-risk tolerance investment profile, she was sold a high-risk portfolio consisting of speculative technology stocks. Rachel's financial advisor failed to properly assess Rachel's financial situation, risk tolerance, and investment goals before making recommendations. As a result, Rachel's investment portfolio experienced significant losses during a market downturn, which put her financial goals at risk.

The failure to act in Rachel's best interest illustrates a clear violation of the best-interest standard. The advisor recommended products that were misaligned with Rachel's stated financial objectives. In this case, the advisor's failure to recommend suitable products led to unnecessary financial stress for Rachel, causing her to reconsider her relationship with her financial advisor. She also explored legal options for recourse.

As a result of these ethical violations, Apex Wealth Advisors faced legal action from affected clients and regulators. The firm was subjected to multiple investigations by the Securities and Exchange Commission (SEC) and state-level regulatory agencies. The firm was ultimately fined for failing to adhere to both fiduciary and best-interest standards, and several advisors lost their securities licenses. Additionally, the firm's reputation was severely damaged, leading to a significant loss of clients and business.

When financial advisors fail to meet fiduciary and best-interest standards, they end up exploiting their position of trust for personal or firm-based gain, which undermines the fundamental principles of fairness and transparency. Clients are entitled to expect that their financial advisors will act in their best interests. It is also reasonable for clients to assume that advice and products are suitable and in alignment with their financial goals. These standards are particularly important in a profession where clients often have limited knowledge of the complex products being offered to them (i.e., information asymmetry exists).

Psychological and Behavioral Insights into Treating Clients Fairly

Protecting clients from mistreatment in the marketplace is a foundational element associated with treating clients fairly. Financial institutions and marketers sometimes exploit clients based on a client's susceptibility to psychological and behavioral biases.[13] Some biases lead people to accept high-interest loans, purchase unnecessary insurance products, and invest in products with hidden and complicated fees. Understanding how certain biases can make a client susceptible to undue influence is one way a financial advisor can help clients make better informed and ethically based decisions. Table 11.2 lists and describes a variety of cognitive, behavioral, and psychological biases (i.e., systematic patterns of thinking and behavior that deviate from rationality in judgment) that can lead some clients to make decisions that are not in their best interest.[14] These biases can make individuals more vulnerable to mistreatment in the financial marketplace, including being misled or exploited by financial institutions, credit providers, or other market actors.

Communication Preferences and Treating Clients Fairly

People have different communication preferences that influence how they like to receive and process information.[15] These preferences can be categorized based on how someone interacts with information. Some people prefer written, verbal, or digital forms of communication. These preferences are associated with whether the person is a visual, auditory, or tactile learner.[16] To treat a client fairly and to make sure that the client feels that they are being treated fairly, it is important to identify each client's communication preference and then match outreach efforts to their preference. The following discussion highlights several of the primary ways clients prefer to receive information. The potential for manipulation in terms of mistreating a client is also presented.

Table 11.2 Fair treatment and common cognitive biases

Bias	Example
Anchoring bias[a]	This bias occurs when people rely too heavily on the first piece of information (the "anchor") they encounter when making decisions. In the financial marketplace, clients may focus on an initial offer or interest rate and fail to compare it properly with other options, leading them to accept unfavorable terms or overlook better deals
Attribution bias[b]	This is the tendency to attribute success to one's own actions and failures to external factors. In the domain of personal finance, this could lead a client to believe they are solely responsible for their financial success while blaming external factors for losses, making it harder to learn from mistakes and protect themselves in the future
Availability bias[c]	This bias occurs when individuals make judgments based on the most readily available information rather than seeking out all relevant information. For example, clients might rely on their own experience or what they have seen in advertisements and avoid comparing multiple financial products or services, leading them to choose suboptimal options
Bandwagon (or herding) effect[d]	The bandwagon/herding effect occurs when individuals make decisions based on what others are doing, rather than their own independent analysis. In financial markets, this could manifest as following popular trends, such as investing in certain stocks or products without fully understanding the risks, because others are doing the same
Confirmation bias[e]	This bias occurs when individuals seek out or give more weight to information that confirms their pre-existing beliefs or decisions. In the financial marketplace, clients might ignore warnings about a particular product or service and focus on information that aligns with their decision to purchase, potentially leading to financial harm
Emotional biases[f]	Emotional biases, such as fear, excitement, or greed, can lead individuals to make impulsive or irrational financial decisions. For example, clients may make hasty financial choices driven by anxiety during economic downturns or by a sense of excitement during a market boom, leading them to overlook risks and fall victim to predatory financial practices
Framing effect[g]	The framing effect refers to the way information is presented. Financial services or products may be marketed with positive framing (e.g., "low monthly payments") that distract from potentially harmful aspects, such as high interest rates or hidden fees. Clients may be influenced by the positive framing and overlook the underlying risks
Loss aversion[h]	Loss aversion refers to the tendency for individuals to prefer avoiding losses over acquiring equivalent gains. This can lead some clients to make poor financial choices, such as avoiding investments that could offer long-term benefits due to the fear of short-term losses. This bias can also cause people to hold on to failing financial products or investments because they fear realizing a loss
Overconfidence bias[i]	Overconfidence bias is the tendency to overestimate one's knowledge or decision-making ability. In financial markets, this may lead individuals to take on more risks or enter into complex financial agreements without fully understanding the terms, increasing the likelihood of mistreatment or poor financial outcomes

(continued)

Table 11.2 (continued)

Bias	Example
Recency bias[j]	This relates to situations when people are influenced by recent events or information rather than considering a broader or longer-term perspective. For example, a client who has recently experienced financial success or a temporary financial setback may make financial decisions based on these recent experiences, overlooking potential risks and resulting in poor financial choices
Status quo bias[k]	This bias describes the preference for things to remain the same rather than change. Financial decisions may lead clients to stick with an existing provider or financial product even when better options are available, simply because the current situation feels safer or more familiar
Sunk cost fallacy[l]	The sunk cost fallacy is the tendency to continue investing in something because of the resources (time, money, effort) already invested, rather than cutting losses. In the financial markets, this could lead a client to hold onto a bad investment, loan, or financial product for too long simply because they have already put money into it

[a] Furnham, A., & Boo, H. C. (2011). A literature review of the anchoring effect. *The journal of Socio-Economics, 40*(1), 35–42

[b] Haggag, K., Pope, D. G., Bryant-Lees, K. B., & Bos, M. W. (2019). Attribution bias in consumer choice. *The Review of Economic Studies, 86*(5), 2136–2183

[c] Tversky, A., & Kahneman, D. (1973). Availability: A heuristic for judging frequency and probability. *Cognitive psychology, 5*(2), 207–232

[d] Schmitt-Beck, R. (2015). Bandwagon effect. *The International Encyclopedia of Political Communication*, 1–5

[e] Peters, U. (2022). What is the function of confirmation bias? *Erkenntnis, 87*(3), 1351–1376

[f] Akinkoye, E. Y., & Bankole, O. E. (2020). Effect of emotional biases on investor's decision making in Nigeria. *International Journal of Business and Management Future, 4*(1), 33–39

[g] Frisch, D. (1993). Reasons for framing effects. *Organizational Behavior and Human Decision Processes, 54*(3), 399–429

[h] Schmidt, U., & Zank, H. (2005). What is loss aversion? *Journal of Risk and Uncertainty, 30*, 157–167

[i] Proeger, T., & Meub, L. (2014). Overconfidence as a social bias: Experimental evidence. Economics Letters, 122(2), 203–207

[j] Durand, R. B., Patterson, F. M., & Shank, C. A. (2021). Behavioral biases in the NFL gambling market: Overreaction to news and the recency bias. *Journal of Behavioral and Experimental Finance, 31*, 100522

[k] Samuelson, W., & Zeckhauser, R. (1988). Status quo bias in decision making. *Journal of Risk and Uncertainty, 1*, 7–59

[l] Friedman, D., Pommerenke, K., Lukose, R., Milam, G., & Huberman, B. A. (2007). Searching for the sunk cost fallacy. *Experimental Economics, 10*, 79–104

Written Communication Preference

Some clients prefer reading information, such as emails, brochures, or contracts, over receiving verbal explanations. They may feel more comfortable processing detailed information at their own pace, allowing for better understanding and recall.

- Potential for Manipulation: Financial services firms can take advantage of this preference by burying key details, such as fees, terms, or risks, in fine print or complex language. Clients may overlook or misunderstand important clauses in a contract, leading to decisions that are not in their best interest.

Verbal Communication Preference

Some clients prefer to have discussions in person or over the phone. They may value real-time interactions and seek to clarify doubts through conversation. This preference is common for those who find it easier to understand information when it is explained to them directly.

- Potential for Manipulation: Financial institutions can manipulate verbal communication by using persuasive or overly complex language during phone calls or face-to-face meetings. Sales representatives may use high-pressure tactics, making it difficult for a client to think critically or ask follow-up questions. Additionally, verbal agreements or promises may be made without written documentation, leaving the client without evidence if issues arise later. Additionally, financial services firms may use scripted messages or manipulate tone and pitch in phone calls, webinars, or advertisements to persuade clients. For instance, they may emphasize reassuring language and manipulate emotions to create urgency, such as pushing for a quick decision by implying that a limited-time offer will soon expire.

Visual Communication Preference

Visual learners tend to prefer information presented in charts, graphs, and other visual formats. They might have difficulty understanding abstract concepts unless they are visually represented.

- Potential for Manipulation: Financial services firms can take advantage of this preference by presenting products or offers in visually appealing ways that simplify complex information, potentially glossing over the risks. For example, a credit card company may emphasize attractive reward points in a brightly colored brochure, downplaying the high interest rates or annual fees associated with the card.

Tactile (Kinesthetic) Communication Preference

Clients with a tactile communication preference prefer learning through hands-on experiences. They like to interact with physical materials or engage in activities requiring movement or touch. They may need to physically manipulate documents, calculators, or models to understand a financial concept.

- Potential for Manipulation: Financial services firms may manipulate this preference by encouraging clients to fill out forms or engage with digital tools without fully explaining the terms. For instance, someone might be asked to sign a document on a tablet without being given enough time to read or understand the fine details. This could lead them to unknowingly agree to unfavorable terms.

Digital Communication Preference

Due to its convenience and speed, many clients prefer digital communication, such as online chat tools, social media, and email.[17] They also like to manage their financial situation through mobile apps or online platforms.

- Potential for Manipulation: Financial services firms can exploit this preference by bombarding clients with targeted ads, notifications, or emails that create a sense of urgency or excitement. For example, pop-up ads for financial products might highlight a "limited-time offer" or "exclusive access" but fail to provide clear details about hidden fees or risks. Furthermore, using automated systems or bots to interact with clients can make clarifying questions or seeking personalized advice difficult, potentially leading to poor decisions.

Nonverbal (Body Language) Communication Sensitivities

Nonverbal communication, such as body language, gestures, and facial expressions, plays a significant role in face-to-face interactions.[18] Some clients are particularly sensitive to the nonverbal cues provided by others during communication.

- Potential for Manipulation: In face-to-face meetings, a financial representative may use certain nonverbal cues, like maintaining eye contact or nodding reassuringly, to influence the client's decision-making process. Subtle cues can make the client feel pressured or manipulated into agreeing with the representative's suggestions without fully considering their own needs or alternatives.

Cultural Sensitivities

Cultural background can influence how clients communicate and interpret information.[19] Some cultures may emphasize indirect communication and respect for authority, while others prefer directness and transparency.

- Potential for Manipulation: Financial institutions may exploit cultural differences by tailoring their marketing and communication approaches in ways that resonate with certain cultural values. For example, in cultures where authority figures are highly respected, clients might be more likely to defer to a financial advisor's recommendations without questioning them. Alternatively, clients from cultures where decisions are often made in groups might feel excluded or isolated when decisions are presented in a way that requires quick, individual action.

Decision Paralysis

Decision paralysis, also known as *analysis paralysis*, is a psychological state in which a person is unable to make a decision due to the overwhelming number of choices, information, or potential consequences being presented.[20] This condition can occur when someone feels overwhelmed by the options available, fears making the wrong choice, or is unsure of how to weigh competing factors. In the context of financial decision-making, decision paralysis can lead to delays, inaction, or suboptimal choices. Decision paralysis can significantly affect financial decision-making, often leading clients to avoid making choices altogether due to overwhelming options, fear, and complexity, which can impact feelings of fairness.

Financial product complexity can create further hesitation, especially when clients struggle to compare product details. Additionally, balancing competing priorities, such as saving for retirement, paying off debt, and building an emergency fund, can add to decision-making challenges.

Cognitive overload is another factor associated with decision paralysis.[21] Exposure to new financial information, marketing materials, and advice from various sources, including financial advisors, family, friends, and online content, can overwhelm clients, making it harder for them to process and prioritize information. For example, someone researching investment strategies may encounter conflicting recommendations, leading to confusion and indecision. Emotional factors, such as anxiety or guilt, can also play a role in decision paralysis, especially for those who easily recall past financial mistakes. These emotions can cloud judgment, making clients hesitant to make decisions they associate with previous failures.

Lastly, the paradox of choice comes into play when an overwhelming number of options causes dissatisfaction and indecision.[22] This phenomenon can be particularly problematic when making financial decisions, as clients may struggle to identify the best option for their needs. For example, a person examining various mutual funds may freeze because they are unsure of which option to choose.

Helping a client overcome decision paralysis is one way to practice fairness. One practical approach involves simplification. Simplifying decision choices means reducing the number of options available or helping a client focus on the most important factors of a product or service. Breaking down complex decisions into smaller, more manageable steps makes the decision-making process less daunting.

Artificial Intelligence and Treating Clients Fairly

Artificial intelligence (AI) is transforming the financial services profession. AI is being utilized at various stages of the investment, insurance, and financial planning business and product life cycle. AI is being used in product development, marketing, sales, underwriting, pricing, policy servicing, claims management, and fraud detection.[23] AI helps improve efficiency, accuracy, client service, and the development of innovative products. However, the use of AI also presents risks, such as inaccuracy, unfair discrimination, data vulnerabilities, and a lack of transparency.

AI is prompting fairness questions that regulators and policymakers are scrambling to address.

The National Association of Insurance Commissioners (NAIC) adopted the Principles of Artificial Intelligence in 2020.[24] These principles are used to guide insurance companies when AI systems are used. The NAIC principles focus on issues of fairness, ethics, and transparency. Current and future regulatory frameworks will need to ensure that decisions informed by AI are accurate, not arbitrary, or discriminatory. Financial service firms and advisors must implement appropriate governance and risk management internal controls and verification and testing methods to identify bias and errors in AI systems to reduce the risk of adverse outcomes. The scope and rigor of these controls must reflect the danger posed by AI systems, considering factors such as decision types, potential harm to clients, human involvement in decision-making, transparency, and reliance on third-party data. By adopting policies similar to those of the NAIC, financial services firms can help ensure that AI is used responsibly and in compliance with legal and regulatory standards.

Chapter Summary

Fair treatment of clients is a multifaceted concept that blends standards of practice, regulatory compliance mandates, an ethical outlook, and a psychological understanding of a client's thoughts and actions. Treating clients fairly is one way to enhance client satisfaction, build long-term relationships, and uphold a firm's reputation. Through the lens of relationship marketing, this chapter reviewed consumer protection laws and regulatory frameworks that help a financial services professional understand what it means to provide fair services to clients. Detailed case studies and practical examples were presented to provide insight into real-world applications of fairness principles. The cases and resulting discussions highlighted how firms and financial advisors can balance business objectives with ethical practices. Additionally, the chapter addressed factors like cognitive biases and decision paralysis that sometimes hinder the fair treatment of clients.

Chapter Resources

- Consumer Financial Protection Bureau: consumerfinance.org
- Federal Reserve: https://www.federalreserve.gov/
- National Association of Insurance Commissioners: https://content.naic.org/
- Overview of Regulation Best Interest: https://www.sec.gov/
- Securities and Exchange Commission (SEC): https://www.sec.gov/

Notes

[1] Worthington, S., & Devlin, J. (2013). Fairness and financial services in Australia and the United Kingdom. *International Journal of Bank Marketing, 31*(4), 289–304.

[2] United States Department of State: https://americanenglish.state.gov/files/ae/resource_files/business_ethics_ch10.pdf

[3]Christopher, M., Payne, A., & Ballantyne, D. (2013). *Relationship marketing*. Routledge.

[4]Although the North American Securities Administrators Association (NASAA) adopted a model rule in 2025 that prohibits broker-dealer agents from using the titles "advisor" or "adviser" unless they are also registered as investment adviser representatives, in this book, a broad definition of financial advisor is retained. A financial advisor advises clients on managing their finances to help them achieve specific financial goals. This advice can cover many areas, including investment management, retirement planning, estate planning, tax planning, insurance needs, debt management, and wealth building.

[5]Karsono, B. (2023). Good corporate governance: Transparency, accountability, responsibility, independency and fairness (Literature Review). *Dinasti International Journal of Management Science, 4*(5), 811–821.

[6]Hagen, J. U., & Schürenkrämer, U. (2015). *Client centricity: Relationship management in banking*. Murmann Publishers GmbH.

[7]Howells, G., & Weatherill, S. (2017). *Consumer protection law*. Routledge.

[8]https://www.ftc.gov/business-guidance/resources/how-comply-privacy-consumer-financial-information-rule-gramm-leach-bliley-act

[9]https://www.federalreserve.gov/pubs/complaints/laws.htm

[10]Román, S. (2003). The impact of ethical sales behaviour on customer satisfaction, trust and loyalty to the company: An empirical study in the financial services industry. *Journal of Marketing Management, 19*(9–10), 915–939.

[11]Madhani, P. M. (2020). Ethics in sales and marketing: Key advantages. *Marketing Mastermind, 17*(5), 53–58.

[12]Craswell, R. (2006). Taking information seriously: Misrepresentation and nondisclosure in contract law and elsewhere. *Va. L. Rev., 92*, 565.

[13]Langevoort, D. C. (1996). Selling hope, selling risk: some lessons for law from behavioral economics about stockbrokers and sophisticated customers. *Cal L. Rev., 84*, 627.

[14]Korteling, J. E., & Toet, A. (2021). Cognitive biases. In *Encyclopedia of Behavioral Neuroscience*. Elsevier Science.

[15]Yuan, S., Hussain, S. A., Hales, K. D., & Cotten, S. R. (2016). What do they like? Communication preferences and patterns of older adults in the United States: The role of technology. *Educational Gerontology, 42*(3), 163–174.

[16]Gilakjani, A. P. (2012). Visual, auditory, kinesthetic learning styles and their impacts on English language teaching. *Journal of Studies in Education, 2*(1), 104–113.

[17]Dronia, I. (2024). "Born to be digital": Communication preferences of Society 5.0. *Language, Technology, Humanities in Society 5.0, 11*, 87.

[18]Hall, J. A., Horgan, T. G., & Murphy, N. A. (2019). Nonverbal communication. *Annual Review of Psychology, 70*(1), 271–294.

[19]Fitch, K. L., & Sanders, R. E. (1994). Culture, communication, and preferences for directness in expression of directives. *Communication Theory, 4*(3), 219–245.

[20]Langley, A. (1995). Between "paralysis by analysis" and "extinction by instinct." *MIT Sloan Management Review, 36*(3), 63–76

[21]Adriatico, J. M., Cruz, A., Tiong, R. C., & Racho-Sabugo, C. R. (2022). An analysis on the impact of choice overload to consumer decision paralysis. *Journal of Economics, Finance and Accounting Studies, 4*(1), 55–75.

[22]Schwartz, B. (2015). *The paradox of choice. Positive psychology in practice: Promoting human flourishing in work, health, education, and everyday life* (2nd ed.). Wiley.

[23]https://idoi.illinois.gov/content/dam/soi/en/web/insurance/companies/companybulletins/CB2024-08.pdf

[24]https://content.naic.org/sites/default/files/inline-files/AI%20principles%20as%20Adopted%20by%20the%20TF_0807.pdf

Real-World Case Studies in Ethics and Compliance

12

Chapter Outcomes
This chapter focuses on helping learners develop the ability to:

1. Evaluate real-world case studies involving unauthorized trading, hidden revenue-sharing, cultural collusion, corruption, data breaches, and sales misconduct.
2. Articulate how ethical and compliance failures erode client trust, damage firm reputation, and destabilize financial markets.
3. Explain the importance of regulatory oversight, transparency, and whistleblower safeguards in preventing and addressing ethical and compliance issues.
4. Describe the significance of fostering an ethical firm culture and protecting client data to maintain trust and integrity in the financial services profession.
5. Assess best practices for building and maintaining compliant and ethical organizations that integrate regulatory requirements, cultural interventions, and behavioral strategies.
6. Identify strategies to mitigate biases such as complacency, groupthink, and greed to promote ethical decision-making.
7. Demonstrate how ethical decision-making contributes to developing trust and market integrity through the broader themes of accountability and resilience.

Note: This chapter was copyedited using Grammarly™ and generative AI tools to enhance clarity, grammar, and overall readability. While these tools provided suggestions and assistance in refining the text, the ideas, content, and arguments presented remain the sole work and responsibility of the authors. Any errors or inaccuracies in the final version are also the authors' responsibility.

W. Heo, J. E. Grable, *Ethics and Compliance in Financial Services*,
https://doi.org/10.1007/978-3-032-14449-2_12

Introduction

Ethical and compliance failures in the financial services profession occur regularly. Failures have a significant impact on clients and can have far-reaching consequences. For example, ethical and compliance failures can erode public trust, weaken the reputation of firms and advisors, and disrupt the stability of financial markets. This chapter brings together the concepts and examples from previous chapters through real-world case studies. These cases have been written to provide a lens through which ethical and compliance failures at the advisor, firm, and market level can be understood. The cases presented in this chapter illustrate how lapses in oversight, transparency, and cultural integrity allow misconduct to escalate.

This chapter examines six cases from U.S. history: JPMorgan's oversight failures, Edward Jones's hidden revenue-sharing, UBS's culture of collusion, the 1MDB scandal, Morgan Stanley's data breach, and sales misconduct at Wells Fargo. Some of these cases were presented in previous chapters. The intention of reviewing them again is that each case reveals how systemic weaknesses in governance, compliance systems, and corporate culture can enable misconduct and cause harm. Unlike the presentations in earlier chapters, the analysis of these cases in this chapter highlights the practical lessons that financial professionals and organizations can draw from to prevent similar failures in the future.

Building on the regulatory foundations established in Chaps. 5 and 6, the case-specific discussions in Chap. 9, and cultural and behavioral insights from Chaps. 4, 7, and 8, this chapter transitions from identifying failures to proposing solutions. Lessons are synthesized across cases, emphasizing oversight, transparency, ethical culture, client protection, and support for whistleblowers. Best practices are then outlined. The practices demonstrate how regulatory systems, cultural reinforcement, and behavioral strategies can work together to ensure compliance and foster trust. The goal of this chapter is to reinforce the notion that the ethical practice of delivering financial advice depends on strong systems, ethical leadership, and an awareness of behavioral risks.

Perspective

Ethical and compliance failures are often portrayed as the work of isolated individuals. However, this is rarely the case. As the following hypothetical case illustrates, systemic factors at the firm and regulatory levels play crucial roles in creating environments where ethical practices and regulatory compliance can be compromised. This case shows how weak regulatory oversight, misaligned compensation incentives, and a toxic firm culture can combine to create conditions in which unethical behavior becomes normalized.

In this fictional scenario, GlobalFinance Corp (GFC), a sprawling international bank, becomes entangled in a cascade of interconnected ethical and operational failures that culminate in one of the largest financial implosions in history. Here is the story:

GFC's aggressive expansion strategy emphasized cross-selling financial products to boost revenue. The strategy devolved into widespread sales misconduct, where employees, under immense pressure to meet sales quotas, opened unauthorized accounts and enrolled clients for unwanted services (mirroring the fake accounts crisis at Wells Fargo). This toxic sales culture fostered a broader environment of collusion (similar to UBS), where internal teams manipulated benchmarks and shared sensitive information to inflate profits. These activities often occurred in coordination with external partners. Oversight lapses, akin to JPMorgan's failures, exacerbated the issues. Specifically, inadequate monitoring of employee communications and third-party vendors, including failures in recordkeeping and background checks, allowed misconduct to go undetected for years. Hidden revenue-sharing deals with mutual fund providers, reminiscent of regulatory lapses at Edward Jones, created undisclosed conflicts, prioritizing kickbacks over client interests and steering investments toward high-fee products.

The scandal reached its peak with GFC's entanglement in a massive embezzlement scheme involving a sovereign wealth fund, echoing the 1MDB affair, where billions were siphoned through shell companies and laundered via the bank's networks. Compounding the damage, a series of data breaches exposed the personal information of millions of clients. These intertwined failures, rooted in a profit-driven culture that incentivized unethical practices, resulted in regulatory probes across multiple countries, billions of dollars in fines, executive oustings, and a profound erosion of public trust. In total, the cascade of failures compelled GFC to undergo a government-brokered restructuring.

While this case narrative is fictional, the events in the case represent real-world examples. Based on the information provided in the case and what has been presented in earlier chapters, how would you answer the following questions?

- Question 1: How can financial institutions prevent oversight failures, such as those involving inadequate monitoring and recordkeeping seen in this case?[1]
- Question 2: What strategies can mitigate hidden revenue-sharing conflicts like the undisclosed agreements with mutual fund providers described in this case?[2]
- Question 3: How can financial institutions address sales misconduct driven by aggressive quotas?[3]

The following section presents the six cases that serve as the foundation for the hypothetical GFC scenario.

Learning from the Past: Real-World Ethical and Compliance Failures

The following cases are presented as a means to analyze past events and identify potential tools for reducing the likelihood of similar failures in the future. These cases represent real-world scenarios involving ethical or compliance failures, their consequences, and the resulting regulatory responses.

Case 1: JPMorgan Chase and the "London Whale"

In 2012, JPMorgan Chase's Chief Investment Office (CIO) in London accumulated massive positions in credit derivatives, primarily driven by trader Bruno Iksil, who became known as the "London Whale." Initially, these trades were intended to hedge the bank's broader credit exposure; however, they grew so large and convoluted that they essentially turned into speculative bets. Weak internal oversight and pressure to maintain profits allowed this portfolio of bets to expand unchecked. When market participants recognized these vulnerabilities and acted against the positions, JPMorgan suffered losses exceeding $6.2 billion.[4]

This episode inflicted severe reputational damage on JPMorgan, which had long positioned itself as a leader in risk management. Investor confidence fell sharply as senior executives, including CEO Jamie Dimon, were called to testify before U.S. congressional hearings, and several managers lost their jobs. The bank ultimately paid $920 million in combined fines to the Securities and Exchange Commission (SEC), the Commodity Futures Trading Commission (CFTC), the Office of the Comptroller of the Currency (OCC), and the United Kingdom's Financial Conduct Authority (FCA). The CIO position was restructured, and the bank improved its internal reporting and risk-monitoring processes.

Regulators concluded that JPMorgan provided misleading information concerning the scale of its exposures, thus violating securities disclosure rules. The SEC's enforcement action reinforced the bank's fiduciary duty to disclose material risks to investors, while the CFTC and FCA emphasized the necessity for accurate reporting of derivative exposures. This case contributed to the enactment of the Volcker Rule, a provision of the Dodd-Frank Act that restricts proprietary trading.[5] A key takeaway from this case is that strategic goals, like maintaining profit targets, can sometimes overshadow effective risk management systems when governance and compliance are not fully integrated.[6] JPMorgan prioritized short-term earnings over transparent communication with stakeholders, undermining fairness and client trust.[7]

The case also presents several behavioral insights. As discussed in Chap. 4, JPMorgan's senior management exhibited overconfidence and groupthink that distorted their judgment. Traders and senior managers displayed overconfidence by assuming that their models and market expertise could manage the risks they were taking, even in the face of warning signs. Meanwhile, groupthink within the CIO team and broader leadership silenced internal dissent. Risk managers who raised early concerns were marginalized as the prevailing narrative characterized the trades as defensible hedges. In other words, the normalization of complexity became standard. The CIO trades became so technically intricate that executives and regulators underestimated their actual risks. This complexity functioned as a shield, dulling critical oversight and enabling staff to rationalize their positions as "sophisticated hedges" rather than speculative bets.[8]

What Would You Do?

You are a newly promoted executive at a global investment bank. The Chief Investment Office (CIO) reports that its large credit derivative positions are considered "strategic hedges," which reduces the bank's exposure to broader market risks. These positions have already generated substantial profits, and senior leadership cites them as evidence of effective risk management. However, during a routine review, you notice troubling signs:

- The positions are extraordinarily complex, making them challenging for even senior managers to explain fully.
- The size of the exposure is so large that it could destabilize the bank if market conditions turn.
- Some risk managers have quietly raised concerns, but their voices are being minimized by the CIO team.
- Investor reports describe the positions as routine hedges, but you are not convinced this description is accurate.

The board is pressuring you to maintain strong quarterly profits, and your peers believe the strategy is sound. Raising concerns could put you at odds with powerful colleagues, damage relationships with leadership, and even jeopardize your career. On the other hand, ignoring the risks may put the bank's reputation, as well as that of its investors and clients, in jeopardy if things unravel.

What Should You Do?

(A) Stay Silent: Trust that your colleagues know what they are doing, accept the "hedge" explanation, and allow reporting to investors to continue as-is.

(B) Quietly Escalate Internally: Push for an independent internal review of the CIO's portfolio and request tighter oversight, even if doing so curbs short-term profits.

(C) Raise the Issue with Investors and Regulators: Recommend more accurate external disclosures about the scope and nature of the derivative exposures, even if this shocks investors and draws regulatory scrutiny.

(D) Propose Restructuring or Downsizing the Positions: Take action to reduce risk, knowing that your actions may generate short-term losses, even if doing so could protect the bank's long-term reputation.

Insight

Answers B and D are correct. Internal escalation paired with risk reduction is the most ethically defensible path forward. This approach aligns with your duty to stakeholders while promoting long-term client protection. Answer A is incorrect because this approach violates principles of transparency; the approach also prioritizes short-term profits over client trust. Answer C is incorrect because this may erode investor confidence and harm the firm's reputation.

Additional Things to Consider

- Profits today may erode trust tomorrow.
- Strong governance protects both clients and the institution.
- Ethical leadership often means challenging peers and superiors when risks are being concealed.
- Investors and clients rely on accurate information.

- Misleading disclosures violate fiduciary obligations.
- Leaders should create a culture where risk managers can question decisions without fear of reprisal.
- Complexity in financial strategies should never obscure accountability.
- Risk controls must evolve in tandem with trading strategies.

Case 2: UBS and the LIBOR Manipulation Scandal

In 2012, UBS was found to have manipulated the London Interbank Offered Rate (LIBOR), a global benchmark at the time for short-term interest rates used in loans, derivatives, and other financial instruments. Traders at UBS, often colluding with counterparts at other major banks, submitted false rate estimates to benefit their own trading positions and to present the bank as financially healthier than it actually was. Internal communications later revealed a culture in which manipulation was normalized, with traders openly requesting favorable rate submissions from colleagues and external brokers.

The manipulation of LIBOR distorted the pricing of trillions of dollars in financial contracts worldwide. The scandal highlighted how conflicts of interest and weak governance typically result in large-scale harm. UBS paid penalties totaling $1.5 billion to regulators in the United States, the United Kingdom, and Switzerland, making it one of the largest settlements in banking at that time.[9] The reputational damage was severe, with the UBS name becoming synonymous with benchmark rigging. The bank's actions undermined public trust in global markets. Several UBS traders faced criminal charges, and senior managers were forced to resign. This scandal accelerated the worldwide effort to phase out LIBOR and replace it with alternative benchmarks like SOFR.[10]

The UBS case illustrates how market manipulation undermines fairness and transparency, which are fundamental to the smooth functioning of the global financial system. Regulators on both sides of the Atlantic, including the U.K. Financial Conduct Authority (FCA), the U.S. Commodity Futures Trading Commission (CFTC), and Switzerland's FINMA, coordinated enforcement actions. The scandal once again revealed how regulatory frameworks often evolve only after major crises.

This case also demonstrates the importance of disclosure as a tool that signals firm integrity. The scandal reflected not only individual misconduct but also a broader culture of failure among those in the firm and among federal regulators. UBS traders treated market manipulation as routine and even joked about collusion in their internal messages. The behavior of UBS traders and executives eroded confidence in the financial profession, highlighting the necessity for transparency, not only in client-facing interactions but also in institutional practices that impact global markets.

Like the situation at JPMorgan, behavioral biases were evident at UBS. Overconfidence and groupthink dominated the decision-making process. Traders overestimated their ability to evade detection (overconfidence) and normalized misconduct through a collusive culture (groupthink). This case also shows the adverse effects of social proof and normalization, where repeated messages of collusion, such as "everyone is doing it," served as justifications for continued manipulation.

Another aspect worth noting is the theme of incentive-driven bias, where the compensation structure rewarded short-term trading profits. Finally, the UBS LIBOR scandal illustrates a deeper cultural failure on the part of firm executives and regulators. At UBS, the organizational environment tolerated and even normalized rate manipulation, shaping collective attitudes toward misconduct. Ethical failures thrived and escalated within UBS's culture because dishonesty was deemed acceptable. The firm created psychological mechanisms, such as conformity bias and diffusion of responsibility, as the operating norm, making employees less likely to challenge wrongdoing.

What Would You Do?

Assume you are a senior financial advisor at UBS in 2012, responsible for advising institutional clients who rely on interest rate benchmarks like LIBOR to price loans and derivatives. You become aware, through conversations and internal communications, that some traders may be influencing UBS's LIBOR submissions. Although you do not have evidence, the messages you have seen suggest that rate submissions are being adjusted to benefit trading desks. You are now faced with the following dilemmas:

- On the one hand, LIBOR is the global benchmark underlying trillions of dollars in contracts. If manipulated, the quote rate will directly affect the costs of borrowing for your clients, destabilize their hedging strategies, and destroy the trust they place in your guidance.
- On the other hand, LIBOR manipulation appears to be normalized within UBS and across other banks. Colleagues shrug it off, saying, "Everyone is doing it." Speaking out could isolate you, damage your career, or even put you at odds with influential executives. It is possible that you could lose your job.
- Meanwhile, your clients continue to make financial decisions, assuming LIBOR is a fair and objective measure.

What Should You Do?

(A) Stay Silent: Accept that LIBOR submissions are industry practice and maintain client relationships without raising concerns.

(B) Raise Concerns Internally: Report your suspicions to UBS compliance and risk management teams, even if you fear retaliation or being ignored.

(C) Be Transparent with Clients: Disclose to clients that benchmark rates may not fully reflect actual market conditions, which could undermine trust in UBS and jeopardize your job at the bank.

(D) Escalate Externally: Blow the whistle to regulators, risking your job and reputation but potentially protecting global markets and restoring fairness.

Insight

Financial advisors should escalate issues internally first to compliance/risk management teams. If ignored or suppressed, external escalation becomes ethically defensible. This approach aligns with the principles of transparency and fairness in financial markets. Answer A is incorrect because complicity in misconduct, while protecting your career in the short run, violates your duties to stakeholders and exposes clients to harm. Answers C and D are incorrect because these actions may breach your obligations to your employer and subject you to career risk. Answer D may be an option if working internally fails.

Additional Things to Consider

- Financial advisors have a fiduciary responsibility to ensure clients base their decisions on accurate information.
- Financial advisors also have a fiduciary duty to their employer.
- Professionalism requires resisting the normalization of misconduct, even when it risks personal or career consequences.
- A toxic employment culture that rewards short-term gains fosters systemic misconduct.
- Ethical business cultures align incentives with integrity.
- Manipulating LIBOR may appear "technically appropriate," but doing so can have global consequences, eroding confidence in financial markets and harming borrowers worldwide.
- Sometimes, the only way to stop widespread misconduct is to bring concerns to external regulators when internal channels fail.

Case 3: The 1Malaysia Development Berhad Scandal

The 1Malaysia Development Berhad (1MDB) scandal involved the embezzlement of over $4.5 billion from a Malaysian state investment fund between 2009 and 2015. Funds that were intended for national development were diverted through a network of shell companies and offshore accounts, with the assistance of bankers, including traders and executives at Goldman Sachs. Instead of being used to finance infrastructure, the money funded luxury real estate, artwork, and even Hollywood films, such as The Wolf of Wall Street.

Investigations revealed that Goldman Sachs bankers helped raise $6.5 billion in bonds for 1MDB, collecting unusually high fees in the process. Internal controls failed to identify obvious red flags in Know-Your-Customer (KYC) and Anti-Money Laundering (AML) processes. This scandal became one of the most significant cases of global corruption and money laundering, involving authorities in the United States, Malaysia, Singapore, and Switzerland.[11]

As a result, Goldman Sachs agreed to pay over $5 billion in global settlements, which included $2.9 billion to the U.S. Department of Justice (this represented the largest penalty ever paid under U.S. anti-corruption laws). Two Goldman bankers were convicted of crimes related to the scandal. One, Tim Leissner, pleaded guilty, while another, Roger Ng, was sentenced for conspiracy to launder money. Politically, the scandal led to the ousting of Malaysian Prime Minister Najib Razak, who was later convicted of corruption and sentenced to prison.[12] Goldman Sachs's reputation as a leading global bank suffered significantly, raising doubts about its governance culture.

The scandal illustrates the importance of AML and KYC regulatory frameworks in preventing institutional abuses. Regulators concluded that Goldman Sachs failed to apply adequate due diligence in its role as the underwriter of 1MDB bonds, ignoring red flags in exchange for lucrative fees. Additionally, the 1MDB case highlighted the lack of system-wide regulatory oversight seen in other global financial scandals. Following this case, regulators intensified scrutiny of cross-border capital flows and raised compliance expectations in emerging markets. The U.S. DOJ's use of the Foreign Corrupt Practices Act (FCPA), alongside AML enforcement, demonstrates the reach of extraterritorial regulation in a globalized economy.

From an ethical perspective, this case represents a profound failure of fiduciary responsibility and stakeholder trust. Goldman bankers prioritized profits over compliance and knowingly facilitated questionable transactions. Beyond the legal misconduct, the scandal negatively impacted Malaysian citizens by diverting public funds from education, healthcare, and infrastructure. Moreover, this misconduct exacerbated social inequities, illustrating how failures at elite financial institutions can amplify corruption and directly harm vulnerable populations.

Similar to the other cases discussed in this chapter, the 1MDB scandal exemplifies how behavioral biases contribute to ethical failures. Overconfidence and rationalization were evident, with Goldman Sachs executives displaying obvious signs of greed-driven ethical fading. They rationalized their actions by focusing on the lucrative nature of the fees, convincing themselves that, because regulators and internal compliance teams had not intervened, the transactions must be acceptable. Their behavior represents a form of motivated blindness, where individuals overlook ethical red flags in pursuit of personal or institutional gain. Another behavioral insight is the diffusion of responsibility; because the scandal spanned multiple jurisdictions, politicians and firm executives felt that oversight was someone else's duty. This diffusion allowed individuals to justify inaction even as misconduct escalated. Together, these dynamics illustrate how global complexity can weaken ethical accountability.

What Would You Do?

Assume you are a firm executive at a global investment bank. Your team has been asked to help underwrite bonds for a sovereign wealth fund in Africa. The deal is extraordinarily secretive. Your bank could earn unusually high underwriting fees, which are far higher than typical for similar transactions. As you review the proposal, you notice several red flags, including:

- The fund's leadership is politically connected, and news reports have raised concerns about corruption and misuse of funds.
- The client has a vague development plan with limited transparency regarding how the billions raised will actually be spent.
- Your compliance team has flagged unusual shell-company structures and offshore accounts associated with the fund.

Your colleagues argue that the bank should proceed because "everyone else is doing deals in emerging markets" and because internal compliance has not formally stopped the transaction. Senior leadership at the bank pressures you to approve the deal quickly, warning that if you hesitate, a rival bank will capture the business. You may also lose your job if you do not act soon. You must decide what to do.

What Should You Do?

(A) Approve the Deal As-Is: "Move forward with the underwriting to secure profit," rationalizing that compliance has not blocked it, and competitors would do the same.

(B) Push for Stronger Due Diligence: Delay the deal and demand more rigorous KYC/AML checks, risking tension with leadership and the loss of a highly profitable opportunity.

(C) Express Concerns to Regulators: Proactively report suspicious activity to external regulators, prioritizing fiduciary responsibility but exposing your bank to scrutiny and backlash.

(D) Decline the Deal Entirely: Recommend walking away, protecting the bank's reputation and long-term integrity, but sacrificing immediate profits and possibly angering top executives.

Insight

Strengthening due diligence (Answer B) is the most prudent initial course. If serious red flags persist or are ignored, escalation (Answer C and D) may become ethically necessary to protect market integrity and vulnerable stakeholders. Answer A is incorrect because this action directly ignores AML/KYC red flags, which will expose the bank to legal penalties, reputational harm, and long-term damage to stakeholder trust.

Additional Things to Consider

- Financial professionals must prioritize the integrity of markets and the welfare of stakeholders (including citizens impacted by public funds) over short-term profits.
- Ignoring AML/KYC red flags undermines regulatory obligations and exposes firms to massive penalties and reputational harm.
- Standing against pressured approval requires moral courage.
- Silence or complicity enables systemic corruption.

- Motivated blindness ("if compliance hasn't stopped it, it must be fine") and diffusion of responsibility ("oversight is someone else's job") often erode ethical judgment.
- Immediate profit can cause lasting institutional damage; reputation, regulatory trust, and stakeholder relationships are more valuable long-term assets.

Case 4: Edward Jones Revenue-Sharing Scandal

In 2004, the U.S. Securities and Exchange Commission (SEC) charged Edward D. Jones & Co. (Edward Jones) with failing to disclose revenue-sharing agreements with seven mutual fund companies. Under these agreements, Edward Jones received payments and other benefits for directing clients toward specific funds. The firm's advisors marketed these funds as "preferred" choices, presenting them as selections based on merit and client benefit, while withholding information about the financial incentives influencing their recommendations.

The case highlights how conflicts of interest can creep into business practices. Edward Jones advisors were encouraged to promote higher-fee products, creating a misalignment between client outcomes and the firm's revenues. Clients believed they were receiving unbiased advice, but hidden incentives actually influenced the recommendations.[13]

As a result, Edward Jones agreed to pay $75 million in penalties, which included $37.5 million in disgorgement and $37.5 million in civil fines. The firm was also required to enhance its disclosure practices, implement compliance reforms, and inform clients about potential conflicts of interest related to fund selection. This scandal damaged public trust in Edward Jones, especially given the firm's longstanding self-promotion as a client-focused and ethical organization.

The case led to regulatory action and reforms, as the SEC enforced the Investment Advisers Act of 1940, which prohibits misleading statements and mandates the disclosure of material conflicts. Subsequently, Congress and the SEC called for greater transparency at the firm level throughout the financial services profession. Alongside the Sarbanes-Oxley reforms, the Edward Jones case signaled to the market that those with undisclosed conflicts of interest when giving financial advice would face severe enforcement actions.

This scandal also illustrates how standards of best interest and fiduciary duty can be compromised when firms and financial advisors fail to disclose revenue-sharing arrangements. Edward Jones advisors violated standards of integrity, fairness, accountability, and transparency, inflicting reputational and economic harm. Ethically, this misconduct eroded the foundation of trust not just among clients, but also across the general investing public.

As seen in similar cases, a variety of behavioral dynamics contributed to the misconduct. First, there was an incentive bias. Edward Jones advisors were influenced by compensation structures that favored revenue-sharing products. The way employees were paid led them to rationalize recommendations as "suitable," even when other options might have been better for clients. A framing effect bias was also apparent, as labeling funds as "preferred" reframed biased recommendations as legitimate, making it easier for financial advisors and clients to overlook conflicts of interest. Additionally, ethical fading occurred. Over time, revenue-sharing became normalized within the firm's culture, causing financial advisors to no longer view the lack of disclosure as unethical, since it had been institutionalized.

As was the case with 1MDB, diffusion of responsibility also played a role in the ethical failures. Individual advisors rationalized that conflicts were "approved" at the firm level, which diminished their personal sense of accountability. These behavioral insights demonstrate that firm-wide conflicts of interest, combined with cultural normalization, can erode individual ethical awareness, allowing misconduct to persist in client-facing roles.

What Would You Do?

Assume you are a financial advisor at a national investment firm. Your firm has a set of "preferred" investments that you are encouraged to recommend to clients. Senior management emphasizes that these investments are "high quality" and appropriate for nearly all clients. The investments appear prominently in marketing materials.

You discover that your firm receives significant revenue-sharing payments from the investment underwriters. You are confused because the fees are not clearly disclosed to clients. This means that when you recommend one of these "preferred" investments, the firm (and indirectly, you) benefits financially.

You face the following dilemmas:

- Your clients trust you to provide unbiased advice. You know that some clients would receive better outcomes by investing in other assets, including lower-cost funds that are not on the "preferred" list.
- Your managers pressure you to promote the "preferred" investments, noting that "everyone else does it" and that compliance has approved the practice.
- The managers stress that every advisor has a sales quota to meet and that an element of this quota involves selling a minimum amount of the preferred investments.
- If you disregard the firm's direction, you risk alienating leadership and forfeiting bonuses tied to sales. You may also lose your job. If you follow along, you may be misleading your clients about why these funds are being recommended.

What Should You Do?

(A) Follow Firm Guidance: Continue recommending the "preferred" investments, rationalizing that the assets remain suitable and that compliance has approved this practice.
(B) Disclose the Conflict with Clients: Inform clients that your firm receives compensation for selling certain funds, even if this level of transparency is not required.
(C) Recommend Non-preferred Investments: Prioritize lower-cost or better-performing funds, even if it means going against firm pressure and possibly losing financial incentives based on sales quotas.

(D) Escalate Concerns Internally: Raise the issue with the firm's compliance office or management, requesting clearer disclosures and more client-centered practice.
(E) Refuse Participation: Decline to recommend revenue-sharing products altogether, knowing that taking this stand could hurt your career at the firm but preserve your professional integrity.

Insight

Begin with internal escalation (Answer D) and full disclosure to clients (Answer B). If the firm resists or minimizes your concerns, you may need to refuse participation (Answer E), although doing so will likely result in employment termination. Answer A is incorrect because this course of action is legally risky and ethically problematic. The behavior normalizes conflicts of interest and undermines client trust. Answer C is incorrect because this course of action places you in direct conflict with employer instructions.

Additional Things to Consider

- Financial advisors must disclose conflicts of interest and prioritize client outcomes over compensation structures.
- Financial advisors who are not Registered Investment Advisers or Registered Investment Adviser Representatives have a fiduciary obligation to their employer.
- Failure to make complete disclosures undermines the integrity of financial advice and erodes long-term client trust.
- Incentive bias, framing, and ethical fading normalize practices that can cloud ethical judgment.
- Sometimes ethical responsibility requires challenging firm norms or escalating concerns to higher levels, even at the risk of losing one's job.
- From a regulatory perspective, disclosure and transparency are not optional; these are central concepts used to maintain fairness in the financial markets and to meet regulatory standards.

Case 5: Wells Fargo Fake Accounts Scandal

In 2016, Wells Fargo was discovered to have generated more than 3.5 million unauthorized deposit and credit card accounts without customer consent. Employees, pressured to meet aggressive cross-selling sales targets, opened accounts using customer information and sometimes transferred funds without approval. This misconduct was systemic, spanning over a decade, and was driven by unrealistic incentive structures that prioritized the number of accounts opened over the quality of customer relationships.[14]

The regulatory fallout was significant. Wells Fargo paid $185 million in fines to the Consumer Financial Protection Bureau (CFPB), the Office of the Comptroller of the Currency (OCC), and the Los Angeles City Attorney. CEO John Stumpf resigned following congressional hearings, and senior executives forfeited tens of millions in compensation. The scandal undermined Wells Fargo's long-standing reputation as a trusted retail bank. Millions of customers closed their accounts, resulting in a declining stock price. The reputational harm extended well beyond retail banking. In addition to fines, Wells Fargo spent billions on legal settlements and compliance reforms in the years that followed.

The Wells Fargo case illustrates that effective regulation is not only about enforcing laws but also about overseeing incentive structures. In this situation, Wells Fargo's governance failures created an environment that encouraged employee misconduct. The enforcement actions by the CFPB and OCC highlight the need for sales practices to align with consumer protection principles, which connect directly to fiduciary-like standards of practice. The scandal also revealed that inadequate governance and compliance frameworks can amplify operational risks. Wells Fargo's sales culture represented a risk that was neither recognized nor managed.

Although this case has been discussed throughout this book, it is worth revisiting because it serves as a textbook example of ethical failure in client-facing roles. Employees at Wells Fargo prioritized sales quotas over client outcomes, violating the principles of fairness, accountability, and transparency. In moral terms, the harm extended beyond financial losses. The credit scores of customers were damaged, trust was eroded, and employees found themselves in situations where unethical conduct became a survival strategy.

This case also highlights the role of cognitive, behavioral, and psychological biases in explaining unethical behavior. Like the other cases discussed, overconfidence, groupthink, and ethical fading were present in the Wells Fargo scandal. The dominant behavioral driver of these failures was a toxic incentive culture that resulted in goal-setting biases, normalization of deviance, diffusion of responsibility, and overall cultural failure. Managers at Wells Fargo set unrealistic sales targets, distorting employee behavior. As more employees engaged in account fraud to meet these quotas, unethical practices became the norm. Employees rationalized their misconduct by citing systemic pressure from leadership. Most importantly, this case demonstrates how organizational culture can function as a powerful behavioral force. Leadership at Wells Fargo celebrated cross-selling metrics without questioning how sales goals were achieved. This culture fostered conformity bias, silenced dissent, and normalized misconduct.

What Would You Do?

Assume you are a branch manager at a large retail bank. Senior executives have launched a corporate initiative "to increase the number of accounts per customer significantly." You and your team are under intense pressure to meet daily and weekly cross-selling quotas.

Some employees have started opening accounts for customers without their consent, transferring small sums of money to make the accounts appear active. When you raise concerns, colleagues shrug and say, "This is how everyone is hitting their targets. Leadership wants numbers, not excuses." Now, you are faced with the following dilemma:

- If you refuse to push aggressive sales, your branch risks being labeled as underperforming, and you may lose your position.
- If you encourage your staff to meet targets by "any means necessary," you know it could harm customers, damage trust, and expose the bank to regulatory scrutiny.

- If you speak out, you may be ignored, punished, or even seen as disloyal to the firm.

What Should You Do?

(A) Meet Sales Goals as Directed: Encourage your employees to meet sales quotas, justifying this approach by pointing out that these practices are common and have implicit leadership approval.
(B) Quietly Resist: Encourage your team to avoid unethical behavior, but keep your resistance low-profile, so you do not attract unwanted attention from leadership.
(C) Raise Concerns Internally: Present your concerns to compliance managers or higher-level executives, arguing that current sales practices are harming customers, risking your career, and jeopardizing the firm's reputation.
(D) Promote Transparency with Clients: Inform customers about sales pressures and ensure clients participate in important account decisions, even if doing so slows down account creation and branch profitability.
(E) Become a Whistleblower or Exit the Firm: Report misconduct to regulators or leave the firm if internal change proves impossible, sacrificing your position but protecting client interests.

Insight

The best course of action is to begin with internal escalation (Answer C) to the firm's compliance department and senior leadership. If ignored or retaliated against, becoming a whistleblower (Answer E) becomes an option. Promoting transparency with clients (Answer D) may also be a future course of action if the firm fails to respond appropriately to your concerns. Answer A is incorrect because while complying with leadership expectations, the action normalizes fraud, harms customers, and guarantees long-term regulatory and reputational damage. Answer B is incorrect because while doing so reduces immediate personal risk, it does little to change firm-wide misconduct, which may allow harm to continue unchecked.

Additional Things to Consider

- Financial advisors and managers must protect client interests above sales incentives.
- Hidden information clearly violates the principles of fairness and transparency.
- Toxic sales cultures normalize misconduct.
- Ethical leadership requires challenging incentive structures that push employees toward fraud.
- Meeting short-term quotas may temporarily protect a job, but it creates lasting reputational and financial harm for the firm.
- Speaking up or resisting unethical norms may feel risky, but doing so protects customers and the integrity of the financial system.
- Incentive structures are governance issues; leaders must design compensation systems aligned with ethical behavior, not just profits.

Case 6: Morgan Stanley Data Breach

In 2016, the U.S. Securities and Exchange Commission (SEC) fined Morgan Stanley Smith Barney for failing to protect sensitive client data belonging to approximately 730,000 clients. The breach occurred when an employee copied confidential client information, including names, addresses, and account numbers, onto personal devices and transferred some of this data to a third-party server that was subsequently hacked. This incident revealed significant weaknesses in the bank's cybersecurity safeguards and internal access controls.[15]

As a result of the data breach, Morgan Stanley agreed to pay a $1 million penalty to settle charges with the SEC. The data breach raised concerns about the firm's ability to protect client information. It also cast doubt on the firm's reputation as a wealth manager. In addition, Morgan Stanley faced lawsuits from affected clients who claimed negligence in data protection. As a result, the firm took steps to improve its data and cybersecurity policies, monitoring tools, and employee training to prevent future breaches.

This case demonstrates the significance of regulatory frameworks, such as the privacy provisions in the Gramm-Leach-Bliley Act (GLBA). Regulators concluded that Morgan Stanley failed to adopt adequate written policies and safeguards to protect client data, violating GLBA's data protection rules. From an ethical perspective, the scandal shows how lapses in ethical responsibility erode trust. Protecting client information is an ethical obligation tied to a firm's fiduciary duty. Morgan Stanley's failure to implement basic safeguards undermined transparency and accountability, exposing clients to risks of identity theft and fraud. At its core, the case demonstrates that ethical responsibility extends beyond financial products to the integrity of information systems.

Similar to the other cases featured in this chapter, the data breach shared many of the same behavioral dynamics associated with other ethical failures. Employees and management underestimated the risks of insider misuse of data, assuming existing controls were sufficient. Protecting data was seen as an IT problem rather than a shared organizational duty. Furthermore, staff and leadership treated cybersecurity as a technical compliance requirement rather than a core ethical obligation to clients. Unlike Wells Fargo (sales culture) or UBS (cultural collusion), Morgan Stanley's failure arose from a culture of complacency. The case shows that ethical blind spots can emerge even in areas perceived as technical rather than client-facing.

What Would You Do?

Assume you are a compliance officer at a major wealth management firm. During a routine audit, you discover that employees have been copying client data, including names, account numbers, and addresses, onto personal devices. The employees are doing this for convenience (they want to work at home to keep pace with work demands). You also learn that some of this data was uploaded to a personal cloud storage service. While no data breach has yet occurred, you know that such practices could expose clients to identity theft or fraud if the data were hacked. You now face the following dilemma:

- If you ignore the behavior, the firm risks a significant data breach, regulatory penalties, lawsuits, and damage to client trust.
- If you act decisively, you may upset employees who rely on data processing shortcuts for efficiency, and you could face pushback from management that views cybersecurity as "just IT's problem."
- You must decide whether to intervene immediately, escalate to senior leadership, or implement stricter policies, balancing operational convenience, employee resistance, and ethical responsibility to clients.

What Should You Do?

(A) Take No Immediate Action: Assume convenience practices are low risk and rely on existing IT controls.

(B) Strengthen Internal Policies and Training: Restrict access to sensitive data, enforce device policies, and require mandatory cybersecurity training for all staff.

(C) Escalate to Senior Leadership and Compliance Committees: Recommend a full review of data access and implement monitoring systems to prevent misuse, even if it disrupts workflow.

(D) Inform Clients Proactively: Notify clients of the potential risk, even before a breach occurs, prioritizing transparency over operational simplicity.

(E) Implement a Reporting and Accountability System: Create mechanisms for employees to report unsafe practices anonymously and enforce accountability for violations of data-handling rules.

Insight

Answers B and C, in combination, are correct. These actions strengthen firm policies and training protocols while informing firm leadership of risky behavior. Answers D and E come into play if appropriate actions at the firm level are not taken. Answer A is incorrect because the action ignores clear risks, which violates your duty to stakeholders; it is also a violation of regulatory requirements.

Additional Things to Consider

- Protecting sensitive client information is a core ethical and legal responsibility.
- Data breaches undermine confidence and can cause direct harm to clients and the firm.
- Cybersecurity is not just an IT problem; all employees share responsibility for the ethical stewardship of client data.
- Addressing data and cybersecurity vulnerabilities before a breach occurs demonstrates ethical foresight and protects the firm's reputation.
- Complacency, underestimation of risk, and treating cybersecurity as a technical issue can create ethical blind spots.
- Ethical decisions may temporarily inconvenience employees or disrupt workflow, but long-term client protection and regulatory compliance outweigh short-term convenience.

Lessons Learned

The six case studies examined in this chapter reveal how ethical lapses and compliance failures occur in institutions, markets, and cultural contexts. Despite their differences, these cases share recurring themes that offer lessons for financial firms, financial advisors, and regulators. These lessons, grounded in practical applications and behavioral insights from earlier chapters, underscore the need for robust oversight, transparency, ethical culture, client protection, and whistleblower safeguards to build resilient and trustworthy risk management and compliance systems. The following discussion reviews some of the most important lessons learned from these cases.

Robust Oversight Prevents Systemic Failures

Weak oversight, as seen in JPMorgan's "London Whale" trading debacle and Morgan Stanley's data breach situation, creates fertile ground for risky and unethical behavior. Regular audits, independent compliance teams, and proactive monitoring are needed to identify and mitigate risks before they escalate. As highlighted in Chap. 7, institutionalized risk management systems that include technical controls and clear accountability structures are essential for detecting issues early. Appropriate oversight is also necessary in spotting complacency and overconfidence biases that can undermine vigilance.

Transparency Serves as a Foundation for Trust

Non-disclosure of conflicts of interest, as exemplified in the Edward Jones case, can erode client trust. A lack of transparency can also expose firms to reputational, legal, and financial risks. Complete transparency in fees, incentives, and conflicts is vital for sustaining long-term firm (and market) credibility. As discussed in Chap. 8, financial advisors who adhere to the fiduciary duty must provide clients with clear practice and product disclosures. Disclosure rules also apply broadly to those who follow the best-interest standard of care. Because disclosure serves as a regulatory obligation and a trust-building tool, ethical training can help professionals recognize and resist the temptation to engage in behaviors that reduce information sharing.

Ethical Culture Acts as a Bulwark Against Misconduct

Toxic organizational cultures, exemplified by the UBS case and the systemic corruption of the 1MDB scandal, normalize unethical behavior and desensitize employees to wrongdoing. These cases highlight the need for firm leadership to champion ethical standards that prioritize integrity over short-term profits. As will be noted in Chap. 13, incentive structures must be designed to promote ethical practices and foster an environment of employee and staff dialogue. Firms (and regulators) need to be vigilant in combating groupthink and social proof biases that lead to normalized illegal practices. Deliberate cultural interventions, such as ethics-focused training and leadership accountability, are crucial for disrupting these dynamics and promoting ethical decision-making.

Client Protection Is a Core Dynamic of Professional Practice

Failures in anti-money laundering (AML) and know-your-customer (KYC) protocols, as in the 1MDB scandal, or cybersecurity lapses, as in Morgan Stanley's data breach scenario, directly harm clients and undermine the profession's reputation. Disregarding client protections can also be costly in terms of regulatory penalties. Protecting client assets, data, and interests must be of primary importance at the advisor, firm, and professional level. As noted in Chaps. 5 and 10, robust compliance systems that prioritize client suitability, AML/KYC procedures, and data privacy are today non-negotiable for firms wishing to align operations with normative ethical standards. Senior firm management must be on guard to counteract greed-driven decisions and misaligned fiduciary priorities. These two biases are common factors in nearly all ethical and regulatory compliance failures.

Whistleblower Protections Enhance Accountability

As seen in the UBS and 1MDB cases, timely whistleblowing could have significantly reduced the scope of harm. Creating a safe environment for employees and other stakeholders to raise ethical concerns is therefore essential. However, whistleblower protections are not universal. Many employees remain silent out of fear of retaliation. As discussed in Chap. 6, the Dodd-Frank reforms have made it easier for firms to establish channels for reporting ethical issues. Even so, concerns about career risks and conflicts of loyalty often prevent action. In the 1MDB case, such fears delayed early intervention. Organizations that cultivate a supportive culture and value truth-tellers are crucial for identifying and addressing misconduct before it escalates.

Integrating Lessons for Resilient Risk Management and Compliance Systems

The cases in this chapter highlight the complex interplay between a firm's ethical culture, employee and client cognitive, behavioral, and psychological biases, compliance frameworks, and regulatory oversight. Ethical failures rarely result from isolated situations or one or two "bad actors." Instead, failures emerge from system-wide weaknesses in culture, incentive structures, and decision-making biases. If left unchecked, these weaknesses can escalate into broad imbalances, increasing the risk of ethical breaches and regulatory violations. As the financial services profession adapts to technological advancements and global risks, vigilance against ethical complacency is becoming increasingly critical. Strong oversight, transparent practices, client-centered priorities, and robust whistleblower protections are no longer optional; they are foundational elements for building trustworthy and resilient financial systems.

Best Practices for Building an Ethical and Compliant Financial Advisory Practice

The case studies in this chapter highlight lessons that can be used to build an ethical and regulatory-compliant financial advisory practice. The following best practices integrate regulatory requirements, organizational culture, and behavioral strategies that align with the material presented throughout this book. The list presents strategies in a normative manner, meaning that these actions are needed to ensure a firm is operating at the highest level.

Implement Comprehensive Compliance Systems

Firms should establish strict policies covering trade surveillance, AML/KYC verification, and data security protocols. Automated RegTech solutions, such as transaction monitoring, identity verification platforms, and real-time anomaly detection, can strengthen these controls. Clear escalation procedures to ensure red flags are addressed swiftly and independently are also needed.

Example: Regular audits and reconciling trading records with client authorizations could have prevented JPMorgan's "London Whale" losses. Comprehensive compliance systems can be used to promote accountability and integrity, reducing the risk of unchecked misconduct.

Foster a Culture of Ethics

Building an ethical firm culture requires initiative-taking leadership, mandatory ethics training, and performance metrics that reward client-centered decisions rather than sales quota metrics. Firm leaders should model ethical behavior consistently. Training programs can be used to present case studies and role-playing exercises to address real-world dilemmas.

Example: Embedding ethics training into annual evaluations and performance measures, and encouraging open dialogue, helps counteract groupthink and greed-driven biases. Regular workshops that provide an analysis of misconduct cases can be used to reinforce responsibility expectations and teach employees to resist pressures to normalize unethical behavior.

Enhance Transparency and Disclosure

Clear, client-friendly disclosures of fees, commissions, and conflicts of interest are essential for firms and financial services professionals whose number one goal is to develop client trust. Using plain language, summary tables, and examples of how fees affect returns helps clients make informed decisions. Disclosures should also explain the advisor's duties and conflict management processes.

Example: Transparent revenue-sharing disclosures could have prevented the negative outcomes associated with the Edward Jones case. Prioritizing clarity of disclosure statements not only meets regulatory requirements but also strengthens firm and advisor credibility.

Strengthen Risk Management Frameworks

Regular stress tests and scenario analyses (e.g., simulating market crashes, client withdrawals, and regulatory probes) should be used to identify firm vulnerabilities related to AML/KYC, data security, and capital adequacy. Automated alerts and enhanced due diligence for high-risk accounts, including politically exposed persons, could have prevented illicit fund flows like those in 1MDB.

Example: Reporting results to senior management strengthens internal controls, reduces overconfidence, and improves risk perception. Implementing strong risk management frameworks enables firms to anticipate and mitigate hidden data and cybersecurity risks.

Encourage Whistleblowing and Reporting

Secure and anonymous reporting channels that allow employees and other stakeholders to report ethical concerns should be a high priority for all firms operating in the financial services field. These channels can consist of encrypted hotlines, third-party platforms, or ombudsperson offices. Regardless of the channel, creating an open pathway for whistleblowers is a way to allow employees to raise concerns without fear of retribution. Strong non-retaliation policies, supported by firm leadership, protect whistleblowers. It is important, as well, to monitor the monitors. Independent compliance teams should review and escalate reports to senior management or regulators as needed.

Example: Early detection of UBS's LIBOR manipulation behavior could have reduced widespread harm. By addressing fear-driven silence and fostering accountability, it might have been possible for UBS to have created a culture that prioritized ethical responsibility.

Invest in Continuous Education

Ongoing regulatory updates and ethical standards training are important factors in creating an ethical firm culture. Annual certifications, case-based modules, and workshops on dilemmas such as data protection lapses help employees remain vigilant. Interactive sessions that describe cognitive, behavioral, and psychological (e.g., overconfidence and ethical fading) tend to help staff understand when they are being manipulated or succumbing to biases that weaken ethical safeguards.

Example: Linking training to performance evaluations reinforces ethical awareness and ensures compliance with evolving firm and regulatory standards, minimizing lapses that undermine trust.

Summary of Best Practices

These practices demonstrate that compliance and ethics are inseparable. While firm compliance systems help reduce risk, culture, education, and transparency sustain trust. By combining structural safeguards with behavioral insights, financial services firms and financial professionals can create practices that are compliant and ethically resilient. Protecting clients and maintaining professional integrity in an evolving financial landscape is the ultimate outcome. Table 12.1 provides a summary of the best practices described above.

Table 12.1 Best practices for building an ethical and compliant financial practice

Best practice	Key actions	Examples/case relevance	Behavioral and ethical focus
Implement comprehensive compliance systems	Continuous trade surveillance; AML/KYC verification; data security protocols; clear escalation procedures	JPMorgan "London Whale": reconciling trades with client authorizations could have prevented losses	Accountability, integrity, and reducing unchecked misconduct
Foster a culture of ethics	Visible leadership commitment; mandatory ethics training; performance metrics rewarding client-centered decisions; open dialogue and workshops	UBS tax evasion schemes: using role-playing and case studies to recognize real-world dilemmas	Counteracting groupthink and greed-driven biases; reinforcing fiduciary responsibility
Enhance transparency and disclosure	Clear, plain-language client disclosures; explain fees, commissions, conflicts; clarify fiduciary duty	Edward Jones revenue-sharing: clear disclosures could have prevented client mistrust	Prevent rationalization of non-disclosure; build client trust
Strengthen risk management frameworks	Stress tests and scenario analyses; automated alerts for high-risk accounts; enhanced due diligence for PEPs; reporting to senior management	1MDB: early detection of risky accounts could have prevented illicit fund flows	Reduce overconfidence; improve risk perception; anticipate systemic risks
Encourage whistleblowing and reporting	Secure, anonymous reporting channels; non-retaliation policies; independent compliance review and escalation	LIBOR manipulation: early whistleblowing could have limited widespread harm	Address fear-driven silence; foster accountability and ethical responsibility
Invest in continuous education	Training in regulatory updates, ethics, behavioral biases; case-based modules and workshops; link training to performance evaluations	Data protection lapses (Morgan Stanley): interactive sessions on ethical fading and overconfidence	Maintain vigilance; challenge assumptions; reinforce ethical awareness

Chapter Summary

This chapter examined six ethics and compliance case failures in the financial services profession: JPMorgan's oversight lapses, Edward Jones's revenue-sharing practices, UBS's cross-border collusion, the 1MDB scandal, Morgan Stanley's data breach, and Wells Fargo's sales culture abuses. While each case occurred in a different context, all revealed systemic weaknesses in oversight, transparency, organizational culture, client protection, and accountability.

The following lessons emerged from these cases. First, weak oversight can encourage excessive risk-taking, while a lack of transparency erodes client trust. Second, a strong ethical culture is critical for preventing misconduct. Protecting client interests must be the central purpose of the firm and advisors operating in the financial services field. Third, adequate whistleblower protections are essential for uncovering wrongdoing early. Collectively, the lessons learned from the cases show that ethical failures are rarely isolated incidents. Failures result from broader organizational, cultural, and behavioral dynamics.

The chapter also highlighted best practices for preventing similar failures in the future. Firms should implement robust compliance systems, foster an ethical culture, provide clear and transparent disclosures, strengthen risk management systems, encourage whistleblowing, and invest in ongoing employee education.

Finally, as these real-world examples demonstrate, regulatory compliance extends beyond following rules. Compliance is deeply connected to organizational values. Preventing ethical lapses requires that risk management systems be in place, ethical leaders exhibit positive behaviors, and employees be incentivized to act ethically. Through the integration of these elements, financial professionals can create practices that are regulatory compliant and trustworthy, fostering resilient client relationships and ensuring long-term professional integrity.

Chapter Resources

- Gramm-Leach-Bliley Act (GLBA): https://www.ftc.gov/business-guidance/privacy-security/gramm-leach-bliley-act
- Consumer Financial Protection Bureau: consumerfinance.org
- Federal Reserve: https://www.federalreserve.gov/
- National Association of Insurance Commissioners: https://content.naic.org/
- Securities and Exchange Commission (SEC): https://www.sec.gov/

Appendix

Concept Check Question

The following questions are designed as self-assessment tools to help readers review and reinforce some of the main facts and takeaways from the cases discussed in this chapter.

1. What was the primary reason for the massive losses incurred by JPMorgan Chase in the "London Whale" scandal?[16]

   (A) Unauthorized trading by external hackers
   (B) Speculative bets disguised as hedges in credit derivatives
   (C) Failure to comply with tax regulations
   (D) Losses from investments in government bonds

2. Which regulatory bodies imposed fines totaling $920 million on JPMorgan Chase for the London Whale incident?[17]

   (A) Federal Reserve, FDIC, and FINRA
   (B) SEC, CFTC, OCC, and FCA
   (C) IRS, SEC, and European Central Bank
   (D) CFTC, OCC, and World Bank

3. What behavioral factor contributed to senior management's failure to address the risks of the CIO's trades?[18]

   (A) Lack of technical expertise in derivatives
   (B) Overconfidence and groupthink
   (C) External pressure from competing banks
   (D) Intentional fraud by the CIO team

4. The JPMorgan Chase London Whale scandal influenced what regulatory change?[19]

   (A) Sarbanes-Oxley Act
   (B) Volcker Rule
   (C) Basel III Accord
   (D) Gramm-Leach-Bliley Act

5. How did the complexity of the CIO's trades impact oversight in the London Whale case?[20]

   (A) It simplified risk assessment for regulators.
   (B) It obscured the actual risks, dulling oversight.
   (C) It led to immediate intervention by the board.
   (D) It reduced the need for internal audits.

6. What was the primary misconduct at UBS in the LIBOR scandal?[21]

   (A) Misrepresenting client investment returns
   (B) Manipulating benchmark interest rate submissions to benefit trading positions
   (C) Hiding losses from subprime mortgage securities
   (D) Engaging in insider trading with government bonds

7. Why was LIBOR manipulation especially damaging to global financial markets?[22]

   (A) It only affected UBS shareholders.
   (B) LIBOR was used to price trillions of dollars' worth of loans, derivatives, and other contracts worldwide.
   (C) LIBOR was a private benchmark used only by UBS traders.
   (D) LIBOR manipulation increased global savings rates.

8. Which behavioral biases were most evident among UBS traders during the LIBOR scandal?[23]

   (A) Anchoring and loss aversion
   (B) Overconfidence and groupthink
   (C) Mental accounting and framing
   (D) Availability bias and recency bias

9. What cultural problem at UBS allowed LIBOR manipulation to continue unchecked?[24]

   (A) Excessive internal regulations and a lack of federal transparency
   (B) A culture that normalized dishonesty, reinforced by conformity bias and diffusion of responsibility
   (C) Overly strict compensation structures that punished risk-taking
   (D) A culture of whistleblowing and strong internal accountability

10. What systemic outcome followed the LIBOR scandal? [25]

    (A) Regulators banned UBS from global markets permanently.
    (B) The LIBOR benchmark was strengthened and became more widely used.
    (C) UBS paid $1.5 billion in fines, several traders were prosecuted, and LIBOR began to be phased out in favor of alternatives, such as SOFR.
    (D) UBS avoided penalties because other banks were also involved.

11. What was the primary wrongdoing in the 1MDB scandal?[26]

    (A) Misreporting quarterly earnings to shareholders
    (B) Embezzlement of billions of dollars intended for national development projects
    (C) Collusion with rating agencies to inflate bond values
    (D) Manipulation of benchmark interest rates

12. Which global bank was most directly implicated in facilitating bond offerings for 1MDB?[27]

    (A) UBS
    (B) Deutsche Bank
    (C) Goldman Sachs
    (D) Credit Suisse

13. What was the total amount Goldman Sachs agreed to pay in global settlements related to the 1MDB scandal?[28]

    (A) $1.5 billion
    (B) $2.9 billion
    (C) $5+ billion
    (D) $10 billion

14. Which behavioral bias BEST explains why Goldman Sachs executives rationalized their involvement despite red flags?[29]

    (A) Anchoring bias
    (B) Motivated blindness
    (C) Framing effect
    (D) Availability bias

15. What broader systemic outcome followed the 1MDB scandal?[30]

    (A) The repeal of the Foreign Corrupt Practices Act (FCPA)
    (B) Tighter global scrutiny of cross-border capital flows and enhanced AML/KYC expectations
    (C) The creation of LIBOR alternatives, such as SOFR, is underway
    (D) The merger of Goldman Sachs with UBS

16. What misconduct led to the SEC charging Edward Jones in 2004?[31]

    (A) Insider trading by senior executives
    (B) Failure to disclose revenue-sharing agreements with mutual fund companies
    (C) Misreporting client account balances
    (D) Manipulating benchmark interest rates

17. Why did the revenue-sharing arrangements create a conflict of interest?[32]

    (A) Advisors were paid directly by clients in cash.
    (B) The funds involved were illegal under SEC rules.
    (C) Advisors were incentivized to recommend higher-fee products, which might not be in clients' best interest.
    (D) The mutual funds performed worse than all competitors.

18. What financial penalty did Edward Jones agree to pay as part of the SEC settlement?[33]

    (A) $25 million
    (B) $50
    (C) million
    (D) $100 million

19. Which regulatory principle was most clearly violated in the Edward Jones case?[34]

    (A) The Glass-Steagall Act's separation of banking activities.
    (B) The Investment Advisers Act of 1940 requires disclosure of material conflicts.
    (C) The Volcker Rule restricts proprietary trading.
    (D) The Dodd-Frank Act's systemic risk provisions.

20. Which behavioral bias BEST explains why Edward Jones advisors normalized recommending "preferred" funds without disclosure?[35]

    (A) Anchoring bias
    (B) Framing effect and ethical fading
    (C) Recency bias
    (D) Representativeness heuristic

21. What was the primary unethical practice uncovered in the 2016 Wells Fargo scandal?[36]

    (A) Manipulating mortgage-backed securities pricing
    (B) Creating unauthorized customer accounts
    (C) Misreporting earnings to shareholders
    (D) Providing insider information to investors

22. Which factor most directly contributed to employees engaging in fraudulent account openings?[37]

    (A) Weak product offerings compared to competitors
    (B) Unrealistic cross-selling sales targets and incentive structures
    (C) Lack of customer demand for new accounts
    (D) High turnover in executive leadership

23. What were the immediate regulatory consequences for Wells Fargo following the scandal?[38]

    (A) The Federal Reserve revoked its banking charter.
    (B) The SEC banned Wells Fargo from selling mutual funds.
    (C) The CFPB, OCC, and Los Angeles City Attorney fined Wells Fargo $185 million.
    (D) Wells Fargo was forced into bankruptcy proceedings.

24. Wells Fargo's actions most clearly violated which ethical principle?[39]

    (A) Beneficence: promoting the well-being of others
    (B) Justice: ensuring equitable treatment of all stakeholders
    (C) Transparency: being truthful, clear, and providing full disclosure
    (D) Loyalty: prioritizing shareholder profits above all else

25. What behavioral bias best explains why Wells Fargo employees continued the misconduct over time?[40]

    (A) Confirmation bias
    (B) Groupthink and normalization of deviance
    (C) Anchoring bias
    (D) Loss aversion

26. What was the primary misconduct in the 2016 Morgan Stanley Smith Barney case?[41]

    (A) Insider trading by executives
    (B) Failure to protect sensitive client data
    (C) Misrepresentation of investment performance
    (D) Unauthorized trading in client accounts

27. Which regulatory framework did Morgan Stanley violate by failing to safeguard client information?[42]

    (A) The Dodd-Frank Act
    (B) The Sarbanes-Oxley Act
    (C) The Gramm-Leach-Bliley Act (GLBA)
    (D) The Investment Advisers Act of 1940

28. Approximately how many clients were affected by the Morgan Stanley data breach?[43]

    (A) 100,000
    (B) 250,000
    (C) 500,000
    (D) 730,000

29. What behavioral issue contributed most directly to Morgan Stanley's failures related to preventing the data breach reported in the case narrative?[44]

    (A) Overconfidence and ethical complacency
    (B) The firm's complacency in viewing cybersecurity solely as an IT problem
    (C) Incentive bias and revenue-sharing conflicts
    (D) Manipulation of benchmark interest rates

30. What was the SEC's penalty against Morgan Stanley in this case?[45]

    (A) $500,000
    (B) $1 million
    (C) $5 million
    (D) $10 million

Notes

[1]Financial institutions should establish comprehensive compliance frameworks that include the mandatory use of approved communication channels for all business activities, along with automated monitoring tools to flag any deviations. Regular independent audits, employee training on regulatory requirements, and swift enforcement of penalties for non-compliance are essential. Additionally, integrating AI-driven surveillance systems can detect patterns of oversight lapses early, while fostering a culture in which supervisors are held accountable for team adherence, thereby reducing systemic risks.

[2]Institutions must prioritize transparency by requiring full disclosure of all revenue-sharing arrangements in client agreements and prospectuses, which should be audited annually by independent third parties. Aligning advisor incentives with client outcomes—such as through fiduciary standards that prohibit conflicted recommendations—helps eliminate biases. Regulatory bodies can enforce stricter reporting rules, and banks should implement internal ethics committees to review partnerships, ensuring that product recommendations are based solely on client needs rather than hidden financial gains.

[3]Financial institutions must shift from volume-based quotas to balanced scorecards that reward ethical behavior, customer satisfaction, and long-term relationships over short-term sales. Provide mandatory ethics training, establish anonymous whistleblower hotlines with protections against retaliation, and conduct regular employee surveys to gauge pressure levels. Leadership must model integrity by tying executive bonuses to compliance metrics, and independent oversight boards should review sales practices quarterly to prevent cultural drift toward misconduct.

[4]https://www.reuters.com/article/business/jpmorgan-blames-risk-management-for-london-whale-loss-idUSBRE90F18G/

[5]https://www.newyorker.com/news/john-cassidy/will-the-london-whale-swallow-jamie-dimon

[6]https://hbr.org/2013/01/the-jp-morgan-whale-report-and

[7]https://www.reuters.com/article/business/jpmorgan-ordered-to-face-london-whale-class-action-in-us-idUSKCN0RT2ZS/

[8]https://www.demos.org/blog/london-whale-tempest-teapot-or-cover

[9]https://www.bbc.com/news/business-20767984

[10]https://archive.nytimes.com/dealbook.nytimes.com/2012/12/19/as-unit-pleads-guilty-ubs-pays-1-5-billion-in-fines-over-rate-rigging/

[11]https://www.justice.gov/archives/opa/pr/united-states-seeks-recover-more-1-billion-obtained-corruption-involving-malaysian-sovereign

[12]https://www.bbc.com/news/world-asia-68137595

[13]https://www.sec.gov/news/press/2004-177.htm.

[14]https://www.consumerfinance.gov/about-us/newsroom/consumer-financial-protection-bureau-fines-wells-fargo-100-million-widespread-illegal-practice-secretly-opening-unauthorized-accounts/

[15]https://www.sec.gov/newsroom/press-releases/2016-112

[16]Correct Answer: B

Explanation: The trades, led by Bruno Iksil, were initially intended to hedge credit exposure but evolved into speculative bets due to their size and complexity, resulting in $6.2 billion in losses.

[17]Correct Answer: B

Explanation: The Securities and Exchange Commission (SEC), the Commodity Futures Trading Commission (CFTC), the Office of the Comptroller of the Currency (OCC), and the United Kingdom's Financial Conduct Authority (FCA) imposed fines for violations, including misleading disclosures.

[18]Correct Answer: B

Explanation: Senior management exhibited overconfidence in their risk models and groupthink, which silenced dissent and allowed the risky trades to continue unchecked.

[19]Correct Answer: B

Explanation: The scandal highlighted the dangers of proprietary trading, contributing to the enactment of the Volcker Rule, a provision of the Dodd-Frank Act that restricts such activities.

[20]Correct Answer: B

Explanation: The technical intricacy of the trades acted as a shield, making it difficult for executives and regulators to recognize the speculative nature and risks, thus undermining effective oversight.

[21]Correct Answer: B

Explanation: UBS traders deliberately submitted false LIBOR estimates to make the bank appear financially stronger and to benefit their own trading positions. This manipulation distorted a key global benchmark.

[22]Correct Answer: B

Explanation: LIBOR served as a global benchmark interest rate at the time, directly influencing the pricing of mortgages, corporate loans, and derivatives. Manipulating it undermined the fairness of contracts across the entire financial system.

[23]Correct Answer: B

Explanation: Traders were overconfident, believing they could manipulate submissions without detection. Groupthink reinforced this misconduct, as collusion and manipulation were normalized within teams and across the banking industry.

[24]Correct Answer: B

Explanation: UBS had a culture where dishonest practices were tolerated and justified as "normal." Social proof ("everyone is doing it"), conformity pressure, and diffusion of responsibility made employees less likely to resist or report manipulation.

[25]Correct Answer: C

Explanation: UBS faced fines of $1.5 billion across multiple regulators, its traders faced criminal charges, and the scandal accelerated the global shift to replace LIBOR with more reliable benchmarks, such as the Secured Overnight Financing Rate (SOFR).

[26]Correct Answer: B

Explanation: More than $4.5 billion was embezzled from 1MDB through shell companies and offshore accounts. Instead of funding schools, hospitals, and infrastructure, the money was diverted into luxury real estate, artwork, and even Hollywood films.

[27]Correct Answer: C

Explanation: Goldman Sachs helped raise $6.5 billion in bonds for 1MDB, collecting unusually high fees while ignoring serious compliance red flags in KYC and AML processes.

[28]Correct Answer: C

Explanation: Goldman Sachs agreed to pay more than $5 billion in global settlements, including $2.9 billion to the U.S. Department of Justice—the largest penalty ever paid under U.S. anti-corruption laws at the time.

[29]Correct Answer: B

Explanation: Executives exhibited motivated blindness, convincing themselves that because regulators or compliance teams had not stopped the deal, it must be acceptable. The lure of unusually high fees also clouded ethical judgment.

[30]Correct Answer: B

Explanation: The scandal accelerated regulatory reforms worldwide. Authorities in multiple countries tightened oversight of capital flows, increased scrutiny of transactions in emerging markets, and reinforced the importance of AML/KYC frameworks.

[31]Correct Answer: B

Explanation: Edward Jones failed to disclose that it had revenue-sharing arrangements with seven mutual fund companies. Advisors marketed these funds as "preferred" without telling clients that the firm received payments for steering them into these products.

[32]Correct Answer: C

Explanation: The revenue-sharing agreements financially incentivized Edward Jones advisors to recommend specific funds. The agreements created a misalignment between client interests (seeking the best product) and firm interests (maximizing revenue).

[33]Correct Answer: C

Explanation: Edward Jones paid a total of $75 million—half as disgorgement of ill-gotten gains and half as civil fines. The firm also had to reform disclosure practices and compliance systems.

[34]Correct Answer: B

Explanation: The SEC cited the Investment Advisers Act of 1940, which requires the disclosure of conflicts of interest and prohibits the making of misleading statements to clients. Edward Jones failed to disclose revenue-sharing payments that influenced fund recommendations.

[35]Correct Answer: B

Explanation: By labeling revenue-sharing products as "preferred," the firm reframed the incentives as legitimate. Over time, ethical fading occurred. Firm advisors ceased to perceive the lack of disclosure as unethical and instead perceived it as a practice that had become institutionalized and widely accepted.

[36]Answer: B. Creating unauthorized customer accounts

Explanation: Wells Fargo employees opened over 3.5 million unauthorized deposit and credit card accounts without customer consent. Aggressive sales quotas and incentive structures drove this misconduct.

[37]Answer: B. Unrealistic cross-selling sales targets and incentive structures

Explanation: Employees were under extreme pressure to meet quotas for accounts per customer. The incentive system rewarded volume over quality, which created conditions where fraud became normalized.

[38]Answer: C. The CFPB, OCC, and Los Angeles City Attorney fined Wells Fargo $185 million

Explanation: In 2016, Wells Fargo agreed to pay $185 million in penalties. Fines included penalties from the Consumer Financial Protection Bureau (CFPB), the Office of the Comptroller of the Currency (OCC), and the Los Angeles City Attorney's Office.

[39]Answer: C. Transparency—providing truthful, clear, and full disclosure

Explanation: Customers were not informed about the unauthorized accounts, funds were transferred without knowledge, and employees concealed the true nature of the practices. These practices violated transparency and fairness, eroding client trust.

[40]Answer: B. Groupthink and normalization of deviance

Explanation: As more employees engaged in fraud to meet quotas, unethical practices became "business as usual." Groupthink discouraged dissent, and the normalization of deviance led employees to view unethical behavior as acceptable and necessary for survival.

[41]Answer: B. Failure to protect sensitive client data

Explanation: An employee copied confidential client information to personal devices and transferred some data to a third-party server, exposing 730,000 clients' sensitive data and revealing weaknesses in internal access controls.

[42] Answer: C. The Gramm-Leach-Bliley Act (GLBA)

Explanation: GLBA requires financial institutions to implement safeguards to protect sensitive client information. Morgan Stanley failed to adopt adequate written policies and safeguards, violating GLBA provisions.

[43] Answer: D. 730,000

Explanation: The breach exposed sensitive information for roughly 730,000 clients, including names, addresses, and account numbers, highlighting the scale and potential risk of the incident.

[44] Answer: B. Complacency and viewing cybersecurity as solely an IT problem

Explanation: Employees and management underestimated the risk of insider misuse and treated data security as a technical compliance issue rather than a shared ethical obligation to clients, creating an ethical blind spot.

[45] Answer: B. $1 million

Explanation: Morgan Stanley agreed to pay a $1 million penalty to settle SEC charges related to its failure to protect sensitive client data and to implement adequate safeguards.

Developing an Ethical Firm Culture in the Financial Services Profession

13

Chapter Outcomes

This chapter focuses on helping learners develop the ability to:

1. Explain why fostering an ethical culture is a strategic firm imperative that goes beyond regulatory compliance.
2. Describe the impact of client culture in shaping client trust and public confidence.
3. Describe strategies that encourage ethical conduct among financial services firm employees.
4. Analyze the role of firm leadership in establishing, modeling, and sustaining ethical standards.
5. Discuss how an ethical firm culture affects individuals, families, businesses, and the macroeconomy in a competitive and litigious economic environment.

Introduction

In recent years, the discussion of unethical behavior in business organizations has gained the attention of those in the media and among politicians. Ethical firm culture, broadly defined, transcends adherence to legal requirements. An ethical firm culture is defined as an environment in which employees are encouraged to make decisions that go beyond minimum moral and regulatory standards.[1] An ethical firm culture is one where employees actively seek solutions that uphold shared values and principles.[2] This culture is shaped by formal systems, such as leadership

Note: This chapter was copyedited using Grammarly™ and generative AI tools to enhance clarity, grammar, and overall readability. While these tools provided suggestions and assistance in refining the text, the ideas, content, and arguments presented remain the sole work and responsibility of the authors. Any errors or inaccuracies in the final version are also the authors' responsibility.

W. Heo, J. E. Grable, *Ethics and Compliance in Financial Services*,
https://doi.org/10.1007/978-3-032-14449-2_13

structures, codes of conduct, and reward mechanisms, and informal elements, including norms, rituals, and language.

Research suggests that organizational culture is among the most significant influences describing ethical or unethical behavior in businesses.[3] An ethical culture aligns formal regulatory and compliance processes with informal traditions, fostering a shared understanding of values that inspire employees to act with integrity.[4] Leaders play a critical role in establishing an ethical culture. Ethical practice comes to the forefront as employees model the ethical behavior of those in leadership roles. Culture is also shaped by engaging others in ethical discussions and reinforcing notions of client relationships based on trust. In this regard, an ethical firm culture is built on some key unifying pillars, including clear communication of ethical standards, consistent enforcement of policies, and organizational customs that reinforce ethical values.

The most successful organizations create environments that align individual and corporate values, promote individuals who exhibit high moral standards, and remove behaviors (and individuals) that are misaligned with core principles. Holding a long-term perspective is a fundamental element within the framework. Successfully managed firms are those where firm managers prioritize an ethical mission and stakeholder's needs over short-term profits. Concepts such as respect, fairness, community, citizenship, and balance dominate the words used to describe ethical firms.

As shown in Fig. 13.1, leadership effectiveness is a key aspect associated with the creation of an ethical firm culture, with senior management acting as role models of integrity and accountability. Ethical leaders address issues transparently, foster open dialogue, and prioritize long-term growth over short-term gains.

Process integrity is also important. Process integrity refers to requiring employees at all levels of the firm to embed ethics into recruiting, training, and operational systems.[5] Reinforcing values through performance appraisals and transparent decision-making is one way managers ensure individual behavior aligns with business level standards of conduct. Governance, supported by independent boards, is also pivotal in fostering an ethical firm culture. The literature is clear in showing that ethical organizations thrive by engaging in ongoing dialogue, respecting diverse needs, and aligning business actions with broader societal responsibilities. These insights reinforce the importance of fostering ethical cultures as a strategic imperative for long-term success in the financial services profession.

The following discussion introduces a framework developed by Jondle and Mitchell[6] that describes what it means to perform in a firm culture of creativity and sustainability. The framework highlights the components of ethical business cultures and provides a guide for enterprise-level leadership to foster an ethical advisor employee base.

The list of ethical attributes and statements shown in Table 13.1 represents the way successful organizations institutionalize ethical principles and cultivate ethical practices. The second column in the table illustrates the types of statements firm employees often express when thinking about their work at a highly ethical firm.

Fig. 13.1 Characteristics associated with ethical firm cultures

Perspective

How does the information in Fig. 13.1 and Table 13.1 apply in practice? The following hypothetical case narrative helps frame what it means to develop and maintain an ethical firm culture. In this case, Northstate Financial Group, a mid-sized wealth management firm, faced a significant reputational challenge following a client complaint that alleged unethical practices by one of its advisor employees. The response by the firm's leadership shows how it is possible to encounter significant reputational harm and reframe it as an opportunity to reflect on an organization's culture. As described below, Northstate Financial Group's executives were able to implement changes to ensure a foundation of integrity, trust, and long-term sustainability.

Northstate's leadership began by rearticulating the firm's mission to prioritize ethical client relationships and sustainable growth over short-term profits. They engaged employees across all levels to identify shared values, which were then codified into an updated code of conduct. The revised mission emphasized respect, fairness, and accountability while aligning with the broader societal responsibilities of the financial services profession.

Table 13.1 Characteristics of ethical firm cultures

Firm characteristic	Characteristic statement examples
Driven by ethical mission and values	• Clarity of mission and values is reflected in ethical guidelines and behavior • Institutionalizes ethical values • Build relationships of trust and respect • Strong culture that actively reduces the role of those who do not share firm values • Corporate values are sustained over extended periods of time
Stakeholder balance	• Consistently balances the needs of stakeholders (e.g., customers, employees, owners, and community) in all decision-making • Deal with all stakeholders on a consistently ethical and value-oriented basis • Good balance of customer value and profit • Giving back to the community in which the company does business • Works to be a good corporate citizen in a global economy • Provides respectful treatment and fair compensation for employees at all levels
Leadership effectiveness	• Ethical culture starts at the top and is conveyed by example • Senior management demands ethical conduct at every level of the company • CEO and senior management live their lives with great personal integrity • When ethical issues arise, the CEO does not "shoot the messenger" but gathers facts and takes action • Managers do what they say they are going to do
Process integrity	• Dedication to quality and fairness in the firm's employees, processes, and products • Invests in ongoing ethics training and communication throughout the organization • Values are reinforced in performance appraisals and promotions • Values are reinforced in everyday execution • Excellent corporate governance processes, supported by Board quality and independence • The mission is internalized in company processes and behavior • Transparent decision-making by the people closest to the question
Long-term perspective	• Places mission above profit, and long term over short term • Acts in the best interests of customers over the long term • The Board takes a long view of managing shareholder value • Connects environmental sustainability, social responsibility, and profit • CEO says they are building an institution that they hope will be here in 50 years

Source: Jondle, D. J., & Mitchell, J. A. (n.d.). *Characteristics of ethical business cultures*. https://files.eric.ed.gov/fulltext/ED501640.pdf

Recognizing that leadership behavior shapes organizational culture, Northstate's executive team committed themselves to leading by example. The CEO initiated quarterly town hall meetings where transparent discussions on ethics and decision-making were encouraged. Senior leaders actively sought employee input, reinforcing a culture of open communication. They also made it a priority to address ethical breaches promptly, ensuring accountability at all levels.

Northstate embedded ethics into its core processes, from hiring to performance reviews. Recruitment focused on identifying candidates whose personal values aligned with the firm's mission. Performance appraisals began to include assessments of ethical behavior alongside traditional metrics like sales targets. Managers were trained to make decisions transparently and involve employees in discussions about ethical challenges, fostering a sense of shared responsibility.

The firm also introduced a comprehensive ethics training program, using real-world scenarios to help employees navigate complex situations. These sessions emphasized the long-term importance of maintaining trust with clients and stakeholders. Additionally, Northstate launched an anonymous ethics hotline, ensuring employees could report concerns without fear of retaliation.

Finally, leadership reinforced the importance of balancing the needs of all stakeholders. For example, clients were assured that their interests would always come before short-term firm profit motives. Employees received equitable compensation and wellness benefits as a way for management to demonstrate the firm's commitment to fairness. Community engagement programs like financial literacy workshops were expanded to align with the firm's broader societal responsibilities.

Within two years, Northstate Financial Group saw measurable improvements across the following business domains:

- Employee Engagement: Surveys indicated that employees felt more empowered and aligned with the firm's values, leading to a 20% reduction in turnover.
- Client Retention: By prioritizing ethical practices, the firm regained client trust, reflected in a 15% increase in retention rates.
- Reputation: Industry recognition as an ethical leader attracted conscientious investors and clients. A prominent trade association awarded Northstate a sustainability and ethics excellence award.

The Importance of Fostering an Ethical Firm Culture

As the Northstate Financial Group case example illustrates, ethical firms have an enhanced capacity to recover from reputational shocks and bounce back stronger than they might have otherwise. Developing and maintaining an ethical culture serves as the foundation for sustainable success in the financial services profession. An ethical culture helps establish a decision-making process that goes beyond mere adherence to legal and regulatory requirements. Key benefits include:[7]

- Building Trust: Ethical organizations inspire trust among clients, stakeholders, and regulators. Trust, once established, enhances client loyalty, attracts new business, and safeguards the institution's reputation.
- Mitigating Risk: Ethical cultures reduce the likelihood of misconduct, fraud, and regulatory violations, thereby minimizing financial penalties and reputational damage.[8]

- Enhancing Employee Morale: Employees in ethical workplaces report higher job satisfaction and engagement. They feel empowered to voice concerns and align their actions with their personal values.
- Driving Long-Term Profitability: Ethical practices align with sustainable business strategies. By prioritizing fair dealings and transparency, organizations attract conscientious employees and clients, ensuring long-term stability and growth.

Strategies for Promoting Ethical Behavior Among Financial Advisors at the Firm Level

To institutionalize ethical behavior within financial organizations, it is essential to adopt holistic strategies that integrate structural frameworks with cultural reinforcements. A foundational element is the establishment of a code of ethics and conduct, which serves as a definitive guide for ethical decision-making.[9] This code should articulate core principles like integrity, transparency, and accountability, offering actionable guidance on resolving industry-specific ethical dilemmas. To remain relevant, the code must be easily accessible, regularly updated, and embedded into onboarding and continuous professional development initiatives.

Ethics training programs further reinforce this foundation by equipping employees with the skills to navigate complex scenarios.[10] Effective programs employ immersive techniques such as real-world case analyses and role-playing, highlighting the organizational, client, and personal repercussions of unethical behavior. Additionally, training programs can be used to proactively address evolving challenges, including artificial intelligence ethics and data privacy concerns.[11]

Fostering a culture of open communication is another critical pillar of cultural ethics, as transparency reduces fear of retaliation and promotes ethical accountability.[12] This is facilitated by establishing anonymous reporting mechanisms, promoting managerial open-door policies, and creating regular forums for discussing ethical issues.

To align behavior with organizational values, recognition and reward systems can incentivize ethical conduct.[13] Key measures include incorporating ethical considerations into performance evaluations, celebrating exemplary ethical actions, and avoiding rewards tied solely to short-term financial performance.

Finally, internal audits and monitoring ensure adherence to ethical standards through continuous oversight. Regular policy audits, data analytics to detect behavioral red flags, and corrective measures informed by past incidents safeguard institutional integrity.[14] Together, these strategies embed ethics into a financial institution's operational and cultural foundation, which helps to create a resilient and principled organizational environment.

The Role of Leadership in Setting Firm Ethical Standards

As noted at the outset of this chapter, firm leadership plays a pivotal role in shaping and sustaining an ethical culture within any financial services firm. Leaders set the tone from the top, influencing the attitudes and behaviors that permeate the workplace. Effective ethical leadership begins with modeling ethical behavior, as leaders must embody the values they seek to instill.[15] This includes demonstrating integrity in decision-making and interpersonal interactions, adhering to the same high ethical standards expected of employees, and transparently acknowledging and learning from mistakes.

Table 13.2 shows the characteristics of ethical role models at the firm level. To be an effective role model, a person must exhibit care, empathy, concern, and compassion for others. The person must also be a leader and willing to take responsibility for the actions of others.[16] Role models must strive to act with integrity, adhering to the same high standards expected of subordinates. They also must transparently learn from mistakes. Role models need to consistently communicate ethical expectations through clear messaging, provide guidance during crises, and direct engagement with others to reinforce a culture of integrity.

Accountability mechanisms are also critical reference points for those who aspire to lead others in ethical behavior. Role models need to take steps to ensure that ethical breaches are addressed impartially while recognizing and rewarding ethical behavior. Additionally, fostering ethical decision-making requires promoting decision, reward, and punishment models that prioritize long-term impacts and client interests.[17] Financial advisors must be aware of these models before being

Table 13.2 Characteristics of ethical role models

<table>
<tr><td>Interpersonal behaviors
• Care, concern, and compassion
• Supports and takes responsibility for others
• Values and maintains relationships
• Hardworking and helpful
• Accentuates the positive
• Accepts others' failures</td><td>Ethical action and expectations of self
• Honesty
• Trustworthiness
• Integrity
• Humility
• Holds self to high ethical standards
• Consistently ethical in public and private life
• Self-sacrificial
• Accepts responsibility for, and is open about, their own ethical failings</td></tr>
<tr><td>Fairness with others
• Resources distributed equitably
• Open to and solicitous of input
• Equal respect; never condescending, even in disagreements
• Offers explanations of decisions</td><td>Articulating ethical standards
• Uncompromising, consistent ethical vision
• Communicates high ethical standards
• Holds others ethically accountable
• Puts ethics above personal/company interests
• Long-term, multiple stakeholder perspective</td></tr>
<tr><td>Contextual foundations
• Frequent interaction
• Respected by others
• Business success is not essential</td><td></td></tr>
</table>

Source: Weaver, G. R., Treviño, L. K., & Agle, B. (2005). "Somebody I look up to": Ethical role models in organizations. *Organizational Dynamics*, *34*(4), 313–330

asked to engage with clients. Doing so enhances judgment and reduces biases. By embodying these principles, firm leaders and ethical role models can create a strong moral foundation that aligns individual advisor actions with organizational values.

Beyond modeling behavior, leaders must actively communicate ethical expectations to ensure alignment across the organization.[18] This involves delivering consistent messages that emphasize the importance of ethics, providing clear guidance on ethical priorities (particularly during crises), and engaging directly with employees to reinforce the organization's commitment to integrity.

To maintain an ethical culture, leaders must also establish accountability mechanisms that address ethical breaches promptly and equitably.[19] Ethical enforcement should be impartial, holding individuals accountable regardless of rank or performance, while recognizing and rewarding exemplary ethical behavior. Collaboration with compliance and risk management teams further upholds ethical standards.

Finally, fostering ethical decision-making is essential to promoting employee engagement, client retention, and firm reputation.[20] Leaders should encourage critical thinking and principled choices by promoting frameworks that prioritize client interests and long-term impacts. Firm leaders and ethics models must also provide employees with resources such as a well-written code of ethics and internal practice standards that can be used to navigate challenging situations and create an environment where diverse perspectives are welcomed to mitigate biases and enhance judgment. Through these actions, firm leaders can define and sustain an ethical organizational culture that aligns with individual and corporate values.

Case Studies: Ethical Firm Culture in Action

This chapter concludes with three hypothetical case studies. The first involves a global bank that implemented a comprehensive ethics training program coupled with a vigorous whistleblower policy. By recognizing employees who upheld ethical standards, the bank saw a significant reduction in compliance violations and an increase in employee satisfaction. The second case discusses a regional credit union that introduced a leadership initiative that required executives to lead monthly ethics discussions. This initiative strengthened trust among employees and customers, resulting in higher account retention rates. The third case illustrates how a firm can respond to a regulatory scandal. The case discusses an insurance company that revamped its incentive structure to reward long-term client satisfaction over sales volume. The firm's reputation rebounded based on these changes, and client complaints decreased dramatically.

Case Study One: Building an Ethical Foundation at Global Bank X

Global Bank X undertook a transformative initiative to cultivate an ethical organizational culture in response to growing regulatory scrutiny and internal feedback. The initiative centered around creating a comprehensive ethics training program and putting into place a rigorous whistleblower policy. This initiative was designed to address compliance challenges, enhance employee morale, and strengthen stakeholder trust, which the execu-

tive team deemed critical for sustainable success if the bank was going to achieve sales and profit targets.

At the core of this transformation was the implementation of a well-thought-out ethics training program. The program was conceived to be a mechanism that could anticipate and deal with issues at all organizational levels. Collaborating with leading academic experts, the bank's training modules ended up integrating real-world examples from the bank's files, industry examples, and role-playing exercises that mirror the complexities of ethical decision-making in client-facing roles. The training emphasized key principles such as integrity, transparency, and accountability. The program also addressed what banking experts considered emerging challenges, including data privacy concerns, sales practices, and the ethical application of artificial intelligence (AI). To ensure sustained engagement at all levels of the bank, executives incorporated ethics training into the firm's onboarding process and mandated annual refresher seminars for all employees.

Complementing the training program was the introduction of a new whistleblower policy. The policy was developed to foster a culture of openness and accountability and reduce the fear of enterprise-level retribution for those courageous enough to point out wrongdoings within the company. The policy included multiple anonymous reporting channels, supported by technology to ensure confidentiality, security, and privacy. Additionally, the bank established a dedicated ethics committee comprised of staff from all company levels to deal with whistleblower reports. The committee was tasked with reviewing reported concerns and recommending corrective actions. The company's commitment to protecting whistleblowers and addressing issues transparently reduced employee fear of retribution. Nearly all employees saw this policy as a sign of increasing fairness within the bank.

To reinforce its ethical culture, bank executives implemented a recognition program that celebrates employees who consistently demonstrate praiseworthy ethical behavior. Since implementing the program, outstanding employees have been publicly acknowledged through awards and internal communications on a monthly basis. Recipients also receive a monetary bonus. Since implementing the recognition program, the company has seen a greater adherence to ethical standards, which the bank executives believe is inspiring a sense of pride and shared responsibility among the bank's workforce.

Overall, the results were transformative. Within two years of the initiative's rollout, Global Bank X reported a substantial reduction in compliance violations. Employee satisfaction surveys revealed marked improvements in morale, with bank staff reporting enhanced trust in leadership and a more substantial commitment to the bank and the bank's mission and vision statements. External stakeholders, including regulators and customers, have also expressed their support for the changes. As one regulator pointed out, "Through its comprehensive approach to ethics training and whistleblower empowerment, Global Bank X is demonstrating the notion that fostering an ethical culture is not only a regulatory necessity but also a strategic value." By putting into place systematically organized and administered ethics programs, the bank positioned itself as a leader in ethical practice, which helped launch the bank to new sales and profit records.

Case Study Two: Ethical Leadership Initiative at Regional Credit Union Y

In a proactive effort to bolster the organization's ethical culture and strengthen stakeholder trust, Regional Credit Union Y introduced an innovative ethics leadership program. This program required organization executives to lead monthly ethics discussions with employees. These discussions aimed to create an environment of transparent, values-driven cooperation among employees. The ultimate goal was to enhance internal engagement and build external customer trust. During the first organization-wide meeting, Regional Credit Union Y's executives shared that the program was being introduced proactively rather than in response to an issue or by regulatory mandate.

The program was structured to ensure meaningful interaction between executives and employees at all levels of the organization. Each month, senior leaders facilitated discussions on core ethical principles such as fairness, accountability, and respect. These sessions incorporated transparent descriptions of the credit union's operations. Executives encouraged employees to provide feedback on "blind spots" that might lead an employee to engage in unethical behavior. Discussions also delved into exploring practical solutions to complex ethical dilemmas. Since implementing the program, topics have ranged from managing conflicts of interest to ensuring equitable treatment of credit union members.

A central element of the ethics initiative was an emphasis on creating open dialogue between senior management and employees. Executives were encouraged to share their perspectives and actively listen to employee concerns and insights. To protect privacy and anonymity, a system was put into place that allows employees to report suspicious activity without disclosing their identity. Based on the notion of fairness, the program has been successful in building a sense of inclusion by making employees feel like valued contributors to the credit union's ethical mission. To reinforce the impact of the program, the executive team has since implemented follow-up actions based on feedback from employees, credit union members, and other stakeholders.

When viewed holistically, the program has had a ripple effect on credit union growth and member satisfaction. By equipping employees with an understanding of the credit union's ethical standards and providing a voice to employees to improve standards, the program has empowered front-line employees to manage member interactions with a greater sense of transparency and empathy. Credit union members, in turn, have reported greater trust and confidence in the organization.

Overall, the program's results have exceeded the executive team's expectations. Internally, employee surveys reveal increased job satisfaction and a stronger alignment with organizational values. Employees report greater trust in the executive team and a deep appreciation for the ability to engage senior leadership in ethical discussions. Externally, the credit union has witnessed measurable improvements in member retention rates and new member growth.

This case illustrates how embedding ethics into the daily operations of a financial services organization through active employee engagement and dialogue can create an organizational culture that is ethics-driven. By positioning senior leaders as role models and creating a platform for ethical reflection, the credit union strengthened its internal cultural norms and enhanced its standing within the community.

Case Study Three: Transforming Incentive Structures at Insurance Firm Z

In the wake of a damaging regulatory scandal that exposed flaws in its sales-driven practices, Insurance Firm Z embarked on a transformative initiative to restore its reputation and realign its operations with core ethical principles. Recognizing that its existing incentive structure, which focused heavily on sales quotas, had unintentionally encouraged advisory staff to sometimes act in conflict with the interests of clients, the firm undertook a comprehensive overhaul of compensation strategies and ethical principles with the goal of prioritizing long-term client retention and satisfaction over short-term revenue.

The revamped incentive framework was designed to provide supplemental bonuses for advisors who exhibit ethical conduct, provide quality service, and sustain client relationships. Sales performance metrics were recalibrated to include measures such as client retention, feedback scores, and the resolution of client conflicts in a manner that prioritizes fairness and transparency. To ensure that the shift in the way advisory staff are paid was meaningful, measurable, and accepted, the firm integrated the new metrics into performance reviews, bonus payout structures, and promotion criteria. This happened across all levels of the firm.

Leadership played a pivotal role in facilitating the compensation transition. Some financial advisory staff expressed concerns about the shift in priorities. Others left the organization. In response, senior executives were aggressive in their communication approach. They organized meetings, workshops, and open-door meeting policies. Their rationale was simple: to reinforce the importance of rebuilding trust with clients, regulators, and stakeholders. As a way to strengthen the executive team's commitment to ethical dealings, the firm implemented training programs aimed at helping advisory and support staff navigate the new incentive system. These sessions included case studies that illustrated the benefits of prioritizing client needs and workshops to develop ethical decision-making skills. Employees who resisted the changes were terminated.

The firm also introduced mechanisms to monitor the incentive program's impact. Not only did senior management want to document the effect on sales and profits, but they also wanted to ensure accountability across the organization. A dedicated ethics and compliance team was created. The team was tasked with conducting regular reviews of client interactions, claims processes, and employee performance. Clients were encouraged (and sometimes incentivized) to provide feedback on their advisor and the firm.

The results of this strategic pivot were swift and significant. Within a year of implementing the new incentive structure, regulatory inquiries and client complaints decreased by 30%. The executive team interpreted this to mean that the program was helping to improve service quality and ethical client engagement. The firm's reputation, once tarnished, began to recover as positive client experiences started to be reported online and on media channels. Employee morale also improved, with advisory and support staff expressing a greater sense of purpose and alignment with the company's values. By prioritizing trust and ethical transparency over short-term sales and profits, Insurance Firm Z mitigated the fallout from a scandal and set a new standard for integrity and accountability in the insurance industry.

Chapter Summary

Developing an ethical culture in the financial services profession is a multifaceted endeavor requiring commitment at all organizational levels. Financial institutions can build trust and accountability by fostering procedural integrity, encouraging open communication, and prioritizing ethical leadership. An ethical culture safeguards clients and employees and ensures long-term success and resilience in an increasingly complex and regulated industry.

This chapter presented a leadership effectiveness framework that can be used to foster dialogue across a firm if the goal is to prioritize long-term growth over short-term gains. The chapter also presented a list of ethical attributes and statements to help guide the development of an ethical firm culture. Finally, the chapter offered a summary of ethical role model characteristics. These tools and the related case studies show that it is possible, through sustained efforts, for financial services firms to incorporate ethical practices that are compatible with growing sales and maximizing profits.

Chapter Resources

- Certified Financial Planner Board of Standards, Inc., Code of Ethics and Standards of Conduct: https://www.cfp.net/ethics/code-of-ethics-and-standards-of-conduct
- Department of Defense Standards of Conduct: https://dodsoco.ogc.osd.mil/Ethics-Program-Resources/Training-Materials/
- United States Agency for International Development Code of Ethics for Insurance Industry Professionals: https://pdf.usaid.gov/pdf_docs/Pnadx421.pdf

Notes

[1]Low, L. S. W., & Mohammed, A. H. (2005). The development of knowledge sharing culture in construction industry. *Proceedings of the 4th Micra Conference*. https://core.ac.uk/download/11777773.pdf.

[2]Hatcher, T., & Aragon, S. (2000a). Rationale for and development of a standard on ethics and integrity for international HRD research and practice. *Human Resource Development International, 3*(2), 207–219.

[3]Trevino, L. (1986). Ethical decision making in organizations: A person-situation interactionist model. *Academy of Management Review, 11*(3), 601–617.

[4]Cohen, D. (1993). Creating and maintaining ethical work climates: A in the workplace and implications for managing change. *Business Ethics Quarterly, 3*(4), 343–358.

[5]https://www.psc.gov.za/documents/reports/2022/FINAL_ETHICS_in_RECRUITMENT_and_SELECTION_REPORT.pdf.

[6]Jondle, D. J., & Mitchell, J. A. (n.d.). *Characteristics of ethical business cultures*. https://files.eric.ed.gov/fulltext/ED501640.pdf.

[7]Sauser Jr, W. I., & Sims, R. R. (2007). Fostering an ethical culture for business. *Human Resource Management: Contemporary Issues, Challenges, and Opportunities*, 253285.

[8]Hamel, R. (2009). Fostering an ethical culture: Rules are not enough. *Health Progress, 90*(1), 10–12.

[9]Enciso, S., Milikin, C., & O'Rourke, J. S. (2017). Corporate culture and ethics: from words to actions. *Journal of Business Strategy, 38*(6), 69–79.

[10]Delaney, J. T., & Sockell, D. (1992). Do company ethics training programs make a difference? An empirical analysis. *Journal of Business Ethics, 11*, 719–727.

[11]Geeta, M., Pooja, J., Mishra, P. N., & Park, K. (2016). Ethical behaviour in organizations: A literature review. *Journal of Research in Business and Management, 4*(1), 1–6.

[12]Gebler, D. (2006). Creating an ethical culture. *Strategic Finance, 87*(11), 28–34.

[13]Hu, Q., Adam, H., Desai, S., & Mo, S. (2024). Turning a blind eye to team members' unethical behavior: The role of reward systems. *Journal of Business Ethics*, 1–20.

[14]Hedley, T. P., & Ben-Chorin, O. (2011). Auditing and monitoring activities help uncover fraud and assess control effectiveness. *The CPA Journal, 81*(6), 68.

[15]Neubert, M. J., Carlson, D. S., Kacmar, K. M., Roberts, J. A., & Chonko, L. B. (2009). The virtuous influence of ethical leadership behavior: Evidence from the field. *Journal of Business Ethics, 90*, 157–170.

[16]Weaver, G. R., Treviño, L. K., & Agle, B. (2005). "Somebody I look up to": Ethical role models in organizations. *Organizational Dynamics, 34*(4), 313–330.

[17]Ibid.

[18]Stevens, B. (1999). Communicating ethical values: A study of employee perceptions. *Journal of Business Ethics, 20*, 113–120.

[19]Beu, D. S., & Buckley, M. R. (2004). Using accountability to create a more ethical climate. *Human Resource Management Review, 14*(1), 67–83.

[20]Laczniak, G. R., & Murphy, P. E. (1991). Fostering ethical marketing decisions. *Journal of Business Ethics, 10*, 259–271.

Emerging Trends in the Financial Services Profession

14

Chapter Outcomes
This chapter focuses on helping learners develop the ability to:

- Identify the five core technologies that are reshaping financial services: artificial intelligence and machine learning (AI/ML), RegTech and SupTech, Distributed Ledger Technology (DLT) and tokenization, open banking and APIs, and cloud/SaaS platforms.
- Evaluate the successes and limitations of technology adoption through various case examples, balancing the efficiency gains with regulatory, operational, and ethical constraints.
- Analyze the behavioral dynamics that influence technology adoption, including trust, overconfidence, resistance to change, risk perception, and gaps in digital literacy.
- Integrate insights from technology adoption and human behavior to understand how innovation can create new opportunities while also introducing new vulnerabilities within the financial services profession.

Introduction

Throughout history, technology has played a central role in shaping and transforming the way businesses and organizations function. This is particularly true in the financial services profession. What end-users experience, whether through seamless mobile banking interfaces, algorithm-driven investment platforms, or real-time

Note: This chapter was copyedited using Grammarly™ and generative AI tools to enhance clarity, grammar, and overall readability. While these tools provided suggestions and assistance in refining the text, the ideas, content, and arguments presented remain the sole work and responsibility of the authors. Any errors or inaccuracies in the final version are also the authors' responsibility.

W. Heo, J. E. Grable, *Ethics and Compliance in Financial Services*,
https://doi.org/10.1007/978-3-032-14449-2_14

fraud detection, is only the visible surface of a much deeper and more profound technological evolution. Beneath consumer-facing innovations lies the technology that is shifting how financial institutions operate, how markets function, and how regulators engage with firms, advisors, and other stakeholders. Today, technological advances are manifestations of broader scientific paradigms that are redefining how financial services are delivered, governed, and trusted.

Previous chapters presented the foundational importance of concepts like fairness, ethical culture, and regulatory compliance when delivering financial services. This chapter turns its attention squarely to the technologies that are influencing the way financial services professionals interact with clients and customers. Across the rapidly evolving financial services and technology landscape, five technological innovations are particularly consequential:

1. Artificial Intelligence and Machine Learning (AI/ML)
2. Regulatory Technology (RegTech) and Supervisory Technology (SupTech)
3. Distributed Ledger Technology (DLT) and Tokenization
4. Open Banking and Application Programming Interfaces (APIs)
5. Cloud Computing and Software-as-a-Service (SaaS) Platforms

These core technologies are not only driving operational efficiency and product innovation, but they are also fundamentally altering the behavior of financial actors, the structure of decision-making processes, and the architecture of trust. For clients, technological advances allow for more product and service choices, including whether to rely on a robo-advisor's recommendations and whether to grant third-party access to sensitive financial data. Technology also shapes feelings of confidence that personal information stored in the cloud remains secure. For institutions, technologies demand a delicate balancing act between leveraging automation and scalability and managing the attendant risks of opacity, systemic fragility, or reputational harm.

This chapter explores the role of technology in the financial services profession. The chapter aims to provide readers with an understanding of the promises of, and the vulnerabilities embedded in, today's digital finance landscape. The discussion also sets the stage for the next chapter, which broadens the perspective to examine the ethical, governance, and oversight frameworks necessary to guide responsible innovation adoption in the digital age.

Perspective

An example of how technological disruption can determine which financial institutions thrive and which fall behind is HSBC's short-lived attempt to compete with fintech disruptors through its digital payments platform, Zing.[1] Launched in early 2024, Zing was HSBC's ambitious foray into the fast-growing space of cross-border digital finance. Zing aimed to challenge market leaders like Wise and Revolut. Designed to offer multi-currency wallets, low-fee international transfers, and a unique mobile user experience, Zing was positioned as a fintech-style brand operating within a traditional banking institution. However, despite an investment of over $150 million in its first 18 months, Zing struggled to gain traction. Monthly active users remained far below expectations (under 9000 in one critical reporting period). The platform failed to deliver a compelling enough value proposition to differentiate itself from HSBC's existing offerings, such as its Global Money service.

The Zing platform's financial performance reflected deeper strategic issues. Zing incurred high operating and development costs while facing intense competition from leaner, more agile fintech players. Moreover, rather than innovating on a blank slate, HSBC had to navigate legacy systems, internal governance hurdles, and regulatory compliance burdens, all of which slowed development and limited flexibility. By early 2025, HSBC quietly shut down Zing, absorbing tens of millions of dollars in losses. HSBC publicly acknowledged that the product could not scale sustainably.[2]

This case serves as a reminder that technological development must be grounded in a clearly differentiated value proposition, strategic alignment with core business capabilities, and a deep understanding of evolving customer expectations. Financial institutions that fail to embrace and integrate innovative technologies with clarity, commitment, and customer-centric design risk being left behind by more nimble competitors. The failure of Zing underscores that launching a digital product is not the same as transforming an organization; true competitive advantage now lies in agility, user experience, and the strategic capacity to evolve alongside technological change.

Core Technologies Reshaping the Financial Services Profession

Technology adoption is no longer a way to remain competitive. Technology development, adoption, and management are now a necessity for firm survival in the financial services profession. Tools like robo-advisors, regulatory technology (RegTech) systems, blockchain-based settlement platforms, open banking ecosystems, and cloud infrastructure are no longer tools that firms hope to use. These tools are now essential elements of successful practice. These innovations are fundamentally reshaping the architecture of financial intermediation. Institutions that strategically integrate new technologies can reduce operating costs, expand access to services, and enhance long-term client relationships. Conversely, those who hesitate risk becoming obsolete in a market where digital fluency increasingly dictates relevance.

However, it is important to note that rapid technology adoption without addressing behavioral and ethical considerations can undermine the potential benefits offered by tools like RegTech and blockchain technology. Technology is not inherently value-neutral; human perceptions and institutional trust influence how technology is used.

Overconfidence in the stability of vendor platforms, client resistance to sharing sensitive data, and misinterpretations of volatility in digital assets are examples of situations where well-intentioned technological adoptions have resulted in negative financial consequences for clients, advisors, firms, and society. In comparison, firms that adopt technology with a strong commitment to transparency, inclusiveness, and client protection are more likely to build a foundation for technological progress and client-centered service models.

For consumers, the language of financial innovation often revolves around familiar terms[3] like artificial intelligence, robo-advisors, big data, blockchain, open banking, and "the cloud." These terms highlight the visible, experiential aspects of technology, including consumer-facing apps that facilitate mobile payments, platforms that automate portfolio management, and tools that allow access to financial data. However, within professional, academic, and regulatory circles, these innovations are categorized more precisely, emphasizing their operational, compliance, and systemic implications.

For instance, what retail investors might commonly refer to as "AI" or "robo-advice" is more rightly defined as artificial intelligence and machine learning (AI/ML). AI/ML encompasses the personalization of financial recommendations, predictive modeling of client behavior, and automation of advisory functions.[4] Similarly, the term "regulatory technology" is formally recognized as RegTech. RegTech includes tools designed to streamline compliance processes, whereas SupTech provides regulators with automated monitoring and supervisory capabilities.[5] The infrastructure supporting cryptocurrencies, tokenized assets, and smart contracts falls under Distributed Ledger Technology (DLT).[6] DLT has implications for trade settlements, custody, and enhancing transactional transparency. Initiatives like Europe's revised Payment Services Directive (PSD2) and Korea's MyData program are part of broader frameworks that are driving trends like open banking, which is supported by standardized APIs[7] that promote interoperability and give clients control over their financial data. Finally, the industry-wide shift from on-premises servers to digital platforms is covered under cloud computing and Software as a Service (SaaS).[8] SaaS developments not only enhance scalability and efficiency but also help firms redefine cybersecurity responsibilities and systemic risk exposures. Each of these technologies is described in more detail below.

Artificial Intelligence and Machine Learning (AI/ML)

For nearly all consumers, the phrase "artificial intelligence in finance" brings to mind specific applications, such as chatbots that handle routine banking inquiries or robo-advisors that create and manage investment portfolios. While these examples are indeed common and increasingly prominent, they represent only a small part of a much larger transformation happening with technological adoptions in financial services firms.

Artificial intelligence (AI) broadly refers to computer systems capable of performing tasks that traditionally required human intelligence, such as recognizing speech, interpreting images, or making decisions in uncertain situations. Among these, machine learning (ML) is the most widely used category in finance. Unlike traditional rule-based systems, ML models detect patterns in data and improve predictive outputs as new information becomes available.[9] This ability to adapt is especially valuable in finance, where markets are constantly changing, consumer behaviors evolve, and risk factors can arise unexpectedly.

At the forefront of these capabilities is Deep Learning, which is a subset of ML. Deep Learning utilizes multi-layered neural networks inspired by human cognitive processes.[10] Deep Learning can analyze vast and unstructured datasets, such as millions of payment transactions, streams of text from earnings calls, or voice data from customer interactions. The outcome for a firm is to improve predictive accuracy that is exponentially better than what existed just a decade ago. For financial institutions, ML and Deep Learning models translate into an unparalleled ability to detect fraud,[11] enhance credit assessments,[12] and anticipate client needs in real time.[13] Other examples of how these technologies are being used include:

- Personalized Advice: Firms are moving beyond static risk-tolerance questionnaires, for example, by combining survey responses with observed behaviors to provide customized recommendations.
- Credit Scoring: ML-driven models utilize vast amounts of non-traditional data, broadening credit access for some groups; insights gained, however, come with ethical concerns about fairness, explainability, and bias.
- Fraud Detection: Real-time anomaly detection helps protect consumers and firms from losses, although similar to credit scoring models, false positives can frustrate clients and undermine trust.
- Predictive Analytics: Firms can now predict life events for clients, including readiness for mortgage refinancing or vulnerability to selling during downturns.

Among the most visible AI/ML applications is what is termed a robo-advisor. Robo-advisors employ algorithms to recommend, construct, and automatically rebalance investment portfolios. By reducing dependency on expensive human advisors, robo-advisors have eliminated barriers to accessing professional guidance. This is particularly true for younger investors and households with modest financial means. Robo-advisors also provide advice efficiently and consistently across thousands of accounts simultaneously, as described in the following case:[14]

> *Robo-advisors such as Betterment,[15] Wealthfront,[16] and KakaoPay Securities[17] demonstrate how AI and machine learning can deliver automated, low-cost investment advice and portfolio rebalancing at scale, significantly reducing advisory costs and broadening access to financial services for mass-market consumers. By lowering barriers and democratizing advice, these platforms reshaped the investment advice industry. These firms also exposed a critical limitation, namely, clients must place trust in opaque algorithms to manage decisions traditionally handled by human advisors. Adoption of robo-advisory services slowed when transparency and assurance were lacking, which underscores the notion that behavioral trust is as essential as technical accuracy in the success of algorithmic financial services.*

Along with client and societal benefits that come from AI/ML and robo-advisors come disadvantages as well. Reliance on algorithms introduces behavioral complexities into advisory relationships. Traditionally, trust has been based on interpersonal relationships. With robo-advisors, trust shifts from a human to an algorithm (a "black box" whose workings are not easily understood). Research indicates that adoption of robo-advisors depends not only on the perceived accuracy of model outputs but also on beliefs about fairness, transparency, and human-like qualities embedded in the AI/ML systems driving the advice.[18] Clients are more inclined to use and trust robo-advisors when recommendations are clearly explained and when the system appears to be unbiased, even if the underlying algorithm's technical superiority is not clear.

Beyond investment management, AI/MI has had (and will continue to) a profound influence on the way people conceptualize behaviors and take action. Consider behavioral nudges. Nudges are subtle prompts intended to improve client outcomes.[19] Examples include reminders to save regularly, alerts about spending patterns, and notifications encouraging diversification. By integrating insights from behavioral finance into everyday financial behaviors, firms can help clients overcome inertia and promote better long-term decision-making. When used responsibly, nudges can democratize access to sophisticated financial guidance and empower clients across the socioeconomic spectrum. Consumer advocates, however, have raised concerns about over-reliance on automation and the lack of algorithmic transparency. For example, clients may follow prompts without doing enough critical evaluation, while firms might not always disclose whether nudges serve the client's interests or primarily benefit the firm.

Regardless of the advantages and disadvantages associated with AI/ML, these technologies will be increasingly used in the future. AI and ML exemplify the dual nature of technological advancement in finance. On the one hand, these tools democratize access, enhance personalization, and reinforce resilience against risks. On the other hand, they present new behavioral, ethical, and governance challenges that must be managed thoughtfully. The future of AI/ML in financial settings will depend not only on technological capabilities but also on how firms, financial advisors, clients, and regulators address these challenges.

RegTech and SupTech

Imagine making a large purchase with a credit card and receiving an instant text message asking for a purchase confirmation, or trying to make an online payment from a new device and being prompted to verify your identity through a mobile notification. These everyday safeguards serve a purpose beyond mere firm convenience. Safeguard systems are used to monitor, flag, and authenticate financial transactions in real time.

While consumers rarely use the term "RegTech," they experience regulatory influence whenever their bank checks their identity, blocks a suspicious payment, or requests additional account verification.[20] Regulatory Technology (RegTech) includes the digital tools that financial institutions use to comply with regulatory requirements. RegTech ranges from customer identity verification to anti-money laundering (AML) monitoring. Closely related is Supervisory Technology (SupTech),[21] which refers to regulators utilizing advanced technologies to oversee financial institutions and markets with greater scope and precision.

It is important to note that RegTech and SupTech are associated with AI/ML.[22] RegTech and SupTech rely heavily on AI/ML models for pattern recognition, cloud computing, scalability, and big data analytics that are used for data aggregation and reporting. For example, automated transaction monitoring employs ML algorithms to differentiate between legitimate consumer behavior and suspicious activity. At the same time, cloud-based regulatory reporting platforms enable institutions to consolidate vast amounts of data quickly and accurately. In this sense, the same algorithmic or data infrastructure can serve different functions depending on whether the model is integrated into a firm's compliance program or into a regulator's supervisory framework. This distinction highlights a broader truth: innovation in the financial services domain is shaped not only by technical capability but also by the roles, responsibilities, and incentives of the actors within the system.

A practical example illustrates how RegTech and SupTech are transforming business practices. In the past, banks relied on rigid, rule-based transaction monitoring systems that often generated excessive volumes of false positives (e.g., flagging routine payroll deposits or international remittances as suspicious). Compliance staff were easily overwhelmed with alerts, which slowed investigations and frustrated clients. ML-driven systems are much more adaptive and less prone to generating false positives. By learning from historical client behavior, these systems reduce reporting errors, which allows compliance teams (and regulators) to pursue genuinely unusual activity.

SupTech is having an equally profound impact in the regulatory field. Instead of relying solely on static, retrospective reports, regulatory agencies can now access near real-time data feeds to monitor liquidity positions, payment flows, and emerging vulnerabilities across institutions. For instance, the cloud-based aggregation of large datasets enables regulators to create more accurate system-wide dashboards that provide early warning signals before risks escalate into crises. This capability has significant implications for market oversight, systemic stability, and crisis prevention.

But as is the case with other technological developments, advancements introduce new challenges. Compliance and oversight, once labor-intensive and paper-based, are now heavily reliant on digital ecosystems and third-party vendors. Financial institutions must navigate increasingly complex relationships with RegTech providers, ensuring that outsourced tools remain reliable, secure, and free from bias. Regulators, in turn, need to trust automated reporting pipelines. Regulators today must rely on machine learning outputs and aggregated data to reflect reality, which involves placing greater trust in algorithms than human investigations to spot non-compliance patterns.

The implications of these developments are twofold. For institutions, the challenge is to integrate RegTech seamlessly into operations without relinquishing accountability for compliance failures. For regulators, the task is to leverage SupTech to strengthen oversight while maintaining transparency, fairness, and public trust. Ultimately, the adoption of RegTech and SupTech illustrates the dual nature of technological adoption in finance; namely, the same underlying infrastructures (i.e., AI, ML, cloud platforms, and data analytics) can be utilized for firm compliance or public oversight. Technology convergence signals a future where compliance and supervision are no longer parallel processes but interconnected, co-evolving across time as the financial system progresses.

Distributed Ledger Technology (DLT) and Tokenization

For most consumers, the concept of distributed ledger technology (DLT) comes from their knowledge of blockchain technology or cryptocurrencies. Bitcoin and Ethereum attract significant public attention, frequently reducing the perception of DLT to behind-the-scenes digital tokens. While blockchain is the most recognized DLT application, big-data experts prefer to use DLT to describe the underlying architecture that supports various applications that extend beyond cryptocurrencies.[23]

At its core, DLT is a decentralized method for recording and synchronizing data across a network of computers. In traditional financial systems, a trusted intermediary, like a bank, clearinghouse, or central securities depository, validates and records transactions. DLT changes this model by enabling multiple participants to maintain synchronized copies of the same ledger. Updates are collectively validated through consensus mechanisms, which can take different forms (e.g., proof-of-work, proof-of-stake, or permissioned voting protocols).

Blockchain is one specific form of DLT, where transactions are grouped into "blocks" that are cryptographically linked in sequence. Blockchain technology creates an immutable chain of records.[24] Other DLT architectures, such as directed acyclic graphs (DAGs), utilize alternative structures to achieve similar objectives of distributed validation and transparency. The underlying principle is that no single entity has exclusive control over the ledger, and any changes require collective agreement across the network.[25] In practice, DLT is used for two reasons:

1. Reduced reliance on centralized intermediaries: Validation and record-keeping can be carried out among participants in the network rather than being dependent on a single trusted authority.
2. Enhanced transparency and resilience: All participants have access to the same verified record, making manipulation, duplication, or fraud more difficult and increasing the system's robustness against single points of failure.

These attributes explain why DLT has garnered interest not only in the cryptocurrency markets but also in mainstream financial applications, such as asset tokenization, payment modernization, and post-trade settlement processes in capital markets.

A notable example of DLT in practice is tokenization. Tokenization occurs when traditional assets, such as bonds, equities, or real estate, are digitally represented on a distributed ledger. Tokenized assets can be issued, transferred, and settled more efficiently than through conventional systems. For instance, in 2021, the European Investment Bank (EIB) issued a €100 million digital bond on the Ethereum blockchain. The bond issue demonstrated the potential for faster and cheaper settlement.[26] However, the issuance also highlighted challenges related to custody, interoperability, and the durability of record-keeping, which remain significant obstacles for wider institutional adoption.

The importance of DLT in the financial services field is twofold: structural and behavioral. Structurally, DLT has the potential to transform market infrastructure by lowering costs, shortening settlement cycles, and challenging the roles of established intermediaries. Behaviorally, DLT adoption largely hinges on trust and perception. For many retail investors, the term "blockchain" still evokes images of speculative cryptocurrency trading characterized by volatility, hype, and risk. In contrast, firms are increasingly focused on programmable finance, which embeds rules, compliance checks, or contractual conditions directly into digital assets. This use of DLT opens the door to automated compliance, issuance of new financial instruments, and innovations in product design.

Open Banking and Application Programming Interfaces (APIs)

From a consumer's perspective, open banking can be seen as a platform that provides conveniences, such as the ability to link multiple bank accounts within a single app or allowing a budgeting tool to access transaction data automatically. For many consumers, the appeal of open banking is the ability to consolidate financial information into one view, which reduces friction and enables more personalized services.[27] From a financial services firm's perspective, what consumers see is just the surface of a much broader technological revolution that is shaping how financial data is governed, shared, and utilized.[28]

Formally, open banking is both a regulatory mandate and a market-driven framework that shifts control of financial data from institutions to consumers. Instead of banks acting as the sole custodians of account information, individuals now have the right to authorize access and portability of their data. The infrastructure that makes this possible is provided by Application Programming Interfaces (APIs).[29] APIs are standardized, secure protocols that allow different platforms to exchange data seamlessly. Unlike earlier practices such as "screen scraping," which required users to share their login credentials with third-party apps, APIs create auditable, transparent, and regulator-approved channels for data movement. The use of APIs results in a balance between consumer empowerment, institutional accountability, and systemic security.

It is important to understand that open banking is not a stand-alone technology like AI/ML. Instead, open banking is best viewed as a framework used for secure data portability. If AI/ML drives financial innovation, open banking provides the infrastructure (the standardized road system) that makes safe and scalable data movement possible. APIs ensure that client data can be transferred securely between institutions, while AI/ML and analytics transform that data into insights, forecasts, and tailored recommendations. In this way, open banking acts as the foundation that allows advanced analytics to function effectively across fragmented financial ecosystems. Globally, open banking has evolved through the following regulatory and market trajectories:

- In the European Union, the Revised Payment Services Directive (PSD2) mandates banks to provide API access to licensed third-party providers; PSD2 laid the groundwork for cross-border competition and innovation.[30]
- The United Kingdom's Open Banking Initiative has gone further by standardizing protocols and fostering an ecosystem of fintech firms that now offer account aggregation, digital lending, and personalized financial planning.[31]
- In Asia, Korea's MyData framework enables consumers to consolidate information across banks, insurers, and investment platforms; the MyData platform facilitates holistic financial management while stimulating competitive service offerings.[32]

Despite how open banking is transforming consumer transactions, open banking presents significant challenges related to liability, trust, and perception. For example, suppose a budgeting app misuses client data or a third-party provider experiences a security breach. In that case, consumers typically blame their bank, even when regulatory frameworks may assign responsibility elsewhere. Adoption of open banking relies not just on technical safeguards, but also on consumer trust in institutions and their perceptions of privacy.

The long-term success of open banking will require more than well-defined APIs and well-crafted regulations. Open banking necessitates a cultural shift in how clients view data ownership, risk, and responsibility in their financial relationships. Consumers must be willing to internalize the notion that financial data is theirs to control, while firms must embrace transparency and accountability in how that data is shared. When these conditions are met, open banking transcends mere consumer convenience to a platform that can serve as the foundation for innovation, competition, and more client-centered financial ecosystems.

Cloud Computing and SaaS Platforms

From a consumer's perspective, cloud computing often appears as an announcement from a bank or other financial institution that the firm has "moved to the cloud." Clients may notice smoother operating mobile apps, faster online banking, or new digital features attached to accounts, but what the consumer does not see are the deep operational issues that cloud platforms entail.[33]

At its core, cloud computing replaces in-house servers and proprietary data centers with infrastructure provided by large-scale external providers such as Amazon

Web Services (AWS),[34] Microsoft Azure,[35] and Google Cloud.[36] Instead of investing in expensive, dedicated hardware, financial institutions can lease computing power, storage, and networking capacity on demand. A closely related concept is Software as a Service (SaaS). SaaS allows firms to subscribe to applications, such as compliance monitoring, customer relationship management, or risk analytics.[37] The applications are then delivered over the internet. Together, these technology models are shifting technological adoption from being a fixed capital expense to a flexible, usage-based service expense.

The benefits of cloud services and SaaS solutions are extensive, including:

- Increased scalability that allows firms to adjust capacity instantly.
- Speed of deployment, which enables new services to be launched in weeks instead of years.
- Accessibility levels the playing field by giving smaller firms access to advanced tools that were once reserved for global institutions.
- Improved efficiency, competition, and innovative support across the financial sector.

It is important to note, however, that these gains come with notable challenges. An increasing number of firms are relying on a limited number of cloud providers. This is known as concentration risk. Concentration risk can manifest if a major cloud provider suffers an outage, cyberattack, or operational failure. If this happens, many institutions could be disrupted simultaneously. Vendor management is also a growing concern, as the responsibility for data security is now shared between a firm and its cloud partner. Regulatory bodies, including the European Banking Authority and U.S. federal agencies, are beginning to place a greater emphasis on the need for cloud services oversight, contractual safeguards, and resilience testing to ensure system-wide stability.

From a consumer perspective, trust is the central issue. Clients must feel confident that their sensitive financial and personal data is secure, private, and handled responsibly. Public perception will play a key role in the further adoption of cloud services and SaaS solutions. Even if technical safeguards are strong, a widely publicized breach at a major provider could undermine confidence across the system. The following case illustrates how consumer trust can be reduced when safeguards fail.

In 2019, Capital One experienced one of the most high-profile cloud-related breaches in banking after migrating much of its infrastructure to Amazon Web Services (AWS).[38] The move had delivered clear benefits—greater scalability, lower IT costs, and faster rollout of digital services—but a misconfigured firewall left sensitive data vulnerable, ultimately exposing the personal information of more than 100 million customers. The incident underscored a critical lesson: while cloud adoption can enhance efficiency and innovation, weak security governance and inadequate vendor oversight can transform technological advantages into systemic risks.

Table 14.1 Case examples of technology in financial services

Case	Application	Success	Limitation
Capital One Cloud Breach	Migration of infrastructure to Amazon Web Services (AWS)	Streamlined operations, reduced IT costs, faster digital service deployment	Data breach from misconfiguration; highlighted vendor oversight and governance risks
EIB Digital Bond	€100 million bond issued on Ethereum using DLT tokenization	Faster settlement, reduced costs, proof of concept for institutional tokenization	Custody challenges, legal recognition issues, and integration with existing infrastructure
UK Open Banking Initiative	Mandated API access for licensed third-party providers	Increased consumer choice, fintech competition, and innovation	Low consumer adoption due to privacy concerns and trust deficits
Robo-advisors	AI/ML algorithms for automated investment advice and rebalancing	Democratized financial advice, lowered costs, expanded access to mass-market clients	Adoption is limited by trust in opaque algorithms, the need for transparency
RegTech in AML	ML-based transaction monitoring to reduce false positives	Improved detection accuracy, lower compliance costs, and more efficient monitoring	Accountability concerns if algorithms miss genuine suspicious activity

In this sense, the future of cloud computing in finance involves the adoption of technological and behavioral insights at the firm level. Technologically, cloud services and SaaS solutions enable agility, innovation, and cost efficiency. Behaviorally, the successful rollout of cloud services and SaaS solutions depends on whether consumers, regulators, and institutions are comfortable with the trade-offs between convenience, security, and systemic reliance on a small number of cloud services and SaaS solutions vendors.

Table 14.1 provides a summary of the ways the emerging technologies discussed in this chapter are being applied in practice. Each row in the table refers to a case, the technological application, the success resulting from the technology adoption, and the limitations. As the table shows, technological innovations can improve efficiency, reduce costs, and expand access. At the same time, technologies consistently introduce new risks related to oversight, legal recognition, trust, and accountability.

Behavioral Dimensions of Technology Adoption in the Financial Services Profession

Technological adoption in the financial services profession goes beyond the need to enhance technical efficiency or regulatory compliance. The success or failure of technology adoption primarily hinges on human behavior. Specifically, how clients, institutions, and regulators perceive, trust, and interact with new technological tools. Across various domains, behavioral factors like trust, overconfidence, resistance to change, perceptions of risk, and gaps in digital literacy consistently influence adoption trajectories. Each of these factors is described below.

Trust and Transparency

Financial technology adoption cannot occur without trust. Clients are more inclined to utilize digital tools, such as robo-advisors, open banking platforms, or cloud-based services, when they believe the systems are transparent, accountable, and fair. In contrast, a lack of transparency and unclear accountability can discourage engagement, regardless of technical competence. For instance, studies conducted in Germany reveal that potential robo-advisor clients tend to be hesitant to use platforms unless they clearly understand how portfolios are built and managed.[39] When firms provide transparent explanations and human-like rationales for their recommendations, adoption rates increase. This suggests that trust hinges not only on accuracy but also on the perceived fairness, clarity, and explainability of technology-mediated financial advice.

Overconfidence in Technology

While some firms, regulators, and other stakeholders tend to be cautious about adopting technological innovations, others demonstrate excessive confidence in technology. For example, firm leadership may mistakenly assume that migrating to the cloud eliminates the need for rigorous internal oversight or that AI-driven compliance tools can completely replace human judgment. This overconfidence can lead to firm-wide vulnerabilities. Numerous global banks, for instance, were early adopters of implementing machine learning-based anti-money laundering (AML) monitoring systems.[40] At the same time, these banks cut staff, expecting algorithms to identify all suspicious transactions.[41] These banks quickly learned that technology is not foolproof. Regulators later penalized these banks for compliance failures, illustrating that automation cannot replace accountability. In this context, overconfidence poses as much of a risk as resistance. Overconfidence undermines resilience and regulatory trust.

Resistance to Change

Resistance to change is a significant barrier to technological adoption. Even when regulatory frameworks and technical safeguards are established, consumers and firms may cling to familiar practices. The United Kingdom's Open Banking Initiative serves as a notable example. Despite the successful implementation of APIs and legal protocols, many consumers were reluctant to share financial data with third-party vendors due to their preference for traditional banking methods.[42] A 2020 survey by the European Banking Authority indicated that a substantial number of EU consumers preferred traditional login methods over API-based authentication under PSD2. Organizational resistance can also be an issue. In Europe, numerous compliance officers in European banks expressed skepticism about RegTech, fearing that automation would undermine their professional judgment and diminish their roles.[43] This internal firm resistance highlights the fact that cultural acceptance often lags behind regulatory and technical readiness.

Risk Perceptions and Volatility

The way clients perceive risk also significantly influences technology adoption. For instance, DLT is often associated with volatile cryptocurrency markets. As such, some retail investors associate DLT with unsafe practices even when DLT is known to offer greater market stability and efficiency. As an example, in Japan, pilot programs for DLT-based securities settlement faced skepticism from retail investors who associated blockchain with cryptocurrency speculation.[44] This reputational bias hindered adoption, even with strong institutional safeguards and stable settlement mechanisms.[45] Here, perception outweighed technical merit, emphasizing the behavioral aspects of innovation risk.

Digital Literacy Gaps

Lastly, disparities in digital literacy create uneven technology adoption patterns. Younger, tech-savvy clients tend to embrace robo-advisors, cloud-based budgeting apps, and mobile-first financial platforms. At the same time, older and less digitally skilled consumers often struggle with aspects like passwords, multi-factor authentication, and app navigation. In the United States, research on budgeting and aggregation apps shows that many older clients hesitate in adopting technology, not due to distrust, but because they feel uncomfortable with digital interfaces. This literacy divide results in an unequal distribution of benefits, where younger, digitally fluent individuals gain early access to innovations, while others are left out. This raises important questions about inclusiveness, fairness, and access in the context of financial innovation.

Chapter Summary

Emerging technologies are transforming every aspect of the financial services profession. While consumers may notice these changes through features like robo-advisors, budgeting apps, or faster online banking, these innovations reflect much more profound shifts in institutional operations, regulatory oversight, and client decision-making processes.

This chapter explored five foundational technologies that are driving the current evolution in the industry:

1. Artificial Intelligence and Machine Learning (AI/ML)
2. Regulatory Technology (RegTech) and Supervisory Technology (SupTech)
3. Distributed Ledger Technology (DLT) and Tokenization

4. Open Banking and Application Programming Interfaces (APIs)
5. Cloud Computing and Software-as-a-Service (SaaS) Platforms

The discussion highlighted clear technological benefits, such as increased efficiency, expanded access, faster transaction settlements, and improved regulatory monitoring. However, the discussion also revealed critical challenges related to governance, legal recognition, and systemic risk. Notably, the chapter emphasized that the successful adoption of financial technologies relies not only on the competency of algorithmic outputs but also on human behavior. Factors such as trust and transparency, overreliance on automation, resistance to change, perceived risks, and gaps in digital literacy significantly influence whether these technological adoptions succeed or fail.

Chapter Resources

- Bank for International Settlements (BIS), https://www.bis.org
- Bank of England, https://www.bankofengland.co.uk
- Competition and Markets Authority (CMA, UK), https://www.gov.uk/cma
- European Banking Authority (EBA), https://www.eba.europa.eu
- European Union/EUR-Lex, https://eur-lex.europa.eu
- Financial Conduct Authority (FCA, UK), https://www.fca.org.uk
- Financial Services Commission (FSC, Korea), https://www.fsc.go.kr/eng
- Financial Stability Board (FSB), https://www.fsb.org
- International Organization of Securities Commissions (IOSCO), https://www.iosco.org
- Organisation for Economic Co-operation and Development (OECD), https://www.oecd.org
- World Bank, https://www.worldbank.org
- World Economic Forum (WEF), https://www.weforum.org

Notes

[1]Dow Jones. (2025, January 22). HSBC to close international payments app Zing a year after launch—financial news. *Dow Jones Institutional News*. Retrieved from https://www.proquest.com/wire-feeds/hsbc-close-international-payments-app-zing-year/docview/3158414116/se-2.

[2]Cruise, S. (2025, January 23). HSBC's payments app closure puts around 400 jobs at risk, source says. *Reuters*. https://www.reuters.com/business/finance/hsbcs-payments-app-closure-puts-around-400-jobs-risk-source-says-2025-01-23/.

[3]Cheryl, C. R., Darryl, G. E., Chris, J., Marc, L., Rena, M. S., David, P. W., Andrew, S. P., Gary, S., Eva, S., & Baird, W. (2020). *Fintech: Overview of innovative financial technology and selected policy issues*. U.S. Congress. https://www.congress.gov/crs-product/R46332?utm_source=chatgpt.com.

[4]Sironi, P. (2016). *FinTech innovation: From robo-advisors to goal-based investing and gamification*. Hoboken, NJ: Wiley.

[5]Arner, D. W., Barberis, J., & Buckley, R. P. (2017). FinTech, RegTech, and the Reconceptualization of Financial Regulation. *Northwestern Journal of International Law & Business, 37*(3). https://heinonline.org/HOL/LandingPage?handle=hein.journals/nwjilb37&div=17&id=&page=.

[6]Zetzsche, D. A., Buckley, R. P., Arner, D. W., & Barberis, J. N. (2020). *The future of data-driven finance and RegTech: Lessons from EU, UK, and Asia* (European Banking Institute Working Paper Series No. 65). European Banking Institute.

[7]An API (Application Programming Interface) is a standardized set of rules (and tools) that allow different software applications to communicate with each other. In the financial services domain, APIs enable secure data sharing and integration.

[8]Financial Stability Board (FSB). (2019). *Third-Party Dependencies in Cloud Services.* https://www.fsb.org/2019/12/third-party-dependencies-in-cloud-services-considerations-on-financial-stability-implications/.

[9]Goodfellow, I., Bengio, Y., & Courville, A. (2016). *Deep Learning.* MIT Press.

[10]Mienye, I. D., & Swart, T. G. (2024). A comprehensive review of deep Learning: Architectures, recent advances, and applications. Information, 15(12). https://www.mdpi.com/2078-2489/15/12/755.

[11]Chen, Y., Zhao, C., Xu, Y., Nie, C., & Zhang, Y. (2025). Deep Learning in financial fraud detection: Innovations, challenges, and applications. *Data Science and Management.* https://doi.org/10.1016/j.dsm.2025.08.002.

[12]Clements, J. M., Xu, D., Yousefi, N., & Efimov, D. (2020). *Sequential deep Learning for credit risk monitoring and tabular financial data.* arXiv, arXiv:2012.15330.

[13]Gupta, A., Dengre, V., Kheruwala, H. A., & Shah, M. (2020). Comprehensive review of text-mining applications in finance. *Financial Innovation, 6*, 39. https://doi.org/10.1186/s40854-020-00205-1.

[14]Abraham, F., Schmukler, S. L., & Tessada, J. (2019). *Robo-Advisors: Investing through machines.* Research & Policy Briefs No. 21, World Bank Group. http://documents.worldbank.org/curated/en/275041551196836758.

[15]Betterment. (n.d.). *Betterment: Smarter investing powered by technology.* Retrieved January 30, 2025, from https://www.betterment.com/.

[16]Wealthfront. (n.d.). *Wealthfront: Automated investing and banking.* Retrieved January 30, 2025, from https://www.wealthfront.com/.

[17]KakaoPay Securities. (n.d.). *KakaoPay Securities.* Retrieved January 30, 2025, from https://www.kakaocorp.com/.

[18]Kofman, P. (2025). Scoring the ethics of AI robo-advice: Why we need gateways and ratings. *Journal of Business Ethics, 198*, 21–33. https://doi.org/10.1007/s10551-024-05753-5.

[19]Leal, C. C., & Oliveira, B. (2024). Nudging financial behavior in the age of artificial intelligence. In Artificial Intelligence in Production Engineering and Management (pp. 115–144). Woodhead Publishing. https://doi.org/10.1016/B978-0-12-819471-3.00002-1.

[20]Arner, D. W., Barberis, J., & Buckley, R. P. (2017). FinTech, RegTech, and the reconceptualization of financial regulation. *Northwestern Journal of International Law & Business, 37*(3), 371–413.

[21]Prenio, J., & Broeders, D. (2018). *Innovative technology in financial supervision (suptech) - the experience of early users.* Financial Stability Institute. FSI Insights No. 9. https://www.bis.org/fsi/publ/insights9.htm.

[22]McArthy, J. (2022). The regulation of RegTech and SupTech in finance: ensuring consistency in principle and in practice. *Journal of Financial Regulation and Compliance, 31*(2), 186–199.

[23]Narayanan, A., Bonneau, J., Felten, E., Miller, A., & Goldfeder, S. (2016). *Bitcoin and cryptocurrency technologies: A comprehensive introduction.* Princeton University Press.

[24]Nakamoto, S. (2008). *Bitcoin: A peer-to-peer electronic cash system.* Bitcoin.com. https://bitcoin.org/en/bitcoin-paper.

[25]Xu, M., Chen, X., & Kou, G. (2019). A systematic review of blockchain. *Financial Innovation, 5*, 27. https://doi.org/10.1186/s40854-019-0147-z.

[26]European Investment Bank. (2021, April 27). *EIB issues its first ever digital bond on a public blockchain.* European Investment Bank. https://www.eib.org/en/press/all/2021-141-european-investment-bank-eib-issues-its-first-ever-digital-bond-on-a-public-blockchain.

[27] World Bank. (2022). *Open banking: How to design for financial inclusion.* World Bank. https://documents.worldbank.org/en/publication/documents-reports/documentdetail/351881625136775280.

[28] World Economic Forum. (2018). *The new physics of financial services: Understanding how artificial intelligence is transforming the financial ecosystem.* World Economic Forum. https://www.weforum.org/publications/the-new-physics-of-financial-services-how-artificial-intelligence-is-transforming-the-financial-ecosystem/.

[29] OECD. (2023). *Shifting from open banking to open finance: Results from the 2022 OECD survey on data sharing frameworks.* OECD Publishing. https://www.oecd.org/content/dam/oecd/en/publications/reports/2023/01/shifting-from-open-banking-to-open-finance_1a650f63/9f881c0c-en.pdf.

[30] European Parliament, & Council of the European Union. (2015). *Directive (EU) 2015/2366 on payment services in the internal market (PSD2). Official Journal of the European Union, L 337,* December 23, 2015, 35–127.

[31] Competition and Markets Authority. (2016). *Retail banking market investigation: Final report.* London: CMA. https://www.gov.uk/cma-cases/review-of-banking-for-small-and-medium-sized-businesses-smes-in-the-uk.

[32] Financial Services Commission. (2021, January 5). *Korea's MyData industry officially takes off* [Press release]. Financial Services Commission, Republic of Korea. https://www.fsc.go.kr/eng/pr010101/75989.

[33] Financial Stability Board. (2019). *Third-party dependencies in cloud services: Considerations for financial stability.* Financial Stability Board. https://www.fsb.org/2019/12/third-party-dependencies-in-cloud-services-considerations-on-financial-stability-implications/.

[34] Amazon Web Services. (n.d.). *Amazon Web Services (AWS).* Retrieved January 30, 2025, from https://aws.amazon.com/.

[35] Microsoft Azure. (n.d.). *Microsoft Azure cloud computing services.* Retrieved January 30, 2025, from https://azure.microsoft.com/.

[36] Google Cloud. (n.d.). *Google Cloud.* Retrieved January 30, 2025, from https://cloud.google.com/.

[37] Armbrust, M., Fox, A., Griffith, R., Joseph, A. D., Katz, R., Konwinski, A., ... & Zaharia, M. (2010). A view of cloud computing. *Communications of the ACM, 53*(4), 50–58. https://doi.org/10.1145/1721654.1721672.

[38] U.S. Department of Justice. (2019, August 15). *United States v. Paige Thompson.* https://www.justice.gov/usao-wdwa/united-states-v-paige-thompson.

[39] Jung, D., Dorner, V., Glaser, F., & Morana, S. (2018). Robo-advisory: Digitalization and automation of financial advisory. *Business & Information Systems Engineering, 60*(1), 81–86. https://doi.org/10.1007/s12599-018-0521-9.

[40] Financial Conduct Authority (FCA). (2019). *Machine learning in UK financial services.* FCA/Bank of England joint report.

[41] European Banking Authority (EBA). (2021). *EBA Report on RegTech in the EU Financial Sector.* See also: https://eba.europa.eu/publications-and-media/press-releases/eba-assesses-benefits-challenges-and-risks-regtech-use-eu-and.

[42] European Banking Authority (EBA). (2020). *Consumer Trends Report 2020/21.* https://eba.europa.eu/publications-and-media/press-releases/eba-assesses-consumer-trends-20202021.

[43] EY (2019). *Open Banking Opportunity Index.* EY Report. https://eyfinancialservicesthoughtgallery.ie/ey-open-banking-opportunity-index-where-open-banking-is-set-to-thrive/.

[44] Bank of Japan (2020). *Payment and Settlement Systems Report.*

[45] IOSCO (2020). *The Use of DLT in Post-Trade Processes.* https://www.ecb.europa.eu/paym/groups/shared/docs/c3c3e-joint-ami-pay-ami-seco-2020-06-29-item-3-fintech-tf-executive-summary-the-use-of-dlt-in-issuance-and-post-trade-processes.pdf.

The Evolving Role of Ethics in a Digital Age

15

Chapter Outcomes

This chapter focuses on helping learners develop the ability to:

1. Explain how a structured and consistent evaluative lens aligns technology adoption at the firm level with global compliance rules and regulations.
2. Identify practice risks and describe how risks can be converted into defined controls to address audits and quality-of-advice assurance checks.
3. Outline a practical approach for financial services firms to enhance ethics compliance processes to ensure technology adoption aligns with organizational goals and regulatory expectations.
4. Assess how technology adoption, guided by ethical compliance processes, supports the broader objectives of financial services firms.

Introduction

The previous 14 chapters provided an overview of the historical roots of ethical practice, a description of the ethical and regulatory compliance landscape, and insight into some of the most important sub-domains associated with ethical practice in the financial services profession. This chapter changes perspectives by helping readers develop the ability to recognize and interpret some of the major technological innovations, shifting market dynamics, and evolving regulatory requirements that are shaping the way firms and financial advisors work with clients.

Note: This chapter was copyedited using Grammarly™ and generative AI tools to enhance clarity, grammar, and overall readability. While these tools provided suggestions and assistance in refining the text, the ideas, content, and arguments presented remain the sole work and responsibility of the authors. Any errors or inaccuracies in the final version are also the authors' responsibility.

W. Heo, J. E. Grable, *Ethics and Compliance in Financial Services*,
https://doi.org/10.1007/978-3-032-14449-2_15

To begin with, it is important to acknowledge that it can be challenging to identify significant trends and future events that will impact the delivery of financial advice in the future. The challenge arises because senior management at firms and financial advisors with client-facing roles tend to be absorbed in day-to-day work that limits their ability to identify events that will change their future.

Consider this parallel example. For much of the twentieth century, Kodak stood as the undisputed leader in film production and photography. Its brand was synonymous with capturing memories, and at its height, the company held a dominant market share in photographic services worldwide. Kodak was so successful that it was a long-time member of the Dow Jones Industrial Average, symbolizing its place among America's corporate elite. Yet despite pioneering early digital camera technology in the 1970s, Kodak failed to embrace the digital revolution. Corporate executives feared that focusing efforts on transforming into a digital leader would cannibalize its lucrative film business. As consumer preferences shifted rapidly toward digital photography in the early 2000s, Kodak clung to its traditional business model while competitors and newcomers seized digital opportunities. In less than a decade, Kodak went from a blue-chip stock held in most household portfolios to filing for bankruptcy in 2012. This example serves as a stark reminder of how even the most established market leaders can falter when they are unable (or unwilling) to adopt new technologies that align with organizational goals, market competition, and regulatory requirements. Firms like Kodak soon disappear in the wake of disruptive innovation.

The adoption of technology is having the same effect on the financial services profession. Some changes are readily apparent, while others are more subtle. How firms and financial advisors anticipate, manage, and adapt to technology will determine if they end up like Kodak or as future market leaders.

This chapter discusses the way the adoption of technology (e.g., generative AI, open-API data sharing, distributed ledgers and tokenization, cloud-native operating models) is building firm efficiencies while simultaneously increasing advisor, firm, and systemic risks.

As will be detailed later in this chapter, the financial services profession is being reshaped by transformative technologies. The rise of artificial intelligence and machine learning (including generative AI), as two primary examples, offer new ways to analyze data, personalize services, and unlock firm efficiencies. Open-API data sharing is breaking down practice silos and enabling connectivity across platforms, while distributed ledgers and tokenization are redefining how assets can be created, transferred, and stored. Cloud-native operating models, in turn, promise scalability, flexibility, and cost savings on a once unimaginable scale.

While each of these innovations comes with opportunities to improve firm performance and client outcomes, risks also exist. These tools introduce new avenues for bias, security vulnerabilities, and operational tensions, all of which can threaten client trust and organizational flexibility.

At the same time, regulators around the world are steadily raising expectations in relation to the way firms and advisors should interact with and use these innovations. Heightened scrutiny around consumer protection, transparency, accountability, and resilience means that firms will need to elevate the role of ethics and regulatory compliance to a more prominent role in organizational structures. The challenge will be not to simply keep pace with innovation but to embed ethical considerations and compliance safeguards directly into the process of technology adoption.

This chapter takes a deliberately practical stance in discussing these innovations. The chapter identifies the changes that are reshaping practices, connects these shifts to the regulatory and fiduciary obligations that financial services professionals must meet, and provides a set of actionable tools to guide daily work with clients.

Perspective

The trends covered in this chapter (i.e., AI, RegTech, tokenization, open banking, cloud computing, and operational resilience) may appear distinct, but they share a familiar pattern. Each creates new opportunities for speed, scale, and automation. Each also introduces new firm and financial advisor risks, including the introduction of biases, the potential to increase the lack of accountability, and the promotion of failure cascades. For front-line financial advisors, it is important to understand how innovative technology is likely to change the way firms operate, learn how to adapt, and ultimately thrive using technology. To do these three things, it is first essential to cultivate a consistent method of analysis.

Rapid technological change can leave even the most seasoned financial services professionals feeling overwhelmed or uncertain. Innovations and tools promise efficiency and innovation, but without a structured way to evaluate technological promises, it is easy to feel lost or fearful of falling behind. As was the case with Kodak, falling behind often means going out of business.

A consistent framework for analyzing market innovations and technological change can help firms and financial advisors navigate uncertainty and maintain regulatory compliance. Three questions serve as the foundation to an analysis framework: (1) What risks does this innovation introduce? (2) What controls are realistic and practical? and (3) What evidence will hold up under regulatory review? These questions provide a framework for understanding fast-moving developments in light of historical reference points.

At a broader level, it is vital to remember that ethics and risk management and compliance are not static beliefs or based simply on filing out checklists. Regardless of the technological innovation that is known or unknown, ethics and regulatory compliance must serve as the foundation of firm and advisor adaptation. While it is true that the firm processes must evolve alongside technology, it is equally valid that evolution must be grounded in ethics. For financial services professionals, credibility with regulators and clients relies less on adopting the latest tool and more on demonstrating that risks have been identified and controls are embedded in daily practice.

Consider, for example, a financial planning firm that is exploring the use of a generative AI system to draft personalized client communications. At first glance, the technology appears to be efficient, saving firm advisors and staff time. However, by asking and answering the three framework questions, it is possible to envision complexities associated with generative AI. For instance, AI may introduce biased language into client communication. AI systems could generate incomplete disclosures or create texts that unintentionally mislead clients. Once these and other risks have been identified, the firm must take steps to identify and implement controls. In this case, the directive may be that all AI-generated communications must be reviewed by a certified human advisor before distribution. Finally, executives at the firm must consider the evidence in anticipation of regulatory compliance, including retaining auditable records of AI prompts, outputs, and human edits.

As this case example illustrates, adopting a structured, repeatable process for assessing technological innovation can transform disruption into opportunity. Rather than merely chasing innovations for their novelty, firms and financial advisors should ground their adoption strategies in an ethical and regulatory compliance framework to enhance client trust.

The Four Innovations and Technologies Shaping Practice Today and in the Future

Artificial Intelligence (AI) and Machine Learning (AI/ML, Including Generative AI)

Artificial Intelligence (AI) and Machine Learning (ML) are extensively used by firms of all sizes operating in the finance sector. AI and ML have already been embedded in credit scoring and fraud detection models. AI is also used for risk modeling, document summarization, and compliance. While these systems enhance efficiency and improve access to credit, regulators have expressed concerns about potential hidden algorithmic biases that could inadvertently disadvantage protected groups. This has led to enforcement actions under fair lending laws.

The use of AI/ML technologies is expected to exponentially increase over the next few decades. As a result, governance issues are coming to the forefront of regulatory compliance discussions.[1] These discussions include addressing bias and fairness issues, explainability of AI and ML models, the role of model learning, data and reporting accuracy, the role of human oversight, and appropriate regulatory documentation. In the United States, guidance on managing these issues and known (and unknown) risks can be found in supervisory standards like the Federal Reserve's SR 11-7 Guidance on Model Risk Management[2] and the National Institute of Standards and Technology (NIST)'s AI Risk Management Framework.[3]

Regulatory Technology (RegTech) and Supervisory Technology (SupTech)

RegTech and SupTech refer to technologies designed to improve compliance and supervisory oversight. These technologies are designed to enhance firm activities such as anti-money laundering and know your client (AML/KYC) screening, digital identity verification, market surveillance, and automated regulatory reporting.[4] The effectiveness of these technologies largely depends on traceability, which involves linking alerts through case management to regulatory outcomes. This point is highlighted in studies conducted by the Financial Stability Board[5] and the Hong Kong Monetary Authority.[6]

Distributed Ledger Technology (DLT) and Tokenization

Distributed Ledger Technology (DLT) and tokenization are expected to significantly transform the financial services profession. DLT is a digital system for recording transactions, where data is stored across multiple computers or nodes rather than in a single centralized database, with blockchains being the most common form of DLT. Tokenization refers to the process of representing real-world or financial assets, such as bonds, real estate, or even artwork, as digital tokens on a distributed ledger. These tokens can be traded, transferred, or settled more efficiently, often with built-in rules or conditions facilitated through smart contracts.

DLT and tokenization form the foundation for programmable assets and smart contracts, which, in the future, will fundamentally reshape how custody, settlement, and control obligations are managed in financial markets. For instance, tokenized bonds, wholesale central bank digital currency (CBDC) pilots, and digital fund structures are already operational at scale, raising new questions about transparency, enforceability, and systemic risk. Programmable assets are digital instruments that embed rules or conditions directly into their design, typically using smart contracts.[7] JPMorgan's JPM Coin exemplifies this potential by enabling instant institutional payments with logic that governs transaction execution. Smart contracts are self-executing agreements written in code on a blockchain that automatically enforces terms without the need for intermediaries. Ethereum-based decentralized finance (DeFi) protocols such as Aave and Compound showcase this model by issuing and repaying loans entirely through code.

These innovations also raise strategic questions concerning custody and settlement. Custody refers to the legal responsibility for safeguarding an asset, while settlement involves completing a transaction and transferring ownership. For example, Coinbase Custody provides institutional-grade storage for digital assets, but it also causes regulatory uncertainties regarding the segregation and protection of customer funds. Wholesale CBDCs (digital forms of central bank money intended for interbank use) are being tested in initiatives such as Project Jura, a collaborative experiment involving the Bank for International Settlements, Banque de France, and the Swiss National Bank.[8] This project successfully settled cross-border securities transactions using wholesale CBDCs, emphasizing both the promise and complexity of this technology.

Tokenized bonds present another example of these changes. Issued in digital form on a blockchain, tokenized bonds allow for near-instant settlement.[9] Issues related to safeguards to protect investor rights and clarify asset control are still being debated. The European Investment Bank's €100 million digital bond issued on Ethereum in 2021 demonstrated this capability by settling in one business day, significantly reducing the traditional five-day timeframe.[10] However, it also raised questions about custody responsibilities and investor protection. In contrast, conventional centralized ledgers that lack distributed consensus or programmable features do not present the same ethical or regulatory dilemmas. Thus, the shift from centralized to distributed models signifies not just a technical change but also a fundamental reevaluation of how trust, accountability, and oversight function in global financial systems.

Open Banking and APIs

Open banking frameworks allow consumers to grant third-party access to their account and product data. This shift in the banking and broader financial services profession is reshaping competition and innovation in the European Union,[11] the United Kingdom, [12] and the United States.[13] Specifically, open banking refers to a system in which banks provide customer account and product data to authorized third parties through standardized Application Programming Interfaces (APIs). An API is a technical interface that enables different software systems to communicate securely and consistently, allowing licensed providers to access data in real time with consumer consent.

As with other technological innovations, policymakers have expressed ethical and regulatory concerns regarding the purpose of these technologies, limitations related to data authentication, the assignment of liability when and if a data breach occurs, and the way regulators will respond across jurisdictions.[14] In the United Kingdom, open banking regulations allow third-party providers (TPPs) to aggregate account data from multiple banks. This enhances consumer choice. However, incidents of disputed liability in cases of fraud highlight the ongoing challenges related to authentication and accountability.

Cloud Computing and Software-as-a-Service (SaaS) and Third-Party Risk

Cloud computing and Software-as-a-Service (SaaS) platforms have revolutionized the operations of financial institutions by providing unparalleled scalability, flexibility, and cost efficiency. Rather than relying solely on on-premises infrastructure, firms can now access computing resources, like storage, servers, and applications, on demand via the internet. SaaS takes this a step further by allowing users to access fully managed applications hosted by third-party providers on a subscription basis, eliminating the need for local installation or maintenance.

While these models offer significant operational advantages, they also introduce new risks that are beyond an institution's direct control. One such risk is concentration risk, which occurs when too many firms depend on the same critical providers. This reliance can create systemic vulnerabilities if a single provider experiences a disruption or failure. Additionally, data residency poses another challenge. Laws and regulations in many jurisdictions specify where sensitive financial data must be stored and processed, potentially limiting cross-border operations.

In response to these challenges, U.S. regulators, including the Federal Deposit Insurance Corporation (FDIC)[15] and the Office of the Comptroller of the Currency (OCC),[16] have established expectations for third-party risk management. Their guidance emphasizes the importance of thorough due diligence before adopting cloud solutions, continuous monitoring of vendor performance, and contingency planning to ensure resilience in the event of outages or breaches. Notably, these requirements primarily apply to outsourced technology arrangements, as fully internal IT systems managed entirely in-house do not raise the same regulatory concerns.

Consider this example. The 2019 Capital One data breach exemplifies the risks involved. A misconfigured cloud service exposed the personal data of over 100 million customers, highlighting how lapses in vendor oversight and technical safeguards can lead to serious vulnerabilities. This incident underscored that cloud adoption is not just a technical choice but also a compliance and governance issue—one that necessitates ongoing vigilance from both institutions and regulators.

Operational Resilience

Operational resilience platforms are now a cornerstone of modern regulatory frameworks. Operational resilience requires financial institutions to go beyond traditional continuity planning. At their core, these frameworks obligate firms to identify the critical business services that are essential to customers and the financial system, establish precise impact tolerances for how long those services can be disrupted, rigorously test the firm's ability to remain within those tolerances, and maintain verifiable evidence of compliance.

Operational resilience differs from conventional business continuity planning, which often focuses primarily on restoring operations after an incident. Instead, operational resilience emphasizes the ability to sustain critical services during disruptions, regardless of whether the cause is a technology failure, a cyberattack, a natural disaster, or a third-party outage. The goal is to minimize customer harm and systemic risk.[17]

Regulators in the United Kingdom, including the Financial Conduct Authority (FCA),[18] the Prudential Regulation Authority (PRA),[19] and the Bank of England have already mandated operational resilience practices, setting a model that other jurisdictions are beginning to follow. Under these rules, generic business continuity plans that lack defined impact tolerances or documented testing evidence fall short of what regulators now demand. The risks of inadequate preparation are clear. In 2021, for example, a major UK retail bank suffered a prolonged outage that left customers unable to access their accounts for several days. This event drew significant public criticism and regulatory scrutiny. Incidents like this underscore the importance of proactively identifying critical services, defining the maximum acceptable level of disruption, and continuously testing the firm's ability to operate within reasonable boundaries. By embedding operational resilience frameworks and practices into risk management and compliance protocols, firms can demonstrate not only compliance but also accountability in the face of rapidly changing technological demands.

A Regulatory Control Framework for Technology Adoption in the Financial Services Profession

In the rapidly evolving financial services landscape, adopting innovative technologies such as AI/ML, blockchain, and data analytics requires a structured approach to ensure regulatory compliance and the mitigation of risks while upholding ethical standards. The following framework can be used when governing technology adoption. The framework is based on a repeatable system consisting of five interconnected elements as described by the U.S. Federal Reserve's *Guidance on Model Risk Management* (SR 11-7):[20] policy, risk assessment, implementation, monitoring, and evidence.[21] This cyclical model translates high-level regulatory principles into practical, day-to-day operations, which enables firms to proactively manage technology-related challenges while demonstrating accountability to stakeholders, regulators, and clients. By embedding this framework into their governance structures, financial institutions can foster innovation without compromising client protection, market stability, or operational resilience. The framework operates as follows:

- Policy: This foundational step establishes the overarching duties and standards that guide technology use, drawing from regulatory expectations such as fiduciary responsibilities, best-interest obligations, principles of fairness, and commitments to honesty and transparency. Policies should be clearly documented, aligned with industry guidelines, and regularly updated to reflect emerging technologies and regulatory changes, serving as the ethical compass for all subsequent actions.
- Risk Assessment: At this step of the process, firms systematically identify potential pitfalls associated with technology adoption, including risks of client harm (e.g., biased algorithms leading to discriminatory outcomes), failures in market integrity (e.g., manipulative trading facilitated by automated systems), or threats to the safety and soundness of the institution (e.g., cybersecurity vulnerabilities). This phase involves comprehensive scenario analysis, stakeholder input, and quantitative modeling to prioritize risks based on likelihood and impact.
- Implementation: Building on identified risks, the next step in the process focuses on deploying concrete controls, assigning defined roles and responsibilities, and establishing operational processes to mitigate those risks. For instance, firms might implement access controls, algorithmic audits, or third-party vendor due diligence protocols, ensuring that technology integrations are seamless, scalable, and aligned with policy objectives.
- Monitoring: At the fourth step, to verify ongoing effectiveness, firms must employ key risk indicators (KRIs) to flag potential issues early, key performance indicators (KPIs) to measure success against benchmarks and regular testing

regimes such as simulations or audits. This continuous oversight allows for real-time adjustments, helping to detect deviations from expected performance and maintain the integrity of technology-driven processes.
- Evidence: The last step in the process involves compiling and maintaining artifacts that provide tangible proof of compliance and diligence, which regulators and auditors can review. Examples include system logs, model validation reports, "model cards" detailing AI/ML system behaviors and limitations, and meeting minutes that document oversight discussions and decisions.

The steps illustrated in Fig. 15.1 create a dynamic and repeatable system that refreshes as new technologies are adopted and evaluated. The process ensures that regulatory compliance aligns with innovations in technology. In addition to following procedures outlined in the Federal Reserve's SR 11-7 policy statement, the process also corresponds with the OCC's *Third-Party Risk Management Handbook*,[22] which emphasizes the importance of vendor oversight in the context of technology adoption and the FCA's Operational Resilience Policy Statement (PS21/3), which centers on enhancing resilience against operating disruptions arising from technological breaches. By adopting this framework, firms can be better prepared to deal with regulatory requirements while improving operational efficiency and fostering trust in technology-driven financial services among clients and other stakeholders.

Here is how the framework shown in Fig. 15.1 can work in practice. This example follows the U.S. Federal Reserve's SR 11-7 guidance requirements that banks (1) define policies for model use; (2) identify risks such as bias or misuse; (3) implement controls for development and validation; (4) monitor performance through

Fig. 15.1 The dynamic and repeatable control loop framework for technology adoption

back-testing and challenger models; and (5) maintain evidence such as validation reports and governance committee minutes. Failure to follow one, some, or all these requirements can result in enforcement actions and loss of reputation at the firm level.

Consider what happened to Capital One. As discussed in Chap. 13, in 2019, the bank suffered a data breach involving a misconfigured cloud service that exposed data from over 100 million customers to hackers.[23] Regulators highlighted weaknesses at steps three (implementation) and four (monitoring) of the control loop framework. While the bank did have policies on third-party risks in place, regulators determined that insufficient controls and a lack of oversight created vulnerabilities. The bank suffered reputation harm and financial losses that could have been mitigated had it followed the framework steps more closely.

Regulatory Practice Standards and Guidelines

Although this book is primarily focused on North America, technology adoption in finance is fundamentally global. Cloud services, AI models, distributed ledgers, and open banking APIs function across borders, and their associated risks and controls extend beyond any single jurisdiction. As finance continues to merge with technology, regulatory frameworks will need to become increasingly interconnected. European Union regulations on AI and operational resilience, UK consumer standards, and U.S. approaches to open banking and model risk influence the same ecosystem. For professionals working in the financial services sector, understanding technology governance requires regional awareness and a comprehensive understanding of how global regulations interact, overlap, and sometimes diverge. The following discussion highlights some of the most important regulatory frameworks impacting the adoption and use of technology in the field.

EU Artificial Intelligence Act (AI Act)

The EU AI Act came into effect on August 1, 2024, with various obligations gradually being implemented throughout 2025 and 2026. This legislation establishes a risk-based framework for artificial intelligence. The Act imposes stricter governance requirements on "high-risk" systems in financial services. Institutions are required to implement controls that focus on documentation, testing, human oversight, and transparency. This act serves as the most comprehensive reference for creating robust AI and machine learning governance programs.[24]

EU Digital Operational Resilience Act (DORA)

DORA took effect on January 17, 2025, across the EU financial sector. This EU policy established requirements for managing information and communication technology (ICT) risks, conducting resilience testing, reporting incidents, and maintaining registers of third-party ICT providers. Financial institutions that operate in the EU are required to incorporate operational resilience testing into their core governance practices. DORA also ensures that vendors that provide ICT services are subject to direct regulatory oversight.[25]

UK Consumer Duty

The UK Financial Conduct Authority (FCA) introduced an initiative called the Consumer Duty starting in 2023. The policy signifies a major regulatory shift that requires firms to move beyond traditional compliance methodologies and actively show that they are delivering positive outcomes for retail customers.

At its core, the Consumer Duty emphasizes fairness, transparency, and the provision of high-quality customer support. Unlike previous regulations that relied heavily on disclosure, Consumer Duty mandates that firms take a proactive approach in monitoring and demonstrating customer outcomes throughout the entire product lifecycle. This means firms must continuously evaluate whether their products and services satisfy the needs of their target market, offer fair value, and operate in a manner that prevents foreseeable harm.

Additionally, the Consumer Duty imposes requirements on governance and reporting. Organizational boards are obligated to review their performance against consumer outcome metrics regularly and to take corrective actions when gaps are identified. In practice, Consumer Duty calls for a cultural shift within firms. Firms must integrate customer-centric thinking into product design, communication strategies, pricing, and post-sale support. The FCA expects firms not only to adhere to the letter of the rule but also to embody the spirit of the Duty by keeping consumer interests at the forefront of their business decisions.[26]

U.S. Open Banking and the Consumer Financial Protection Bureau's §1033 Rule

In November 2024, the Consumer Financial Protection Bureau (CFPB) finalized the Personal Financial Data Rights Rule under Section 1033 of the Dodd-Frank Act.[27] This marked a significant step toward open banking in the United States. The rule establishes a clear framework that grants consumers the right to securely access their financial information and share it with third-party providers of their choice.

On August 22, 2025, the CFPB initiated a formal reconsideration process, reflecting the complexity and ongoing debates surrounding the rule's implementation. The framework is built on several core principles, including security, informed consent, purpose limitation, and equitable access to information. The framework is designed to balance innovation in financial services with robust consumer protections.

While the main elements of the rule are in place, the detailed compliance requirements and phased implementation timelines are still being developed. As a result, financial institutions, fintech companies, and consumer advocates are closely monitoring the situation for further guidance.[7]

The U.S. Model Risk Governance Framework

In the United States, the governance of artificial intelligence (AI) and machine learning (ML) is anchored in guidance provided by the Federal Reserve and the Office of the Comptroller of the Currency, specifically the SR 11-7 Guidance on Model Risk Management discussed earlier in the chapter. This guidance serves as the foundational reference for financial institutions. The guide emphasizes the importance of rigorous model development, independent validation, and ongoing performance monitoring to mitigate risks associated with adopting complex or opaque models.

Building on this foundation, the National Institute of Standards and Technology (NIST) released the AI Risk Management Framework 1.0, along with a dedicated Generative AI Profile.[28] These standards expand the governance perspective beyond traditional model risk to encompass issues like explainability, transparency, fairness, and robustness. The NIST highlights the importance of process documentation, continuous testing, and adaptive oversight as models are adopted and implemented.

Together, these frameworks establish a baseline to help firms deal with AI/ML governance issues in supervisory and regulatory reviews. The frameworks provide a structured approach to demonstrating responsible AI practices, ensuring that models are not only technically sound but also aligned with broader ethical, operational, and compliance standards. For firms implementing AI/ML, following these standards is increasingly viewed as meeting regulatory compliance standards.

U.S. Third-Party Risk Standards

The 2023 Interagency Guidance on Third-Party Risk Management, jointly issued by the Federal Reserve, the FDIC,[29] and the OCC, established a comprehensive framework for how banks (and other financial institutions) should oversee outsourcing and other third-party relationships. This guidance outlines lifecycle expectations that cover every stage of a relationship with a third party, including:

1. Planning: Assessing the business need, potential risks, and alignment with strategic objectives before engaging a third party.
2. Due Diligence: Evaluating a prospective provider's financial condition, operational resilience, compliance practices, and overall ability to deliver services safely and reliably.
3. Contracting: Ensuring that agreements clearly define roles, responsibilities, performance standards, audit rights, and termination provisions.

4. Ongoing Monitoring: Continuously evaluating the third party's performance, security, compliance, and risk profile throughout the duration of the relationship.
5. Termination and Exit: Preparing for an orderly wind-down or transition of services to minimize disruption to critical operations.

The regulations emphasize that financial institutions must document each stage of the technology adoption lifecycle in detail to provide evidence of accountability. This documentation is deemed critical as a way to demonstrate to regulators that risks are being actively managed and that contingency plans are in place in case any issues arise.

Business Continuity and Operational Resilience Standards (U.S./UK)

In the United States, the *FFIEC Business Continuity Management* (BCM) Booklet[30] serves as the primary regulatory reference for continuity planning within the banking sector. BCM guidelines outline supervisory expectations for establishing governance structures, developing comprehensive continuity strategies, and conducting testing programs to ensure that critical operations can withstand and recover from disruptions. The standards emphasize the importance of not only creating continuity plans but also ensuring board-level oversight, implementing risk-based testing, and committing to continuous improvement as threats evolve.

In the United Kingdom, the regulatory approach is a formal operational resilience framework. The Financial Conduct Authority (FCA) and the Prudential Regulation Authority (PRA) issued Policy Statements PS21/3 and PS6/21, which introduced binding obligations for firms to incorporate resilience into their operating models. These regulations require firms to identify their most important business services, set explicit impact tolerances for maximum acceptable disruption, and conduct scenario testing to evaluate their ability to remain within those tolerances. Additionally, firms must compile and maintain detailed evidence packs to demonstrate compliance, document decision-making, and provide regulators with a clear audit trail.

Together, the U.S. and UK approaches reflect a shared recognition that resilience extends beyond traditional disaster recovery. Both frameworks underscore the necessity for comprehensive operational preparedness, continuous monitoring, and accountability at the senior management and board levels. While the U.S. guidance anchors resilience within continuity planning and governance, the UK model promotes a more outcomes-focused approach centered on protecting critical services and minimizing harm to consumers and markets.

Cross-border Data Transfer Standards

In 2023, the European Commission adopted the EU-U.S. Data Privacy Framework (DPF) adequacy decision, which re-established a lawful basis for transatlantic personal data transfers after the previous framework, the Privacy Shield, was invalidated by the Court of Justice of the European Union in the Schrems II ruling.[31] The DPF aims to enhance protections for EU citizens by introducing stronger safeguards, oversight mechanisms, and redress rights for those living in the European Union whose data is transferred to the United States. The DPF requires participating U.S. companies to adhere to enforceable data protection principles, with oversight provided by the U.S. Department of Commerce and the Federal Trade Commission.

For financial institutions and other EU-based firms that depend on U.S. vendors or service providers, the adequacy decision offers a more straightforward legal pathway for cross-border data flows. However, relying solely on the DPF is not enough to meet the comprehensive requirements of EU data protection laws. Firms are expected to complement the framework with contractual assurances, such as data protection agreements and service-level clauses, and to implement ongoing monitoring and due diligence of their third-party vendors. This layered approach helps ensure compliance with the General Data Protection Regulation (GDPR), particularly regarding the principles of accountability, data minimization, and security of processing.

In practice, firms must consider the DPF as a baseline mechanism while maintaining strong internal governance and oversight of third parties. Regulators are increasingly emphasizing that adequacy decisions do not eliminate the need for proactive risk management, especially in sensitive sectors like financial services, where cross-border data transfers are essential for critical operations.

Regulatory Summary

Table 15.1 presents a consolidated overview of the regulatory frameworks and standards discussed in the preceding sections. Collectively, these rules highlight a common regulatory expectation: firms adopting and deploying technology must do so responsibly, balancing innovation with safeguards that protect institutional stability and consumer interests. Effective implementation of technology is not just about improving operational efficiency. Technology adaptation must also enhance client and customer outcomes, strengthen resilience, and align with regulatory requirements.

At the same time, the regulatory environment is growing in complexity and becoming multi-jurisdictional. Firms face obligations that span continuity planning, operational resilience, third-party risk oversight, data privacy, and AI/ML governance. Each framework imposes detailed requirements around governance, documentation, testing, and monitoring, with regulators making clear that accountability rests at the senior management and board levels. The consequences of failing to

Table 15.1 Worldwide regulatory standards

Area	Regulatory/standard source	Core reference point
General Framework (Policy → Risk → Implementation → Monitoring → Evidence)	(U.S.) FRB, SR 11-7, Guidance on Model Risk Management; (U.S.) FDIC and OCC, Third-Party Relationships: Interagency Guidance on Risk Management (2023); (UK) FCA and PRA, Operational Resilience Policies (FCA PS21/3, PRA PS6/21); (U.S.) NIST, Risk Management Framework	Universal control lifecycle applied across domains
A.I./ML (including Generative AI)	FRB SR 11-7; NIST AI RMF 1.0; EU AI Act (2024)	Bias, drift, explainability, validation, and documentation
Reg Tech and Sup Tech	(EU) EU DORA (Digital Operational Resilience Act, 2025); (Int.) FSB and FATF guidance on AML/KYC automation	Traceability, thresholds, testing, and ICT-TPP registers
DLT/Tokenization	(Int.) ICMA DLT Bonds Reference Guide; (HK) HKMA tokenized green bonds (2024); (Prv.) BlackRock USD Institutional Liquidity Fund (BUIDL) (2024–25)	Custody, key management, code quality, and sanctions controls
Open Banking/APIs	(EU) EU PSD3/PSR proposals (2025); (UK) FCA/JROC Open Banking policies; (U.S.) CFPB §1033 Rule - Personal Financial Data Rights (PFDR) Rule (2024–25)	Consent lifecycle, purpose limitation, and liability allocation
Cloud/SaaS and Third-Party Risk	(U.S.) Interagency Third-Party Guidance (2023); (U.S.) OCC Third-Party Handbook; (EU) EU DORA ICT Registers	Concentration risk, exit plans, audit rights, and data residency
Operational Resilience	(UK) FCA/PRA PS21/3 and PS6/21; (U.S.) FFIEC Business Continuity Management Booklet (2019); (UK) Bank of England resilience standards	Impact tolerances, testing, evidence packs, and closure of actions

Note: U.S. = United States; UK = United Kingdom; EU = European Union; Int. = International organization including non-profit organization; HK = Hong Kong; Prv. = private section; FRB = Federal Reserve Board; FDIC = Federal Deposit Insurance Corporation; OCC = Office of the Comptroller of the Currency; FCA = Financial Conduct Authority; PRA = Prudential Regulatory Authority; NIST = National Institute of Standards and Technology; FSB = Financial Stability Board; FATF = Financial Action Task Force; ICMA = International Capital Market Association; HKMA = Hong Kong Monetary Authority; JROC = Joint Regulatory Oversight Committee; CFPB = Consumer Financial Protection Bureau; FFIEC = Federal Financial Institutions Examination Council.

comply can be significant, ranging from financial penalties and reputational damage to direct restrictions on business operations.

Against this backdrop, Table 15.1 serves as a reference guide, distilling the core elements of each regulation into a comparative format. The information in the table is intended to help financial services professionals quickly identify the areas of overlap, divergence, and emphasis to support regulatory compliance planning and strategic decision-making.

From Framework to Practice

Up to this point, the chapter has primarily examined the landscape of regulatory guidelines and supervisory frameworks governing the use of technology in the delivery of financial services. While these standards provide essential structure and oversight, they may appear abstract or detached from the day-to-day realities faced by financial advisors, firm managers, and other practitioners who interact directly with clients. This perceived disconnect underscores the importance of translating regulatory expectations into operationally meaningful practices that support both compliance and effective client service.

Accordingly, the remainder of this chapter shifts focus to the practical application of regulatory requirements, with particular emphasis on how firms can navigate these obligations in the context of adopting emerging and innovative technologies. By exploring the intersection of regulation and practice, the discussion aims to illustrate how complex rules can be operationalized to enhance efficiency, improve customer outcomes, and maintain regulatory alignment. In doing so, the analysis seeks to bridge the gap between the theoretical underpinnings of regulatory frameworks and the applied strategies necessary for their successful implementation within financial institutions.

AI/ML (Including Generative AI)

In practice, the main challenge with AI systems is not just the numbers they produce, but the potential bias those numbers can conceal or their tendency to become unreliable over time. Financial institutions that rely on automated credit scoring or advisory chatbots, for example, must prioritize transparency and fairness. This focus involves documenting the data used to create the model, the criteria for selecting thresholds, and conducting bias testing before implementation. Additionally, allowing a human manager to override an AI model should be a standard operational practice. Doing so serves as a regulatory safeguard. Maintaining a record of these human overrides serves as evidence of responsible use. Post-deployment monitoring is also crucial, as models can drift naturally with market changes. Regulators now expect firms to provide periodic validation reports, showing that the model continues to function within acceptable limits.

RegTech and SupTech

RegTech (regulatory technology) and SupTech (supervisory technology) refer to the use of advanced technologies (e.g., artificial intelligence, machine learning, and data analytics) to enhance regulatory compliance and supervisory oversight. RegTech solutions are typically utilized by financial institutions to streamline their compliance functions, while SupTech tools are employed by regulators to improve supervisory capabilities. Both technologies promise significant efficiency gains;

however, they can also introduce new types of risk if not carefully designed, calibrated, and governed.

A commonly referenced example is the implementation of automated systems for anti-money laundering (AML) monitoring. These systems are intended to flag suspicious transactions for further review. Still, monitoring systems are notorious for generating large volumes of false positives (i.e., alerts that indicate potential issues but ultimately prove to be non-problematic). An excessive number of false positives can overwhelm compliance teams, obscure genuinely critical alerts, and increase the likelihood of missing illicit activity. To address this, firms are encouraged to establish risk-based thresholds tailored to their specific risk profile and to update these thresholds regularly. Best practices also include dual-control reviews, where two individuals verify decisions to ensure a balance between operational efficiency and accountability.

From a regulatory standpoint, demonstrating a transparent and traceable workflow is essential when attempting to remain compliant. Regulators want to see a clear progression from "alert" to "case" to "final decision," supported by a comprehensive audit trail that records how each alert was handled and by whom. Such documentation provides evidence that the systems are functioning as intended and that appropriate human oversight is in place.

Another practical concern is the issue of vendor lock-in. Once a firm integrates a specific vendor's rules engine or compliance platform, switching to another provider can become prohibitively expensive and operationally disruptive. To mitigate this risk, institutions are advised to include exit strategies and data portability provisions in their contracts before implementation begins. This proactive approach helps ensure that the firm retains flexibility and can adapt to evolving regulatory expectations, technological advancements, or changing business needs.

Distributed Ledger Technology (DLT), Tokenization, and Smart Contracts

Distributed Ledger Technology (DLT), tokenization, and smart contracts are transforming the issuance, trading, and management of financial instruments. DLT involves digital systems, like blockchain, that record transactions across a decentralized network of computers. This structure ensures that no single party has unilateral control over data. Tokenization is the process of converting ownership rights to assets, including funds, bonds, or real estate, into digital tokens recorded on a ledger.[32] This process enables faster settlement, fractional ownership, and greater transparency. Smart contracts are self-executing computer programs that automatically enforce contractual terms when specific conditions are met, thereby eliminating the need for manual intervention.

These technologies have advanced beyond the experimental stage. For example, tokenization is no longer a speculative concept. Institutional-scale products, including sovereign green bonds, are now being issued and traded on distributed ledgers. However, the risks associated with these innovations are substantial. Coding defects in smart contracts can lock up assets or trigger unintended transfers. Additionally, weak custody arrangements for private keys (the cryptographic credentials needed to access tokens) can lead to theft or loss, and inadequate sanctions screening of tokenized transfers can expose firms to serious compliance violations.

To mitigate these risks, best practices include requiring independent code reviews of smart contracts, implementing standard operating procedures (SOPs) for private key management, and designing circuit breakers or upgrade mechanisms that allow faulty contracts to be suspended or corrected without destabilizing the larger system. From a client's perspective, firms must also provide clear and explicit disclosures about what "finality" means in the context of blockchain-based transactions. Disclosures should include describing whether and to what extent transactions can be reversed or challenged, and what forms of legal recourse are available, or not available.

Finally, evidence of control can help build client trust and ensure regulatory compliance. Evidence of control can include audit logs that capture the full lifecycle of transactions. These third-party certificates verify code quality or custody procedures and signed client acknowledgments, confirming that risks and limitations have been disclosed and understood. These measures ensure that safeguards are not merely theoretical but are actively implemented in practice.

Open Banking and APIs

The expansion of open banking (a system in which banks, fintech companies, and other third-party providers can access and share consumer financial data through secure Application Programming Interfaces [APIs])[33] is transforming how financial information flows and how services are delivered. While open banking offers opportunities for innovation, it also introduces complex regulatory requirements that vary significantly across jurisdictions, requiring firms to adopt flexible and forward-looking strategies.

In the European Union (EU), proposals for the Payment Services Directive 3 (PSD3) and the Payment Services Regulation (PSR) are still under negotiation. These frameworks are expected to update and expand rules for account access, data sharing, and payment initiation. As a result, firms must design API programs that are adaptable to evolving requirements, particularly with respect to purpose limitation (using consumer data only for explicitly consented purposes), the lifecycle of consent (ensuring that permissions are current and revocable), and liability allocation (clearly defining responsibility in the event of errors or breaches).

In the United Kingdom (UK), the Joint Regulatory Oversight Committee (JROC) and the Financial Conduct Authority (FCA) are guiding the implementation of Variable Recurring Payments (VRPs) models. VRPs allow consumers to authorize automated payments that can vary in amount.[34] Regulators are also developing a centralized access entity to manage and streamline third-party access in the future. For financial institutions, adoption patterns and VRP use cases provide early indicators of where operational and compliance controls will be most critical.

In the United States, the Consumer Financial Protection Bureau (CFPB) is taking a principles-based approach under Section 1033 of the Dodd-Frank Act, which focuses on ensuring consumers' rights to access and share their financial data rather than imposing strict timelines. Key considerations include data security, transparent access rights, and robust consent management. For practitioners, this emphasizes the importance of maintaining strong consent records, drafting clear contracts to delineate liability, and monitoring API activity to ensure compliance as the regulatory landscape continues to evolve.

Across all regions, the common thread is that financial institutions must balance innovation and operational efficiency with consumer protection, transparency, and regulatory adherence. Designing systems with adaptability and strong governance built in from the outset is critical to managing risk while capturing the benefits of open banking.

Cloud Computing, SaaS, and Third-Party Risk

Cloud computing and Software-as-a-Service (SaaS) have emerged as foundational tools in the operations of financial institutions. Cloud computing and SaaS enable scalable infrastructure, rapid application deployment, and improved operational efficiencies. However, reliance on third-party cloud providers brings about outsourcing and concentration risks that cannot be fully reduced or eliminated through internal controls. A disruption at a major cloud vendor, whether due to technical failure, cyberattack, or operational mismanagement, can affect dependent systems and raise systemic and supervisory concerns globally.

To address these risks, firms are encouraged to implement multi-region and multi-cloud architectures where feasible. Diversifying services ensures that critical workloads are distributed across multiple data centers and providers. Firms must also define recovery time objectives (RTOs), which indicate the targeted duration to restore services after an outage, and recovery point objectives (RPOs), which represent the maximum acceptable amount of data loss measured in time. RTOs and RPOs should be regularly evaluated through business continuity and disaster recovery exercises to ensure their effectiveness.

Worldwide, regulators are emphasizing the importance of data residency and sovereignty requirements, which dictate where sensitive customer and corporate data must be stored. Firms are expected to obtain formal written commitments from vendors detailing where data is stored and processed, along with the controls in place to protect it. Equally critical are exit and transfer plans. Firms that rely exclusively on a single SaaS provider without practiced disengagement procedures expose themselves to hidden operational risks, including potential service interruptions and legal or contractual complications.

To demonstrate robust oversight, firms should maintain comprehensive evidence of vendor risk management, including:

- Results from continuity and disaster recovery tests.
- Service-level reports tracking performance and uptime.
- Independent assurance certifications, such as SOC (Service Organization Control) reports and ISO standards, verify operational controls and security practices.

Together, these measures ensure that third-party and cloud-related risks are not only identified but actively monitored and managed, aligning operational practices with regulatory expectations and safeguarding both the firm and its customers from potential disruptions.

Operational Resilience

As described earlier in the chapter, operational resilience refers to an organization's ability to anticipate, withstand, recover from, and adapt to disruptions while continuing to deliver its critical products and services. Resilience concepts have emerged as a top priority for regulators because operational crises, whether cyberattacks, natural disasters, or vendor outages, rarely occur within predefined organizational sectors. Single points of failure, whether involving technology, personnel, or third-party providers, can rapidly escalate into systemic risks that affect not just the firm itself but the broader financial ecosystem.

For firms, building operational resilience begins with the identification of important business services (i.e., those activities whose disruption would have a significant impact on customers, markets, or the firm's viability). Each service should be associated with impact tolerances, which define the maximum acceptable level of disruption in terms of duration, scope, or financial loss. These tolerances serve as operational benchmarks against which the firm can assess its ability to respond effectively.

Practical operational resilience implementation requires regular scenario-based exercises, such as tabletop scenarios, which simulate crises in a controlled environment. These exercises enable senior managers to assess response effectiveness and decision-making. Resilient firms complement internal incident runbooks (i.e., step-by-step guides for employees during disruptions) with customer communication playbooks, ensuring that clients and other stakeholders remain informed and confident even during stressful events.

Regulators also expect firms to track corrective actions to completion. When disruptions occur, organizations must document lessons learned, implement improvements, and provide evidence that changes are embedded in day-to-day operations. This is where tools like exercise reports, incident timelines, and key risk indicator (KRI) dashboards come into play. These tools provide evidence that resilience planning has been translated into operational continuity and risk mitigation practices. The following case study illustrates these concepts.

Case Study

In this hypothetical case study, a wealth management firm launched an AI-driven electronic Know Your Customer (eKYC) system to onboard clients remotely using ID documents, selfies, and video checks. Initially, the system sped up onboarding and flagged more potential issues (alerts), but as usage grew, fraudsters using deepfakes (AI-generated fake videos) slipped through. Firm compliance teams were swamped with low-quality alerts, and a mule account (used for illicit funds) exposed the system's primary flaws: the system favored speed over accuracy, lacked fairness or performance checks, and had poor record-keeping, risking regulatory trouble.

What Went Wrong

The firm implemented a system prioritizing fast onboarding and high alert volumes, but without ensuring the accuracy of these alerts. Thresholds (i.e., criteria for flagging issues) were too lenient. Leniency resulted in missing signs of sophisticated fraud. Fairness audits were lacking, which created an environment that allowed biases (e.g., rejecting clients due to poor lighting) to creep into the model. Distributional drift (i.e., when fraud patterns evolve) was not monitored, which allowed the system to degrade. Weak traceability (i.e., tracking alerts to decisions) left gaps, making audits unreliable.

A Better Approach

The firm could have implemented a more effective electronic Know Your Customer (eKYC) system that both protected client data and ensured regulatory compliance. A robust system would have addressed several key issues before deployment.

- *First, risk-tiered verification is critical: high-risk clients, such as politically exposed persons (PEPs), individuals from high-fraud regions, or clients using complex financial products, require stricter identity checks. These could include challenge-response liveness probes, such as blinking or head movements on cue, and multi-modal verification, which combines identity documents, biometric scans, and device fingerprints (unique device identifiers) to confirm authenticity.*
- *Second, ongoing monitoring and validation of AI models is essential to maintain reliability and fairness. Regular audits can track distributional drift (changes in data patterns), operational performance indicators like alert-to-case conversion rates (the proportion of alerts that result in investigations), and fairness metrics to detect disparities in false rejections. System robustness can be further strengthened using challenger models (i.e., alternative models tested in parallel) and canary datasets, which are synthetic or controlled test cases designed to reveal weaknesses.*
- *Third, a dual-stage triage process ensures accuracy and efficiency. Automated scoring prioritizes alerts, followed by human quality assurance (QA) sampling, where a small percentage of alerts (typically 5–10%) are reviewed to refine model precision.*
- *Fourth, analysts require targeted training to detect sophisticated fraud, including deepfake indicators such as irregular blinks, mismatched audio-video signals, and distorted edges.*
- *Fifth, traceability and auditability are crucial. Every alert should be linked to its corresponding case, analyst decisions, and any overrides, creating a complete evidentiary trail aligned with SR 11-7 (Federal Reserve guidance on model risk) and the NIST AI Risk Management Framework (AI RMF).*

To evaluate system performance, firms should track key metrics, including model precision (the proportion of truly fraudulent alerts), recall (the proportion of frauds detected), false-positive rate (alerts incorrectly flagged), alert-to-case conversion, QA discrepancies, drift signals indicating model degradation, and fairness deltas to identify potential biases by device, network quality, or lighting conditions. In the end, while AI can dramatically enhance eKYC efficiency, speed without oversight introduces risk. A carefully designed system that is risk-tiered, continuously monitored, and fully traceable ensures effective fraud detection, equitable treatment of clients, and regulatory compliance, prioritizing quality and resilience over raw throughput.

Firm Technology Adoption Checklist

The following checklist brings together the information presented in this chapter into six practical, actionable steps that firms can use to guide the adoption of innovative technologies. The purpose of the checklist is to convert broad principles, such as risk identification, control design, and evidence collection, into daily operational practices that regulators, auditors, clients, and other stakeholders can recognize as credible. Each step in the checklist emphasizes not only what to do but also how to demonstrate regulatory compliance.

The first step is to inventory and tier all models and digital tools, including generative AI assistants. Institutions should maintain a complete register that assigns an accountable owner, a risk rating, and links each tool to governance standards such as SR 11-7 and the NIST AI Risk Management Framework (AI RMF). This ensures transparency and proportional oversight, enabling focused risk management.

The second step involves validating systems before deployment. No model or digital tool should go live without a documented validation process, including predefined fairness thresholds, drift tolerances, and a log of all human overrides of automated decisions. Validation packs should be updated regularly to demonstrate ongoing compliance and operational soundness.

Third, institutions must register all ICT third-party contracts, as required under frameworks such as DORA. A centralized third-party provider (TPP) register should document audit rights, data residency requirements, and exit or transition plans. Periodic testing of these plans ensures they are functional and enforceable.

At the fourth step, firms should set impact tolerances for critical services. By identifying essential business functions and defining maximum tolerable disruptions (e.g., downtime or service degradation), organizations can rehearse recovery through tabletop exercises and maintain evidence packs—including incident logs and corrective-action registers—for supervisory review.

Fifth, firms need to enforce consent and purpose limits in open banking. Third-party providers should only access client data for clearly defined purposes, with client consent expiring as scheduled. Continuous diligence is required, including monitoring API performance, latency, and error rates, to ensure compliance and operational reliability.

Finally, firms should take steps to strengthen tokenization pilot tests. Before launching tokenized funds or bonds, firms should embed sanctions screening and Travel Rule compliance, implement key custody standard operating procedures (SOPs), commission independent code audits, and provide explicit client disclosures regarding transaction finality, recourse, and associated risks.

The following checklist can be used to ensure effective management, validation, and compliance of technology-driven systems. The checklist balances automation, risk management, and regulatory compliance:

1. Inventory and Tier Models/Tools
    - **Create a Model Register**: Document all AI models/tools, including:
        - **Owner**: Assign a responsible team or individual for oversight.
        - **Risk Rating**: Classify models by risk level (e.g., high for models handling high-risk clients like PEPs).
        - **Governance Links**: Reference policies, procedures, or frameworks (e.g., SR 11-7, NIST AI RMF).
    - **Update Regularly**: Review and update the register quarterly to reflect new models or changes.
    - **Purpose**: Ensure all models are tracked, prioritized by risk, and aligned with governance standards.
2. Validate Before Deployment
    - **Document Pre-deployment Validation**:
        - Evaluate model performance (e.g., precision, recall, false-positive rates).
        - Set risk-based thresholds (e.g., stricter for high-risk clients).
        - Define human override policies (e.g., when analysts can bypass alerts).
    - **Maintain Validation Packs**: Store test results, threshold settings, and override logs.
    - **Schedule Regular Updates**: Revalidate models quarterly to address drift or new fraud patterns.
    - **Purpose**: Confirm models are effective and fair before use, with evidence for audits.
3. Register ICT Third-Party Contracts
    - **Centralize Contracts**: Maintain a repository of all third-party provider (TPP) contracts for AI systems.
    - **Define Key Clauses**:
        - **Audit Rights**: Ensure access to TPP systems for compliance checks.
        - **Data Protections**: Specify data handling and security requirements.
        - **Exit Strategies**: Outline termination and data transition plans.
    - **Test Transition Plans**: Conduct annual rehearsals to ensure smooth provider switches.
    - **Purpose**: Mitigate risks from third-party dependencies and ensure regulatory compliance.
4. Set Impact Tolerances for Critical Services
    - **Assign Tolerances**: Define acceptable downtime or performance thresholds for critical AI services (e.g., eKYC downtime < 1 hour).
    - **Rehearse Recovery Exercises**: Simulate disruptions (e.g., system outages) to assess recovery plans.
    - **Store Evidence Packs**: Document exercise outcomes, recovery times, and lessons learned.

- **Purpose**: Ensure critical services remain resilient under stress, with proof of preparedness.

5. Enforce Consent and Purpose Limits in Open Banking

   - **Define Access Controls**: Specify what data third parties can access in open banking setups.
   - **Monitor TPP Performance**: Track third-party compliance with consent terms via KPIs (e.g., unauthorized access attempts).
   - **Manage Consent Lifecycles**: Implement systems to renew, revoke, or remove client consents.
   - **Purpose**: Protect client data and ensure compliance with open banking regulations.

6. Strengthen Tokenization Pilots

   - **Integrate Screening**: Embed sanctions and Travel Rule checks (e.g., for crypto transactions) in tokenization processes.
   - **Implement Custody SOPs**: Define standard operating procedures for secure asset custody.
   - **Audit Code**: Regularly review tokenization code for vulnerabilities.
   - **Provide Client Disclosures**: Clearly communicate tokenization risks and limits to clients.
   - **Purpose**: Enhance security and transparency in emerging tech like tokenization.

Table 15.2 consolidates the major themes of the chapter into a risk–control–evidence view, translating what was presented in the chapter into operational steps. Each row identifies a key risk, the corresponding control to mitigate the risk, the monitoring activities that track policy effectiveness, and the types of evidence necessary to demonstrate regulatory compliance. For example, AI bias against specific client segments can be managed through pre-deployment fairness testing and quarterly bias and drift dashboards, monitored through key risk indicators (KRIs) by segment and drift alerts, with evidence including validation reports and remediation tickets aligned with SR 11-7 and the NIST AI Risk Management Framework (AI RMF). Similarly, risks such as misuse of client data by third-party providers (TPPs), smart-contract defects, cloud outages, or alert fatigue in RegTech platforms can be mapped to practical controls, monitoring measures, and evidence that satisfy regulatory expectations.

By moving systematically from "what can go wrong" (risk) to "how to respond" (control) and "how to prove it" (evidence), this matrix reinforces the chapter's central message: assurance in financial technology is not solely achieved through system design but through continuous monitoring, disciplined control, and credible documentation.

Table 15.2 Risks–controls–evidence matrix

Risks (trend)	Control (how)	Monitoring	Evidence (prove it)
AI bias against a client segment	Pre-deployment fairness tests; quarterly bias and drift dashboards	Key risk indicators by client segment; drift alerts versus service-level agreements (SLAs)	Validation report; dashboard snapshots; remediation tickets (SR 11-7, NIST AI RMF): federalreserve.gov; nvlpubs.nist.gov
TPP misusing client data (open banking)	Consent lifecycle management (obtain/refresh/revoke); data minimization; TPP due diligence	Consent revocations; access-scope anomalies	Consent registry; TPP onboarding pack; API logs (JROC/FCA): fca.org.uk
Smart-contract defect	Independent code review; circuit-breaker and patch SOPs	Time-to-patch; incident counts	Code review report; patch runbook; post-incident actions (HKMA tokenized bond precedent): hkma.gov.hk
Cloud outage/ vendor cascade	Multi-region deployment; tested recovery time objective (RTO)/recovery point objective (RPO); exit plan	Disaster recovery (DR) exercise outcomes; SLA breaches	DR test report; SLA evidence; exit-plan drill (DORA/US interagency guidance): eiopa.europa.eu; fdic.gov
Alert fatigue (RegTech)	Risk-based alert thresholds; QA sampling; analyst training	Percentage of true-positive alerts; time-to-resolution	Tuning logs; QA results; training roster

Chapter Summary

This chapter examined how emerging technologies and evolving regulatory expectations are reshaping ethics and compliance in the financial services sector. To bridge the gap between abstract trends and operational practice, the chapter applied a structured lens of policy, risk, implementation, monitoring, and evidence. This framework can be used to translate broad technology adoption concerns into specific, testable controls that meet regulatory requirements and compliance team expectations. Documentation was emphasized as a foundation of regulatory compliance. Firms are increasingly expected to maintain validation reports, override logs, fairness dashboards, and incident records that demonstrate ongoing compliance. Tools such as the risk–control–evidence matrix and the practitioner checklist can be used to obtain actionable reference points (these tools are not intended to replace detailed guidance or case studies).

The overall takeaway from this chapter is that financial innovation and regulatory scrutiny are advancing in parallel. Ethics and compliance are not sustained simply by adopting technology. At the firm level, being regulatory compliant with technology requires embedding risk awareness, disciplined controls, and credible evidence into every stage of adoption and oversight. Firms that operationalize these principles can leverage emerging technologies while maintaining trust, resilience, and regulatory compliance.

Chapter Resources

- Bank of England: https://www.bankofengland.co.uk/
- Business Continuity and Operational Resilience Standards: https://occ.gov/news-issuances/bulletins/2020/bulletin-2020-94.html
- Cross-Border Data Transfer Standards: https://globaldataalliance.org/wp-content/uploads/2021/07/03022021gdacrossborderdatapolicyprinciples.pdf
- EU Artificial Intelligence Act (AI Act): https://artificialintelligenceact.eu/the-act/
- EU Digital Operational Resilience Act (DORA): https://www.eiopa.europa.eu/digital-operational-resilience-act-dora_en
- FCA's Operational Resilience Policy Statement (PS21/3): https://www.fca.org.uk/publications/policy-statements/ps21-3-building-operational-resilience
- Financial Conduct Authority (FCA): https://www.fca.org.uk/
- Model Risk Governance Framework: https://www.federalreserve.gov/supervisionreg/srletters/sr1107.htm
- National Institute of Standards and Technology (NIST) released the AI Risk Management Framework 1.0: https://www.nist.gov/itl/ai-risk-management-framework
- OCC's Third-Party Risk Management Handbook: https://www.occ.gov/news-issuances/bulletins/2023/bulletin-2023-17.html
- Prudential Regulation Authority (PRA) (PS21/3 and PS6/21): https://www.bankofengland.co.uk/-/media/boe/files/prudential-regulation/policy-statement/2021/march/ps621.pdf?la=en&hash=A15AE3F7E18CA731ACD30B34DF3A5EA487A9FC11
- U.S. Federal Reserve's Guidance on Model Risk Management (SR 11-7): https://www.federalreserve.gov/supervisionreg/srletters/sr1107.htm
- U.S. Open Banking and the Consumer Financial Protection Bureau's §1033 Rule: https://www.consumerfinance.gov/about-us/newsroom/cfpb-finalizes-personal-financial-data-rights-rule-to-boost-competition-protect-privacy-and-give-families-more-choice-in-financial-services/
- UK Consumer Duty: https://www.fca.org.uk/firms/consumer-duty

Notes

[1]Simple rule-based IT systems, which do not learn or adapt, are typically not included in discussions about ethics and regulatory compliance.

[2]https://www.federalreserve.gov/supervisionreg/srletters/sr1107.htm.

[3]https://www.nist.gov/itl/ai-risk-management-framework.

[4]It is important to note that general enterprise IT systems, such as payroll or email systems, do not contribute to regulatory or supervisory functions and are not relevant to this discussion. For exam-

ple, the Monetary Authority of Singapore has actively encouraged the adoption of RegTech for anti-money laundering monitoring. This approach enables the tracking of suspicious transaction alerts through to enforcement outcomes, thereby reducing false positives and enhancing supervisory trust.

[5]https://www.fsb.org/.

[6]https://www.hkma.gov.hk/eng.

[7]https://www.imf.org/en/Publications/WP/Issues/2024/08/15/Programmability-in-Payment-and-Settlement-553493.

[8]https://www.bis.org/about/bisih/topics/cbdc/jura.htm.

[9]https://www.bis.org/publ/bisbull107.htm.

[10]https://www.eib.org/en/stories/cryptocurrency-blockchain-bonds.

[11]https://www.europarl.europa.eu/thinktank/en/document/EPRS_BRI(2025)775891.

[12]https://www.fca.org.uk/news/news-stories/fca-shares-feedback-new-standard-setting-body-open-banking.

[13]https://www.consumerfinance.gov/about-us/newsroom/cfpb-launches-process-to-recognize-open-banking-standards/.

[14]Proprietary data feeds or integrations that do not involve consumer consent are typically excluded from regulatory oversight.

[15]https://www.fdic.gov/banker-resource-center/information-technology-it-and-cybersecurity.

[16]https://www.occ.gov/news-issuances/bulletins/2020/bulletin-2020-46.html.

[17]https://occ.gov/news-issuances/bulletins/2020/bulletin-2020-94.html.

[18]https://www.fca.org.uk/publications/policy-statements/ps21-3-building-operational-resilience.

[19]https://www.bankofengland.co.uk/prudential-regulation/prudential-and-resolution-policy-index/banking/operational-resilience.

[20]SR 11-7 describes a framework with governance/policies, risk assessment, model development/implementation/use, ongoing monitoring, and outcomes analysis (serving as evidence).

[21]https://www.federalreserve.gov/supervisionreg/srletters/SR1107.htm.

[22]https://www.occ.gov/news-issuances/bulletins/2023/bulletin-2023-17.html.

[23]https://consumer.ftc.gov/capital-one-data-breach-time-check-your-credit-report.

[24]https://artificialintelligenceact.eu/.

[25]https://www.eiopa.europa.eu/digital-operational-resilience-act-dora_en.

[26]https://www.fca.org.uk/firms/consumer-duty.

[27]https://www.consumerfinance.gov/rules-policy/notice-opportunities-comment/archive-closed/dodd-frank-act-section-1033-consumer-access-to-financial-records/.

[28]https://www.nist.gov/itl/ai-risk-management-framework.

[29]https://www.fdic.gov/news/press-releases/2023/pr23065.html.

[30]https://ithandbook.ffiec.gov/it-booklets/business-continuity-management.

[31]https://ec.europa.eu/commission/presscorner/detail/en/ip_23_3721.

[32]https://www.reuters.com/practical-law-the-journal/transactional/asset-tokenization-2024-06-01/.

[33]https://www.bostonfed.org/publications/payment-strategies/modernizing-us-financial-services-with-open-banking-and-apis.aspx.

[34]https://www.psr.org.uk/publications/working-group-and-payments-forum/variable-recurring-payments-non-sweeping-working-group-terms-of-reference/.

Conclusion and Future Directions

16

Chapter Outcomes
This chapter focuses on helping learners develop the ability to:

1. Explain the importance of ongoing ethical vigilance at the financial advisor, firm, and market levels.
2. Use ethical theories and frameworks, such as deontology, consequentialism, and virtue ethics, to analyze and resolve ethical dilemmas in hypothetical financial services case studies.
3. Identify and assess compliance risks related to technology adoption, insider trading, and data privacy.
4. Apply relevant regulatory standards from bodies like the SEC, FINRA, and GDPR when conceptualizing risk management and compliance situations.
5. Recognize how behavioral biases (e.g., overconfidence, rationalization) and psychological factors contribute to ethical lapses in financial services practice.
6. Evaluate how leadership decisions and firm culture impact ethical outcomes, including transparency, client trust, and compliance in technology-driven and crisis scenarios.
7. Propose practical strategies to address conflicts of interest, ensure transparency, and mitigate risks in financial services, drawing on lessons from case studies.

Introduction

The financial services profession operates in an environment of constant change. Markets evolve, technologies emerge, and regulatory expectations expand. Yet one principle remains unchanged, namely, the profession's ability to function depends on building, managing, and defending trust. Over the course of 15 chapters, this book discusses the theoretical foundations of ethical practice; the role of regulatory frameworks in shaping the delivery of financial services; the cognitive, behavioral,

W. Heo, J. E. Grable, *Ethics and Compliance in Financial Services*,
https://doi.org/10.1007/978-3-032-14449-2_16

and psychological biases associated with unethical behavior; and the technological advances that are shaping the profession. A key takeaway from the book is that regulatory compliance and ethical practice are more than merely legal obligations. Acting ethically by focusing first and foremost on client outcomes should be a strategic imperative for firms and financial services professionals.

Key Themes Across the Chapters

This book explored ethics and compliance in the financial services profession using multiple perspectives. The foundations of ethical practice and regulatory compliance were introduced first. Definitions and frameworks were presented to ground ethical behavior in established norms. Next, core theories associated with ethical practice were presented. Of particular importance were utilitarianism, deontology, virtue ethics, and fiduciary principles. Ethical behavior was then described using psychological and behavioral perspectives, including moral disengagement, ethical fading, overconfidence, and decision-making biases. The discussion highlighted why misconduct can sometimes occur even among well-intentioned professionals. Risk mitigation strategies were presented to help firms and financial advisors deal with potential harm arising from biases. The regulatory environment was then examined to illustrate how laws and regulatory oversight influence financial practices. Historical developments, including the Securities Act, the Investment Advisers Act, and the Dodd–Frank Act, were discussed to illustrate how regulation has evolved to protect investors, stabilize markets, and address systemic market weaknesses. Attention then turned to specific areas of ethical concern, including client-facing roles, insider trading, market manipulation, cybersecurity threats, and the obligation to treat clients fairly. Case-based scenarios underscored the importance of fiduciary and best-interest standards, showing that these principles are not abstract ideals but necessary safeguards in complex financial interactions. The last third of the book focused on the adoption of innovative technologies. The benefits and potential harms associated with technological advancements were discussed.

Case Studies and Practical Applications

The book also presented real-world case studies and practical applications as a way to demonstrate the consequences of ethical lapses. The cases demonstrated that issues related to firm culture, weak regulatory oversight, toxic sales incentives, and organizational compliance lapses can cause harm at the firm, the financial advisor, and the market levels. A core takeaway from the cases presented throughout the book is that misconduct is rarely an isolated event. Instead, ethical misconduct typically reflects system-wide vulnerabilities. Combating fraud and ethical lapses requires vigilant oversight and a strong culture of accountability.

Future technological trends and challenges were considered. A focus of the discussion was on the potential disruptive impact of technology. Artificial intelligence (AI), RegTech, distributed ledgers, open banking, and cloud computing were defined and discussed. As noted throughout the discussion, these technologies promise greater efficiency and the opportunity to democratize access to financial services; however, these same technologies also pose the introduction of risks like biases, disclosure opacity, and operational fragility. The degree to which technological innovations strengthen or undermine the financial services profession will depend on governance frameworks, regulatory adaptation, and institutional resilience.

Looking Forward

The future of the financial services profession, as exemplified by the learning outcomes of this book, is one where ethical integrity, regulatory compliance, and technology adoption converge to redefine trust and accountability. As financial institutions increasingly integrate advanced technologies like artificial intelligence, distributed ledger technology, and cloud platforms, the ability to apply ethical frameworks (e.g., deontology, consequentialism, and virtue ethics) will be a differentiating factor in helping firms navigate complex dilemmas. Regulatory frameworks, informed by history, and regulatory bodies like the SEC, FINRA, and GDPR will need to evolve to address emerging risks, such as data breaches and insider trading. Firms must also adapt by adopting structured evaluative lenses to align innovation with compliance.

Cognitive, behavioral, and psychological insights will continue to play a pivotal role in shaping the way firms and financial advisors deliver financial services. Enabling professionals to mitigate biases like overconfidence and rationalization is something firms and regulators need to focus on in the future. Fostering an initiative-taking compliance culture that prioritizes transparency and client protection will also be of importance. Firm leadership will be instrumental in embedding ethical standards into a firm's culture. The future will see financial services firms not only meet regulatory expectations but also leverage ethical reasoning and risk mitigation strategies to enhance client relationships, safeguard market integrity, and drive sustainable growth in an increasingly competitive and litigious global economy. The following discussion highlights a few of the core takeaways from the previous chapters.

Trust Is the Profession's Currency

The history of financial services has repeatedly shown that trust, once broken, is exceedingly difficult to restore. The collapse of confidence during financial crises demonstrates that client relationships and market stability depend, in large part, on the credibility of firms and financial advisors.

Culture Shapes Compliance

Regulatory frameworks set necessary boundaries to guide the ethical delivery of financial services. Still, compliance failures arise, even with regulatory guidelines in place, when organizational culture and leadership do not reinforce ethical norms. As all the cases presented in this book reveal, rules alone cannot prevent misconduct if incentive structures reward short-term gains over long-term responsibility.

Cognitive, Behavioral, and Psychological Factors Matter

Overconfidence, herd behavior, groupthink, and ethical fading, among a long list of cognitive, behavioral, and psychological biases, were shown to be recurring drivers of misconduct. As described in this book, individuals rarely set out to act unethically. Those who commit fraud slide into misconduct under pressure, ambiguity, or social influence. Recognizing these tendencies in individuals and organizations is essential for prevention.

Integration Is Essential

Rather than viewing ethics, risk management, regulatory compliance, and technology as siloed concepts, this book shows that these issues are, in fact, highly interrelated. Fragmented risk management and compliance approaches invite gaps where misconduct thrives or risks are overlooked. The rise of RegTech, distributed ledgers, and open banking illustrates how innovation creates opportunities and vulnerabilities. Integrating compliance, governance, and technology into unified and coherent frameworks ensures that financial firms (and those who work at firms) remain resilient in the face of ethical disruptions.

Evolving Technologies

Artificial intelligence, machine learning, and tokenization are already reshaping the delivery of financial advice. As discussed throughout this book, AI/ML and automation are being used to improve compliance monitoring but not without reputational costs for firms that either misuse or do not implement technologies appropriately. In the future, firms must pair innovation with explainability, resilience testing, and independent oversight if technology is to enhance rather than erode public trust.

Global Regulation

Increasing regulatory and compliance alignment across jurisdictions is producing a new challenge for firms that are accustomed to operating in one country. ESG reporting standards, anti-money laundering enforcement, and international data privacy frameworks are placing new obligations on firms, which directly shape the way financial advice is delivered. Firms of all sizes will need to implement compliance systems that anticipate regulatory convergence in order to stay competitive and in step with local and international laws.

Client-Centered Standards

As discussed in the book, regulatory and professional bodies are moving beyond suitability tests to reinforce fiduciary and best-interest requirements. The cases in the book demonstrate how lapses in fair treatment harm vulnerable populations, particularly elderly clients who tend to be fraud targets and those who are digitally excluded. Future standards will measure professionalism not just by avoiding harm but by demonstrating equity and inclusion in service delivery.

Ethics as a Strategy

Ethics, once treated as a firm cost, is becoming a differentiator among firms as they compete for clients. Unethical practices reveal how short-term incentives can destroy a firm's and a financial advisor's reputation, as well as sales and profits. Competitive advantage will increasingly shift to firms that embed ethics into branding, governance, and incentive structures.

Education and Continuous Training

As discussed throughout the book's chapters, factors like overconfidence, groupthink, and ethical fading show up time and again as causes of moral lapses. A core takeaway is that misconduct is rarely about ignorance of regulations. Instead, misconduct occurs when risk management and compliance systems fail to remain vigilant. In the future, professional development will likely shift from periodic compliance refresher courses to continuous training in behavioral awareness, ethical decision-making, and adaptive risk management.

Hypothetical Case Studies in Ethics, Compliance, and Technology in Financial Services

This chapter concludes by presenting three hypothetical case studies that integrate the ethical, regulatory, and technological concepts covered in the previous chapters. Each case is followed by five multiple-choice questions designed to reinforce key learning outcomes. The cases and questions are designed to encourage learners to apply ethical frameworks, regulatory knowledge, and risk mitigation strategies to real-world scenarios.

Case Study 1: The AI-Driven Advisory Dilemma

BrightFuture Wealth Management, a mid-sized financial advisory firm, recently implemented an AI-driven robo-advisor platform to provide personalized investment recommendations to clients. The platform promises cost efficiency and scalability, aligning with the firm's goal to expand its client base. However, during an internal audit, it was discovered that the AI system occasionally recommended high-risk investment products to conservative clients. The issue was related to an algorithmic bias favoring higher-commission products. This issue went unnoticed for months because the firm's leadership prioritized rapid technology adoption over thorough testing and compliance checks. Additionally, the firm failed to disclose the AI's decision-making process to its clients, which raised concerns about transparency in disclosure. As a financial advisor in the firm who noticed discrepancies, you faced a dilemma: report the issue to regulators, risking a hit to the firm's reputation, or address the issue internally, potentially facing resistance from leadership focused on short-term profits.

This case draws on themes from Chaps. 1, 2, 3, 9, 12, 13, 14, and 15, including ethical decision-making, transparency, regulatory compliance, technology adoption risks, and the role of leadership in fostering an ethical culture. Based on information from these chapters, answer the following questions:

1. Which ethical framework from Chap. 3 could best guide the junior advisor's decision to report the AI issue?[1]

   (a) Consequentialism
   (b) Deontology
   (c) Virtue ethics
   (d) Utilitarianism

2. What regulatory principle from Chap. 5 is most relevant to the firm's failure to disclose the role of AI in the decision-making process?[2]

   (a) Procedural fairness
   (b) Transparency
   (c) Distributive fairness
   (d) Interactional fairness

3. Which behavioral bias from Chap. 4 likely contributed to the firm's leadership's oversight in evaluating the AI platform?[3]

   (a) Confirmation bias
   (b) Overconfidence
   (c) Herd mentality
   (d) Loss aversion

4. What strategy from Chap. 12 could help BrightFuture Wealth Management foster an ethical culture to prevent such issues?[4]

(a) Implementing stricter sales targets
(b) Encouraging open communication
(c) Reducing compliance training
(d) Outsourcing audit functions

5. How does this case relate to the risks of technology adoption discussed in Chap. 14?[5]

   (a) It highlights the need for digital literacy among clients
   (b) It shows how technology can introduce new compliance vulnerabilities
   (c) It demonstrates the efficiency of AI in reducing costs
   (d) It underscores the irrelevance of regulatory oversight in tech adoption

Case Study 2: The Insider Trading Temptation

Jessica, a senior portfolio manager at GlobalTrust Investments, overhears a conversation at a corporate event about a pending merger between two major clients of the firm. Although the information is not yet public, acting on it could yield significant profits for her clients and boost her performance metrics. Jessica faces pressure from the firm's senior management to deliver strong quarterly results. She rationalizes that using the information could benefit her clients without harming the market. However, she is aware of the legal and ethical implications of insider trading. Meanwhile, the firm's compliance team has been understaffed, which Jessica believes will make it harder for any trading to be uncovered. Jessica must decide whether to act on the information, disclose the information to her compliance officer, or ignore what she heard entirely.

This case connects to Chaps. 1, 4, 5, 6, 8, and 11, addressing insider trading, ethical decision-making, regulatory oversight, behavioral biases, and the importance of compliance culture. Based on information from these chapters, answer the following questions:

1. Which concept from Chap. 8 is most relevant to Jessica's potential decision to act on the merger information?[6]

   (a) Market manipulation
   (b) Insider trading
   (c) Data privacy
   (d) Procedural fairness

2. What psychological factor from Chap. 4 might influence Jessica's rationalization to use the insider information?[7]

   (a) Overconfidence
   (b) Confirmation bias

   (c) Rationalization
   (d) Loss aversion

3. Which regulatory body from Chap. 6 would investigate Jessica's actions if she trades on the information?[8]
   (a) Certified Financial Planner Board (CFP Board)
   (b) Securities and Exchange Commission (SEC)
   (c) Financial Industry Regulatory Authority (FINRA)
   (d) Both b and c
4. What lesson from Chap. 11 could help GlobalTrust Investments prevent such ethical lapses?[9]
   (a) Reducing regulatory oversight
   (b) Strengthening whistleblower safeguards
   (c) Ignoring minor compliance gaps
   (d) Focusing solely on client outcomes
5. How does this case illustrate the importance of a compliance culture from Chap. 5?[10]
   (a) It shows that compliance is unnecessary for senior employees
   (b) It highlights how weak compliance monitoring can enable ethical breaches
   (c) It demonstrates that regulations hinder profitability
   (d) It proves insider trading has no market impact.

Case Study 3: A Data Breach Crisis

SafeHaven Financial, a regional financial planning firm, recently suffered a data breach due to outdated cybersecurity measures. Hackers accessed sensitive client information, including social security numbers and investment portfolios. The breach occurred because the firm delayed upgrading its systems and instead prioritized cost savings (despite warnings from the firm's IT team about vulnerabilities). The firm's senior leadership now faces a crisis. Should they disclose the breach to clients and regulators, risking reputational damage, or should they attempt to resolve the issue internally without notifying clients and regulators? The firm operates in multiple regions, including Europe, where GDPR compliance is mandatory. Senior management knows that this adds complexity to the decision. Internally, employees are concerned about client-eroding trust as the leadership team debates how to balance transparency with minimizing financial fallout.

This case relates to Chaps. 1, 5, 7, 9, 11, 12, and 15, focusing on data privacy, regulatory compliance, ethical culture, risk mitigation, and transparency. Based on information from these chapters, answer the following questions:

1. Which regulation from Chap. 9 is most relevant to SafeHaven's obligations in Europe?[11]

(a) California Consumer Privacy Act (CCPA)
(b) General Data Protection Regulation (GDPR)
(c) Sarbanes-Oxley Act
(d) Dodd-Frank Act

2. What ethical principle from Chap. 7 should guide SafeHaven's decision to disclose the breach?[12]

(a) Procedural fairness
(b) Transparency
(c) Distributive fairness
(d) Interactional fairness

3. Which risk mitigation strategy from Chap. 6 could have prevented the breach?[13]

(a) Reducing IT staff training
(b) Implementing advanced cybersecurity measures
(c) Ignoring IT team warnings
(d) Outsourcing data management

4. How does this case reflect the importance of an ethical firm culture from Chap. 12?[14]

(a) The case shows that cost-cutting always enhances profitability
(b) The case highlights how the priorities of a firm's leadership can undermine ethical standards
(c) The case proves that client trust is irrelevant in data breaches
(d) The case demonstrates that regulations are overly restrictive

5. What lesson from Chap. 11 does this case illustrate?[15]

(a) Data breaches have minimal impact on client trust
(b) Ethical failures can erode client trust and firm reputation
(c) Regulatory oversight is unnecessary for data protection
(d) Internal resolution of breaches is always preferable

Chapter Summary

The conclusion of this book also marks a beginning for those who are working as financial services professionals. Ethical and regulatory compliant behavior is not a one-time, box-checking activity. Practicing ethically reflects one's ongoing commitment to treating clients fairly and always acting with integrity. Ethical practice must be embedded in every aspect of the delivery of financial services. For firms, this means going beyond meeting regulatory requirements to actively cultivating a culture where integrity, transparency, and accountability guide daily decisions. For firm leaders, acting ethically requires modeling ethical behavior and encouraging open dialogue among clients, staff, and firm stakeholders. It also means aligning business strategies with the long-term well-being of both clients and society.

The frameworks, models, and case studies used in this book show how ethical practices can be practical and profitable. Firms that treat ethics as a foundation of practice rather than an afterthought will continue to be better positioned to earn client trust, foster resilience, and succeed in a complex, rapidly evolving profession. In this way, the end of the book is an invitation to begin building organizations where compliance and ethics are not obligations but enduring sources of strength and competitive advantage.

Notes

[1]Correct Answer: (b) Deontology

Explanation: Deontology emphasizes duty-based ethics, such as adhering to professional standards and reporting issues to uphold integrity, regardless of the outcome. Deontological standards require that an advisor prioritize client interests and transparency.

[2]Correct Answer: (b) Transparency

Explanation: Chapter 5 highlights transparency as a key regulatory standard, requiring firms to clearly communicate processes to clients, especially when using automated systems like AI.

[3]Correct Answer: (b) Overconfidence

Explanation: Leadership's rush to adopt the AI platform without thorough testing suggests overconfidence in the technology's reliability, a bias discussed in Chap. 4.

[4]Correct Answer: (b) Encouraging open communication

Explanation: Chapter 12 emphasizes open communication as a strategy to promote ethical conduct, allowing issues like the AI's bias to be reported and addressed internally.

[5]Correct Answer: (b) It shows how technology can introduce new compliance vulnerabilities

Explanation: Chapter 14 discusses how technology adoption, like AI, can create new risks such as algorithmic biases, requiring robust compliance frameworks.

[6]Correct Answer: (b) Insider trading

Explanation: Chapter 8 defines insider trading as using nonpublic information for financial gain, which directly applies to Jessica's situation.

[7]Correct Answer: (c) Rationalization

Explanation: Chapter 4 discusses rationalization as a psychological factor where individuals justify unethical actions such as Jessica believing the information benefits clients without harm.

[8]Correct Answer: (d) Both b and c

Explanation: Chapter 6 notes that both the SEC and FINRA oversee insider trading, with the SEC enforcing federal laws and FINRA monitoring brokerage activities.

[9]Correct Answer: (b) Strengthening whistleblower safeguards

Explanation: Chapter 11 emphasizes whistleblower safeguards as critical for addressing ethical issues, encouraging employees like Jessica to report concerns safely.

[10]Correct Answer: (b) It highlights how weak compliance monitoring can enable ethical breaches

Explanation: Chapter 5 underscores the role of regulatory frameworks in ensuring accountability, which is compromised by GlobalTrust's understaffed compliance team.

[11]Correct Answer: (b) General Data Protection Regulation (GDPR)

Explanation: Chapter 9 highlights GDPR as a key data protection regulation in Europe, requiring firms like SafeHaven to report breaches and protect client data.

[12]Correct Answer: (b) Transparency

Explanation: Chapter 7 emphasizes transparency as critical in client-facing roles, requiring SafeHaven to disclose the breach to maintain trust.

[13]Correct Answer: (b) Implementing advanced cybersecurity measures

Explanation: Chapter 6 discusses integrating risk management with compliance, including adopting measures like encryption to mitigate data privacy risks.

[14]Correct Answer: (b) It highlights how leadership's priorities can undermine ethical standards

Explanation: Chapter 12 notes that leadership plays a pivotal role in sustaining ethical standards, which SafeHaven neglected by prioritizing cost savings.

[15]Correct Answer: (b) Ethical failures can erode client trust and firm reputation

Explanation: Chapter 11 emphasizes that ethical and compliance failures, like data breaches, damage client trust and firm reputation.

Index[1]

A

B

[1] Note: Page numbers followed by 'n' refer to notes.

W. Heo, J. E. Grable, *Ethics and Compliance in Financial Services*,
https://doi.org/10.1007/978-3-032-14449-2

W

The manufacturer's authorised representative in the EU is Springer Nature Customer Service Centre GmbH, Europaplatz 3, 69115 Heidelberg, Germany. If you have any concerns regarding our products, please contact ProductSafety@springernature.com

Printed and bound by CPI Group (UK) Ltd, Croydon, CR0 4YY
10/10/2026
02231329-0016